Critical Thinking and American Government

THIRD EDITION

Kent M. Brudney
Cuesta College

Mark E. Weber
Cuesta College

Australia • Brazil • Canada • Mexico • Singapore
Spain • United Kingdom • United States

Critical Thinking and American Government
Third Edition
Kent M. Brudney and Mark E. Weber

Executive Editor, Political Science: David Tatom
Associate Development Editor: Rebecca Green
Editorial Assistants: Eva Dickerson, Cheryl Lee
Technology Project Manager: Michelle Vardeman
Marketing Manager: Janise Fry
Marketing Assistant: Teresa Jessen
Project Manager, Editorial Production: Lori Johnson
Creative Director: Rob Hugel
Executive Art Director: Maria Epes

Print Buyer: Rebecca Cross
Permissions Editor: Joohee Lee
Production Service and Compositor: Integra
Text Designer: LAD Design, Lee Anne Dollison
Copy Editor: Carol Reitz
Illustrator: Integra
Cover Designer: Bartay
Cover Image: Panoramic Images/Getty Images
Text and Cover Printer: Thomson/West

© 2007 Thomson Wadsworth, a part of The Thomson Corporation. Thomson, the Star logo, and Wadsworth are trademarks used herein under license.

ALL RIGHTS RESERVED. No part of this work covered by the copyright hereon may be reproduced or used in any form or by any means—graphic, electronic, or mechanical, including photocopying, recording, taping, Web distribution, information storage and retrieval systems, or in any other manner—without the written permission of the publisher.

Printed in the United States of America
1 2 3 4 5 6 7 10 09 08 07 06

Library of Congress Control Number: 2005936959

ISBN 0-495-00746-3

Thomson Higher Education
10 Davis Drive
Belmont, CA 94002-3098
USA

For more information about our products, contact us at:
Thomson Learning Academic Resource Center
1-800-423-0563

For permission to use material from this text or product, submit a request online at **http://www.thomsonrights.com**.
Any additional questions about permissions can be submitted by e-mail to **thomsonrights@thomson.com**.

Table of Contents

Preface vi

Introduction vii

CHAPTER 1 Governing Principles and Ideologies 1

Exercise 1.1	Reading the Constitution	1
Exercise 1.2	The Framers of the Constitution and Republicanism	9
Exercise 1.3	Contemporary American Political Ideologies	11
Exercise 1.4	Direct Democracy: Electronically	17

CHAPTER 2 Federalism 21

Exercise 2.1	Creating Federalism	21
Exercise 2.2	Federal Education Aid to State and Local Governments: Should Strings Be Attached?	27
Exercise 2.3	The Amendment Process	37
Exercise 2.4	Who's in Charge of the Minimum Drinking Age—The Federal Government or the States?	45

CHAPTER 3 Public Opinion and the Mass Media 51

Exercise 3.1	Public Confidence in American Institutions	51
Exercise 3.2	Bias and Accuracy in the News Media: The Case of CBS News and President Bush's Military Record	55
Exercise 3.3	How Do You Want Your News: Hard or Soft?	59

CHAPTER 4 Political Parties and Elections 65

Exercise 4.1	The Presidential Election of 2004: Why It Wasn't the Economy	65
Exercise 4.2	Gerrymandering	77
Exercise 4.3	To Vote or Not to Vote?	83
Exercise 4.4	Alternative Voting Systems	97

CHAPTER 5 — Interest Groups — 105

Exercise 5.1	AARP Versus Generation X: Mismatched Interest Group Power	105
Exercise 5.2	The Discreet Charm of Pork-Barrel Spending: The Political Side of Punxsutawney Phil	113
Exercise 5.3	Campaign Finance Reform and the Newest Loophole—527 Groups	119

CHAPTER 6 — Congress — 127

Exercise 6.1	What is the Proper Role of the Representative?	127
Exercise 6.2	Why We Hate Congress but Love Our Member of Congress	133
Exercise 6.3	Blacks in Congress	141
Exercise 6.4	Legislative Apportionment	151

CHAPTER 7 — The Presidency — 159

Exercise 7.1	The Electoral College	159
Exercise 7.2	Evaluating Presidential Performance	175
Exercise 7.3	The Power of the Sword	181
Exercise 7.4	Distinguishing Fact from Opinion in an American Presidential Campaign	195

CHAPTER 8 — Bureaucracy and the Regulatory Process — 203

Exercise 8.1	The Fourth Branch	203
Exercise 8.2	The National Security State	211
Exercise 8.3	How Much Regulation Is Enough? How Much Is Too Much?	219

CHAPTER 9 — The Judiciary — 225

Exercise 9.1	Establishing Judicial Review	225
Exercise 9.2	Judicial Activism Versus Judicial Restraint: The Supreme Court and the Juvenile Death Penalty	235
Exercise 9.3	What Role Should the Senate Play in Judicial Appointments?	241
Exercise 9.4	Beating the Odds on Judicial Appointments	249

CHAPTER 10 — Civil Rights — 257

Exercise 10.1	Mandating Racial Segregation by State Law	257
Exercise 10.2	Same-Sex Marriage: The New Civil Right?	267
Exercise 10.3	The Gender Wage Gap	275
Exercise 10.4	The End of Affirmative Action?	283

CHAPTER 11 — Civil Liberties — 289

Exercise 11.1	The Tension between Civil Liberties Advocates and Civil Rights Advocates: Campus Hate Speech Codes	289
Exercise 11.2	Random Drug Testing in Public Schools	297
Exercise 11.3	Homosexuals and the Right to Privacy	303
Exercise 11.4	Jerry Falwell and *Hustler* Magazine: Libel and the Slippery Slope of Censorship	309

Appendix 1	*For Instructors: A Guide to Using This Textbook*	313
Appendix 2	*Tools in Political Analysis*	317
Appendix 3	*Constitution of the United States*	323

Preface

We have made several key changes in this new (third) edition of *Critical Thinking and American Government*. We've updated the exercises, inserting material on a number of important political events that have occurred in the three years since the second edition was published. There are new exercises, for example, that focus on the presidential election of 2004, loopholes in campaign finance after McCain–Feingold, the president's war power, civil rights for gays and lesbians, and trends in voter turnout. We've pared the number of exercises and streamlined many of those retained from the second edition. We have included for teachers, in Appendix 1, a guide to integrating the critical thinking approach into introductory American Government and Politics courses.

We are indebted to reviewers, faculty members, and students for the new approaches, exercises, and topics they suggested for this edition. We thank them, too, for pointing out inconsistencies in the second edition, allowing us to clarify and amend where necessary. Dionne Brooks was particularly helpful in reviewing several of the most difficult exercises. Of course, any remaining sins of omission or commission are ours alone. Our thanks to the professionals at Wadsworth: Our editor, David Tatom, could not have been more encouraging; Eva Dickerson, Lori Johnson, and Janis Fry ensured smooth production at their end. We are especially grateful for the good eye of our copyeditor, Carol Reitz. Most of all, thanks to John Culver for coauthorship of the first two editions. He was sorely missed in the third edition, but his good work is still evident in several exercises.

Introduction

Critical Thinking and American Government was written for students who come to the study of American government unaccustomed to thinking critically and analytically about politics. It was also written for Advanced Placement and college instructors who want their students to grasp American politics in greater depth and with more practical applications than standard survey textbooks provide.

We suggest that students and teachers consider a few elements that underpin the critical thinking approach to the study of American politics incorporated in this text.

The first element is *discipline-based* critical thinking. Many colleges and universities require students to take a class in critical thinking as one of their degree requirements. Unfortunately, those classes are often taught in isolation from any academic discipline, which is a bit like teaching writing without a language to work with. This text grounds the development of critical and analytical thinking skills in the discipline of political science.

Second is the *integration* of critical thinking into the introductory American politics course. The critical thinking exercises in this text are grouped in chapters that match those in most standard survey texts. The exercises allow students and teachers to delve critically and analytically into topics typically covered in the introductory course. Examples include tracing African-American representation in Congress using data sets, analyzing the electoral college through popular and electoral vote results, assessing the president's war power by categorizing and quantifying the use of armed force abroad, and investigating incumbency using data on reelection rates. Students and teachers will find that the exercises complement their studies in class and in the standard text.

The third element in our approach is the *regular assignment* of critical thinking exercises. This text allows students to *practice* analytical inquiry within political science on a regular basis, thereby deepening their knowledge and understanding of the discipline and course material. We recognize that the term *homework* conjures up in many students' minds images of bleak, unending drudgery. But that won't be the case here. These critical thinking exercises offer a wide variety of approaches that our students find interesting and challenging.

The fourth element is *actively engaging* the subject. The introductory American government course is often constrained by its reliance on the instructor's description and analysis of the subject matter. But no matter how effective a survey text—or how dynamic a teacher—description without active engagement hauls students up short. Our students want to confront, apply, manipulate, and actively problem-solve within the discipline. This text provides that opportunity.

For teachers in the natural sciences and mathematics, it's a self-evident truth that students must embrace the subject—actively and regularly—to learn it. Imagine teaching math by describing numeric problems with a Microsoft® PowerPoint® presentation, and not requiring students to practice solving problems that embody the concepts and relationships explicated in class. Science students have their labs; math students have their homework; why should a midterm and final exam alone suffice for students of American politics?

A note on the structure of the text. Each critical thinking exercise begins with an introduction, one to three pages long, broadly explaining the topic and preparing students to tackle the critical thinking assignment. The introduction is followed by critical thinking questions based on a wide variety of primary sources: Supreme Court opinions, legislation, the Federalist Papers, public opinion polls, apportionment and population tables, presidential and congressional election results, data on campaign spending, among others. The critical thinking questions are calibrated carefully to lead students to successfully engage these sources. The exercises focus on data interpretation and analysis, the discovery of basic relationships among variables, and the ability to read critically, to summarize information concisely, to formulate generalizations and hypotheses, to draw logical inferences, to assess the strength of opposing arguments and positions, and to practice obtaining and analyzing *reliable* sources on the Internet.

An important note to teachers. Appendix 1 is a guide to using this critical thinking approach. It includes suggestions on selecting and assigning exercises, integrating the exercises into the introductory class, getting students started, employing the exercises as group work, and evaluating the exercises.

CHAPTER 1

Governing Principles and Ideologies

EXERCISE 1.1 Reading the Constitution

INTRODUCTION

The U.S. Constitution establishes the fundamental principles, processes, and structures of the American political system. Among them are representative government, republicanism, popular sovereignty, and individual rights; the process of checks and balances; and the structures of separation of power and federalism. The Constitution grants power to government institutions, to officeholders, and to citizens, and constrains all of them in their exercise of power. Under the Constitution, sovereignty is divided among the people, the state governments, and the national government, preventing a concentration of power that could endanger the liberties of citizens.

That the Constitution has endured for more than two centuries is a function of four extraordinary innovations in the theory and practice of republican government. First, American constitutions were written. This innovation was employed in creating state constitutions and later the Articles of Confederation and the Constitution of 1787. Written constitutions were a significant departure from the British model, a vague body of law and precedent, some written and some not. During the colonial and revolutionary periods, Americans had found that an informal constitution was a weak and unreliable guarantor of citizens' liberties. So they insisted that their constitutions be written.

Second, the American constitutions were separate from and superior to the government they sought to restrain. This too was a departure from the British model. In England, citizens customarily looked to Parliament to protect their liberties from the abuse of power by the king. But Americans learned from their experience with state governments between 1776 and 1787 that duly elected legislatures and even citizens themselves might abuse power and had to be restrained by a higher authority. Their written constitutions would be that separate and paramount authority.

The third innovation was a process for creating and then amending the written documents. A constitution separate from and superior to the government could not be created or altered by the government it was meant to control. So Americans located the power to create and alter the Constitution of 1787 in special conventions of citizens that were separate from the national and state governments in existence at the time.

Article V of the Constitution of 1787 divides the amendment power between the national and state governments, on the one hand, and popular conventions of citizens, on the other. Popular conventions have been employed only once since the adoption of the Constitution, when the Twenty-First Amendment, which repealed Prohibition, was ratified by popularly elected conventions in the states in 1933. But their inclusion in the Constitution illustrates the Americans' conviction that fundamental law must be separate from the institutions of government.

The fourth innovation was *judicial review*, the power of judges to say what a constitution means and to strike down government actions that conflict with the authority of the Constitution. Judicial review was rooted in the belief that the nation's fundamental law is both separate from and superior to the government: Clearly, government officials cannot evaluate their own performance against the standards set forth in the Constitution. The framers, or authors, of the Constitution could have made the people the instrument for assessing the government's compliance with the Constitution. But they, like many Americans at the time, held a dim view of democracy and feared the consequences of locating power in the citizenry.

Actually, judicial review is nowhere mentioned in the Constitution of 1787. But the concept of a fundamental law that binds the government pointed to the need for interpretation by some impartial body. Judges at the state government level were the first to exercise judicial review. In 1803, the U.S. Supreme Court asserted the power for the first time, striking down a law passed by Congress. In *Marbury v. Madison*, Chief Justice John Marshall claimed for the Supreme Court the power to interpret the Constitution: "A law repugnant to the Constitution is void." The exercise of judicial review confirmed that Americans had elevated the fundamental law above their government and had found a practical way to maintain that separation.

The framers intended the Constitution to be the foundation for "A New Order of the Ages," yet it is a surprisingly brief and often ambiguous document. Both its brevity and ambiguity suggest the wisdom of its authors: They did not want the document to be so detailed that it would constrain policymakers in future generations, tying them to the interests and issues of the founding period. The framers knew that a free people facing ongoing political change would cast off any document that could not be adapted to new circumstances. The spareness of the Constitution has helped it endure as the fundamental law in the United States for over two hundred years.[1]

Some of the matters on which the Constitution is ambiguous are important. The interests of those at the Constitutional Convention were often too diverse to reconcile through bargaining and compromise. Ambiguous language allowed the parties to agree on issues that if dealt with specifically would have deadlocked the convention. Since 1787, ambiguities in the Constitution have been sorted out in the practice of American political life and through interpretation by the federal courts. Still, the meanings of certain phrases—"necessary and proper" (Article I, Section 8) and "equal protection" (Fourteenth Amendment), for example—are likely always to be contested.

On a number of important matters the Constitution is silent. The framers did not explicitly confer the right to vote on anyone. Until the Fifteenth Amendment was ratified in 1870, state governments alone determined who could vote. Subsequent amendments granted the right to vote to women and citizens age 18 or older. The framers did not set out the role political parties should play in the political system or a process for canceling treaties. Over the years, state legislatures and Congress have defined in law the functions and responsibilities of parties in the electoral arena. And it wasn't until the late 1970s that the treaty issue was resolved. In 1978, President Jimmy Carter abrogated (canceled) a mutual defense treaty with Taiwan without securing the approval of the Senate. A group of senators challenged the president's action in court. In *Goldwater v. Carter* (1979), the Supreme Court ruled that the case involved a political question and refused to decide

---

[1] By contrast, many state constitutions suffer from excessive detail. They often run on for hundreds of pages, arcane specifications confused by scores of amendments. They are commonly documents that only legislators, lawyers, and judges can make sense of.

the matter. With both the Constitution and the Supreme Court silent on the authority to abrogate treaties, it seems that authority is now the president's by virtue of a president's having claimed it and successfully exercised it.

The Constitution offers neither law nor much guidance on certain difficult social issues. It was the Supreme Court that legalized abortion in *Roe v. Wade* (1973). And the courts are just now beginning to examine and rule on laws governing the right to die. Judges will have to look deeply into the Constitution and their own notions of truth and justice to confirm or strike down those laws.

ASSIGNMENT, PART A: THE CONSTITUTION'S BASIC PROVISIONS

The following questions should familiarize you with the organization of the Constitution and several of its provisions. Consult the Constitution in Appendix 3 at the back of this textbook. In your answers, always cite the number of the relevant article or amendment. Preview the questions below before you read the Constitution so that you know what to be looking for as you read the document.[2]

1. Read each article of the Constitution. In just one sentence, state the general purpose or subject of each article.

Article I: _____

Article II: _____

Article III: _____

Article IV: _____

Article V: _____

Article VI: _____

Article VII: _____

2. In the Constitution of 1787—the unamended document—how many times do the words *slave* and *slavery* appear?

---

[2] A valuable Internet resource on the Constitution is at http://www.library.unt.edu/govinfo/law/constitutions.htm.

3. The powers the Constitution specifically grants to the branches of government or to officeholders are called *enumerated powers*.

a. Identify one enumerated power of the president.

b. Identify one enumerated power of the vice president.

c. Identify one enumerated power of Congress.

4. a. How were U.S. senators chosen before the Seventeenth Amendment was ratified in 1913?

b. How have U.S. senators been chosen since 1913?

5. a. Identify one power the Constitution prohibits to Congress.

b. Identify one power the Constitution prohibits to the states.

6. According to the principle of checks and balances, each branch of government must have some degree of scrutiny and control over the other branches. With the exception of the judiciary, the Constitution accomplishes that by giving each branch roles in the affairs of the others.[3] Look at the first two articles of the Constitution, and identify one of each of the following types of checks and balances:

a. A power that the executive branch holds over the legislative branch

b. A power that the executive branch holds over the judicial branch

c. A power that the legislative branch holds over the executive branch

d. A power that the legislative branch holds over the judicial branch

---

[3] The Constitution specifies no role for the judiciary in the functions of the legislative or executive branches. The power of judicial review was claimed by Chief Justice John Marshall in his decision in *Marbury v. Madison*, 1803. See Exercise 9.1.

7. a. What are the two ways that amendments to the Constitution can be proposed?

b. What are the two ways that amendments to the Constitution can be ratified?

8. Article V of the Constitution of 1787 singles out two matters that are beyond the reach of the amendment process. What are they?

9. Identify by number one amendment that
a. extended individual rights.

b. extended civil rights (including voting rights).

c. prohibited certain practices by the states.

10. The Twenty-Fifth Amendment describes the sequence of events that would install the vice president as acting president against the will of the president. Outline that sequence of events.

11. Identify one term in the Constitution that you do not understand. Look up the meaning of the term, and define it here.

ASSIGNMENT, PART B: MAJORITY AND SUPERMAJORITY

Essential to the functioning of government and to balancing the relative powers of its three branches are the numeric requirements the Constitution sets forth for overriding a presidential veto, ratifying treaties, and carrying out other tasks and procedures. The three numeric requirements specified in the Constitution are the simple majority and two supermajority levels, two-thirds and three-fourths. The simple majority and two-thirds margins apply to the number of House and Senate members actually casting votes, not to the total number of votes residing in each body. For example, the requirement for passing legislation in the House is a simple majority, or 50 percent plus one, of the number of votes cast. There are 435 members in the House, so a simple majority is 218. But 218 votes are needed to pass a bill only if all 435 members vote. If only 400 members vote on a bill, then 201 votes would satisfy the simple-majority requirement.

The Constitution makes an additional stipulation that can affect the minimum number of votes required to pass a bill: The House and the Senate are required to have a majority of their members present (a quorum) to conduct legislative business.

1. a. What bodies have the power to override a presidential veto?

b. What margin is required to override a presidential veto?

2. a. What body has the power to ratify treaties?

b. What margin is required to ratify treaties?

3. *To impeach* means "to bring charges against" or "to indict."

a. What body has the power to impeach the president?

b. What margin is required to impeach a president?

4. a. What body has the power to convict the president of charges brought against him in the impeachment process and thereby remove him from the presidency?

b. What margin is required to convict and remove a president?

EXERCISE 1.1 READING THE CONSTITUTION   7

5. a. What body has the power to accept or to reject a president's nominations to the Supreme Court?

_____

b. What margin is required to elevate a president's nominee to a seat on the Court?

_____

6. a. If no candidate for the presidency wins a simple majority of the total number of electoral votes, what body has the power to choose the president?

_____

b. What margin is required to choose the president?

_____

7. If the House can muster only the minimum requirement for a quorum, what number of votes would be needed to pass a bill?

_____

8. The Constitution specifies a three-fourths majority for just one process. What is it?

_____

EXERCISE 1.2 The Framers of the Constitution and Republicanism

INTRODUCTION

The U.S. Constitution established a republic. The framers chose the republican form of government over all other forms, including monarchy, aristocracy, and democracy.

Americans have often differed over the practice of republican government. But they have agreed in large part on the fundamental principles and elements of republican government:

- *Republican government is limited*. The powers of government are circumscribed to reduce the possibility of tyranny. In the Constitution, the framers set limits on the powers exercised by the national government over the states and over individuals.
- *Republican government is representational*. The exercise of power by government over citizens is legitimate only when citizens are represented by legislative assemblies. The framers admired the representative institutions of the Roman Republic. They even named the U.S. Senate for the Roman Senate. But Republicanism offered no standard position on four difficult issues:
  1. How many constituents should each legislator represent?
  2. Should legislators be responsible to their constituents, to their own conscience, or to the public interest?
  3. Should representatives of the people be elected by the people themselves or by intermediate institutions?
  4. Who should be eligible to vote for their legislators?

  On the issue of the direct popular election of representatives (3, above), the framers were divided. The Constitution always has provided for the direct popular election of members of the House, but U.S. senators were chosen by members of their state legislature until after the Seventeenth Amendment was ratified in 1913. Remember that the framers didn't think too highly of the public's ability to handle political power wisely. So they chose not to expand the right to vote beyond the voting qualifications the states had established for the largest branch of each state's legislature. Later, a series of constitutional amendments, Supreme Court decisions, and popular movements democratized representation and expanded the eligible electorate.
- *In republican government, the people are sovereign*. Republicans believe that the people at large create, authorize, and empower government, and that government must be accountable to the people. A government rooted in the people cannot act without the consent of the people. The word *republic* comes from the Latin *res publica* ("the public thing"), which means that government is a common enterprise, originating from and belonging to the people. Thomas Jefferson made the principle of popular sovereignty clear in the Declaration of Independence: "Governments are instituted among Men, deriving their just powers from the consent of the governed. . . . Whenever any Form of Government becomes destructive of these ends, it is the Right of the People to alter or to abolish it, and to institute new Government."

ASSIGNMENT

The following questions require a close reading of the Constitution. Consult the Constitution in Appendix 3 at the back of this textbook.

1. Identify three significant elements of the Constitution (including amendments) that embody the republican principle of limited government. Explain and support your answers.

_____

_____

_____

CHAPTER 1 GOVERNING PRINCIPLES AND IDEOLOGIES

_____
_____
_____
_____

2. Three institutions in the new government embodied the framers' commitment to the principle of representation: the House of Representatives, the Senate, and the presidency. Identify below the system of representation the framers established for each institution by answering this question: Was it representation by direct popular election, or was representation filtered through the choice of some intermediate body? If the latter, identify that intermediate body and describe its role.

House of Representatives: _____
_____
_____

Senate: _____
_____
_____

President: _____
_____
_____

3. Identify three amendments to the Constitution that expanded democratic representation, and explain what each amendment has accomplished.

_____
_____
_____
_____
_____

4. Identify one passage in the Constitution that expresses the republican principle of popular sovereignty.

_____
_____

EXERCISE 1.3 Contemporary American Political Ideologies

INTRODUCTION

The labels we use to describe political thought are often loaded with connotations either positive or negative—depending on who's wielding the label as a political weapon and on who's listening. Republicans, for example, have turned *liberalism* into a term of disparagement by associating that label with big government, moral irresponsibility, and a lack of will to defend the nation. Democrats have tried to discredit *conservatism* by linking that label to practices such as racism, the oppression of women, religious fanaticism, and favoritism for the rich.

A *political ideology* is a set of coherent, deeply felt political beliefs and values through which individuals interpret political events and decide what is politically right and wrong. Despite the utility of the labels in making sense of political issues and actors, most Americans are not ideologues: They may hold ideological positions on particular issues, but they do not think of themselves in terms of a political ideology. Most Americans are pragmatists—positioned in the middle of the political spectrum—and are unlikely to judge issues or candidates by a set of consistent political beliefs. Indeed, Americans historically have rejected political movements and candidates that appeared too ideological. Some public opinion polls, however, suggest that Americans have become increasingly ideological in the first decade of the twenty-first century (see Exercise 4.1).

Ideological labels do help voters sort out a bewildering array of political arguments, and to some extent they do reflect political positions, especially among political elites, which tend to be more ideological than other Americans. But the task of identifying ideological positions has become more difficult in recent decades as the relatively simple divisions of the New Deal era—based largely on the economy and the role of government in the economy—have fragmented into ever-more diverse and complex thinking about the economy; moral, religious, and social issues; and foreign policy, especially in the wake of 9/11 and the war on terrorism.

Below are brief definitions of six ideologies prominent on the American political landscape today. Recognize that the descriptions are simplified.

Liberalism Liberals generally support strong government action in a broad array of contemporary issues, from economic policy to civil rights. But liberals are likely to oppose strong government action when they believe it threatens civil liberties—freedom of speech, for example, or the individual's right to privacy. Liberals believe that government must play an active role in creating equal opportunity, through antidiscrimination laws, through affirmative-action programs, and through initiatives to assist the disadvantaged. Liberals pin their hopes for a just and progressive society on action by the national government because of its superior power and resources. Liberals favor progressive income taxes as a means of assisting the most disadvantaged, and they believe that all levels of government should prevent and punish market practices that hurt consumers and threaten the environment. Liberals want foreign and defense policies that depend less on military and unilateral action and more on diplomacy and multilateralism, especially through the United Nations.

The Left Wing From the 1930s to the 1960s, the American Left supported socialist, or Marxist, economics (public ownership of the means of production and the redistribution of wealth to foster economic equality); opposed American imperialistic, interventionist foreign policy; and sought to eradicate racism in America. In the decades since, with the increasingly conservative trend in American politics and the end of the cold war, the left has splintered into a number of movements, each with its own passionate critique or indictment of American society. Among those left-wing movements are radical feminism (denouncing patriarchal relationships), radical environmentalism (damning the ethos of acquisitiveness and the rape of nature), and radical multiculturalism (censuring social, economic, and belief systems that marginalize people of color). Recently, left-wing organizations have attacked economic globalization, which they believe cheats developing nations and damages the environment. The left wing has vehemently opposed the Bush administration's doctrine of preemptive, unilateral action in world affairs.

Conservatism Conservatives want to reduce the role of government in the nation's economic affairs. For conservatives, government's chief roles are to defend the nation from foreign attack, maintain law and order, and protect citizens from immediate threats to their health and safety. Conservatives decidedly favor government spending on national security over social programs. Although many conservatives have made peace with the main components of the welfare state—Social Security and Medicare—many want those programs to be contained or even scaled back and partially privatized. Conservatives today are split on budgetary policy. Supply-siders, like President George W. Bush, advocate across-the-board tax cuts—even a flat tax—which, they believe, will stimulate economic growth. Fiscal conservatives, on the other hand, worry about budget deficits. Rather than cut government revenues, they want to see existing programs downsized. Conservatives argue that affirmative action improperly creates special rights for minority groups. Most conservatives believe that individual liberties must be balanced against the government's responsibilities to maintain law and order and to defend core American values (for example, the war on terrorism) or Judeo-Christian values (for example, government support to religious organizations that render social services). Conservatives support a foreign policy that muscularly advances American interests abroad and protects American prestige—unilaterally and preemptively if necessary. Conservatives worry that multilateral organizations, like the United Nations, may undermine U.S. sovereignty and constrain America's freedom to act on the world stage.

Neoconservatism Neoconservatism has taken a prominent place in American foreign policy, especially after 9/11. Neoconservatives want to secure and advance the cultural and moral traditions of the United States—particularly freedom and democracy. The justification for American intervention in Iraq was largely the result of strong neoconservative voices in the Bush administration. Neoconservatives call for a renewed commitment to individual responsibility—a value that they believe has been eroded by liberal policies. Nevertheless, neoconservatives are less enamored of strict free-market solutions to economic problems than their conservative brethren.

Christian Conservatism/Evangelical, Born-Again Christianity Evangelical, born-again Christians are a major political force in the United States, having contributed significantly to George W. Bush's election in 2000 and his reelection in 2004 (see Exercise 4.1). Adherents of this ideology/theology promote so-called traditional moral values against a perceived assault on them by a hedonistic, media-driven culture. Christian conservatives believe that America was founded on and owes its greatness to Judeo-Christian principles. They oppose abortion rights, favor government aid to students who attend religious schools, and have lately been galvanized in opposition to gay marriage.

The Right Wing The American Right includes groups with different agendas, but it is united in its opposition to social diversity and to governmental encroachments on private property rights. Right-wing ideologues contend that the national government has established a tyranny over the individual; white Christian males are believed to be those most oppressed. Many right-wing groups embrace doctrines of racial supremacy; others are anti-Semitic. In recent years, several right-wing groups have come to believe that armed resistance—including terrorism—is necessary to liberate the United States from perceived sources of oppression.

ASSIGNMENT

1. Go the Directory of U.S. Political Parties at http://www.politics1.com/parties.htm.[1] The site briefly describes the ideologies of the two major political parties in the United States, Democratic and Republican, and more than thirty minor parties. The site also provides a link to each party's website. Search the directory for a political party that exemplifies each of the political ideologies identified above. Explain and support your answers.

---

[1] Website URLs sometimes change. Try an external search (e.g., Google) to find the website. Configurations of a website often change. Try an internal search of the site to locate the information. Sometimes websites and pages within websites are removed. In that case, move on to the next question.

EXERCISE 1.3 CONTEMPORARY AMERICAN POLITICAL IDEOLOGIES

Liberalism: _____

_____

_____

The left wing: _____

_____

_____

Conservatism, or neoconservatism, or Christian conservatism: _____

_____

_____

The right wing: _____

_____

_____

2. Go to the websites of the following organizations. Identify the ideology each organization exemplifies. Explain and support your answers. You might need to navigate around the website to determine the ideology.

Religious Freedom Foundation: http://www.rfcnet.org/news/default.asp

_____

_____

_____

American Liberty Foundation: http://www.americanlibertyfoundation.org/

_____

_____

_____

Project for the New American Century: http://www.newamericancentury.org/

_____

_____

_____

United for a Fair Economy: http://www.faireconomy.org/

_____

_____

_____

Earth First: http://www.earthfirst.org/about.htm

_____
_____
_____

Council of Conservative Citizens: http://www.cofcc.org/

_____
_____
_____

3. Listed below are five hypothetical statements. Identify the ideology each statement reflects. Explain and support your answers.

a. "Marriage must be legally defined as only between a man and a woman."

_____
_____
_____

b. "If elected, I will get government off your backs and release the great energy of the American people."

_____
_____
_____

c. "So long as I am president, no American shall go to bed hungry, no American shall suffer the burden of discrimination, and no American shall fall ill without the benefit of medical help."

_____
_____
_____

d. "To make America safe from terrorism, we must first make the Islamic world safe for democracy."

_____
_____
_____

e. "The war on terrorism should not provide a pretext for a governmental assault on the liberties of the American people."

_____
_____
_____

4. Take the "World's Smallest Political Quiz" at http://www.self-gov.org/quiz.html. What was the result? Do you think the quiz was accurate about you? Why or why not?

EXERCISE 1.4 Direct Democracy: Electronically

INTRODUCTION

In a direct democracy, every citizen is a ruler: Citizens—not elected representatives—make law. Direct democracy was practiced in the ancient Greek city-state of Athens, but large segments of the population were excluded: women, slaves, the foreign-born, and the young. The Athenian statesman Pericles (ca. 495–429 BC) said, "We do not say that a man who takes no interest in politics minds his own business; we say that he has no business here at all."[1] The major theoretical defense of direct democracy was made by philosopher Jean-Jacques Rousseau (1712–1778), who argued, in *The Social Contract*, that the moment citizens surrender their will to a representative, they become slaves to that representative. Only the individual can represent his or her own will.

The framers of the Constitution were vehemently opposed to direct democracy and excluded it from the Constitution. In "Federalist No. 10," Madison wrote: "such democracies have ever been spectacles of turbulence and contention; have ever been found incompatible with personal security and the rights of property; and have in general been as short in their lives as they have been violent in their deaths." The U.S. Constitution continues to reflect Madison's view; the Constitution has not been amended to allow direct democracy.

In contrast, since about the beginning of the twentieth century, Americans have been enthusiastic practitioners of direct democracy in many of their state and local governments. Many state constitutions provide for the *initiative*, which allows voters to originate and enact laws irrespective of their elected representatives, and the *referendum*, which allows voters to approve or repeal laws passed by their representatives. Neither practice conforms precisely to the Athenian understanding of direct democracy because citizens do not assemble to debate the legislation. In fact, many citizens today are woefully ill informed about the ballot measures they pass judgment on. Moreover, measures that do pass are subject to modification or even nullification by the courts. Still, vestiges of pure direct democracy survive in parts of the United States—especially New England—where town business, such as spending and local ordinances, are decided by citizens directly in public meetings.

ASSIGNMENT

Direct democracy of the Athenian or New England town meeting variety could be practiced only in small political communities.[2] There are two reasons for this: First, the logistics—too many citizens would make assemblies impossible and too vast a territory would make it unlikely that many citizens could travel to the assemblies. Second, smaller communities facilitated the establishment of trust and friendship among citizens, bonds that were important in the exercise of direct political power. The size and complexity of the modern nation-state would seem to prohibit the practice of direct democracy today. Not so, say the supporters of direct democracy, who point to the possibility of using electronic technology to simulate the assembly of a community of citizens. Reading 1.4.1 presents one vision of electronic direct democracy. Study the model and answer the questions that follow.

READING 1.4.1 A MODEL OF ELECTRONIC DIRECT DEMOCRACY

The national government, at public expense, would provide all eligible voters with an electronic voting machine for use in the privacy of their places of residence. The electronic voting machines would allow voters to choose *yes*, *no*, or *abstain*. The machines would be tied into regional computers. Public voting stations would be established for the homeless and for people who are away from home on election day. To prevent voter fraud, access to voting machines would be allowed only through a thumbprint scanner, and access would be cut off after the individual had

---

[1] Thucydides, *The Peloponnesian War* (Baltimore: Penguin Books, 1954), p. 119.
[2] Athens at its most populous had about 100,000 residents, some 20,000 of whom were citizens.

voted. To prevent mischief from hackers, hard copies of the vote would be printed out for the voter and for election officials.

Legislative initiatives could be placed on the electronic ballot by an act of Congress, by executive order of the president, or by citizens' petition. The petition route would require a number of verified signatures equal to 5 percent of all eligible voters. Legislative initiatives would be written in clear and concise language. For example, the voters might be asked, "Should all Americans be guaranteed insurance that covers 80 percent of their health-care costs annually?" or, perhaps, "Should the United States send troops to Iran to force compliance with nuclear nonproliferation agreements?" By a simple majority (50 percent plus one vote) results of the electronic vote would be binding on the nation.

To be effective, this system of direct democracy would require modifying the existing structure of government. First, the courts would be stripped of the power of judicial review—no more striking down the will of the majority by activist judges. Second, although citizens would continue to elect members to a unicameral (one house) Congress—to write specific legislation to carry out the result of the popular electronic vote and to appropriate funds—the power of Congress would be substantially diminished. The president, who would remain commander in chief, would retain emergency power to deploy troops. But even the exercise of that power would be subject to a later nationwide referendum.

Unrestricted media campaigns for and against electronic ballot measures would be allowed. In addition, a bipartisan commission, appointed by the president with the consent of Congress, would be responsible for arranging televised debates about each initiative or referendum in the week preceding the vote. Participants in each debate would include spokespersons for the pro and con positions and an independent analyst, who would provide an expert opinion on the consequences and costs of the measure. This model of electronic direct democracy would require a new constitutional convention, according to the procedures outlined in Article V of the Constitution (see Appendix 3 at the back of this textbook).

Electronic voting would take place on Friday night. So crack a six-pack and get ready to push that voting button.

---

1. Do you support or oppose the idea of direct democracy, whether in its electronic or in its small-community form? That is, do you think it's a good idea for citizens to make law? Explain and support your position.

_____

_____

_____

_____

_____

_____

_____

_____

_____

2. What particular features of the model of *electronic* direct democracy do you like? Explain and support your answer.

_____

_____

_____

_____

_____

3. What particular features of the model of *electronic* direct democracy do you dislike? Explain and support your answer.

_____

_____

_____

_____

_____

CHAPTER 2

Federalism

EXERCISE 2.1 Creating Federalism

INTRODUCTION

In 1781, American forces defeated the British at Yorktown. A year later Great Britain agreed to recognize the independence of the United States; and in 1783, it signed the Treaty of Paris. The war over, Americans were able to give their full attention to this question: What form of government would be most suitable for the newly independent republic?

In 1777, the colonies joined together to fashion America's first national government under the provisions of the Articles of Confederation. Americans were in no mood in 1777 to create a strong central government that might abuse power and suppress the liberties of citizens as the British government had done. A central feature of the new government was that states would retain their sovereignty, unless the power was expressly delegated to the Congress of the Confederation. The colonies were stingy in their grants of power to the new government, denying to it powers that Americans today take for granted. That first national government, for example, had no executive or judicial branch: All power was vested in Congress, but a weak Congress, without the power to tax or to regulate foreign or domestic commerce.

By 1787, many Americans recognized the folly of their experiment with a central government too weak to maintain order, conduct foreign relations, or provide for the general welfare of the citizens of the Republic. That year, proponents of a stronger central government gathered in Philadelphia to consider revising the Articles. Instead, the delegates to the Constitutional Convention went considerably further: They produced a new constitution that vested in the national government many of the powers denied to it under the Articles of Confederation.

Proponents of the new government faced the formidable task of persuading citizens in the thirteen states to ratify the new Constitution. Those proponents, who would have been described most accurately as nationalists, instead called themselves *federalists*. They wanted to emphasize that state governments would retain considerable powers under the new

Constitution. Federalists also emphasized that the new national government would be limited and restrained by the separation of powers and checks and balances. Opponents of the new Constitution, called *antifederalists*, objected, insisting that the document proposed to empower the new national government largely at the expense of state governments. For example, under the Articles of Confederation, the states reserved exclusively to themselves the power to tax. Under the new Constitution—for the first time—the national government would have the power to tax directly. Antifederalists favored decentralized government and the preservation of the powers and prerogatives of the states.

A debate raged in the new nation over the transfer of power to the national government as well as over many other features of the new Constitution. Because the ratification of the proposed Constitution was by no means a foregone conclusion, Alexander Hamilton, John Jay, and James Madison—all federalists—wrote public arguments, under the pseudonym Publius, to defend and promote the Constitution. Eighty-five of their articles were reprinted as *The Federalist* in 1788, a collection usually referred to as *The Federalist Papers.* The degree to which the arguments advanced in *The Federalist* persuaded the public of the time is debatable, but today the collection remains an essential explanation of the structure and functions of the government established by the Constitution.

ASSIGNMENT

The Articles of Confederation were written in 1777 and in full force with Maryland's ratification in 1781. Study Reading 2.1.1, which contains excerpts from the Articles, and then answer the questions that follow it.

READING 2.1.1 Excerpts from the Articles of Confederation

I. Stile [legal designation] of this Confederacy shall be "The United States of America".

II. Each state retains its sovereignty, freedom, and independence, and every power, jurisdiction, and right, which is not by this Confederation expressly delegated to the United States, in Congress assembled.

III. The said States hereby severally enter into a firm league of friendship with each other, for their common defense, the security of their liberties, and their mutual and general welfare, binding themselves to assist each other, against all force offered to, or attacks made upon them, or any of them, on account of religion, sovereignty, trade, or any other pretense whatever....

V. ... In determining questions in the United States in Congress assembled, each State shall have one vote.

---

1. a. Confederations have been likened to alliances. Alliances are organizations in which the member nation-states act in concert only when they agree to act together. What language in the Articles suggests an alliance of the states rather than a union of the states?

b. In a unitary form of government, power flows from the central government. In a federal form of government, some powers belong to the central government and some to regional or state governments. In a confederal form of government, power flows from regional or state governments. What language in the Articles suggests that power flows from the states?

c. What language tells us that, under the Articles of Confederation, states were represented, not people?

_____

_____

d. What institution under the U.S. Constitution to this day embodies the representational principle of the Articles?

_____

_____

"Federalist No. 45," written by James Madison, appeared in the *New York Packet* on January 29, 1788. In the article, Madison sought to dispel the fear that the new constitution would undermine the powers and prerogatives of the state governments. Study Reading 2.1.2, which contains excerpts from "Federalist No. 45," and then answer the questions that follow it.

READING 2.1.2 Excerpts from "Federalist No. 45" by James Madison

Having shown that no one of the powers transferred to the federal government is unnecessary or improper, the next question to be considered is, whether the whole mass of them will be dangerous to the portion of authority left in the several States.

... [I]f the Union, as has been shown, be essential to the security of the people of America against foreign danger; if it be essential to their security against contentions and wars among the different States; if it be essential to guard them against those violent and oppressive factions which embitter the blessings of liberty, and against those military establishments which must gradually poison its very fountain; if, in a word, the Union be essential to the happiness of the people of America, is it not preposterous, to urge as an objection to a government, without which the objects of the Union cannot be attained, that such a government may derogate from the importance of the governments of the individual States? Was, then, the American Revolution effected, was the American Confederacy formed, was the precious blood of thousands spilt, and the hard-earned substance of millions lavished, not that the people of American should enjoy peace, liberty, and safety, but that the government of the individual States, that particular municipal establishments, might enjoy a certain extent of power, and be arrayed with certain dignities and attributes of sovereignty? ...

We have seen, in all the examples of ancient and modern confederacies, the strongest tendency continually betraying itself in the members, to despoil the general government of its authorities, with a very ineffectual capacity in the latter to defend itself against the encroachments. Although, in most of these examples, the system has been so dissimilar from that under consideration as greatly to weaken any inference concerning the latter from the fate of the former, yet, as the States will retain, under the proposed Constitution, a very extensive portion of active sovereignty, the inference ought not to be wholly disregarded....

The State governments may be regarded as constituent and essential parts of the federal government; whilst the latter is nowise essential to the operation or organization of the former. Without the intervention of the State legislatures, the President of the United States cannot be elected at all. They must in all cases have a great share in his appointment, and will, perhaps in most cases, of themselves determine it. The Senate will be elected absolutely and exclusively by the State legislatures.[1] Even the House of Representatives, though drawn immediately from the people, will be chosen very much under the influence of that class of men, whose influence over the people obtains for themselves an election into the State legislatures. Thus, each of the principal branches of the federal government will owe its existence more or less to the favor of the State governments, and must consequently feel a dependence, which is much more likely to begat a disposition too obsequious than too overbearing towards them....

The powers delegated by the proposed Constitution to the federal government are few and defined. Those which are to remain in the State governments are numerous and indefinite. The former will be exercised principally on external objects, as war, peace, negotiation, and foreign commerce; with which last the power of taxation will, for the most part, be connected. The powers reserved to the several States will extend to all the objects which, in the ordinary course of affairs, concern the lives, liberties, and properties of the people, and the internal order, improvement, and prosperity of the State.

The operations of the federal government will be most extensive and important in times of war and danger; those of the State governments in times of peace and security. As the former periods will probably bear a small proportion to the latter, the State governments will here enjoy another advantage over the federal government. The more adequate, indeed, the federal powers may be rendered to the national defence, the less frequent will be those scenes of danger which might favor their ascendancy over the governments of the particular States.

---

2. a. Identify two arguments Madison made to support his contention that a strong central government with independent powers is necessary.

b. Identify three arguments Madison made to support his contention that the Constitution is not a threat to the powers and prerogatives of the state governments.

The distribution of power between the national and state governments in the United States today is governed by several key passages in the Constitution, the Supreme Court's interpretation of those passages, and legislation enacted by Congress and the state legislatures. Two clauses in the

---

[1] The Twelfth Amendment (1804) provided for the election of the president by electors chosen by the public, and the Seventeenth Amendment (1913) provided for the direct election of U.S. senators.

Constitution are particularly important. Go to the copy of the Constitution in Appendix 3 at the back of this textbook. Study Article I, Section 8. Pay close attention to the last clause, which gives Congress the power "to make all Laws which shall be necessary and proper for carrying into Execution the foregoing Powers, and all other Powers vested by this Constitution in the Government of the United States, or in any Department or Officer thereof." Look next at the Tenth Amendment: "The powers not delegated to the United States by the Constitution, nor prohibited by it to the States, are reserved to the States respectively, or to the people." Compare these provisions with Article II in the Articles of Confederation: "Each State retains its sovereignty, freedom and independence, and every power, jurisdiction, and right, which is not by this confederation expressly delegated to the United States in Congress assembled."

3. a. Article II of the Articles of Confederation uses the phrase *expressly delegated* to limit the power of the central government. Even though the Tenth Amendment was meant to protect the power of the states, its authors omitted the word *expressly*, so that it refers to only the powers "delegated to the United States," not "expressly delegated." What is the significance of the omission of the word *expressly*?

___

b. In Article I, Section 8, of the Constitution, how does the last paragraph—the *necessary and proper* clause—pave the way for the expansion of national power?

___

EXERCISE 2.2 Federal Education Aid to State and Local Governments: Should Strings Be Attached?

INTRODUCTION

Who's in charge of what our schools teach? Who determines whether or not students have learned their lessons?

Early in the Republic's history, parents and private schools controlled the practice of education. As public school systems expanded during the nineteenth and early twentieth centuries, local and state governments added their influence. The federal government, however, did not claim a significant role in determining educational policy until after World War II.

The creation of the Department of Health, Education and Welfare (HEW) in 1953 signaled that educational policy had become a matter of national concern. That concern escalated into a crisis of confidence after the Soviet Union launched Sputnik—the world's first orbiting satellite—on October 4, 1957. Many Americans feared that the Soviets might rocket ahead of the United States to conquer outer space. As part of a broad response to ensure that the United States would not be left behind, President Dwight Eisenhower proposed, and Congress approved, federal funding for the expansion of science, mathematics, and foreign language education. As indicated by its title, the National Defense Education Act of 1958 was sold to Congress and the public as a national security measure. The act endorsed a greater federal role in determining national educational policy by increasing federal funding for schools and universities. Not only were many students now receiving federal aid, but many colleges and universities, in order to be eligible for federal dollars, responded to the federal government's interest in expanding their curricula in science and mathematics.

The expansion of the national government's role in education continued as a result of President Lyndon Johnson's War on Poverty. In the Educational and Secondary School Act of 1965, Johnson sought to expand and equalize educational opportunity by providing federal aid in the form of *categorical grants* to states and to school districts. Categorical grants fund specific projects, and they come with strings attached, thereby giving the national government greater control over educational policy. By 1979, during Jimmy Carter's presidency, the federal role in education had become so large that Congress established a separate Department of Education.

During Ronald Reagan's presidency (1981–1989) and later during the Republican ascendancy in Congress (beginning in 1995), conservatives led a backlash against the growing role of the national government in traditionally state and local government affairs, including education policy. As part of the rebellion against "big government," Republicans sought to provide a larger percentage of federal aid to education in the form of *block grants*, which give state and local officials more control over how federal money is spent than categorical grants.

How to improve the nation's schools—and particularly who would direct and control that effort—was a prominent issue in the 2000 presidential campaign. The issue had taken center stage because of Americans' declining confidence in K–12 education. Widespread concern about education can be traced to the U.S. Department of Education's stinging critique of the performance of the nation's public schools in its report, *A Nation at Risk* (1983). With mounting evidence of declining test scores and complaints from employers about the lack of math, science, and writing skills in the workforce, candidate George W. Bush charged that President Bill Clinton and Vice President Al Gore were responsible for an "education recession."

Bush advocated a hybrid approach to federal aid to education, containing both categorical and block grant elements. Criticizing Democratic candidate Al Gore's proposals as imposing too many federal mandates on the states, Bush appeared to tilt toward the block grant approach. But Bush's position that schools that failed to meet standards should lose their federal aid and that their students should then be free to transfer to successful schools was closer to the intrusive, strings-attached approach usually associated with Democrats. Bush especially insisted that public schools be held accountable for improving test scores for racial and ethnic minorities. Lack of

BOX 2.2.1 Three Ways the Federal Government Has Delivered Aid to State and Local Governments

Revenue sharing. The federal government returned federal tax dollars to the states with few strings attached. The states could use the money as they wished to supplement state revenues. Though started as a Republican approach in the Nixon administration to end heavy-handed federal regulations on the use of federal funds, revenue sharing was abolished during the Reagan administration: With his tax-cut plan and his proposal to increase federal spending on defense, Reagan argued that the federal government could no longer afford to distribute revenue-sharing funds.

Block grants. These grants have been the Republican approach to federal funding to the states since the Reagan administration. Funds are awarded in general policy areas (e.g., highway construction funds), but the states may decide on which programs to use the funds. Block grants come with relatively few restrictions.

Categorical grants. Beginning in the Johnson administration, funds were delivered directly to projects at the local level, including school districts. Funds are awarded for local projects' consistency with federal policy objectives. Categorical grants come with abundant rules, regulations, and accountability procedures. Usually categorical grants require matching funds from the governmental entity seeking the funding. Most federal aid is still delivered in the form of categorical grants—over 80 percent.

---

funding has led some states to claim that the program is an unfunded federal mandate, which Congress prohibited in 1995.[1] Bush also favored a school voucher program that would allow students in poorly performing schools to use federal funds to enroll in private schools. Except for the school voucher proposal, Bush's plan was signed into law as the No Child Left Behind (NCLB) Act of 2001.

Because the NCLB Act has never been fully funded, transfers of funds to successful schools have been difficult, especially in large urban districts, where successful schools are already overenrolled. Lack of funding combined with higher standards has raised concerns in many states. Utah has since enacted a law that exempts the state from provisions that conflict with Utah's own educational goals or that require additional funding by the state. Nevertheless, leaders of several minority groups in Utah have defended the NCLB Act and worry that Utah's new law will negate some of the gains made by minorities in that state.[2] One recent study suggests that although student scores have improved since the implementation of the NCLB Act, the rate of improvement has begun to decline.[3]

ASSIGNMENT

This assignment asks you to think of the NCLB Act in terms of the ongoing dispute over federal versus state and local control of public education. Study Reading 2.2.1, "Riley Says No to Education Block Grants" (Richard W. Riley was secretary of education in the Clinton administration), and Reading 2.2.2, "Federal Block Grants Require More Voter Responsibility." Then answer questions 1–3.

---

[1] In 2005, the largest teachers' union and several school districts across the country sued the Department of Education for requiring states to meet standards without providing the necessary funding. See Sam Dillon, "Teachers' Union and Districts Sue Over Bush Law," *New York Times*, April 21, 2005, p. A.1. As of this writing, several states, including Connecticut, are considering similar suits.

[2] Sam Dillon, "Utah Vote Rejects Part of Education Law," *New York Times*, April 20, 2005, p. A.14.

[3] Greg Winter, "Study Finds Shortcoming in New Law on Education," *New York Times*, April 13, 2005, p. A.15.

READING 2.2.1 RILEY SAYS NO TO EDUCATION BLOCK GRANTS; REPORT SHOWS 96 PERCENT OF FEDERAL DOLLARS GO TO LOCAL COMMUNITIES (MAY 4, 1998)[4]

U.S. Secretary of Education Richard W. Riley [in the Clinton administration] today said some members of Congress have lost sight of the goal of federal investment in education.

"We must stay focused on the priorities—supporting education reform, raising standards, and providing special assistance for children in need," Riley said. "Any legislation that just dumps federal money into general state operating funds is not serving the needs of children. It would be a diversion and would likely lead to less money going to the schools and students in the most need."

Riley said that, in fact, a greater share of federal education funds reach the classroom than state or local funds and that overall, the great majority of federal education money is used for instruction and instructional support at the local level. He cited a recent study, *The Use of Federal Education Funds for Administrative Costs,* prepared by the Education Department's Planning and Evaluation Service at the direction of Congress, that found across more than 20 large state formula grant programs, an average of only 4 percent of funds were held at the state level; the rest went to school districts and other service providers. The same report found that the Department spends the equivalent of 0.5 percent of elementary and secondary funds for administration.

Riley said proposals to collapse federal education funds into block grants to states would be a step in the wrong direction. "We've been down that road before," Riley said, referring to block grants in the mid-1970s and the early 1980s, "and the result was lack of focus and lack of accountability."

A General Accounting Office report issued in January, *State and Federal Efforts to Target Poor Students,* found that federal funds are eight times more likely than state funds to target disadvantaged students. Riley also noted that in state after state, the federal money helped to close the gap in spending between the richest and poorest districts.

"We want to make sure that every child has a real opportunity to learn—in a safe, well equipped classroom and a class small enough to assure the teacher can spend time with each child." The administration supports legislation that would leverage some $22 billion in interest-free bonds for school construction—funds that could be used to repair or replace dilapidated schools and to modernize existing facilities. President Clinton has also called for a national effort to reduce class sizes, especially in the early grades.

In addition, Riley noted that the U.S. Department of Education has eliminated one-third of previous departmental regulations over the past 3 years, and two-thirds of those which governed elementary and secondary education programs. The Clinton administration has also proposed an expansion of Ed-Flex status to all states, giving them the opportunity to waive additional federal requirements.

"I'm asking the Congress to keep the needs of children first and foremost in mind. Let's move beyond partisan rhetoric and do what's right for their future," said Riley.

---

[4] Source: Department of Education press release: http://www.ed.gov/PressReleases/051998/money.html.

READING 2.2.2 FEDERAL BLOCK GRANTS REQUIRE MORE VOTER RESPONSIBILITY (MARCH 3, 2003)[5]

The primary question is: At what level of government are the best decisions about what's good for the citizens of our states and communities made? The answer, we feel, is at the level that is closest to the people who will be most affected.

That is why the concept of including Head Start, Title I, No Child Left Behind and other federal educational money in block grants to the states appeals to us. It takes the federal government out of the decision-making process and places it at the state level—one step closer to the people.

For too long the states have been forced to accept the one-size-fits-all approaches taken by the federal government in dealing with national problems, and experience has shown us that doesn't work. Just look at our system of social welfare that makes it more viable for single mothers to go on the welfare rolls than to get a job because as welfare recipients they can get insurance, food stamps and other benefits not available to the working poor.

The needs of the individual states vary significantly. In New Hampshire, for example, Head Start works well as currently funded, but child welfare and the Medicaid systems are in shambles. Providing federal dollars in lump-sum block grants will allow states to use the money in ways that address their unique challenges, thereby maximizing the impact of those dollars.

However, there are several caveats that must be imposed on any block grant system that is established. First and foremost, the federal government cannot decrease the total amount the state gets for individual federal programs now when the block grant system is established. It cannot be used to cost-shift: to move federal expenses onto the states and communities.

There is also a concern being voiced by many child advocates and others that federal money now earmarked for specific programs will not get to those programs under the block grant system, but will go to reducing budget deficits and to funding other state initiatives. Citing Gov. Craig Benson's support for the block grant approach because it allows the state more flexibility in the use of federal funds, Ellen Shimetz, president of the Children's Alliance of New Hampshire, said she disagreed with the governor's assessment.

"We do not believe this is enhancing flexibility or local decision-making," Shimetz said. "This is a clear effort to gut Head Start and dismantle the program that is universally celebrated across party lines."

We're not convinced that Shimetz's opposition is grounded in anything other than a distrust of state government in general. But it brings up a second caveat that we believe is critical to the block grant system working effectively.

The citizens of every state will have to concentrate harder on electing representatives to state governments who best reflect the views of their constituents. It will be up to those representatives to determine how block grants are spent, and voters will have to give as much thought—perhaps even more—to the priorities of those they elect to state office than they currently give to those vying for federal positions.

The block grant system for distributing federal funds offers an immense opportunity, but also brings with it increased voter responsibilities. Block grants put federal money closer to those who initially generated those dollars, but unless close attention is paid to electing people at the state level the statement expressed so eloquently in the Who song, "Won't Get Fooled Again," will come to pass.

---

[5] Editorial reprinted with permission of the *Portsmouth (New Hampshire) Herald*.

It will truly be "Meet the new boss, same as the old boss," and Americans will be no better off than they are today.

---

1. What, according to Riley (Reading 2.2.1), are the disadvantages of the block grant approach to education?

2. What, according to the editorial (Reading 2.2.2), are the advantages of the block grant approach to education?

3. Are you persuaded by the arguments for or against block grants? Explain and support your position.

The Bush administration argues that the No Child Left Behind Act incorporates the block grant principle of flexibility for state and local governments. Yet, opponents of the NCLB Act argue that its approach is heavy-handed because it imposes unrealistic testing requirements and punishes schools that fail to live up to those requirements. One such opposition group is the National Teachers Association (NEA). Study Reading 2.2.3, "Unprecedented State and Local Flexibility," which presents the Bush administration's case, and Reading 2.2.4, "Changes to NCLB Help But More Needs to Be Done," which states the NEA's case. Then answer questions 4–6.

READING 2.2.3 THE BUSH ADMINISTRATION CASE: UNPRECEDENTED STATE AND LOCAL FLEXIBILITY[6]

Problem

— For too long, federal education programs have come with unfunded federal mandates, one-size-fits-all approaches, and unnecessary and duplicative paperwork.

— When the Elementary and Secondary Education Act was reauthorized in 1994, for example, states were required to regularly test public school students in reading and math. But this federal requirement did not come with the necessary flexibility and resources for states to focus their education strategies on what works to improve student achievement.

Solution

— The No Child Left Behind Act provides unprecedented new flexibility for all 50 states and every local school district in America in the use of federal education funds. It will revitalize the "flexibility for accountability" agreement with States first struck by President George H. W. Bush during his historic 1989 education summit with the Nation's Governors at Charlottesville, Virginia. While prior flexibility efforts have focused on waiving some program requirements, the NCLB Act moves beyond this limited approach to give States and school districts unprecedented flexibility in the use of Federal education funds in exchange for strong accountability for results. No Child Left Behind in essence moves decision making away from Washington, D.C., and empowers states and local districts to make more decisions with federal funds for goals such as teacher quality, English language proficiency, technology, and after school enrichment.

— The Department of Education administers four major state grant programs—Teacher Quality State Grants, Educational Technology, Innovative Programs, and Safe and Drug-Free Schools. New flexibility provisions in the NCLB Act will allow every school district in America to transfer up to 50 percent of the federal funding they receive between any one of these programs or to Title I. This will allow school districts to put resources into the programs that most closely match their unique local needs. States will be permitted to transfer up to 50 percent of their State administrative funding this way.

— The new law also includes a competitive State Flexibility Demonstration Program that permits up to seven States to consolidate the State administration and State activity funds from a variety of ESEA programs, including: the Innovative Programs Block Grant; the state administration components of Title I, Part A Grants (Education for the Disadvantaged); and the state administration and state activities components of Title I Part B (Reading First and Even Start). Participating States must enter an agreement with the Secretary covering the use of the consolidated funds, which may be used for any educational purpose authorized under the ESEA. As part of their plans, States also must enter into up to ten local performance agreements with districts, which will enjoy the same level of flexibility granted under the separate Local Flexibility Demonstration Program.

— A new Local Flexibility Demonstration Program would allow up 150 school districts to consolidate funds received under Teacher Quality State Grants, Educational Technology State Grants, Innovative Programs, and the Safe and Drug-Free Schools programs. Participating districts would enter into performance agreements with the Secretary of Education, and would be able to use the consolidated funds for any ESEA-authorized purpose.

---

[6] Source: White House website: http://www.whitehouse.gov/infocus/compassionate/education.html.

READING 2.2.4 THE NATIONAL EDUCATION ASSOCIATION CASE: CHANGES TO NCLB HELP BUT MORE NEEDS TO BE DONE[7]

U.S. Education Secretary Rod Paige has now made four substantive changes to regulations that govern implementation of the so-called "No Child Left Behind" federal education law.

The latest change relaxes the requirement that 95 percent of all students in each subgroup in a school must take the test in order for the school to make Adequate Yearly Progress (AYP).

NEA has welcomed the Department of Education's recognition that the law as written is inflexible and needs to be changed. But much more remains to be done.

None of the announced changes addresses a fundamental flaw of NCLB—measuring schools and holding them accountable based just on two test scores on one day.

There is no flexibility to utilize multiple measures of student achievement. Even in basing accountability just on test scores, NCLB limits how tests scores are utilized, basing everything on a snapshot on one day of what percent of students are proficient. Growth or value added models are not allowed.

NCLB also fails to give schools credit for moving students from below basic to basic, or from proficient to advanced. NCLB is still too focused on punishments and sanctions, treating a school that falls just a bit short on one of the 37 required criteria the same as a school that fails to meet all 37.

Moreover, none of the announced or proposed changes ensure that paraprofessionals will not have to pay out of their own pocket for college courses or tests required of them. The changes also fail to ensure that civil rights laws apply to supplemental service providers. And, finally, NCLB still fails to provide the resources necessary for improving student achievement.

4. On what grounds does the Bush administration rest its case for NCLB flexibility?

_____

_____

_____

_____

5. On what grounds does the NEA rest its case for NCLB inflexibility?

_____

_____

_____

_____

---

[7] Source: NEA website: http://www.nea.org/esea/flexibilitynclb.html.

6. What changes in the NCLB Act does the NEA advocate?

_____

_____

_____

7. Go to and read the Department of Education's summary of the NCLB Act: http://www.ed.gov/nclb/overview/intro/execsumm.html.[8] Which case is better supported by the actual provisions of the act: the Bush administration's characterization of the NCLB Act as flexible, or the NEA's characterization of the NCLB Act as inflexible? Support your answer with evidence from the summary of the NCLB Act.

_____

_____

_____

_____

_____

_____

_____

_____

Questions 8–13 are based on Table 2.2.1, "Revenues for Public Elementary and Secondary Schools (1939–1940 to 1999–2000)."

8. a. What percentage of total K–12 funding in 1939–40 came from the federal government?

_____

b. What percentage of total K–12 funding came from the federal government in 1999–2000?

_____

c. What is the percentage increase in the federal share of K–12 funding from fiscal year 1939–1940 to 1999–2000? (To find the percentage increase, subtract the 1939–1940 number from the 1999–2000 number. Then divide the result by the 1939–1949 number.)

_____

9. a. What percentage of total K–12 funding in 1939–40 came from state governments?

_____

b. What percentage of total K–12 funding came from state governments in 1999–2000?

_____

---

[8] Website URLs sometimes change. Try an external search (e.g., Google) to find the website. Configurations of a website often change. Try an internal search of the site to locate the information. Sometimes websites and pages within websites are removed. In that case, move on to the next question.

TABLE 2.2.1 Revenues for Public Elementary and Secondary Schools (1939–1940 to 1999–2000)

School Year	Federal percent of education funding	State percent of education funding	Local percent of education funding
1939–40	1.8	30.3	68.0
1941–42	1.4	31.4	67.1
1943–44	1.4	33.0	65.6
1945–46	1.4	34.7	63.9
1947–48	2.8	38.9	58.3
1949–50	2.9	39.8	57.3
1951–52	3.5	38.6	57.9
1953–54	4.5	37.4	58.1
1955–56	4.6	39.5	55.9
1957–58	4.0	39.4	56.6
1959–60	4.4	39.1	56.5
1961–62	4.3	38.7	56.9
1963–64	4.4	39.3	56.3
1965–66	7.9	39.1	53.0
1967–68	8.8	38.5	52.7
1969–70	8.0	39.9	52.1
1970–71	8.4	39.1	52.5
1971–72	8.9	38.3	52.8
1972–73	8.7	39.7	51.6
1973–74	8.5	41.4	50.1
1974–75	9.0	42.0	49.0
1975–76	8.9	44.4	46.7
1976–77	8.8	43.2	48.0
1977–78	9.4	43.0	47.6
1978–79	9.8	45.6	44.6
1979–80	9.8	46.8	43.4
1980–81	9.2	47.4	43.4
1981–82	7.4	47.6	45.0
1982–83	7.1	47.9	45.0
1983–84	6.8	47.8	45.4
1984–85	6.6	48.9	44.4
1985–86	6.7	49.4	43.9
1986–87	6.4	49.7	43.9
1987–88	6.3	49.5	44.1
1988–89	6.2	47.8	46.0
1989–90	6.1	47.1	46.8
1990–91	6.2	47.2	46.7
1991–92	6.6	46.4	47.0
1992–93	7.0	45.8	47.2
1993–94	7.1	45.2	47.8
1994–95	6.8	46.8	46.4
1995–96	6.6	47.5	45.9
1996–97	6.6	48.0	45.4
1997–98	6.8	48.4	44.8
1998–99	7.1	48.7	44.2
1999–2000	7.3	49.5	43.2

SOURCE: U.S. Department of Education.

c. What is the percentage increase in the state share of K–12 funding from fiscal year 1939–1940 to 1999–2000? (To find the percentage increase, subtract the 1939–1940 number from the 1999–2000 number. Then divide the result by the 1939–1949 number.)

10. What's the long-term trend? (Are elementary and secondary schools coming to rely more on federal or state dollars? Does the growth in the federal share of K–12 funding versus the growth in the state share of K–12 funding confirm the notion of an expanding federal role in education?)

To answer questions 11–13, you'll need a list of presidents with their years in office. A list of presidencies is available at http://www.enchantedlearning.com/history/us/pres/list.shtml.

11. Between which successive school years did the largest increase in the federal share of K–12 funding occur? Who was the president at that time?

12. Between which successive school years did the largest decrease in the federal share of K–12 funding occur? Who was the president at that time?

13. Are your answers to questions 11 and 12 consistent with the assessment that Republicans favor a smaller and Democrats favor a larger federal role in education?

EXERCISE 2.3 The Amendment Process

INTRODUCTION

Many forces have propelled constitutional change: social and political movements, public opinion, political leadership, and court decisions, among others. The framers recognized that an amendment process was necessary to make the Constitution's fundamental law both flexible and enduring. The functions of government and the allocation of political power would have to be adjusted as the nation evolved and faced new challenges. The threat of tyranny—the abuse of power—surely would arise from quarters and situations the framers had not anticipated, and the Constitution would have to be able to meet that threat.

The problem, of course, was where to locate the immense power to alter the nation's fundamental law. To vest the power of amendment exclusively in elected officials would be foolish: A primary objective of the Constitution is to restrain those very officials. To vest the power of amendment directly in the citizens would raise the threat of majority tyranny and would likely result in transitory popular interests corrupting the nation's fundamental law. In the end, to guard against abuse of the amendment power, the framers divided it more extensively than any other power and subjected it to a supermajority requirement found nowhere else in the Constitution. James Madison claimed in "Federalist No. 53" that the amendment mechanism guarded "equally against that extreme facility, which would render the Constitution too mutable, and that extreme difficulty, which might perpetuate its discovered faults."

The amendment process established by Article V consists of two distinct phases: proposal and ratification. Changes to the Constitution do not take effect until the requirements of both phases have been satisfied. There are two ways to satisfy the requirements of each phase. Amendments to the Constitution can be *proposed* by a two-thirds vote in the House and Senate or by a constitutional convention called by Congress at the request of two-thirds of the states—this latter route to bypass an unresponsive Congress. All twenty-seven amendments to the Constitution have been proposed by Congress. The *ratification* phase of the amendment process requires approval by three-fourths of the state legislatures or by special ratifying conventions in three-fourths of the states. Congress decides which path a proposed amendment will follow in the ratification phase. (See Figure 2.3.1 for a diagram of the amendment process.)

The three-fourths requirement for ratification is extraordinary: It is the most stringent margin in the Constitution. It makes changing the nation's fundamental law a very difficult task, one that can be accomplished only with widespread support in Congress and the states. It also increases the probability that changes to the Constitution will prove enduring, that transitory popular passions are unlikely to be written into fundamental law. And for the most part, that has been the case. Only the Eighteenth Amendment has been repealed. Of course, the supermajority requirement also can block what's right and just: It took women well over a century to obtain the right to vote through the Nineteenth Amendment (1920).

One authority estimates that over 11,000 amendments have been introduced in Congress.[1] Recent amendments that were not approved by Congress include one to allow devotional Bible reading in public schools and one to prohibit burning the American flag as a form of protest. Only thirty-three amendments have completed the proposal phase of the amendment process. Of those, only twenty-seven have been ratified. The first ten amendments—the Bill of Rights—were proposed by the First Congress as a gesture of conciliation to the remaining opponents of the new government. They were ratified by the state legislatures in 1791. The seventeen subsequent amendments were adopted between 1795 and 1992.

The states have never achieved the two-thirds requirement (thirty-four states) necessary for Congress to call a second constitutional convention. They came close when opposition

---

[1] J. W. Peltason, *Understand the Constitution* (New York: Harcourt, 1997), p. 188.

FIGURE 2.3.1

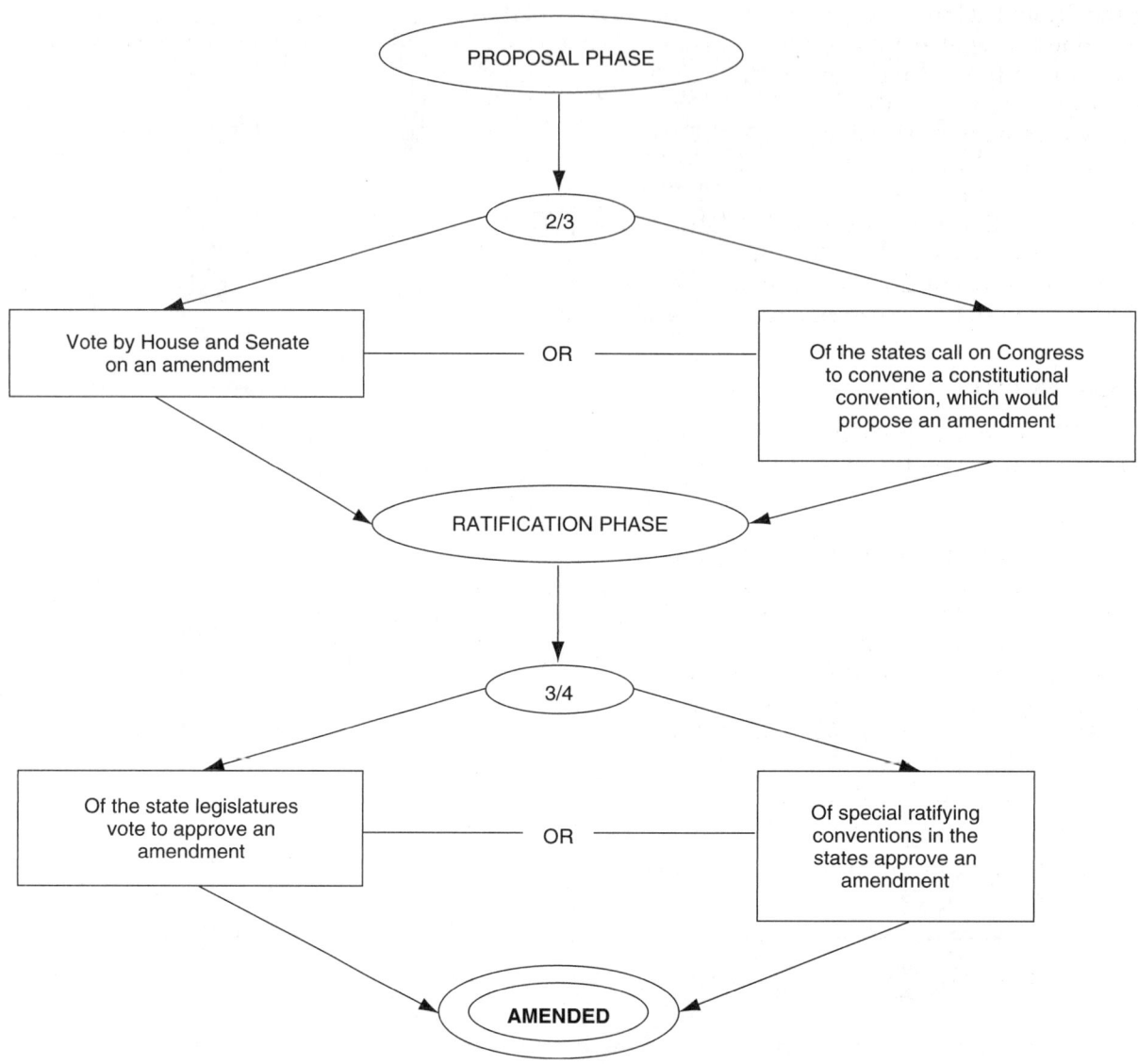

developed to the Supreme Court's decision in *Reynolds v. Sims* (1964), which required the reapportionment of state legislatures on the basis of population (see Exercise 6.4). By 1967, thirty-three state legislatures had petitioned Congress to call a constitutional convention. Their objective: to use the amendment process to reverse the ruling in *Reynolds*. But a thirty-fourth state legislature never gave its assent.

All amendments but one have been ratified by the state legislatures. The Twenty-First Amendment (1933), which repealed the Eighteenth, was routed by Congress through and then approved by special ratifying conventions in three-fourths of the states. Members of Congress believed that supporters of Prohibition (the "drys") controlled too many state legislatures, and that repeal would be more likely if the matter was decided in special ratifying conventions. Delegates to the ratifying conventions ran on "wet" or "dry" slates, so the conventions reflected the voters' will in each state.

Great power can be achieved by amending the Constitution, but proponents of constitutional change often have found their victories less than complete. In the case of Prohibition, the amendment was later repealed. Advocates of women's suffrage were disappointed following the ratification of the Nineteenth Amendment in 1920 that the voting rate for women remained below that for men until the 1950s. The Supreme Court narrowed the scope of the Fourteenth Amendment (1868) so severely in the late nineteenth century that racial discrimination remained a legal reality in the South until the 1960s. The Fifteenth Amendment (1870), which guarantees the voting rights of blacks, was not implemented across the nation for nearly one hundred years after its ratification. Even today, efforts to suppress the African-American vote are widespread.[2] These examples show that constitutional change is effective only in the presence of political and social change.

Congress has charged the National Archives and Records Administration (NARA) with managing the ratification process. NARA's website (www.nara.gov/fedreg/amdhome.html) offers information that should help you understand the amendment process. The website also has links to the Treasures of Congress exhibit, which offers additional information on the Bill of Rights and the Thirteenth, Seventeenth, and Nineteenth Amendments.

ASSIGNMENT

The Constitution stipulates two-thirds and three-fourths majorities for the proposal and ratification phases of the amendment process. We might assume, then, that changing the Constitution requires the support of a very large number of the nation's citizens. Questions 1–6 test that assumption. To answer these questions you'll need to consult Table 2.3.1 which lists the population of each state and its representation in the House based on the 2000 census.

Consider an amendment to the Constitution that would change the basis of representation in the House. Under this amendment, the bargain struck at the Constitutional Convention between the large and small states—the Great Compromise—would be nullified. The amendment under consideration here would revise Article I, Section 2, abolishing population-based representation in the House and instead making representation there equal for every state by increasing the size of the House to 500 members and awarding ten seats to each state. (An amendment to the Constitution requiring population-based representation in the Senate would be unconstitutional unless each state consented to it. This is specified in Article V of the Constitution, and it essentially freezes into the Constitution a non–population-based Senate.)

1. How many seats in the House would California lose under the terms of the proposed amendment?

2. How many seats would Alaska gain under the proposed amendment?

3. Consider first the fate of the amendment in the *proposal* phase of the amendment process. The proponents of the amendment introduce it in the House and Senate, hoping to marshal the required two-thirds support.

a. Use the data in Table 2.3.1 to determine the number of votes that would be cast in the House and Senate for and against *proposing* the amendment. Assume that members of Congress vote solely on the basis of the amendment's effect on their state's voting power in the House, that they do not consider other issues raised by the amendment. Virginia, for example, would vote against the amendment because its delegation in the House would be reduced by one member. Assume that Massachusetts, the only state with ten representatives in the House—and so nothing to gain or lose—votes in favor of the amendment.

---

[2] See, for example, "The Long Shadow of Jim Crow: Voter Intimidation and Suppression in American Today" at www.naacp.org.

TABLE 2.3.1	Population and Representation in the House by State, 2000 Census Data	
State	Population	Number of Representatives in the House
Alabama	4,461,130	7
Alaska	628,933	1
Arizona	5,140,683	8
Arkansas	2,679,733	4
California	33,930,798	53
Colorado	4,311,882	7
Connecticut	3,409,535	5
Delaware	785,068	1
Florida	16,028,890	25
Georgia	8,206,975	13
Hawaii	1,216,642	2
Idaho	1,297,274	2
Illinois	12,439,042	19
Indiana	6,090,782	9
Iowa	2,931,923	5
Kansas	2,693,824	4
Kentucky	4,049,431	6
Louisiana	4,480,271	7
Maine	1,277,731	2
Maryland	5,307,886	8
Massachusetts	6,355,568	10
Michigan	9,955,829	15
Minnesota	4,925,670	8
Mississippi	2,852,927	4
Missouri	5,606,260	9
Montana	905,316	1
Nebraska	1,715,369	3
Nevada	2,002,032	3
New Hampshire	1,238,415	2
New Jersey	8,424,354	13
New Mexico	1,823,821	3
New York	19,004,973	29
North Carolina	8,067,673	13
North Dakota	643,756	1
Ohio	11,374,540	18
Oklahoma	3,458,819	5
Oregon	3,428,543	5
Pennsylvania	12,300,670	19
Rhode Island	1,049,662	2
South Carolina	4,025,061	6
South Dakota	756,874	1
Tennessee	5,700,037	9
Texas	20,903,994	32
Utah	2,236,714	3
Vermont	609,890	1
Virginia	7,100,702	11
Washington	5,908,684	9
West Virginia	1,813,077	3
Wisconsin	5,371,210	8
Wyoming	495,304	1
Total national population	281,424,177	435

EXERCISE 2.3   THE AMENDMENT PROCESS

Vote in the House:

_____

Vote in the Senate:

_____

b. Does the vote in the House meet the two-thirds requirement?

_____

c. Does the vote in the Senate meet the two-thirds requirement?

_____

d. Will the amendment be forwarded to the states for possible ratification and incorporation into the Constitution?

_____

e. Why is the outcome of the vote in the Senate strikingly different from the vote in the House? Explain and support your answer.

_____

_____

_____

_____

_____

_____

4. Now consider the fate of the amendment in the *ratification* phase of the amendment process. Assume that each state legislature votes solely on the basis of the amendment's effect on the state's voting power in the House, as you did in question 2.a. above.

a. How many state legislatures would vote to ratify the amendment, and how many would be opposed?

_____

b. Is the number of state legislatures in favor of the amendment sufficient to change the Constitution?

_____

5. a. Using the data in Table 2.3.1, calculate the approximate population of the twelve largest states.

_____

b. Calculate the approximate population of the thirty-eight smallest states.

_____

c. What percentage of the nation's population lives in the twelve most populous states?

d. What percentage of the nation's population lives in the thirty-eight smallest states?

6. On Figure 2.3.2, plot the relationship between population and political power in the House. Begin with the group of twelve states with the largest populations. On the vertical axis of the graph, locate the total number of votes in the House that these states command. On the horizontal axis, locate the percent of the population in these states. From the location you established on the vertical axis, draw a line to the right, stopping when it intersects the line you'll draw up from the location you established on the horizontal axis. Repeat the same process for the group of thirty-eight states with the smallest populations. Label each rectangle: small states and large states.

FIGURE 2.3.2 Population and Political Power in the House

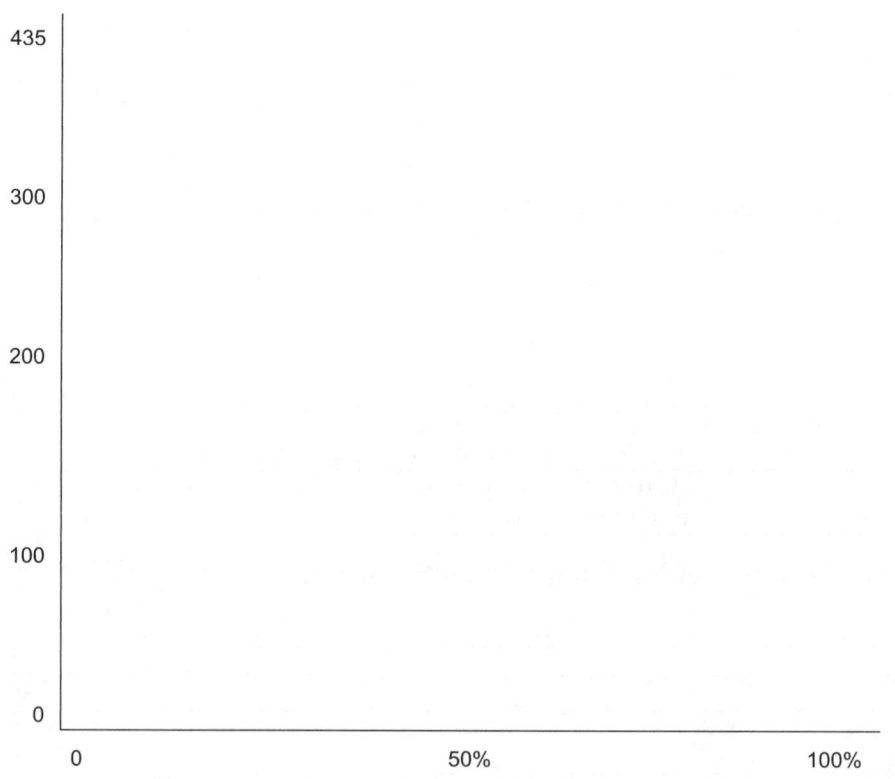

On Figure 2.3.3, plot the relationship between population and political power in the Senate for the group of twelve states with the largest populations and for the group of thirty-eight states with the smallest populations. Follow the same process you used for the graph on the House. Label each rectangle.

FIGURE 2.3.3 Population and Political Power in the Senate

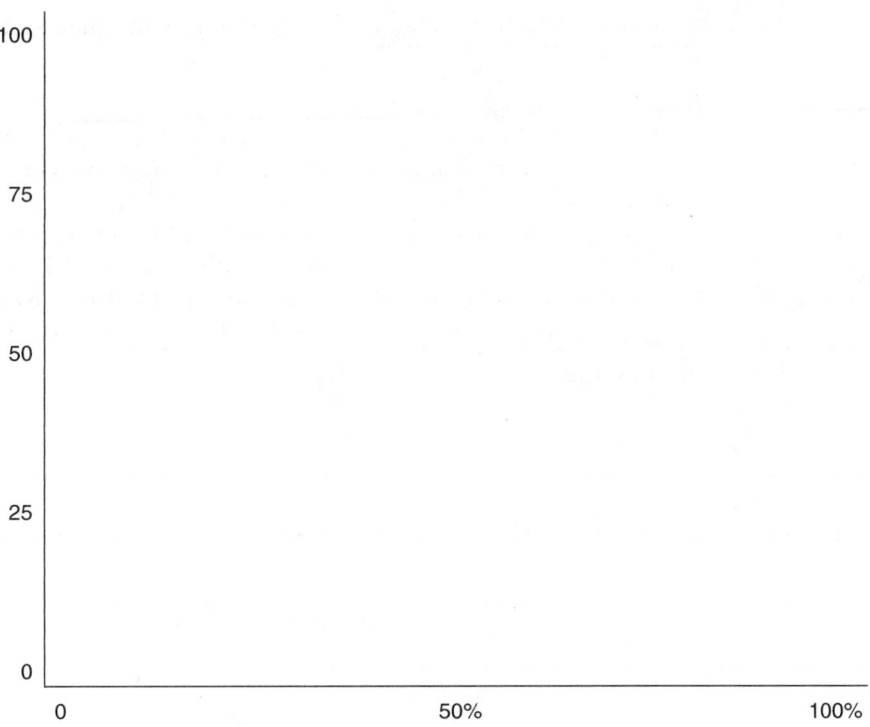

a. Explain why the shapes of the two rectangles on the House graph are similar.

_____
_____
_____
_____
_____

b. Explain why the shapes of the two rectangles on the Senate graph are so strikingly different.

_____
_____
_____
_____
_____

7. What percentage of the nation's population would support the amendment? Assume that popular support is determined by whether a state gains or loses seats in the House under the terms of the amendment.

_____

8. Suppose that this amendment was put to a nationwide popular vote. Assume that voters cast their ballots based on whether their state gains or loses seats in the House. What would the result of the vote be? Explain and support your answer.

9. a. Design and explain an alternative to the Constitution's amendment process that gives a less prominent role to the states and that is more consistent with the principles of representative democracy.

b. Make an argument in support of your alternative amendment process.

c. Make an argument against your alternative amendment process.

EXERCISE 2.4 Who's in Charge of the Minimum Drinking Age—The Federal Government or the States?

INTRODUCTION

The Constitution delegates certain powers to the national government and others to the states. Some areas of responsibility are clearly specified in the Constitution: Article I, Section 8, for example, enumerates the powers that belong to Congress and hence to the national government. Other responsibilities are not as clear. The Tenth Amendment (1791) states: "The powers not delegated to the United States by the Constitution, nor prohibited by it to the States, are reserved to the States respectively, or to the people." American political history is replete with disputes centering on the distribution of those powers.

The Supreme Court is the final arbiter in those disputes. But because the political landscape constantly is changing in response to international and domestic events, the Court has not been consistent in its interpretation of the respective powers of the national and state governments. Still, from the mid-1930s to the mid-1990s, the Court consistently found for the national government. At times it would cite implied powers to support federal claims to power over the states. According to the Court, *implied powers* are those that Congress rightfully infers as its own from the necessary and proper clause of the Constitution. For example, the Court has held it proper for Congress to pass legislation prohibiting racial discrimination in hotels, motels, and restaurants.[1] According to the Court, that authority is implied by the Constitution, which grants Congress the authority to regulate interstate commerce. The Court reasoned that because travelers make use of public accommodations as they go from one state to another, the businesses are engaged in interstate commerce and therefore are subject to federal regulation.

In the 1980s, the national government used its allocation of highway funds to the states to restrict the sale of alcoholic beverages. At issue: the minimum drinking age. Although most states set the minimum age at 21, several allowed the consumption of some types of alcoholic beverages at ages ranging from 18 to 20. The national government eventually adopted the argument of Mothers Against Drunk Driving (MADD) that an under-21 drinking age in one state creates an incentive for young people to drive from bordering states to purchase and consume alcoholic beverages and then to return to their home states. Actuarial tables showed that arrests for driving under the influence and drunk-driving accidents among 18- to 21-year-old drivers increased in states that bordered a state with a lower minimum drinking age. Congress subsequently enacted the National Minimum Drinking Age Amendment of 1984. (The Reagan administration, despite its dislike of federal meddling in state affairs, eventually supported the law.) That statute directed the secretary of transportation to withhold 5 percent of federal highway block grants (see Exercise 2.2) from states where those under 21 could legally purchase or consume alcoholic beverages.

South Dakota, which allowed those 19 years or older to purchase and consume 3.2 percent beer, filed suit in federal court seeking a declaratory judgment that the statute violated the Twenty-First Amendment to the U.S. Constitution, which gives the states the power to impose restrictions on the sale of liquor. South Dakota also contended that the statute violated the spending clause in Article I, Section 8, of the U.S. Constitution because it permitted the federal government to withhold block grant money available to other states. The federal district court rejected South Dakota's claim and was upheld by the U.S. court of appeals. South Dakota then appealed to the U.S. Supreme Court. South Dakota was the plaintiff; the respondent was Elizabeth Dole, then the secretary of transportation. In a 7–2 vote, the justices rejected South Dakota's claim.

Since that decision, all states have raised their minimum drinking age to 21, partly because of the lobbying efforts of MADD and partly because the states could not afford to look the gift horse of federal highway grants in the mouth. Recently, a debate has begun in Vermont about lowering its drinking age. Vermont stands to lose $9.7 million if the current age minimum of 21 is repealed.[2]

---

[1] See *Atlanta Motel v. United States* (1964) and *Katzenbach v. McClung* (1964).

[2] Pam Belluck and Kay Zazima, "Vermont Considers Lowering Drinking Age to 18," *New York Times*, April 13, 2005, p. A.13.

The decision in *South Dakota v. Dole* was typical of the Court's deference to federal over state power that prevailed between the mid-1930s and the mid-1990s. But from 1995 to 2005, the Rehnquist Court, led by a pro-states' rights majority—typically found for the states in federal–state disputes. The shift began with *United States v. Lopez* (1995), in which the Court held that a federal law (the Gun-Free Schools Act of 1990) prohibiting the possession of a gun within 1,000 feet of a school was unconstitutional because it was not within the meaning of commerce that can be regulated by Congress. Nevertheless, in the most controversial case in recent years, *Bush v. Gore* (2000), the Court held that the state of Florida could not recount ballots cast in the 2000 presidential election because a recount would violate the equal protection clause of the Fourteenth Amendment. This departure from the Rehnquist Court's usual deference to states led some critics to claim that the Court's majority was less committed to the principle of states' rights than to a conservative, pro-Republican political agenda.

ASSIGNMENT

Excerpts from the opinion of the Court (Chief Justice Rehnquist) and the dissenting opinion (Justice O'Connor) in *South Dakota v. Dole* (1987) are reprinted in Reading 2.4.1. Study the decision and answer the questions that follow it.

READING 2.4.1 *SOUTH DAKOTA V. DOLE*, 483 U.S. 203 (1987)

Mr. Chief Justice Rehnquist delivered the opinion of the Court.

In this Court, the parties direct most of their efforts to defining the proper scope of the Twenty-first Amendment.... South Dakota asserts that the setting of minimum drinking ages is clearly within the "core powers" reserved to the States under §[Section]2 of the Amendment.... The Secretary in response asserts that the Twenty-first Amendment is simply not implicated by §158 [the National Minimum Drinking Age Amendment]; the plain language of §2 [of the Twenty-First Amendment] confirms the States' broad power to impose restrictions on the sale and distribution of alcoholic beverages but does not confer on them any power to *permit* sales that Congress seeks to *prohibit*. That Amendment, under this reasoning would not prevent Congress from affirmatively enacting a national minimum drinking age more restrictive than that provided by the various state laws; and it would follow a fortiori that the indirect inducement involved here is compatible with the Twenty-first Amendment.

These arguments present questions of the meaning of the Twenty-first Amendment, the bounds of which have escaped precise definition.... Despite the extended treatment of the question by the parties, however, we need not decide in this case whether that Amendment would prohibit an attempt by Congress to legislate directly a national minimum drinking age. Here, Congress has acted indirectly under its spending power to encourage uniformity in the States' drinking ages. As we explain below, we find this legislative effort within constitutional bounds even if Congress may not regulate drinking ages directly.

The Constitution empowers Congress to "lay and collect Taxes, Duties, Imposts, and Excises, to pay the Debts and provide for the common Defence and general Welfare of the United States." Art. I, §8, Cl. 1. Incident to this power, Congress may attach conditions on the receipt of federal funds, and has repeatedly employed the power "to further broad policy objectives by conditioning receipt of federal moneys upon compliance by the recipient with federal statutory and administrative directives." ... The breadth of this power was made clear in *United States v. Butler*... where the Court, resolving a long-standing debate over the scope of the Spending Clause, determined that "the power of Congress to authorize expenditure of public moneys for public purposes is not limited by the direct grants of legislative power found in the Constitution." Thus, objectives not thought to be within Article I's "enumerated legislative fields," ... may nevertheless be attained through the use of the spending power and the conditional grant of federal funds.

The spending power is of course not unlimited ... but is instead subject to several general restrictions articulated in our cases. The first of these limitations is derived from the language of the Constitution itself: the exercise of the spending power must be in pursuit of "the general welfare." ... In considering whether a particular expenditure is intended to serve general public purposes, courts should defer substantially to the judgment of Congress.... Second, we have required that if Congress desires to condition the States' receipt of federal funds, it "must do so unambiguously ..., enabl[ing] the States to exercise their choice knowingly, cognizant of the consequences of their participation." ... Third, our cases have suggested (without significant elaboration) that conditions on federal grants might be illegitimate if they are unrelated "to the federal interest in particular national projects or programs." ...

South Dakota does not seriously claim that §158 is inconsistent with any of the first three restrictions mentioned above. We can readily conclude that the provision is designed to serve the general welfare, especially in light of the fact that "the concept of welfare or the opposite is shaped by Congress...." Congress found that the differing drinking ages in the States created particular incentives for young persons to combine their desire to drink with their ability to drive, and that this interstate problem required a national solution. The means it chose to address this dangerous situation were reasonably calculated to advance the general welfare. The conditions upon which States receive the funds, moreover, could not be more clearly stated by Congress.... And the State itself, rather than challenging the germaneness of the condition to federal purposes, admits that it "has never contended that the congressional action was ... unrelated to a national concern in the absence of the Twenty-first Amendment." ... Indeed, the condition imposed by Congress is directly related to one of the main purposes for which highway funds are expended—safe interstate travel.

This goal of the interstate highway system had been frustrated by varying drinking ages among the States. A Presidential commission appointed to study alcohol-related accidents and fatalities on the Nation's highways concluded that the lack of uniformity in the States' drinking ages created "an incentive to drink and drive" because "young persons commut[e] to border States where the drinking age is lower." ... By enacting §158, Congress conditioned the receipt of federal funds in a way reasonably calculated to address this particular impediment to a purpose for which the funds are expended.

The remaining question about the validity of §158—and the basic point of disagreement between the parties—is whether the Twenty-first Amendment constitutes an "independent constitutional bar" to the conditional grant of federal funds.... Petitioner, relying on its view that the Twenty-first Amendment prohibits direct regulation of drinking ages by Congress, asserts that "Congress may not use the spending power to regulate that which it is prohibited from regulating directly under the Twenty-first Amendment." ... But our cases show that this "independent constitutional bar" limitation on the spending power is not of the kind petitioner suggests. *United States v. Butler*..., for example, established that the constitutional limitations on Congress when exercising its spending power are less exacting than those on its authority to regulate directly.

We have also held that a perceived Tenth Amendment limitation on congressional regulation of state affairs did not concomitantly limit the range of conditions legitimately placed on federal grants.

These cases ... establish that the "independent constitutional bar" limitation on the spending power is not, as petitioner suggests, a prohibition on the indirect achievement of objectives which Congress is not empowered to achieve directly. Instead, we think that the language in our earlier opinions stands for the unexceptionable proposition that the power may not be used to induce the States to engage in activities that would themselves be unconstitutional. Thus, for example, a grant of federal funds conditioned on invidiously discriminatory state action or the infliction of cruel and unusual punishment would be an illegitimate exercise of the Congress's broad spending power. But no such claim can be or is made here. Were South Dakota to succumb to the blandishments offered by Congress and raise its drinking age to 21, the State's action in so doing would not violate the constitutional rights of anyone.

Even if Congress might lack the power to impose a national minimum drinking age directly, we conclude that encouragement to state action found in §158 is a valid use of the spending power. Accordingly, the judgment of the Court of Appeals is affirmed.

Justice O'Connor dissenting.

The Court today upholds the National Minimum Drinking Age Amendments ... as a valid exercise of the spending power conferred by Article 1, §8. But, §158 is not a condition on spending reasonably related to the expenditure of federal funds and cannot be justified on that ground. Rather, it is an attempt to regulate the sale of liquor, an attempt that lies outside Congress' power to regulate commerce because it falls within the ambit of §2 of the Twenty-first Amendment.

My disagreement with the Court is relatively narrow on the spending power issue: it is a disagreement about the application of a principle rather than a disagreement on the principle itself.

The Court reasons that Congress wishes that the roads it builds may be used safely, that drunken drivers threaten highway safety, and that young people are more likely to drive while under the influence of alcohol under existing law than would be the case if there were a uniform national drinking age of 21. It hardly needs saying, however, that if the purpose of §158 is to deter drunk driving, it is far too over and under inclusive. It is over-inclusive because it stops teenagers from drinking even when they are not about to drive on interstate highways. It is under-inclusive because teenagers pose only a small part of the drunken driving problem in this Nation.

When Congress appropriates money to build a highway, it is entitled to insist that the highway be a safe one. But it is not entitled to insist as a condition of the use of highway funds that the State impose or change regulations in other areas of the State's social and economic life because of an attenuated or tangential relationship to highway use or safety. Indeed, if the rule were otherwise, the Congress could effectively regulate almost any area of a State's social, political, or economic life on the theory that use of the interstate transportation system is somehow enhanced....

As discussed above, a condition that a State will raise its drinking age to 21 cannot fairly be said to be reasonably related to the expenditure of funds for highway construction. The only possible connection, highway safety, has nothing to do with how the funds Congress has appropriated are expended. Rather than a condition determining how federal highway money shall be expended, it is a regulation determining who shall be able to drink liquor. As such it is not justified by the spending power.

The immense size and power of the Government of the United States ought not obscure its fundamental character. It remains a Government of enumerated powers.... Because 23 USC 158 ... cannot be justified as an exercise of any power delegated to the Congress, it is not authorized by the Constitution. The Court errs in holding it to be the law of the land, and I respectfully dissent.

---

1. What are the three restrictions on Congress's spending power identified in Chief Justice Rehnquist's opinion?

2. On what grounds did the Court find that Congress was not in violation of those three restrictions when it withheld a percentage of block grant highway funds from South Dakota?

_____
_____
_____
_____

3. The Twenty-First Amendment makes the states responsible for regulating the sale of alcohol. But the Court took the position that the Twenty-First Amendment does not present an "independent constitutional bar" to the federal government's effort to encourage the states to raise their minimum drinking age by withholding block grant funding. What was the basis for the Court's conclusion that the Twenty-First Amendment did not stand in the way of the National Minimum Drinking Age Amendment of 1984? Explain and support your answer by citing language from the Court's decision.

_____
_____
_____
_____

4. Congress did not attempt to legislate directly a uniform minimum national drinking age. Does Rehnquist indicate in the Court's decision whether this direct approach would violate the Twenty-First Amendment? Explain and support your answer by citing language from the Court's decision.

_____
_____
_____
_____

5. In her dissent, Justice Sandra Day O'Connor holds that the National Minimum Drinking Age Amendment of 1984 is not "reasonably related to the purpose for which the funds are expended." How does she justify her position? Explain and support your answer by citing language from the Court's decision.

_____
_____
_____
_____

6. In your view, should the national government be allowed to use the conditional grant of federal funds to pressure states to increase their drinking age to 21—despite the specific language of the Twenty-First Amendment? Explain and support your position.

CHAPTER 3

Public Opinion and the Mass Media

EXERCISE 3.1 Public Confidence in American Institutions

INTRODUCTION

Politicians use opinion polls to gauge the public's view of their performance in office, to assess public support for particular policies, and to determine the strengths and weaknesses of candidates as elections draw near. Some pundits claim that the national obsession with opinion polls has made our political life a popularity contest and turned our electoral campaigns into horse races.

The key to a credible public opinion poll is questioning a statistically significant number of people; most nationwide polls survey anywhere from 600 to 2,000 respondents. The procedure called *random sampling* is based on the mathematical probability that random surveying (for example, using randomly generated telephone numbers) of a large number of citizens will approximate the views of the whole population. Most polls have a margin of error of 3 percent. For example, several polls taken just before the 2004 election showed George W. Bush's support at 49 percent and John Kerry's at 47 percent. That was a statistical dead heat because Bush's support—given the margin of error—might have been as low as 46 percent and Kerry's as high as 50 percent. These polls proved quite accurate: Bush ended up wining with approximately a 3 percent margin.

Some polls are more problematic than others. A question can be phrased so that it is likely to elicit a favorable or a negative response. Pollsters have found that even the positioning of a question can make a difference. Because many respondents have little interest in or commitment to any of the alternatives posed in a survey, they may "merely choose the option that was mentioned last."[1] Another problem is that some respondents don't answer honestly, and some answer even though they are uninformed.

---

[1] David W. Moore, "Questionnaire Experiments," *The Gallup Monthly*, December 1995, p. 36.

The least credible polls are so-called *straw polls*. Local media and college newspapers often use straw polls to gauge the popularity of politicians and policies. A straw poll may involve asking as few as fifty people going into a local market who they think is the best candidate in the town's upcoming mayoral election. Even though straw polls interest many people, they are not scientific and not reliable.

ASSIGNMENT

Polls regularly ask Americans about their level of confidence in different institutions. The responses can be charted over time, allowing us to see how public confidence changes in response to major events.

Questions 1–4 are based on Table 3.1.1, "Confidence in Selected American Institutions, 1979–2004."

TABLE 3.1.1 Confidence in Selected American Institutions, 1979–2004

	Percent Responding "Great Deal" or "Quite a Lot"									
Institution	1979	1981	1984	1986	1988	1991	1993	1995	2001*	2004
Military	54	59	58	63	58	69	68	64	66	75
Religion	65	64	64	57	59	56	53	57	60	64
Presidency	NA	NA	NA	NA	NA	50	43	45	48	52
Supreme Court	45	46	51	54	56	39	44	44	50	52
Banks	60	46	51	49	49	30	37	43	44	53
Public schools	53	42	47	49	49	35	39	40	38	41
Newspapers	51	35	34	37	36	32	31	30	36	30
Organized labor	36	28	30	29	26	22	26	26	26	31
Congress	34	29	29	41	35	18	18	21	26	30
Big business	32	20	29	28	25	22	22	21	28	24
Television news	38	25	25	27	27	24	21	NA	34	30

NOTE: NA = not available
SOURCE: Adapted from "Confidence in Institutions—Trend," *Gallup Poll Monthly*, May 1995, 13; and "Military Retains Top Position in Americans' Confidence," *Gallup Poll Analyses*, June 25, 2001, and May 23, 2004. Used by permission of The Gallup Organization.
*Poll taken before the events of 9/11/2001.

1. Which institutions enjoyed an increase in confidence from 1979 to 2004?

2. Which institutions saw a decrease in confidence from 1979 to 2004?

3. Students of public opinion agree that the Watergate scandal and the defeat of the United States in the Vietnam War undermined public confidence in American institutions in the quarter-century after these major national crises, 1975–2000. Are the data consistent with that view? (Use the 1979 and 1995 columns in Table 3.1.1.) Explain and support your answer.

4. Students of public opinion believe that the terrorist attacks of 9/11 and the subsequent war on terrorism have rebuilt public confidence in American institutions—possibly because of the tendency during wartime to rally around the flag. Compare the data for 2001 (poll taken before 9/11) and 2004. Do the data show an increase in public confidence? Explain and support your answer.

Questions 5–7 are based on Table 3.1.2, "Trust in Federal Government." The data in this table differ in two ways from the data in Table 3.1.1: The data in Table 3.1.2 focus on the federal government only and cover a shorter period of time.

TABLE 3.1.2 Trust in Federal Government

"How much of the time do you think you can trust the government in Washington to do what is right: just about always, most of the time, or only some of the time?"

	PERCENT RESPONDING				
	Just About Always	Most of the Time	Only Some of the Time	Never	No Opinion
9/02	8	38	52	2	—
6/02	6	39	51	3	1
10/01	13	47	38	1	1
7/00	4	38	56	2	—
2/99	5	29	64	2	—
2/98	6	33	59	2	—
6/97	3	29	65	2	1

SOURCE: The Gallup Poll, Sept. 13–15, 2004. Used by permission of The Gallup Organization.

5. In which month/year was the largest increase in those respondents who trusted the government in Washington "just about always" and "most of the time"?

6. Does that increase confirm the notion that the events of 9/11 led to a "rally around the flag" effect of a national crisis? Explain and support your answer.

7. Historically, public confidence tends to decline as the "rally around the flag" effect plays itself out. Do the data indicate that this has occurred? Explain and support your answer.

EXERCISE 3.2 Bias and Accuracy in the News Media: The Case of CBS News and President Bush's Military Record

INTRODUCTION

Negative perceptions of the news media are widespread. One poll by the Council for Excellence in Government showed that 29 percent of the respondents blamed the media for "what's wrong with government today"; only "special interest groups" got more blame (38 percent).[1] A Gallup Poll showed public confidence in the news media below that for all major institutions, except "big business" and health maintenance organizations (HMOs).[2] The public's view of the news media has become even more negative over the past four years, continuing a long-term decline in media credibility.[3] Recent scandals about plagiarized, fabricated, and false stories in print and television news media have fueled the decline.

Part of the news media's credibility problem is the belief that reporters and news organizations are biased—that coverage is slanted to further a political agenda. One study found that 78 percent of the public perceived the news media as biased.[4] The perception of bias in the news media, however, sometimes stems from the viewer's bias. One study by the nonpartisan Pew Research Center for the Study of the People and the Press found that party loyalty correlates strongly with confidence in particular news providers. For example, among viewers of cable news networks, Republicans tend to find Fox News what it claims to be: "fair and balanced," whereas Democrats have more confidence in CNN.[5]

Conservative Republicans claimed liberal bias in a CBS News *Sixty Minutes* segment, broadcast on September 8, 2004, during the heated and highly partisan presidential race. Dan Rather—the CBS anchor and target of conservative critics for his alleged liberal bias—reported that CBS News had obtained a document proving the oft-repeated charges that George W. Bush received favorable treatment in the Texas Air National Guard because of his family connections and that his performance and participation in training were not up to par. For days, Rather defended the authenticity of the incriminating document despite allegations that it was a forgery. Subsequently, CBS News admitted that it was unable to prove the authenticity of the document. The resulting firestorm of criticism engulfed Rather, Mary Mapes (the segment's producer), and CBS News in charges that they were out to get Bush. CBS subsequently appointed an independent panel to review its handling of the story. The panel's report—sections of which are included in this exercise—found numerous sins of commission and omission. Dan Rather retired as anchor of the *CBS Evening News* on March 9, 2005.

Although conservatives charge that CBS is afflicted with political bias, many experts on journalism argue that the real problem is *commercial bias*. According to those critics, the mistakes in the Bush National Guard story stemmed less from political bias than from the high level of competition among news organizations to break a story. Competitive pressures led CBS News to air the story before other news organizations could run it, which compromised the news organization's ability to properly check the story. Many have also noted that the substance of the story—Bush's poor record in the Texas Air National Guard—was never found to be false and that the document was never proved to be a forgery.

ASSIGNMENT

Study Reading 3.2.1, which includes sections of the "Report of the Independent Review Panel on the September 8, 2004, *60 Minutes Wednesday* Segment, 'For the Record', Concerning President Bush's Air National Guard Service." The questions that follow the reading assess possible political and commercial bias in the Rather story.

---

[1] Poll conducted February 9–16, 2004.

[2] Poll conducted May 21–23, 2004.

[3] Harris Poll, conducted February 9–16, 2004. (Previous polls conducted January 2001, January 2002, and December 2002.)

[4] American Society of News Editors, "Examining Our Credibility," August 10, 1999 (http://www.asne.org/kiosk/reports/99reports/1999examiningourcredibility/p27-32_Bias.html).

[5] June 8, 2004, http://people-press.org/reports/display.php3?PageID=833.

READING 3.2.1 REPORT OF THE INDEPENDENT REVIEW PANEL, BY DICK THORNBURGH AND LOUIS D. BOCCARDI[6]

Part X. Whether There Was a Political Agenda Driving the September 8 Segment

There has been widespread speculation in the media that the September 8 Segment was motivated, in whole or in part, by an anti-Bush political agenda....

The question of whether a political agenda played any role in the airing of the Segment is one of the most subjective, and most difficult, that the Panel has sought to answer. The political agenda question was posed by the Panel directly to Dan Rather and his producer, Mary Mapes, who appear to have drawn the greatest attention in terms of possible political agendas. Both strongly denied that they brought any political bias to the Segment. The Panel recognizes that those who saw bias at work in the Segment are likely to sweep such denials aside. However, the Panel will not level allegations for which it cannot offer adequate proof.

The Panel does not find a basis to accuse those who investigated, produced, vetted or aired the Segment of having a political bias. The Panel does note, however, that on such a politically charged story, coming in the midst of a presidential campaign in which military service records had become an issue, there was a need for meticulous care to avoid any suggestion of an agenda at work. The Panel does not believe that the appropriate level of care to avoid the appearance of political motivation was used in connection with this story.

It should be noted that 60 Minutes Wednesday was hardly alone in pursuing the story. Other mainstream media, including USA TODAY, The New York Times and The Associated Press, were pursuing the same story in what was clearly a competitive race to be first. In fact, USA TODAY on September 9 published a similar story relying on the same Killian documents, but has not been as criticized for its story as CBS News has been for the September 8 Segment. The Panel recognizes that some will see this widespread media attention not as evidence that 60 Minutes Wednesday was not motivated by bias but instead proof that all of mainstream media has a liberal bias. That is a perception beyond the Panel's assignment....

The Panel believes that additional factors in the production of the September 8 Segment rebut the notion that it was politically motivated. The most significant factors are discussed below.

1. The Previous Work of Rather and Mapes

The Panel asked Rather directly to comment on whether he was motivated in any way by a political animus in pursuing the September 8 Segment. He responded: "absolutely, unequivocally untrue." Rather related that over his long career, he has done tough stories on a number of Presidents, both Republican and Democrat, including: Lyndon Johnson and the Vietnam War; Richard Nixon and Watergate; Jimmy Carter and the Iran hostages; George H. W. Bush and Iran Contra; and Bill Clinton and Monica Lewinsky. With respect to the September 8 Segment, Rather said that he had full confidence in the people who put the story together and that he had no indication at the time that the documents were not authentic.

Mapes told the Panel that she was motivated by "proximity, not politics." Mapes has lived in Texas for 15 years and at least six of her thirty 60 Minutes Wednesday stories before the September 8 Segment had a Texas nexus. The Panel was told by many at 60 Minutes Wednesday and CBS News who worked with Mapes that she was motivated by reporting on a significant story and that they did not believe that political ideology became a part of her stories. Mapes stridently believed in both the authenticity of the documents and their content, and, indeed, told the Panel that she still does.

---

[6] Source: http://wwwimage.cbsnews.com/htdocs/pdf/complete_report/CBS_Report.pdf.

The senior producers and management, Murphy, Howard and West, as well as the other vetters [fact checkers], all told the Panel that they were comfortable in broadcasting the September 8 Segment because they believed at the time that the Killian documents and their content had been authenticated. They recognized the political sensitivity of the story and took steps to make it more balanced. The Panel finds no evidence that any of these individuals were motivated by political considerations.

2. *The Editing Process Added Balance*

The management structure at CBS News and within 60 Minutes Wednesday is intended to serve as a mechanism to ensure that stories are reported fairly and accurately. Thus, the President of the CBS News Division [Heyward], the Senior Vice President, Prime Time, CBS News [West] and the Executive Producer of 60 Minutes Wednesday [Howard] can dictate that changes be made to a story and each has veto power over any story. The producer and correspondent cannot force a show to air over the veto of any of these executives.

With respect to the September 8 Segment, Heyward, West and Howard all were involved before the Segment aired to ensure that it was fair and balanced, although their degree of involvement varied. At least two specific changes in the September 8 script were ordered by some or all of these individuals: 1) the deletion of Colonel Hackworth's interview excerpts, including his characterization that then-Lieutenant Bush "was AWOL for a whole bunch of his service"; and 2) the inclusion of additional statements from the interview with White House Director of Communications Dan Bartlett that further rebutted the allegations against President Bush. These changes were designed to make the Segment more balanced.

3. *Assuming the Killian [the alleged author of the incriminating] Documents Were Authentic, They Added New Data to the Bush TexANG [Texas Air National Guard] Record*

The September 8 Segment addressed some items pertaining to President Bush's TexANG service record that were not previously known and thus could be considered newsworthy. Significant among them were:

1. Lieutenant Colonel Killian on May 4, 1972 ordered Bush to report for his annual physical no later than May 14, 1972.
2. Lieutenant Colonel Killian on August 1, 1972 suspended Bush from flying status on August 1, 1972 not only for failing to take his physical, but also for "failure to perform to USAF/TexANG standards...."
3. Lieutenant Colonel Killian wrote on August 18, 1912 that General Staudt, the then-former TexANG Chief of Staff, was pressuring Major General Hodges and Lieutenant Colonel Harris to "sugar coat" an evaluation of Lieutenant Bush.

If true, these statements appear to have constituted newsworthy information in which the public could have an interest. These documents would have, again if true, been the basis for a legitimate story in the Panel's view, as attested to by the fact that other national media were pursuing the same story. It is a large part of an investigative reporter's mandate to provide this kind of provocative information to viewers or readers, assuming it has been properly reported and vetted, regardless of the reporter's political affiliation or motives.

Part XI. [Excerpts from] the Panel's Recommendations

Competitive pressures are a fact of life in journalism and may impact the timing of a news story. The leadership of CBS News, however, should make clear to all personnel that competitive pressures cannot be allowed to prompt the airing of a story before it is ready. It would have been better to "lose" the story on the Killian documents to a competitor than to air it short of investigating and vetting to the highest standards of fairness and accuracy.

CHAPTER 3 PUBLIC OPINION AND THE MASS MEDIA

1. In one sentence, state the panel's conclusion on whether Rather's news report stemmed from an anti-Bush bias.

The panel did not believe that the appropriate level of care to avoid the appearance of political motivation was used in connection w/ the story.

2. What evidence did the panel provide for its conclusion?

- That mainstream media has a liberal bias
- That mainstream media is competitive in a race to be the first in reporting a breaking story

3. How did the panel respond to the charge that all the mainstream media are biased?

4. Do you find the panel's conclusion convincing and its evidence sufficient? Explain and support your answer.

5. What does the panel say about the role competitive pressures (commercial bias) played in CBS's decision to air the story?

EXERCISE 3.3 How Do You Want Your News: Hard or Soft?

INTRODUCTION

Media analysts and political scientists make distinctions between hard and soft news. *Hard news* covers significant international and national events. *Soft news* features human-interest and celebrity stories. Soft news also includes "news you can use"—for example, stories about lifestyle issues, such as nutrition and exercise. Soft news is sometimes called *infotainment*—news that entertains rather than informs Americans about vital issues of the day. Indeed, infotainment has become so pervasive that candidates for president—and a candidate for governor of California—now make use of entertainment shows to reach prospective voters. Witness George W. Bush on *Dr. Phil*, Al Gore on *The Oprah Winfrey Show*, and Arnold Schwarzenegger announcing his gubernatorial candidacy on *The Tonight Show with Jay Leno*. Young people, aged 18–29, appear particularly to favor infotainment. In 2004, according to one study, 21 percent said they prefer comedy outlets, such as *The Daily Show*, as their primary source of campaign information.[1]

Television, because it provides sound, sight, and movement, is much more effective at delivering soft news than either newspapers or news magazines. The upshot? Network television's news coverage is increasingly diluted—some would say contaminated—by matters that are entertaining and interesting but not necessarily newsworthy. Critics charge that news broadcasters are surrendering their traditional role—reporting and analyzing facts—to peddle entertainment. That transformation allegedly stems from the increased competition among the networks for ratings and profits. Indeed, many of the networks are now subsidiaries of entertainment corporations; for example, the Disney Corporation owns ABC.

The increased coverage of soft news on network broadcasts makes it harder for citizens to know what's important and what's not. The extensive coverage of the Michael Jackson trial was clearly soft news, a spectacle of celebrity and sordid charges. Several questions below ask you to determine, from a sampling of newspapers, whether the print media are prone to similar excesses.

ASSIGNMENT

This assignment asks you to examine news coverage in the broadcast (television) and print (newspapers) media. If you don't have television, monitor the home page of television news websites. You can use any search engine to find the URL of the media source.

Over three weeknights, watch the evening news on three of the major networks (ABC, CBS, CNN, CNN Headline News, FOX News, or NBC). As you watch, fill in the chart with the amount of time spent on each type of news. In the parentheses at the head of each column, identify the news networks you monitored. Apply the definitions of hard news and soft news from the first paragraph of the Introduction to this exercise.

Based on the observations you recorded in the chart, answer the following questions.

1. Combining all three nights of observation, what percentage of total broadcast time (including commercials) did each network devote to hard news stories, both international and national?

Network 1:_____

Network 2:_____

Network 3:_____

---

[1] Melanie McFarland, "Young People Turning Comedy Shows into Serious News Source," *Seattle Post-Intelligencer*, January 22, 2004. The survey is by The Pew Research Center for the People and the Press.

Network News Stories									
	News Network 1 ( )			News Network 2 ( )			News Network 3 ( )		
	Day 1	Day 2	Day 3	Day 1	Day 2	Day 3	Day 1	Day 2	Day 3
International hard news stories									
National hard news stories									
Total minutes of hard news									
Soft news stories									
Total minutes of soft news									
Total minutes of commercials									

2. Combining all three nights of observation, what percentage of total hard news broadcast time (excluding commercials) did each network devote to international news?

Network 1: _____

Network 2: _____

Network 3: _____

3. Did the networks follow up on hard news stories that had been aired the previous night? Did one network stand out for follow-up stories? If so, which one? What was the story?

_____

_____

_____

_____

_____

4. Which network do you think did the best job covering hard news stories? Explain and support your answer.

_____

_____

_____

_____

_____

5. Which network newscast most consistently held your attention? Why did it hold your attention?

_____

_____

_____

_____

_____

Using the Internet, examine the homepage for the *New York Times* (http://www.nytimes.com)[2] and the homepage of a newspaper from your hometown or your college town. (You can find the URL using any search engine.) Monitor the home pages of these two newspapers for three days during the week. Enter the topics of the news stories in the chart. In the parentheses at the head of the third column, write the name of the local newspaper you monitored.

Newspaper Stories						
	NEW YORK TIMES			LOCAL NEWSPAPER ( )		
	Day 1	Day 2	Day 3	Day 1	Day 2	Day 3
International hard news stories						
National hard news stories						
Soft news stories						

---

[2] Website URLs sometimes change. Try an external search (e.g., Google) to find the website. Configurations of a website often change. Try an internal search of the site to locate the information. Sometimes websites and pages within websites are removed. In that case, move on to the next question.

Based on the observations recorded in the chart, answer the following questions.

6. Did the *New York Times* or the local newspaper cover more hard news (international and national)?

_____

7. Did the *New York Times* or the local newspaper cover more international hard news?

_____

8. Which newspaper did the better job of following up on its hard news stories?

_____

9. Identify a story covered in both the *New York Times* and the local paper. Analyze each paper's coverage of that story. Which paper's coverage was superior? Explain and support your answer.

_____

_____

_____

_____

_____

_____

_____

_____

10. Based on your observations and analysis, write a paragraph explaining the respective advantages and disadvantages of newspaper and television news coverage. (You may distinguish among the networks and between the *New York Times* and the local newspaper.)

_____

_____

_____

_____

_____

EXERCISE 3.3 HOW DO YOU WANT YOUR NEWS: HARD OR SOFT? 63

CHAPTER 4

Political Parties and Elections

EXERCISE 4.1 The Presidential Election of 2004: Why It Wasn't the Economy

INTRODUCTION

Voters without strong party ties and without strong ideologies—independent and moderate voters—often determine the outcome of presidential races. While loyalist liberal Democrats and loyalist conservative Republicans routinely vote for their party's candidate, so-called *swing voters* move between the two major parties' presidential candidates according to their assessment of the economy. In what's called *retrospective voting*, swing voters ask themselves the question Ronald Reagan posed to voters in 1980: "Are you better off now than you were four years ago?" In 1992, when the economy was in recession, Bill Clinton's advisors posted a large sign in the campaign headquarters: "It's the economy, stupid." The purpose? To remind Clinton to stay focused on the poor state of the economy, which voters—rightly or wrongly—blamed on the incumbent president, then George H. W. Bush. That strategy put Bill Clinton in the White House.

Whereas the economy has played a major role in the outcome of so many presidential races, beginning with Franklin Roosevelt's victory over Herbert Hoover during the Great Depression, it was not the decisive factor in 2004. Observers have offered several explanations for George W. Bush's victory.

- Even though George W. Bush was the first president to post a net loss of jobs since Herbert Hoover's term at the beginning of the Great Depression, there was no clear consensus among voters that the economy was as bad as John Kerry portrayed it. When economic growth and job creation improved in 2004, Kerry's case that the economy was in such trouble that the incumbent should be kicked out of office was undermined. Those voters who thought that the economy was the issue that mattered most and who thought that their economic situation had deteriorated in the past four years favored Kerry by a large margin. But there were not enough of those voters to put Kerry in the White House.

- Whereas swing voters—moderates and independents—usually determine the outcome of a presidential election, their influence was diminished in 2004. That's because in a close race, like 2004, the rate at which party loyalists turn out to vote often decides the contest. Recognizing this, both parties invested heavily to mobilize their core supporters. Moreover, President Bush's style and ideology polarized many voters into Bush and anti-Bush camps; fewer voters than usual identified themselves as undecided—a common attribute of moderates and independents.
- The events of 9/11 and the subsequent war on terrorism focused attention on national security issues. Many voters, reluctant to change course during a time of national emergency, perceived Bush as a strong, effective guardian of national security. Consequently, many were willing to overlook troubling news from Iraq during the campaign.
- Many voters perceived John Kerry as a weak presidential candidate. His lack of a clear message, his seeming "flip-flopping," and the fact that he was relatively unknown to Americans outside of Massachusetts allowed the Bush campaign and allied groups to define him negatively. Many Kerry voters were more anti-Bush than they were pro-Kerry. To defeat an incumbent president, an opponent must make a compelling case for change and convince a majority of voters that he can be trusted to do better than the incumbent. Kerry failed to make that case.[1] That Kerry had a liberal voting record in the U.S. Senate and that he was from the Northeast worked against him in potentially competitive border states, such as Missouri, and in southern states, such as Louisiana. After the 1960s, only middle-of-the-road Democratic presidential candidates from the South—Jimmy Carter and Bill Clinton—have won electoral votes in those states.
- The prominence of the gay marriage issue and the presence of anti–gay marriage initiatives on eleven state ballots led to unusually high voter turnout among self-identified Christian evangelicals, and an overwhelming majority of them voted for Bush. President Bush's endorsement of a constitutional amendment to prohibit gay marriage no doubt helped him among those voters. The gay marriage issue prompted many voters to embrace morality as the major issue in the campaign. So-called moral issues—like gay marriage, abortion, sexuality in the media, and secularism in public life—tend to favor Republican candidates.[2]

Despite long lines and glitches on election day, voter turnout was higher than in any other national election since 1968—more than 60 percent of eligible voters. The number of competitive states, the political parties' efforts to mobilize their core voters, and the polarizing effect of President Bush's first term helped account for the relatively high turnout. It remains to be seen whether or not the 2004 election signals the beginning of a new era of increased citizen attentiveness to and participation in politics.

ASSIGNMENT

Questions 1–5 following the exit poll data in Tables 4.1.1 and 4.1.2 ask you to test the interpretations, above, of the 2004 presidential election and to compare and contrast the presidential elections of 2000 and 2004.

---

[1] The narrowness of Bush's victory was more of a surprise than his reelection. Political science models showed him winning with 53–57 percent of the two-party vote. (He won with slightly less than 51 percent.) Bush had the narrowest percentage margin of victory of all Republicans reelected in the past one hundred years. See Mark Danner, "How Bush Really Won," *New York Review of Books*, January 13, 2005, pp. 48–53.

[2] See Curtis Gans, "President Bush, Mobilization Drives Propel Turnout to Post-1968 High; Kerry, Democratic Weaknesses Shown," Committee for the Study of the American Electorate, Press Release, November 4, 2004.

TABLE 4.1.1 Exit Poll, Presidential Election of 2000*

	Percent total vote	Percent Bush	Percent Gore
Party:			
Democrat	39	11	86
Republican	35	91	8
Independent/other	25	47	45
Ideology:			
Liberal	20	13	80
Moderate	50	44	52
Conservative	29	81	17
Part of Christian conservative movement?			
Yes	14	79	18
No	83	41	54
Issue that mattered most:			
World affairs	12	54	40
Medicare/RX drugs	7	38	60
Health care	8	33	64
Economy/jobs	18	37	59
Taxes	14	80	17
Education	15	44	52
Social Security	14	39	59
Family financial situation compared to four years ago:			
Better	50	36	61
Worse	11	33	62
Same	38	60	35
Population of area:			
City over 50,000	29	35	61
Suburb	44	49	47
Small town/rural	28	59	38

*Does not include Pat Buchanan and Ralph Nader.
SOURCE: Exit poll data from MSNBC (http://www.msnbc.com/m/d2k/g/polls.asp?office=P&state=N1).

TABLE 4.1.2 Exit Poll, Presidential Election of 2004*

	Percent total vote	Percent Bush	Percent Kerry
Party:			
Democrat	37	10	89
Republican	37	93	7
Independent/other	26	47	50
Ideology:			
Liberal	21	13	86
Moderate	45	44	55
Conservative	33	83	16

TABLE 4.1.2 (Cont.)

	Percent total vote	Percent Bush	Percent Kerry
Religion:			
White evangelical/ born-again Christians	22	77	22
All others	78	42	57
Was your vote for president mainly:			
For your candidate	69	58	41
Against his opponent	25	29	79
Do you consider the war in Iraq:			
Part of war on terrorism	54	80	19
Separate from war on terrorism	43	11	88
Issue that mattered most:			
Moral values	22	80	18
Economy/jobs	20	18	80
Terrorism	19	86	14
Iraq	15	26	73
Health care	8	23	77
Taxes	5	57	43
Education	4	26	73
Who would you trust to handle terrorism?			
Only Kerry	31	1	99
Only Bush	48	97	3
Both of them	9	23	75
Neither of them	9	15	79
Family financial situation compared to four years ago:			
Better today	31	79	20
Worse today	28	19	80
Same	39	48	50
Population of area:			
City over 50,000	30	43	56
Suburbs	46	51	48
Small town/rural	24	56	43

*Does not include Ralph Nader.
SOURCE: Exit poll data from MSNBC (http://www.msnbc.msn.com/id/5297138).

1. Consider voters' views of the economy. Examine the category "Issue that mattered most" in 2000 and 2004.

a. What percentage of voters responded that the economy mattered most to them?

In 2000: _____

In 2004: _____

b. What percentage of those voters cast their ballot for the Democratic candidate (Gore or Kerry)?

In 2000: _____

In 2004: _____

Examine the category "Family financial situation compared to four years ago" in 2000 and 2004.

c. What percentage of voters responded that their family situation was worse than four years ago?

In 2000: _____

In 2004: _____

d. What percentage of those voters cast their ballot for the Democratic candidate?

In 2000: _____

In 2004: _____

e. What do the data you assembled in parts a–d tell you about the role of the economy in 2000 and 2004? Explain and support your answer.

_____

_____

_____

_____

2. Consider the ideological polarization and party loyalty of the electorate in 2000 and 2004. Examine the "Ideology" category in 2000 and 2004.

a. Do the data support the conclusion that voters were more divided into the liberal and conservative camps—with fewer moderates—in 2004 than in 2000? (Look at the "Percent total vote" column to answer this question.) Explain and support your answer.

_____

_____

_____

b. Conservatives are likely to vote Republican, and liberals are likely to vote Democratic. Were conservatives more likely to vote for the Republican presidential candidate and liberals for the Democratic presidential candidate in 2004 than in 2000?

_____

_____

_____

c. Examine the "Party" category in 2000 and 2004. Were self-proclaimed Democrats and self-proclaimed Republicans more likely to support their party's presidential candidate in 2004 or in 2000? Explain and support your answer.

d. Which party's voters were more united behind its candidate in 2000 and 2004?

e. Compare and contrast how moderates and independents split their votes in 2000 and 2004.

f. Do the data support the interpretation that moderate and independent voters, usually the decisive factor in a presidential election, were not decisive in 2004? Explain and support your answer.

g. In light of your responses to parts a–f, do the data support the interpretation that the electorate was more ideologically polarized and exhibited more party loyalty in 2004 than in 2000? Explain and support your answer.

3. Consider the interpretation that the war on terrorism became the dominant issue in the 2004 election and that it worked to Bush's advantage. Examine the "Issue that mattered most" category.

a. Was terrorism mentioned in survey responses in 2000?

b. In 2000, what percentage of voters thought that world affairs was the issue that mattered most?

c. In 2004, what percentage of voters thought that terrorism was the issue that mattered most?

d. Of those voters who thought that terrorism mattered most, what percentage cast their ballot for Bush?

e. In 2004, what percentage of voters thought that Iraq was the issue that mattered most?

f. Of those voters who thought that Iraq mattered most, what percentage cast their ballot for Kerry?

For 2004, examine the exit poll categories "Who would you trust to handle terrorism" and "Do you consider the war in Iraq."

g. What percentage of voters trusted only Bush to handle terrorism?

h. What percentage of voters trusted only Kerry to handle terrorism?

i. What percentage of those who trusted only Bush voted for Bush?

j. What percentage of voters thought that Iraq was part of the war on terrorism?

k. Of those voters who thought that Iraq was part of the war on terrorism, what percentage cast their ballot for Bush?

l. Do the data you examined in parts a–k support the interpretation that the issue of terrorism helped to put Bush back in the White House? Explain and support your answer.

4. Consider the interpretation that Kerry was not a strong candidate. Examine the 2004 exit poll category "Was your vote for president mainly."

a. What percentage of voters who cast their ballot "For your candidate" voted for Kerry?

b. What percentage of voters who cast their ballot "Against his opponent" voted for Kerry?

c. Do the data support the interpretation that Kerry was a weaker candidate than Bush? Explain and support your answer.

5. Consider the interpretation that moral issues worked to Bush's advantage in 2004. Examine the "Issue that mattered most" category in 2004.

a. What percentage of voters thought that moral values mattered most in 2004?

b. Of those voters who thought that moral values mattered most, what percentage cast their ballot for Bush?

Examine the "Part of Christian conservative movement" category in 2000 and the "Religion" category in 2004.

c. What percentage of voters in 2000 identified themselves as part of the Christian conservative movement?

d. Of those voters, what percentage cast their ballots for Bush?

e. In 2004, what percentage of voters identified themselves as "White evangelical/born-again Christians"?[3]

f. Of those who identified themselves as "White evangelical/born-again Christians," what percentage cast their ballot for Bush?

g. Do the data support the contention that so-called moral issues helped to put Bush back in the White House in 2004? Explain and support your answer.

6. Find the state-by-state results of the Bush–Gore race in 2000 and the Bush–Kerry race in 2004. (A good source for the results is the National Archives and Records Administration: http://www.archives.gov/federal-register/electoral-college/votes/2000_2005.html#2004.[4] The year 2000 is at the top of the page; scroll down for 2004.)

On the maps in Figure 4.1.1 (Bush–Gore, 2000) and Figure 4.1.2 (Bush–Kerry, 2004), shade the states Gore won in 2000 and the states Kerry won in 2004; leave blank the states Bush won in 2000 and 2004. Then answer the following questions:

---

[3] Note that the "White/evangelical born-again Christians" identification in 2004 is both more inclusive and less inclusive than the "Christian conservative" identification in 2000. The 2000 category excludes evangelicals and born-again Christians who are not conservatives. The 2004 category excludes non-white Protestants and all Catholics who support at least some of the positions of the Christian conservative movement.

[4] Website URLs sometimes change. Try an external search (e.g., Google) to find the website. Configurations of a website often change. Try an internal search of the site to locate the information. Sometimes websites and pages within websites are removed. In that case, move on to the next question.

EXERCISE 4.1 THE PRESIDENTIAL ELECTION OF 2004: WHY IT WASN'T THE ECONOMY 73

FIGURE 4.1.1 Bush–Gore, 2000

FIGURE 4.1.2 Bush–Kerry, 2004

74   CHAPTER 4   POLITICAL PARTIES AND ELECTIONS

a. Which states did the Republican candidate—Bush—win in both 2000 and 2004 (the so-called red states because they're usually colored red on electoral vote maps)?

_____

_____

_____

_____

_____

b. What characteristics are shared by the states (region, size of electoral vote, and the like) that supported Bush in both elections? (Review the "Population of area" category in Tables 4.1.1 and 4.1.2.)

_____

_____

_____

c. If you were the Republican Party chair, would you be confident about Republican prospects in future presidential elections? Why or why not?

_____

_____

_____

_____

_____

d. Which states did the Democratic candidates—Gore and Kerry—win in both 2000 and 2004 (the so-called blue states because they're usually colored blue on electoral vote maps)?

_____

_____

_____

_____

e. What characteristics are shared by the states (region, size of electoral vote, and the like) that supported the Democratic candidates? (Review the "Population of area" category in Tables 4.1.1 and 4.1.2.)

_____

_____

_____

f. If you were the Democratic Party chair, would you be confident about Democratic prospects in future presidential elections? Why or why not?

_____

_____

_____

_____

EXERCISE 4.2 Gerrymandering

INTRODUCTION

Legislative districts come in many shapes, from the compact and ordinary to the distended and bizarre. Describing a legislative district forged in the shape of a salamander, the editor of the *Boston Centinel* in 1811 coined the term *gerrymander*. The governor of Massachusetts who approved the salamander-shaped district was Elbridge Gerry. Since then, Gerry's name has been used to describe the drawing of exotically shaped legislative districts designed to yield political advantage for parties, interests, or incumbents.

Representation in the House is population based: States are awarded seats according to the relative size of their populations. The framers of the Constitution recognized that state populations would change and that the distribution of seats in the House would have to be adjusted accordingly. The Constitution requires that the reapportionment—the reallocation—of seats in the House take place every ten years based on the results of the federal census. The addition or subtraction of one or more of a state's seats in the House usually requires redrawing the boundaries of many—if not all—of the House districts in the state. That's because in 1964, the Supreme Court ruled that the equal protection clause of the Fourteenth Amendment requires that legislative districts be roughly equal in population—the standard of "one-person, one-vote."[1]

The task of redistricting usually is carried out by the state's legislature, which also redraws the boundaries of state legislative districts when necessary. If a state's legislators and governor cannot agree on a redistricting plan, the task reverts to the courts or a commission. As of 2005, there were twelve states that located the final authority for redistricting in some body other than the state legislature. Arkansas's redistricting commission, for example, consists of the governor, secretary of state, and state attorney general. The redistricting boards and commissions of other states have much more complicated membership criteria.[2]

State legislators are keenly aware that redistricting is inherently political, easily turned to the advantage of a particular political party or interest, or to incumbents generally. In drawing new legislative districts, geographic coherence, demographic similarity, and fairness often are subordinated to politics. Although some redistricting schemes may be more egregiously political than others, no one can dodge the fact that grouping voters in legislative districts necessarily works to the advantage of some and to the disadvantage of others.

Those disadvantaged by redistricting often go to court. The round of redistricting that followed the 2000 census triggered over 150 lawsuits in at least forty states, according to the National Conference of State Legislators. Redistricting litigation focuses on three questions:

- How much variation in population between districts is permissible?
- Can states redistrict more often than once within a decade?
- Does partisan gerrymandering violate the equal protection clause of the Constitution?

The Supreme Court remains reluctant to become entangled in the political thicket of redistricting, ruling that the matter is best left to the citizens and their elected representatives. Recent decisions indicate that the Court remains split on two important points: whether claims against political gerrymandering fall under the Court's jurisdiction, and what standards the Court would use to adjudicate those claims.[3] No gerrymander has yet been struck down by the Court solely on the grounds that it gives an unconstitutional political

---

[1] *Wesberry v. Sanders; Reynolds v. Sims.*

[2] Details on the various state redistricting boards and commissions, and other information about redistricting, can be found on the website of the National Conference of State Legislatures: http://www.ncsl.org/programs/legman/elect/law-article.htm.

[3] *Davis v. Bandemer*, (1986); *Vieth v. Jubelirer* (2004).

78 CHAPTER 4 POLITICAL PARTIES AND ELECTIONS

advantage to one party at the expense of another. The Court has, however, ruled against gerrymanders that dilute the power of racial minorities and against the creation of districts with voting majorities of racial or ethnic minorities when race or ethnicity was the deciding factor in drawing the district lines.

Recent events have increased public scrutiny of gerrymandering. In 2003, the Republicans in the Texas state legislature rammed though a second redistricting of the state that cost four Texas Democrats their seats in the House. During the ensuing battle, Texas Democrats fled the state in an attempt to deny Republicans a quorum in the state legislature. In California, Governor Arnold Schwarzenegger placed before the state's voters in the 2005 special election a proposal to hand redistricting to a panel of three retired judges. Finally, the reelection rate for incumbents has climbed to a level that many voters find obscene (see Exercise 6.2 on incumbency). In the 2004 election in California, for example, of the 53 House seats and 100 seats in the state legislature that were up for grabs, not even one changed party hands. Gerrymandering has become the incumbent's best friend partly because of the increasing sophistication of computer programs that enable incumbents to predict with near certainty how voters will cast their ballots.

ASSIGNMENT

To better understand the politics of gerrymandering, examine the model in Figure 4.2.1. This hypothetical state is entitled to four seats in the House of Representatives. Figure 4.2.1. shows one method of dividing the state into its four legislative districts. The method seems *nonpartisan*, undertaken without regard for the interest of a political party. The state has been divided into four quadrants, each square and equal in population. The districts appear to be neutral and impartial, drawn solely on the basis of simple geometry.

In answering the questions below, assume the following: *Republicans (R) and Democrats (D) vote by party affiliation; they never cross party lines; and they never vote for minor-party candidates.* Voting behavior in the real world, of course, is much less certain and much more complicated. But this simple model of voting behavior should make the politics of gerrymandering easier to grasp.

FIGURE 4.2.1 A Hypothetical State

	D	D	R	R	R	R	R	D	R	D	
	D	D	R	R	R	R	R	R	D	D	
A	D	D	R	R	R	R	R	D	D	D	B
	D	D	R	R	R	R	R	D	R	R	
	R	D	R	R	R	D	R	D	R	R	
	R	D	D	D	D	D	D	D	D	R	
	R	R	D	D	D	D	D	R	D	R	
C	R	R	R	R	D	R	D	D	R	D	D
	R	D	R	D	D	R	D	R	R	D	
	R	R	D	R	D	D	R	R	R	R	

1. a. Under the districting plan in Figure 4.2.1, what percentage of the state's seats does the Republican Party command?

b. What percentage of the state's seats does the Democratic Party command?

---

2. Under the districting plan in Figure 4.2.1, how does each party's share of the state's seats compare with the percentage of Republican and Democratic voters in the state? In other words, is each party's share of the state's seats roughly proportional to its share of voters in the state? Explain and support your answer.

---

3. Under the districting plan in Figure 4.2.1, which party's hold on its seats is more secure? Explain and support your answer by specifying the margin by which each party holds its seats. Use whole numbers—not percentages.

---

4. Under the districting plan in Figure 4.2.1, in which two districts is the incumbent most secure? Explain and support your answer by specifying the incumbent's margin of control in those two districts. Use whole numbers—not percentages.

---

5. a. The next figure shows the same distribution of voters as in Figure 4.2.1. Gerrymander the state to give a greater margin of protection to the two Republican and two Democratic incumbents who hold the seats under the districting plan in Figure 4.2.1. In other words, alter the district boundaries so that the Republican incumbents in Districts A and B and the Democratic incumbents in Districts C and D can count on a greater margin of victory on election day. In drawing the boundaries of the

D	D	R	R	R	R	R	D	R	D
D	D	R	R	R	R	R	R	D	D
D	D	R	R	R	R	R	D	D	D
D	D	R	R	R	R	R	D	R	R
R	D	R	R	R	D	R	D	R	R
R	D	D	D	D	D	D	D	D	R
R	R	D	D	D	D	D	R	D	R
R	R	R	R	D	R	D	D	R	D
R	D	R	D	D	R	D	R	R	D
R	R	D	R	D	D	R	R	R	R

new legislative districts, be sure that each district contains twenty-five voters and that each district is continuous (unbroken) in shape. Label your new districts A, B, C, and D.

b. Fill in the chart below with the former margin of victory and the new margin of victory for each incumbent. Use whole numbers—not percentages.

District	Former Margin of Victory	New Margin of Victory
A		
B		
C		
D		

6. a. The next figure shows the same distribution of voters as in Figure 4.2.1. Gerrymander the state to give the Republican Party the maximum possible number of the state's four seats. In drawing the boundaries of the new legislative districts, be sure that each district contains twenty-five voters and that each district is continuous (unbroken) in shape. Label your new districts A, B, C, and D.

```
D  D  R  R  R  R  R  D  R  D
D  D  R  R  R  R  R  R  D  D
D  D  R  R  R  R  R  D  D  D
D  D  R  R  R  R  R  D  R  R
R  D  R  R  R  D  R  D  R  R
R  D  D  D  D  D  D  D  D  R
R  R  D  D  D  D  D  R  D  R
R  R  R  R  D  R  D  D  R  D
R  D  R  D  D  R  D  R  R  D
R  R  D  R  D  D  R  R  R  R
```

b. According to your redistricting, what is the maximum number of seats you can award to the Republican Party?

c. How does the Republican Party's share of the state's seats compare with the percentage of Republican voters in the state? Explain and support your answer by contrasting the Republican Party's percentage of the seats in the state with its percentage of voters in the state.

7. a. The figure below shows the same distribution of voters as in Figure 4.2.1. Gerrymander the state to give the Democratic Party the maximum possible number of the state's four seats. In drawing the boundaries of the new legislative districts, be sure that each district contains twenty-five voters and that each district is continuous (unbroken) in shape.

D	D	R	R	R	R	R	D	R	D
D	D	R	R	R	R	R	R	D	D
D	D	R	R	R	R	R	D	D	D
D	D	R	R	R	R	R	D	R	R
R	D	R	R	R	D	R	D	R	R
R	D	D	D	D	D	D	D	D	R
R	R	D	D	D	D	D	R	D	R
R	R	R	R	D	R	D	D	R	D
R	D	R	D	D	R	D	R	R	D
R	R	D	R	D	D	R	R	R	R

b. According to your redistricting, what is the maximum number of seats that you can award to the Democratic Party?

_____

c. How does the Democratic Party's share of the state's seats compare with the percentage of Democratic voters in the state? Explain and support your answer by contrasting the Democratic Party's percentage of the seats in the state with its percentage of voters in the state.

_____

_____

_____

8. Explain how you approached the redistricting in question 7. Your answer should demonstrate that you were thinking about political advantage and party interest. To demonstrate that you are thinking politically, you must do more than repeat the directions in the questions. Think about your political purpose in realigning the Republican and Democratic voters and the efficiency with which you rose to the challenge.

_____

_____

_____

_____

_____

_____

EXERCISE 4.3 To Vote or Not to Vote?

INTRODUCTION

Voting has always been a problem for American democracy, and it remains so today. The unamended Constitution and the Bill of Rights did not explicitly confer on any American the right to vote.[1] For *most* of the Republic's history, *most* Americans could not vote. A succession of battles for the right to vote eventually made universal suffrage the law. Yet the 2000 and 2004 elections proved how difficult it remains for many citizens to cast their ballots unimpeded by dysfunctional electoral machinery and outright efforts to suppress voting.[2] But most problematic for American democracy is the choice made by many citizens to not vote.

The electoral system and the voting process confound many Americans. That's partly because state and local governments have wide discretion in conducting elections. The nation's election machinery is so decentralized, for example, that the supervisor of elections in Palm Beach County, Florida, Theresa LePore, decided on her own authority to experiment with a new ballot format in the 2000 election. That many voters couldn't fathom the so-called "butterfly ballot"—and consequently miscast their votes for Pat Buchanan instead of for Al Gore—made news around the world and helped put George Bush in the White House in 2001. Within the federal limits explained below, state governments have authority to establish voter eligibility requirements, voter registration procedures, and how and when voters will cast their ballots. The variation among these state electoral systems is striking—a testament to the vitality of federalism, in the view of some. Others see the diversity as federalism run amok—the root of confusion and unfairness in national elections.

State government restrictions on voter eligibility—formal and informal—long barred a broad swath of the population from casting ballots: especially poor whites, minorities, and women. Amendments to the Constitution, Supreme Court decisions, and federal legislation slowly overcame state restrictions, expanding and securing the franchise for almost all. The Fifteenth Amendment, the Nineteenth Amendment, *Smith v. Allwright*,[3] the Voting Rights Act of 1965, and the Twentieth-Sixth Amendment were milestones in the battle for universal suffrage. Today, all citizens 18 years of age and older are eligible to vote, with two general exceptions: those who fail to meet state residency requirements, and convicted felons and the mentally incompetent.[4] In the 1970 extension of the Voting Rights Act, the national government limited states to a maximum thirty-day residency requirement. But the federal government has not yet restricted the right of states to deny the franchise to convicted felons and the mentally incompetent.[5]

Although eligibility barriers have come down, voting registration remains a hurdle for many citizens. In the United States, the burden of registration rests entirely on the citizenry. Other democracies place the burden on government. According to one critic of the American system: "Every other democracy acknowledges an obligation on the part of the state to assemble the list of registered voters, either by imposing a duty to register to vote or by taking responsibility for assembling the lists. If Great Britain, Canada, France, and Germany assume the task of assembling lists of eligible voters, why shouldn't the United States adopt similar policies?"[6]

---

[1] The right to vote is implicit, for example, in the Constitution's guarantee that every state will have a republican form of government and in the Constitution's references to the election of representatives, senators, and the president.

[2] See, for example, "The Long Shadow of Jim Crow: Voter Intimidation and Suppression in American Today" at www.naacp.org.

[3] In April 1944, the Supreme Court decided by an 8-to-1 majority that all-white primary elections in the South had the practical effect of disfranchising African American voters in the general election.

[4] New Hampshire does not require any minimum period of residency in the state to register or to vote. Residency requirements and restrictions on voting by felons vary by state. To view state requirements and restrictions, go to www.civicyouth.org and click on the Youth Voting State by State Map. More detailed information about the varied state restrictions on voting by felons is at www.righttovote.org. Two states allow felons to vote while incarcerated.

[5] On November 8, 2004, the Supreme Court declined to hear two cases on whether state disfranchisement of felons violates the federal Voting Rights Act.

[6] Burt Neuborne, "Reclaiming Democracy," *The American Prospect*, Volume 12, Issue 5, March 12–March 26, 2001.

The federal government, in 1993, directed the states to facilitate voter registration. The so-called Motor Voter Bill required states to make voting registration available at selected state and local government offices and by mail. But many states did not fully fund or comply with the Motor Voter Law. The Department of Justice responded by taking many states to court to secure their compliance. For the most part, however, state registration processes and requirements remain beyond the reach of the federal government and continue to vary significantly by state, posing differing degrees of difficulty to prospective voters.

North Dakota is the only state that does not require voters to register. In 1975, Governor Arthur Link vetoed a bill that would have established the registration of voters in North Dakota. In his veto message, Governor Link stated that "this legislation offers no improvement in our election law. Rather, it appears to be a significant movement away from securing more active participation of the electorate. The low percentage of eligible voters who actually vote clearly indicates we do not need complicated registration legislation which [sic] will tend to reduce even further the number of citizens who vote. A need for voter registration could exist if there were irregularities or fraud in North Dakota elections. There has been no indication or evidence of such election problems to justify this legislation. We need legislation to make the ballot more accessible to citizens. We do not need additional roadblocks to keep voters from the polls."[7]

All it takes to cast a ballot on election day in North Dakota is identification proving residency in the precinct. In the other forty-nine states, citizens must complete the registration process before voting. Six states allow voters to register on election day: Idaho, Maine, Minnesota, New Hampshire, Wisconsin, and Wyoming. The state of Mississippi, in contrast, requires new voters, or those whose name or address has changed since the last election, to complete a registration form and return it to the county clerk at least thirty days prior to the election—the maximum interval allowed by federal law, as noted above.

Texas is one of several states experimenting with alternative voting arrangements aimed at increasing turnout. Texas and nineteen other states allow voters to cast their ballots at the county clerk's office, or in some cases at the local polling place, anywhere from fourteen to forty days before the election. Oregon's effort to increase turnout is unique: All Oregon voters are required to cast their ballots by mail. Finally, many states have long offered voters the opportunity to cast absentee ballots by mail without restriction.

Despite these efforts to increase turnout, many citizens who are registered to vote decide to sit out election day. All sorts of factors are involved. Some people have experienced or heard of crowded and inconvenient polling places, voting machinery that doesn't work, incorrect registration rolls, or efforts to intimidate voters. Other potential voters check out because candidates failed to connect with them, negative campaigning turned them off, or favored issues were not addressed. Finally, some of those registered find themselves genuinely unable to get to the polls; others find ways to justify and rationalize their absence.

ASSIGNMENT, PART A: VOTER TURNOUT

The voting rate is a quantitative measurement of the extent to which Americans turn out to vote or participate in elections, and it is often viewed as a key indicator of the health and viability of American democracy. The voting rate can be calculated on different bases and reported in various ways. Questions 1–5 are based on Table 4.3.1, "Voting-Age and Voting-Eligible Populations, 2004."[8]

1. The column in Table 4.3.1 labeled "Voting Age Population (VAP)" specifies the number of citizens in each state who are 18 years of age or older. The next column specifies the percentage of each state's VAP who are *not* citizens.

---

[7] Go to www.state.nd.us/sec/electvote/voting/vote-history.html?print=y.

[8] Table 4.3.1 was adapted from the United States Elections Project at http://elections.gmu.edu/.

TABLE 4.3.1 Voting-Age and Voting-Eligible Populations, 2004

	Voting Age Population (VAP)	Percent Noncitizens in VAP	Total Ineligible Felons	Voting Eligible Population (VEP)	Turnout*
U.S. Total	221,285,099	7.92	3,205,137	203,864,860	122,293,720
Alabama	3,425,842	1.09	55,216	3,333,450	1,883,415
Alaska	470,024	3.98	8,061	443,254	312,598
Arizona	4,194,395	12.21	69,011	3,613,391	2,012,585
Arkansas	2,069,578	1.71	40,135	1,993,991	1,054,945
California	26,647,974	18.28	273,699	21,502,515	12,419,857
Colorado	3,456,281	7.91	25,644	3,157,395	2,129,630
Connecticut	2,684,496	6.96	23,124	2,474,586	1,578,769
Delaware	629,012	4.78	16,869	582,050	375,190
District of Columbia	448,818	9.84	0	404,651	227,586
Florida	13,441,589	11.46	229,125	11,672,341	7,609,810
Georgia	6,534,901	5.0	281,332	5,927,030	3,301,867
Hawaii	980,145	8.06	5,635	895,484	429,013
Idaho	1,025,470	3.26	24,264	967,761	598,376
Illinois	9,518,511	7.78	43,186	8,734,675	5,275,415
Indiana	4,635,693	0.99	22,576	4,567,371	2,468,002
Iowa	2,274,202	3.43	21,937	2,174,215	1,506,908
Kansas	2,049,542	4.33	20,430	1,940,330	1,187,756
Kentucky	3,157,230	0.81	38,297	3,093,509	1,795,860
Louisiana	3,358,475	1.69	79,495	3,222,149	1,943,106
Maine	1,038,834	1.34	4,960	1,019,972	740,752
Maryland	4,200,864	8.08	76,866	3,784,457	2,386,678
Massachusetts	4,956,251	9.1	10,511	4,494,501	2,912,388
Michigan	7,616,370	3.68	49,524	7,286,565	4,839,252
Minnesota	3,872,377	4.6	66,571	3,627,805	2,828,387
Mississippi	2,139,838	1.35	31,916	2,079,049	1,152,365
Missouri	4,344,701	1.88	73,674	4,189,455	2,731,364
Montana	715,516	1.05	3,440	704,593	450,434
Nebraska	1,316,507	5.0	13,959	1,236,680	778,186
Nevada	1,737,785	12.01	20,733	1,508,328	829,587
New Hampshire	1,000,677	3.67	2,483	961,505	677,662
New Jersey	6,573,016	11.36	103,602	5,723,017	3,611,691
New Mexico	1,403,012	6.16	16,648	1,300,005	756,304
New York	14,790,563	12.02	121,767	12,891,280	7,391,036
North Carolina	6,414,826	4.52	92,592	6,032,533	3,501,007
North Dakota	490,193	1.5	1,168	481,655	312,833
Ohio	8,680,824	2.39	45,831	8,427,425	5,627,903
Oklahoma	2,664,546	2.21	41,214	2,564,424	1,463,758
Oregon	2,766,949	5.89	12,422	2,591,580	1,836,782
Pennsylvania	9,615,192	3.11	40,545	9,275,167	5,769,590
Rhode Island	842,974	8.04	16,926	758,276	437,134
South Carolina	3,174,275	1.91	47,481	3,066,155	1,617,730
South Dakota	576,223	1.03	3,059	567,215	388,215
Tennessee	4,516,712	4.14	54,794	4,274,705	2,437,319
Texas	16,263,943	12.45	482,488	13,755,786	7,410,749
Utah	1,645,373	4.76	5,594	1,561,513	927,844
Vermont	488,177	1.4	0	481,325	312,309
Virginia	5,695,264	5.86	60,399	5,301,155	3,198,367

TABLE 4.3.1 (Cont.)

	Voting Age Population (VAP)	Percent Noncitizens in VAP	Total Ineligible Felons	Voting Eligible Population (VEP)	Turnout*
Washington	4,732,168	6.54	102,796	4,319,948	2,859,084
West Virginia	1,430,277	0.44	12,139	1,411,867	755,887
Wisconsin	4,192,517	3.05	62,000	4,002,710	2,997,007
Wyoming	386,177	0.49	4,718	379,570	243,428

*Number who voted for a presidential candidate.

a. What's the voting rate of California's VAP? To make this calculation, divide the total number who voted in California (that's the last column) by California's VAP.

b. California has the highest percentage of noncitizens in its VAP: 18.28 percent, or 4,871,249. The VAP in California who are citizens is 21,776,725. What's the voting rate of California's VAP who are citizens?

c. Which provides the more accurate measurement of voter turnout: the voting rate of the VAP or the voting rate of the VAP who are citizens? Explain and support your answer.

2. A state's felon population, which is generally ineligible to vote, may also affect the measurement and reporting of the voting rate. Texas, for example, has the largest number of felons ineligible to vote.

a. What's the voting rate of Texas's VAP who are citizens?

b. The column labeled "Voting Eligible Population (VEP)" excludes not only noncitizens but also felons who are ineligible to vote. What's the voting rate of Texas's VEP?

c. Which provides the more accurate measurement of voter turnout: the voting rate of the VAP who are citizens or the voting rate of the VEP? Explain and support your answer.

3. In California, 16,557,273 citizens were registered to vote at the time of the 2004 election.

a. What was the voting rate in California as a percentage of registered voters?

b. What was the voting rate in California as a percentage of the VEP?

c. Which figure provides the more accurate measurement of voter turnout: the voting rate as a percentage of registered voters or the voting rate as a percentage of eligible voters? Explain and support your answer.

4. Listed below are the six states that allowed election-day voter registration in 2004, and the voting rate for each of these states as a percentage of their VEP.

Idaho	61.8
New Hampshire	70.5
Maine	72.6
Minnesota	73.0
Wisconsin	74.9
Wyoming	64.2

a. What was the average voting rate of these six states?

b. What does a comparison of the average voting rate of these six states with the national voting rate of 60 percent suggest about the relationship between election-day registration and turnout?

5. Listed below are the six states with the highest voting rates in 2004 that did *not* allow election-day registration, and the voting rate for each of these states as a percentage of the VEP.

Alaska	70.5
Colorado	67.4
Iowa	69.3
Michigan	66.9
Ohio	66.8
South Dakota	68.4

a. What was the average voting rate of these six states?

_____

b. Given that the average voting rate in these six states is above the national average, What factors other than election-day registration might account for the voting rate in these states?

_____

_____

_____

_____

Questions 6 and 7 are based on Table 4.3.2, "Reported Rates of Voting and Registration by Selected Characteristics: November 2002."[9]

TABLE 4.3.2 Reported Rates of Voting and Registration by Selected Characteristics: November 2002

Characteristic	Reported Voted
	Percent
Age	
18 to 24 years	19.3
25 to 34 years	31.8
35 to 44 years	44.8
45 to 54 years	53.4
55 to 64 years	60.1
65 to 74 years	65.1
75 years and over	60.0
Marital Status	
Married-spouse present	55.0
Married-spouse absent	33.3
Widowed	50.7
Divorced	39.6
Separated	30.0
Never married	28.7
Educational Attainment	
Less than 9th grade	29.9
9th to 12th grade, no diploma	26.7
High school graduate or GED	39.6
Some college or Associate degree	47.9

---

[9] The data in Table 4.3.2 come from the Census Bureau's Current Population Survey. Voters do not disclose to election officials, of course, information about their income, education, or any other characteristic, when casting their ballots. Consequently, exit polls and surveys are the only means of identifying the characteristics of voters. The Current Population Survey is rigorous, includes a large sample, and is conducted within two weeks of the election. Many of those surveyed (perhaps 10 percent) are reluctant to admit that they declined to do their civic duty and falsely report having voted. This makes it impossible to know exactly how many voters, for example, fall within a particular income bracket or any of the other selected characteristics in Table 4.3.2. The 2002 election is the most recent one for which Census Bureau data were available at the time of publication. Voter turnout is, of course, lower in mid-term elections than in presidential election years.

TABLE 4.3.2 (Cont.)

Characteristic	Reported Voted
	Percent
Bachelor's degree	60.5
Advanced degree	68.9
Annual Family Income*	
Total family members	48.4
Less than $5,000	26.4
$5,000 to $9,999	24.5
$10,000 to $14,999	35.9
$15,000 to $24,999	38.6
$25,000 to $34,999	43.8
$35,000 to $49,999	47.1
$50,000 to $74,999	53.2
$75,000 and over	59.3
Income not reported	41.2
Employment Status	
In the civilian labor force	45.2
Employed	46.0
Unemployed	31.0
Not in the labor force	48.0
Tenure	
Owner-occupied units	52.2
Renter-occupied units	27.6
No cash rent units	35.7
Duration of Residence**	
Less than 1 month	20.5
1 to 6 months	26.5
7 to 11 months	29.3
1 to 2 years	38.3
3 to 4 years	48.9
5 years or longer	59.5
Not reported	3.6

*Limited to people in families.

**Data on duration of residence were obtained from responses to the question "How long has (this person) lived at this address?"

SOURCE: U.S. Census Bureau, Current Population Survey, November 2002.

6. Table 4.3.2 indicates a 45.8-point difference between the percentage of 18–24-year-olds who reported voting and the percentage of 65–74-year-olds who reported voting. Let's call this the "turnout gap."

a. What's the turnout gap (in percentage points) between those earning less than $5,000 annually and those earning $75,000 and over?

b. What's the turnout gap (in percentage points) between those with less than a ninth-grade education and those with a bachelor's degree?

c. For which characteristic is the turnout gap greatest: age, income, or education?

90 CHAPTER 4 POLITICAL PARTIES AND ELECTIONS

7. Which characteristics other than age, income, and education specified in Table 4.3.2 help account for the low voter turnout of those 18–24 years of age? In other words, which characteristics associated with low rates of voting might disproportionately affect and depress the turnout of those 18–24 years of age?

___

___

___

Questions 8–11 are based on Table 4.3.3, "Reasons for Not Voting by Age: November 2002."

8. a. Which reason for not voting has the largest percentage point gap between 18–24-year-olds and those 65 years of age and over?

___

b. What's that percentage point gap?

___

9. a. Which reason had the second largest percentage point gap between 18–24-year-olds and those 65 years of age and over?

___

b. What's that percentage point gap?

___

10. Which age cohort (group) appears to be most forgetful?

___

11. According to the responses in Table 4.3.3, which age group found "registration problems" to be most difficult?

___

ASSIGNMENT, PART B: THE YOUTH VOTE

The age qualification for voting has traditionally been set by state governments at 21 years. During World War II, many citizens felt that if 18-year-olds could be drafted and die in combat, they should be able to vote as well. In 1943, Georgia lowered its voting age to 18; Kentucky followed suit—but not until 1955. When Alaska and Hawaii became states in the late 1950s, their constitutions had voting ages of 19 and 20, respectively.

The discrepancy between the draft and voting ages arose again during the Vietnam War. One provision of the Voting Rights Act of 1970 established a voting age of 18 in all federal, state, and local elections. Several states objected to the national government overriding the traditional state prerogative of regulating the conduct of state and local elections. In 1970, in *Oregon v. Mitchell*, the Supreme Court ruled that Congress had the authority to set the voting age *only* in elections for Congress and the presidency. The daunting prospect of having voting age requirements vary by state and type of election prompted Congress to propose, and the states to ratify, the Twenty-Sixth Amendment, which states that "the rights of citizens of the United States, who are eighteen years of age or older, to vote shall not be abridged by the United States or by any state on account of age."

Given a political climate in the 1960s charged by the antiwar, civil rights, women's, and environmental movements, many observers expected America's newly enfranchised youth to

TABLE 4.3.3 Reasons for not Voting, by Sex, Age, Race and Hispanic Origin, and Educational Attainment: November 2002 (In thousands)

REASONS FOR NOT VOTING	TOTAL NON-VOTING REGISTERED POPULATION		AGE							
			18 to 24 years		25 to 44 years		45 to 64 years		65 years and over	
	Number	Percent	Number	Percent	Number	Percent	Number	Percent	Number	Percent
All reasons	39,251	100.0	5,773	100.0	17,534	100.0	10,910	100	5,035	100.0
Illness or disability (own or family's)	5,143	13.1	160	2.8	1,244	7.1	1,511	13.8	2,228	44.3
Out of town or away from home	4,085	10.4	880	15.2	1,517	8.7	1,276	11.7	413	8.2
Forgot to vote (or send in absentee ballot)	2,242	5.7	367	6.4	1,103	6.3	595	5.5	176	3.5
Not interested, felt vote would not make a difference	4,715	12.0	649	11.2	2,174	12.4	1,349	12.4	543	10.8
Too busy, conflicting schedule	10,631	27.1	1,703	29.5	6,059	34.6	2,595	23.8	274	5.4
Transportation problems	656	1.7	84	1.4	202	1.2	170	1.6	200	4.0
Did not like candidates or campaign issues	2,848	7.3	242	4.2	1,164	6.6	1,012	9.3	431	8.6
Registration problems	1,595	4.1	341	5.9	854	4.9	288	2.6	112	2.2
Bad weather conditions	283	0.7	13	0.2	97	0.6	76	0.7	97	1.9
Inconvenient polling place or hours or lines too long	559	1.4	76	1.3	288	1.6	144	1.3	52	1.0
Other reason, not specified	3,544	9.0	453	7.9	1,684	9.6	1,052	9.6	355	7.0
Refused or don't know	2,951	7.5	806	14.0	1,147	6.5	842	7.7	155	3.1

SOURCE: U.S. Census Bureau, Current Population Survey, November 2002. Internet Release date: July 28, 2004.

storm the polls in the election of 1972. They did not. Fewer than half of the newly enfranchised 18–20-year-olds turned out to vote in 1972, and the youth voting rate has declined precipitously since then. According to Census Bureau figures, only 36 percent of 18–20-year-olds reported voting in the 1980 election, and only 28 percent in the 2000 election.

To answer questions 1 and 2, go to The Center for Information and Research on Civic Learning and Engagement (CIRCLE) at www.civicyouth.org.[10] Click on New Fact Sheets and study the report titled "Youth Voter Turnout 1992 to 2004: Estimates from Exit Polls."

1. According to the CIRCLE report, how did youth voter turnout in the 2004 election compare with the 1996 and 2000 elections? Cite figures from the report to support your answer.

_____

_____

_____

_____

_____

2. According to the CIRCLE report, what are some of the problems with estimating youth voter turnout?

_____

_____

_____

_____

_____

_____

To answer questions 3 and 4, study Reading 4.3.1, "Barriers to Student Voting," published by the Brennan Center for Justice at NYU School of Law. [11]

READING 4.3.1 BARRIERS TO STUDENT VOTING

Background on Student Voting

Research dating back to the 1940s has consistently shown that young citizens vote at lower rates than older citizens and are less likely to feel connected to the electoral process. Low voter turnout among young citizens has grown more acute since 1972, when 18–21-year-olds were first permitted to vote. According to the Center for Information and Research on Civic Learning and Engagement (CIRCLE) at the University of Maryland, voter turnout of 18–24-year-olds dropped by at least 13 percent (from 55% in 1972 to 42% in 2000), a much higher rate of decline than that of their elders.

---

[10] Website URLs sometimes change. Try an external search (e.g., Google) to find the website. Configurations of a website often change. Try an internal search of the site to locate the information. Sometimes websites and pages within websites are removed. In that case, move on to the next question.

[11] Reprinted with permission from the Brennan Center for Justice at NYU School of Law; all rights reserved. For more information about the Brennan Center's work in voting and representation, go to www.brennancenter.org. For questions on student voting, contact Jennifer Weiser, Associate Counsel, at (212) 998-6745 or at jennifer.weiser@nyu.edu.

This lack of representation at the polls means that young people's issues are being virtually ignored by political candidates.

The reality is that younger citizens are not voting in large numbers. But the problem is not as clear-cut as it initially seems. Too often, the low voter turnout is taken as conclusive evidence that young people are not engaged in social or political change or don't care about their communities. Yet, young people are volunteering and protesting at higher numbers today than in previous generations. For a large number of young people, refraining from voting is a conscious decision for various reasons, such as rejection of the system or a belief that their vote will not make a difference. However, a great many young people, particularly students, who want to vote are unable to do so because of legal or administrative barriers that make it extremely difficult or impossible to vote in their college communities.

Law on Student Voting

College students, like all individuals, are entitled to register and vote in the community that they regard as their principal residence. Under most states' laws, voting residence is synonymous with domicile, which is determined by physical presence and intent to make that place home. Thus, if a student considers her college community to be her primary residence and has no present intent to leave, she is entitled to register to vote in that community. The student need not be certain as to her residence after graduation, so long as she has no present intention of returning to her parents' home. The fact that a student resides in a dormitory is irrelevant to her intent to make her school address home.

In several jurisdictions, constitutional or statutory provisions provide that no person shall be deemed to have gained or lost a residence for voting purposes by reason of her presence or absence while a student at an institution of learning. These "gain or loss" provisions mean that a student's voting residence cannot be determined by physical presence alone; voting residence depends on the student's connections to the community in which she desires to vote.

States have established varying standards and tests for determining a person's intent with respect to voting residence. In New York, for example, the standard is whether the place is the "center of the individual's life now, the locus of primary concern." If this standard were fairly and uniformly applied by election officials, most college students seeking to vote as residents of their colleges would be permitted to do so because most students live principally in their college communities. They eat, sleep and carry out the daily activities of their lives in those communities; they are often deeply involved in part-time employment and community activities within the college community; and they are far more affected by the acts and omissions of local officials in their college community than they are by the acts of local officials in some distant parental community.

In the 1970s and 80s, many states incorrectly presumed that students were residents of their parents' communities unless they could prove otherwise. To overcome the presumption of non-residency, the burden was on students to present evidence of their intent to make the college address their new residence. Such presumptions against student voting generally have been invalidated by courts under the equal protection clause. For example, in *Williams v. Salerno*, the Second Circuit held that a letter sent by the Westchester County Board of Elections to student applicants, which stated that "[a] college dorm cannot be considered a fixed, permanent or principal home," created an unconstitutional rule or presumption against student residency.

The equal protection clause precludes states from subjecting students to more rigorous registration requirements than are generally applied to other citizens. A few courts have held that a state may make an additional inquiry in a good faith attempt to determine residency, so long as it does not require students to meet a different standard from any other person seeking to register to vote. However, if the inquiry is designed to elicit irrelevant information that is unnecessary to assess fairly whether the student considers the college community to be her primary residence (e.g., where the student's car is registered), it creates a per se rule against residence in the college community, which violates the equal protection clause.

Barriers to Student Voting

College students across the country are facing barriers to voting in their college communities. [In the 2004 election cycle there were] several incidents in which local officials... attempted to impede the ability of students to register to vote in their college or university towns through intimidation, refusal to process registration forms, or local ordinances establishing next-to-impossible residency standards. For example, the district attorney of Waller County, Texas, threatened to prosecute students at Prairie View A&M University who attempted to register in the local March 9, 2004 primary, claiming erroneously that college students cannot establish permanent residency at school. The registrar of the town of Williamsburg, Virginia, adopted a policy that made it almost impossible for William and Mary students to demonstrate residency to vote in local elections. Until June 2004, the Oneida County Board of Elections in Utica, New York, was sending college students a form letter encouraging them to register to vote as residents of the communities in which their parents live and automatically rejecting their registration applications. All of these incidents have required the intervention of lawyers in order to safeguard student voting rights. While some cases of local voter suppression can be attributed to misinformation due to a lack of guidance from the state, most are the result of concerted efforts to prevent students from affecting local politics.

The problems with student voting are not just local. A new federal law, the Help America Vote Act ("HAVA"), requires first-time voters who register by mail to provide identification. Unless a state specifies that a student identification card is an acceptable form of ID, students (particularly, those who live in dormitories) may be unable to meet HAVA's ID requirement. One way to avoid disenfranchising students who do not have identification that reflects their school address is to encourage, as Minnesota does, schools to provide local elections officials with a list of matriculated students, which can be used to verify students' residence.

Many states also have in-person voting or address matching requirements that disproportionately burden students. For example, Michigan state law requires that citizens' voter registration address match the address on their drivers' license. Students who do not wish to change their drivers' license to reflect their school address, which is common, will be unable to vote in Michigan unless they travel to their parents' home because state law also requires first-time voters to vote in person, rather than by absentee ballot.

At a time when voter turnout for young people has reached catastrophically low rates, it is critically important to remove all legal and administrative barriers to student voting. State and local elections officials must make clear that students have the right to register to vote in their college communities, if they consider that to be their primary residence. If students cannot register the first time they attempt to vote, they will be less likely to participate in elections in the future and politicians will continue to be unresponsive to their interests. The health of American democracy requires that our young voters become engaged in electoral politics.

---

3. In your view, what's the most significant barrier to student voting identified in the Brennan Center article?

4. How do the in-person voting or address-matching requirements of many states disproportionately burden students?

_____

_____

_____

_____

_____

EXERCISE 4.4 Alternative Voting Systems

INTRODUCTION

Nothing matters more in an election than the rules under which votes are cast and counted.[1] Americans learned this lesson in the contested presidential election of 2000, when the candidate who came in second in the popular vote won the Oval Office. Of course, the presidential election is governed by the electoral college and its web of rules and procedures prevailed. In most elections in the United States, ballots are cast and counted according to the rules of the plurality voting system (which is explained below). Most Americans take the plurality system for granted, even though few other democracies employ it and even though there are a number of viable alternatives to it.

Our examination of alternative voting systems will consider these questions: Does the system fairly and accurately gauge popular preferences? Which interests and viewpoints does a particular system reward, and which does it penalize? What effect does a voting system have on voter turnout? How does a system of casting and counting ballots shape citizens' views of the political system?

ASSIGNMENT

Described below are several different voting systems. Study each system and answer the questions that follow.

The Plurality Voting System In a plurality voting system, the candidate who receives the most votes wins. A plurality is different from a simple majority. To win a simple majority, a candidate must receive 50 percent of the total votes cast plus one more. In a plurality system, there is no minimum number of votes necessary to win.

Candidates from minor parties—the Libertarian Party or the Reform Party, for example—find it difficult to win political office in the United States because of the interplay between the plurality voting system and *single-member districts*. In American elections, voters in a congressional district or state legislative district elect just one official. The system is known as *winner-take-all, single-member district* because the winner of the election takes possession of the sole public office being contested in the election. There is no prize for the runners-up: The candidate with the most votes wins it all.[2] Winners are almost always members of the two major parties, Democrat and Republican, which monopolize political power in the United States. The two-party monopoly dates to the beginning of the Republic and continues to shape the expectations and voting behavior of citizens and candidates alike.

1. Go to the website of the Socialist Party USA, www.sp-usa.org.[3] Click on Who We Are and read "The Two Party Problem." Then click on Principles. Scroll down to "Socialist Strategy" and read about the party's stand on electoral action. In the space below, briefly summarize the Socialist Party USA's criticism of the two-party monopoly.

_____

_____

_____

_____

_____

---

[1] Source material from the *Los Angeles Times*, August 16, 1995.

[2] The only exceptions are run-off elections in some primaries. We discuss those elections below.

[3] Website URLs sometimes change. Try an external search (e.g., Google) to find the website. Configurations of a website often change. Try an internal search of the site to locate the information. Sometimes websites and pages within websites are removed. In that case, move on to the next question.

2. Explain how the combination of winner-take-all and the plurality voting system works against third-party candidates and discourages citizens from voting for those candidates.

_____

_____

_____

_____

_____

_____

The Run-Off System The run-off system described here is used in primary elections in nine southern states. Under the rules, a candidate must win a simple majority of the popular vote to win the party's nomination. If no candidate wins a simple majority in the first primary election, the top two finishers compete in a second primary, a *run-off primary*, which again is decided by a simple-majority vote.

3. Complete the table below by specifying the percentage of the popular vote each candidate would need to receive in the first primary election to produce a run-off election between Candidates A and B, and then the percentage of the popular vote Candidate A would need to win the run-off election. (There are many percentage figures that will produce the result you're seeking.)

First Primary Election	
Candidates	**Percent of Vote Needed to Go On to Run-off Election**
A. Republican Party	
B. Republican Party	
C. Republican Party	
D. Republican Party	
Run-off Primary Election	
Candidates	**Percent of Vote Needed to Win the Nomination**
A. Republican Party	
B. Republican Party	

4. Under which system, plurality or run-off, would a minority candidate—for example, an African-American—have a greater chance of winning? Explain and support your answer. (Remember that the run-off is used in party primaries, so there is no two-party monopoly.)

_____

_____

_____

The Approval Voting System Under the approval voting system, voters may decide to cast no votes at all or to cast one vote for any candidate on the ballot who they find acceptable. The requirement for winning the election could be plurality or simple majority (with the contingency of a run-off election). The United Nations, by the way, uses this system to select its secretary-general.

5. Five candidates are running for state representative:

Candidate A: Democrat, liberal, pro-choice

Candidate B: Democrat, moderate, pro-choice

Candidate C: Republican, moderate, pro-choice

Candidate D: Republican, moderate, pro-life

Candidate E: Republican, conservative, pro-life

Consider the position of an independent voter strongly in favor of abortion rights (pro-choice) and moderate to conservative on most other issues. Which candidates would this voter support under the approval voting system? Explain your answer.

6. Under the approval system of casting and counting ballots, the candidate who is acceptable to, but not necessarily the enthusiastic choice of, the greatest number of voters wins the election. Obviously this type of candidate would attract support from a wide variety of voters. Very few voters would be deeply committed to the candidate, but just as few would be repelled by the candidate. Describe the likely characteristics of this type of candidate and the positions he or she probably would take on abortion rights, gun control, and environmental protection.

The Cumulative Voting System Under the cumulative voting system, citizens can cast as many votes as there are candidates in the race, distributing the votes in any way they choose. For example, if there are six candidates on the ballot, a voter can cast all six votes for a strongly favored candidate, or one or more votes to each candidate the voter finds acceptable. Here, too, candidates may win with a plurality or with a simple majority (and a contingency run-off election).

7. Consider the following candidates on the ballot:

   Candidate A: Democrat, left-wing liberal, white, female

   Candidate B: Democrat, liberal, white, female

   Candidate C: Democrat, moderate, black, female

   Candidate D: Republican, moderate, white, male

   Candidate E: Republican, conservative, black, male

   Candidate F: Republican, right-wing conservative, white, male

   How would a lifelong Democrat, active in the party and on behalf of liberal and feminist causes, most likely cast her six votes? Explain and support your answer.

   _____

   _____

   _____

   _____

   _____

   _____

   _____

8. The cumulative voting system would hand victory in an election to a candidate who can generate deep and enthusiastic support from a particular segment of the electorate. Those voters presumably would be so committed to their candidate that they would throw all of their votes to him or her. Describe the likely characteristics of this type of candidate and the positions he or she probably would take on abortion, gun control, and environmental protection.

   _____

   _____

   _____

   _____

   _____

   _____

The Transferable-Vote System This is the most complex of the systems examined here, but some mathematicians maintain that it most accurately takes into account voters' preferences and that it, of all voting systems, is most likely to end in the election of a consensus candidate. The Associated

Students of the University of California at Berkeley, by the way, uses this system to elect its officers. Under the transferable-vote system, voters rank each candidate, assigning the number 1 to the candidate they favor most strongly, the number 2 to the next most favored candidate, and so on. An initial tally is made to determine how many number 1 rankings each candidate received. The candidate receiving the fewest is eliminated from the contest, and the number 1 rankings he or she received are transferred to the candidates those voters ranked number 2. This process of eliminating the candidate with the fewest number 1 rankings and distributing those votes to the voters' number 2 choice is repeated until all candidates but one have been eliminated. That candidate is the winner.

In a plurality election, a vote cast for any candidate other than the winner plays no affirmative role in determining the outcome of the election. That could leave voters who cast their votes for losing candidates feeling that their preferences did not shape the outcome of the contest—that they wasted their vote. The transferable-vote system eliminates this problem because under this system, every vote plays an affirmative role in shaping the outcome of the election.[4]

9. Make one argument in favor of the transferable-vote system.

_____

_____

_____

_____

_____

10. Make one argument against the transferable-vote system.

_____

_____

_____

_____

_____

Proportional Representation All of the voting systems examined above are candidate-based, winner-take-all systems. By contrast, some nations employ political party–based systems, multimember election districts, and proportional representation. In these systems each party fields a slate (list) of candidates, and voters cast their ballots for the party they prefer. Seats in the legislature are awarded to each party according to the percentage of votes the party captures in the election. The party then elevates the appropriate number of candidates from its slate to seats in the legislature. Typically, parties that receive just a small percentage of the vote (for example, less than 6 percent) are not awarded seats in the legislature. Under the proportional representation system, one party often is unable to capture an outright majority of the seats in the legislature. Coalitions between parties must then be formed to achieve the majority needed to control the legislature and, hence, to govern.

11. Fill in the right-hand column of the table below by allocating the 100 seats in Parliament on a proportional basis—in other words, according to the percentage of the vote each party received. Assume that parties that win less than 6 percent of the vote receive no seats in the legislature.

---

[4] For more information about the transferable-vote system and about other voting systems in general, go to the website of the Labour Campaign for Electoral Reform, www.electoralreform.org.uk/, and click on Voting systems, or go to www.electionmethods.org.

Party	Percent of Vote	Seats in Parliament (100)
A	38	
B	26	
C	20	
D	9	
E	4	
F	3	

12. Identify the possible coalitions of parties that would achieve majority control of Parliament.

_____

_____

Alternative Voting Systems The following project will let you test how alternative voting systems might have worked in the 2004 presidential election. It assumes, of course, that the presidency is determined not by the electoral college system, but by the nationwide popular vote.

13. Ask ten people—friends, family members, classmates—to vote under each of the systems, except proportional representation. The proportional system does not apply here because this election is candidate-centered, not party-centered, and because it's for a single executive office, not for a legislative body. Then fill in the table to show which candidate emerged victorious under each system.

Candidate	Plurality	Run-off	Approval	Cumulative	Transferable
George W. Bush (Republican)					
John Kerry (Democrat)					
Ralph Nader (Independent)					
Michael Badnarik (Libertarian)					
Michael Peroutka (Constitution)					
David Cobb (Green)					

14. Which of the voting systems examined in this exercise do you think is best? Explain and support your position.

CHAPTER 5

Interest Groups

EXERCISE 5.1 AARP Versus Generation X: Mismatched Interest Group Power

INTRODUCTION

Many citizens magnify their political power by joining or forming interest groups. Many others—for lack of knowledge, resources, or motivation—decline to do so. Interest group membership, like the voting rate,[1] varies according to factors such as age, education, and economic position. The interests of Americans over age 50, for example, are represented muscularly—some would say notoriously—by AARP. Formerly called the American Association of Retired Persons, now it's known simply as AARP to acknowledge that many members are not retired. In fact, AARP recruits members as young as 50 who would have at least ten to fifteen working years until retirement.

Because elected officials and the media often equate an interest group's power with the size of its membership, numbers count. AARP's membership of 35 million is daunting—far surpassing that of any other public interest group. By comparison, the National Rifle Association boasts a membership of about 4 million. Although its membership is a mere fraction of the AARP's, the NRA has the advantage of near unanimity among its members on the group's central issue: protecting a citizen's right to own firearms unimpeded by government regulation. Because AARP's objective of advancing the security of older Americans is quite broad, its members often part company on just how to achieve that objective.

In 2003, AARP's leadership was reminded of the perils of taking policy positions for a membership that's notably diverse. AARP surprised its traditional Democratic allies in Congress and many of its members by backing President George W. Bush's proposal for a Medicare prescription drug

---

[1] In the 2000 presidential election, 28 percent of those aged 18–20 voted. By contrast, 67 percent of those over age 65 voted. See Exercise 4.3 for information on youth turnout in the 2004 election.

benefit. Two components of the president's proposal had long been opposed by AARP: an experiment with limited privatization of the drug benefit and a means test requiring wealthy recipients to pay a bigger share of their premium. AARP members reacted by burning their membership cards outside the group's headquarters in Washington, DC, and demanding that AARP chief William Novelli be fired from his $420,000-a-year job. Eighty-five House Democrats expressed their outrage by announcing that they would resign from AARP, or refuse to join in the future. One Florida resident interviewed by the *New York Times* said, "I'm going to resign from AARP. Its support of this drug plan tipped the balance. They're more sympathetic to the big drug and insurance companies than to ordinary seniors who want a simple solution."[2]

AARP is usually categorized as a public—as opposed to a private—interest group. But the distinction between the two types of interest groups is not always clear. Generally, public interest groups advocate for broad political and social causes as opposed to seeking narrow material benefits for their members—the purpose of private interest groups such as the American Farm Bureau Federation, for example. AARP claims its mission is to enhance "the quality of life for all as we age," which would seem to anchor it securely in the public interest camp. Yet AARP also provides particular financial benefits to its members and makes money doing so. The American Automobile Association (AAA)—whose 45-million-strong membership trumps AARP's—is generally considered a private interest group because it provides emergency and other road services to members.[3] Few AAA members are aware that the group lobbies against environmental, auto safety and public transportation initiatives.[4]

How effectively interest groups deploy their resources and how genuinely they serve the interests of their members are controversial matters—particularly in the case of AARP. Dale Van Atta, a trenchant critic of AARP and author of *Trust Betrayed: Inside the AARP*, argues that government policymakers and journalists have overestimated the power of AARP and that other seniors' organizations are more effective at lobbying Congress.[5] Van Atta and other AARP critics skewer the organization as a money-making machine run by fat cats that often works against the interests of its members. Yet despite its critics, AARP remains widely perceived as the voice of the elderly and the mother of all interest groups.

A striking disparity in power and influence exists between AARP and groups that have struggled for years to organize and advocate for Americans in their 20s and 30s—a demographic group usually referred to as Generation X.[6] One group that's now defunct—but had more staying power than most—was Third Millennium: Advocates for the Future. Third Millennium was founded in 1993 by young adults to promote sustainable reform of Social Security and Medicare. Launched with a foundation grant of $9,200 and operated out of the bedroom of one of its founders during its first several months, the group by 2000 claimed to have an annual operating budget in excess of $500,000 (AARP's budget is about 1,500 times greater). In 1994, Third Millennium commissioned a poll that found that more Americans 18–34 years of age believed that UFOs exist (46 percent) than believed that Social Security would exist by the time they reached retirement age (28 percent). This "UFO factoid" is often cited as evidence of the generational divide on the problem of Social Security reform. Among a long list of accomplishments, Third Millennium hosted conferences on Social Security reform, published reports and opinion pieces on the issue, and provided testimony to congressional committees. But by 2003, Third Millennium was out of business—a casualty of the difficulties of sustaining the organization of Generation X.

A more recent effort to organize young adults for advocacy flowered and died even more rapidly than Third Millennium. The 2030 Center was founded in 1997 to advocate for the economic interests of young adults, but emphasized the need to bridge the generation gap on difficult issues such as Social Security reform. The group's name referred to Americans in their 20s and 30s as well as to the

---

[2] Robert Pear, "Florida Elderly Feel Let Down by Medicare Drug Benefit," *New York Times*, November 30, 2003, p. 1.34.

[3] *Public Interest Group Profiles, 2005–2005* (CQ Press, 2004) lists AARP as a public interest group, but not the AAA.

[4] Ken Silverstein, "Smitten with a Club: Your AAA Dues Fuel Pollution and Sprawl," *Harpers Magazine*, May 2002.

[5] Dale Van Atta, *Trust Betrayed: Inside the AARP* (Washington, DC: Regnery Publishing, 1998). The organizations Van Atta cites as being more effective than AARP are the National Committee to Preserve Social Security, the Seniors Coalition, and the National Council of Senior Citizens.

[6] Generation X is generally considered to include those born between 1964 or 1965 and 1980. The baby boom generation is generally considered to include those born between 1946 and 1964 or 1965. For an introduction to the controversies involved in defining generations, consult www.webster-dictionary.org/definition/generation%20X.

year 2030, a demographic benchmark when the leading edge of Generation X will begin claiming its Social Security retirement benefits. In 1999, the 2030 Center commissioned a poll of Generation X members; it purported to show that "an antagonistic political battle between older people, baby boomers, and young people is largely a myth."[7] Among other accomplishments, the group published a manual for strengthening Social Security for young workers, testified before congressional committees, and received significant media attention. The 2030 Center folded sometime in 2002.

The disparity in power and influence between interest groups representing seniors and those representing Generation X affects the future of Social Security. Most observers believe that Social Security requires substantive reform to meet its long-term obligations to future retirees. The fundamental problem is demographic. As the baby boom generation reaches retirement age, the number of retirees drawing Social Security benefits will increase; the number of workers paying into the system will decrease. For example, in 1940, the ratio of workers paying into Social Security to retirees drawing benefits was 42 to 1. By 2000, the ratio had dropped to 3 to 1. By 2044, the ratio is projected to be 2 to 1. Also straining the system is the increasing longevity of retirees.[8]

AARP is quick to point out that it seeks a solution to the Social Security problem that is fair to younger generations as well as to seniors. Perhaps that's because AARP doesn't want to alienate the generations it will be recruiting from in the not so distant future. It might be a sobering prospect indeed for members of Generation X to consider they too will one day be eligible for membership in AARP.

ASSIGNMENT

The questions below explore the structure and functions of AARP and its position on Social Security reform.

1. Broadly speaking, what characteristics of those over age 50 make older Americans more effective interest group members than those of Generation X? In other words, why have efforts to organize older Americans been so much more successful than efforts to organize members of Generation X?

___

___

___

___

2. Take a few minutes and explore AARP's website at www.aarp.org.[9] Generally speaking, does the website give more emphasis to services and benefits for AARP members or to the group's work on political advocacy and its positions on public issues?

___

___

---

[7] Americans for Generational Equity (AGE), founded in 1985, was the first organization to promote the notion of "future intergenerational conflict." Christopher Cuomo argued in 1997 that the divide between the young and old was a myth promoted by conservatives who sought to weaken Social Security. See "The Generation Gambit: The Right's Imaginary Rift Between Young and Old," Fairness & Accuracy in Reporting (FAIR), March/April 1997, at http://www.fair.org/index.php?page=1379.

[8] A brief and accessible introduction to the history of Social Security and the challenges the system faces is at www.ssa.gov/history/brief.html.

[9] Website URLs sometimes change. Try an external search (e.g., Google) to find the website. Configurations of a website often change. Try an internal search of the site to locate the information. Sometimes websites and pages within websites are removed. In that case, move on to the next question.

108 CHAPTER 5 INTEREST GROUPS

To answer questions 3–8, click on "About AARP" (on AARP's homepage) and then on "AARP History."

3. What does AARP claim its mission to be?

4. Who does AARP claim to represent?

5. How does AARP finance its operations?

6. How does AARP communicate with its members?

7. How does AARP develop its policy positions?

8. What advocacy efforts does AARP undertake?

To answer questions 9 and 10, study the article "What's the Big Idea?" by Thomas N. Bethell. Conduct a search for the article on AARP's website. Also study Reading 5.1.1, "Where AARP Stands on Social Security."

READING 5.1.1 WHERE AARP STANDS ON SOCIAL SECURITY[10]

As Congress grapples with Social Security's future, many ideas are on the table, with issues of solvency defining the debate. AARP remains open to many options and, above all, is firmly committed to protecting and strengthening the system.

AARP supports:

- Offering individual retirement accounts in addition to Social Security
- Raising the cap on wages subject to Social Security tax so that 90 percent of wages nationwide would be covered
- Making the Social Security system universal, with everyone sharing its obligations and benefits
- Investing a portion of the trust fund in a total market index fund to increase the return. By law, the trust fund now may be invested only in government bonds.

AARP opposes:

- Creating "carve-out" private accounts that divert payroll contributions away from Social Security
- Indexing benefits to prices instead of wages
- Reducing the COLA
- Increasing the retirement age

9. Notice that AARP opposes four of the nine solutions that Bethell examines in the article. What do those four solutions have in common, and why does AARP oppose them?

10. AARP has not taken a position on increasing the payroll tax rate. Why not? To answer this question, think about the present and future membership of the organization.

---

[10] From AARP's website, April 2005.

Questions 11–14 are based on Reading 5.1.2, an excerpt from "A Management Study of the Communications of the American Association of Retired Persons."

READING 5.1.2 A MANAGEMENT STUDY OF THE COMMUNICATIONS OF THE AMERICAN ASSOCIATION OF RETIRED PERSONS[11]

Many on the staff [of the AARP]... expressed confusion about the diversity of AARP membership demographics. They are uncomfortable with a population [of AARP members] that includes the affluent, the needy, retired people, those still working, the mature, the old, the old old, the feeble elderly, active seniors, etc. As membership characteristics become more pronounced, the issues gain complexity.

The question for many: "Who is AARP's constituency, and how does it best serve them?" As a result, we found growing tension over tactics and a deepening rift between two camps: membership growth/service and advocacy on public policy issues.

The service camp says that taking sides and speaking out on issues will polarize members and alienate potential members. They feel the mounting advocacy campaigns will subject AARP to increased criticism, ultimately retard membership growth and curtail the delivery of services to members.

The advocacy faction believes AARP members must be outspoken... and lead the national dialogue about issues important to the aging. They fear the low-profile, don't-rock-the-boat attitude of the services [membership growth] camp will prevent them [the advocacy faction] from being heard on key issues. They fear that AARP will be seen as "money-making fat cats."

We encountered some *destructive static*—not healthy tension—between these two opposing views of AARP's mission.

---

11. How does the management study describe the diversity of AARP's membership?

_____

_____

_____

_____

12. According to the management study, what conflict exists within AARP as the organization tries to grapple with the diversity of its "membership demographics"?

_____

_____

_____

---

[11] Conducted by outside consultants, Chester Burger & Co., Inc., September 1985. The study is cited in Dale Van Atta, *Trust Betrayed: Inside the AARP* (Washington, DC: Regnery Publishing, 1998), p. 117.

13. What's ultimately at stake for AARP if advocacy undermines membership growth and the sale of services?

14. If you were the executive director of AARP, would you side with the service or advocacy faction? Explain and support your position.

EXERCISE 5.2 The Discreet Charm of Pork-Barrel Spending: The Political Side of Punxsutawney Phil

INTRODUCTION

Members of Congress often are accused of bringing federal dollars home to benefit their districts or states at the expense of the national interest. The common term for this use of federal funds is *pork-barrel spending*, implying that the projects are wasteful and serve mainly to enhance the reelection prospects of the representative who is "bringing home the bacon."[1]

Presidents are among the loudest critics of Congress' penchant for pork-barrel spending. A president's national constituency and budget perspective seem to put the president above the narrow constituencies clamoring for federal dollars. But presidents are not above playing politics with pork. They tend to be more enthusiastic about cutting pork-barrel spending in districts and states controlled by the other party than in those controlled by their own party.

Congress often prevails in battles with the president over pork-barrel spending. Why? Two factors are particularly important in explaining how representatives protect their slice of the pork. First, members of Congress use their positions on key committees and subcommittees to protect special interests. Congressional committees exercise immense power by determining which bills are left to die in committee and which are forwarded to the full chamber for a vote. And the *quid* for that *quo*? Special interests in the representative's district or state support those members of Congress at election time. Presidents find it difficult, if not impossible, to break the ties that bind powerful members of Congress to organized interests back home that benefit from the pork. Second, even though most members of Congress have no direct stake in any other member's pork, they'll often vote for it to ensure that their own pork-barrel programs are funded. This kind of reciprocal arrangement is called *logrolling*. Logrolling is required to achieve majority support for projects that by themselves are too particular, and have too little to do with the national interest, to win approval.

On December 7, 2004, Punxsutawney Phil, the famous groundhog whose shadow (or lack thereof) signals the coming of spring, joined Representative John Peterson (Republican, Pennsylvania) in Washington, DC, for a rally. The purpose of the rally was to defend a federal appropriation (in the 2005 Omnibus Appropriations bill) of $100,000, a small piece of pork by federal standards, for the Punxsutawney Weather Discovery Center in Peterson's district. The money would allow the center to secure the services of an exhibit design firm. The Weather Discovery Center is part of the town of Punxsutawney's effort to use Punxsutawney Phil's weather forecasting acumen to establish itself as Weather Capital of the World. The press and public interest groups like to publicize the more bizarre examples of pork-barrel expenditures, and Rep. Peterson had been the target of some bad publicity in the national press about his appetite for pork. In fact, Citizens Against Government Waste gave one of its 2005 "Oinkers" award, "The Burrowing a Hole in Our Wallets Award," to Peterson.

ASSIGNMENT

In this assignment you will examine the politics of pork through the case study of the Punxsutawney Weather Discovery Center. Start with learning about Representative Peterson and his district. Go to Rep. Peterson's website at http://www.house.gov/johnpeterson/.[2] Then answer the questions that follow.

---

[1] Origin of the term *pork barrel*: "Slave owners on special occasions, or whenever they were feeling particularly charitable (some did it regularly in the binding spirit of noblesse oblige—a code the best owners lived by), would put out salt pork in big barrels at a certain time on an announced day. And like the Oklahoma settlers waiting for the firing of a gun to rush and seize a claim of land, the slaves would rush to the barrels and grab what they could" (*BBC News*, December 29, 2003: http://news.bbc.co.uk/1/hi/programmes/letter_from_america/3354949.stm).

[2] Website URLs sometimes change. Try an external search (e.g., Google) to find the website. Configurations of a website often change. Try an internal search of the site to locate the information. Sometimes websites and pages within websites are removed. In that case, move on to the next question.

114   CHAPTER 5   INTEREST GROUPS

Click on and read the following material:

"About the Representative"

   Biography
   Committees
   Legislation
   Rural Caucus
   Western Caucus

Then scroll down to read:

"Discover Pennsylvania"

   5th District

1. When was Peterson first elected to the House of Representatives? How many terms will he have served at the end of 2006?

_____

_____

_____

2. Identify the important characteristics of Peterson's district. For example, is the district predominantly urban or rural? What's the economy of the district based on?

_____

_____

_____

3. What two committees does Peterson serve on? What subcommittees of each committee?

_____

_____

_____

4. How are Peterson's committee assignments related to the characteristics of his district and his ability to support projects important to his constituents? You can find a list of committees and their jurisdictions at http://clerk.house.gov/committee/index.html.

_____

_____

_____

_____

5. Based on the legislation Peterson sponsored (not cosponsored) in the 109th Congress (2005–2006), what are his legislative interests?

_____

_____

6. How are Peterson's legislative interests related to the characteristics of his district and his constituents' interests?

_____

_____

_____

_____

7. What is the Rural Caucus? What is the Western Caucus?

Rural Caucus: _____

_____

_____

Western Caucus: _____

_____

_____

8. a. Why is Peterson a member of the Rural Caucus?

_____

_____

b. Why is he a member of the Western Caucus? Pennsylvania, after all, isn't exactly a western state.

_____

_____

Go to the websites of the Punxsutawney Weather Discovery Center: http://www.groundhogweather.com/ and http://www.punxsutawney.com/weathercenter/. Explore both sites to answer questions 9–11.

9. What is the mission of the Weather Discovery Center?

_____

_____

_____

10. What kinds of events and services does the Weather Discovery Center provide?

_____

_____

_____

11. In what ways would the center's functions benefit Rep. Peterson's constituents?

_____

_____

_____

Go to http://councilfor.cagw.org/site/PageServer?pagename=reports_Ratings_House. There Citizens Against Government Waste rates members of the House of Representatives according to their affinity for pork. Note the rating scale near the top of the page. Then scroll down to the Pennsylvania delegation to the House and find Rep. Peterson.

12. a. What is Rep. Peterson's rating for 2003? What is his lifetime rating?

2003: _____

Lifetime: _____

b. Does Citizens Against Government Waste consider Peterson to be a problem porker? (Refer back to the rating scale at the top of the website.)

_____

13. Is Peterson's sponsorship of the $100,000 of federal funds for the Weather Discovery Center in his district consistent with his CAGW rating? Explain your answer.

_____

_____

14. Here's some old wisdom about American politics: "Everyone wants a balanced budget, but nobody wants the balancing to be done at his or her expense." Do Peterson's CAGW rating and his support for the $100,000 expenditure for his district lend credence to that wisdom? Explain your answer.

_____

_____

_____

Following is Rep. Peterson's press release announcing Punxsutawney Phil's visit to Washington, DC, to defend the $100,000 expenditure for the Weather Discovery Center:

"The Punxsutawney Weather Discovery Center is a unique museum that presents the history, science, technology and folklore of weather in an interactive setting that is not only educational for young people, but fun for the whole family. This one-of-a-kind museum will help promote tourism in a beautiful, historic region of the country that has been struggling economically. To cry 'pork' without knowing anything about the project only serves to undermine the credibility of otherwise reputable organizations, and I hope they will take time to visit Punxsutawney with their families and join the thousands of others who have experienced the unique Weather Discovery Center for themselves."

15. Are you persuaded by Rep. Peterson's defense of the expenditure? Explain and support your answer.

_____

_____

_____

_____

16. Do you think that many of residents of the 5th District of Pennsylvania would be persuaded by their representative's defense of the expenditure? Explain your answer.

_____

_____

_____

_____

EXERCISE 5.3 Campaign Finance Reform and the Newest Loophole—527 Groups

INTRODUCTION

Time and again, efforts to regulate cash flowing into federal election campaigns have foundered. Reforms have been enacted only to be circumvented through the latest loophole. Campaign finance regulations have so far been unable to check the powerful attraction between private wealth and candidates running for office.

Reacting to the discovery of vast amounts of illegal money in Richard Nixon's reelection campaign of 1972, Congress in 1974 amended the Federal Election Campaign Reform Act to establish for the first time public finding of presidential election campaigns. In the presidential primary election, the new system provided federal matching funds for candidates who limit themselves to private individual contributions of $250 or less. Those contributions are then matched dollar for dollar from the Presidential Election Campaign Fund. The new system also provided public funding for the major-party presidential candidates in the general election. Candidates who accept this public money cannot take private contributions during the general election.

The decision to accept federal matching funds in the primary election or public funding in the general election is made by each presidential candidate. All major-party candidates have so far accepted the general elections funds, knowing that their campaigns would be supplemented by money funneled through the loopholes discussed in this exercise.[1] But not all candidates have accepted the primary matching funds. George W. Bush refused matching funds in 2000 and 2004 because he believed that he could raise more money on his own, and he did—$60 and $240 million, respectively. John Kerry also refused primary matching funds, raising slightly less than Bush for the 2004 primaries.

What is the rationale for publicly financed presidential campaigns? The less candidates rely on soliciting funds from rich donors and special interests, the more responsive and accountable they are to the American people. Congress also placed limits on the amount individuals, Political Action Committees (commonly known as PACs), and political parties can contribute directly to candidates in congressional campaigns. The purpose of these limits was to curtail the influence of wealthy donors and special interest groups.

No legislative reform is perfect. The federal election reforms adversely affected the interests of many individuals and organizations. They responded by contesting the provisions of the new law and searching for loopholes in the language of the legislation. In 1976, in *Buckley v. Valeo*, the U.S. Supreme Court handed opponents of the new legislation a significant victory by ruling that political campaign contributions in some cases are protected speech under the First Amendment. That decision led to the proliferation of *independent spending campaigns,* in which individuals spend unlimited amounts on *behalf* of candidates for federal office. (Wealthy individuals were also allowed to bankroll their own campaigns for federal office.)

The federal election reform legislation also created the Federal Elections Commission (FEC), which was charged with enforcing the reforms. Ambiguous language in the bill allowed candidates, parties, individuals, and interest groups to circumvent the restrictions Congress had established. Unfortunately for the advocates of reform, the FEC has consistently upheld these spending loopholes.[2]

The distinction between hard-money and soft-money campaign contributions is critical to understanding the source of loopholes in campaign financing.

- *Hard-money contributions* are made directly to the campaign of a candidate running for federal office and are limited under law. The limitations depend on who's giving (an individual, a PAC, or the Presidential Election Campaign Fund) and on who's receiving

---

[1] George W. Bush and John Kerry each received about $75 million in federal funds to run their general election campaigns. Source: Federal Elections Commission.

[2] Many critics of the FEC believe that it must be reformed. Their argument: The Commission is appointed by party leaders in Congress (three Republicans and three Democrats) and is, therefore, often less interested in reform than in making regulations that benefit the parties and their candidates.

(a congressional candidate, a presidential candidate, or a political party). For example, the current law limits hard-money contributions by individuals to congressional candidates to $2,000 per candidate per election. (See Table 5.3.1 below.)

- *Soft-money contributions* flow from donors to the national party organizations (prohibited since 2002) and now to *527 groups*, named after that numbered provision of the IRS code. Individuals, unions, and corporations—otherwise restricted by hard-money limitations—can donate as much money as they wish to 527 groups. The 527s then spend their vast store of money on ads, voter mobilization drives, and other activities that support their favored presidential or congressional candidates. One noteworthy example is the Swift Boat Veterans for Truth, which, in 2004, ran attack ads questioning Kerry's military record.

The upshot? Presidential candidates, congressional candidates, and political parties can have their cake and eat it, too: They agree to limit themselves to the hard money allowed by law, but they know that their campaigns will be supplemented by hefty sums of soft money.

After the 1996 campaign, which included ever more sophisticated attempts to circumvent the intent of the 1974 campaign reforms, voices of reform began to be heard. Chief among them was that of Senator John McCain (Republican, Arizona), who made campaign finance reform the center of his battle for the Republican presidential nomination against the eventual winner, George W. Bush. On March 27, 2002, a reluctant President Bush signed into law the first major campaign finance reform since 1974, the Bipartisan Campaign Reform Act of 2002. The president then flew off to raise funds for the 2002 congressional elections before new limits on fundraising would take effect (in November 2002). The Supreme Court eventually upheld the law in *McConnell v. Federal Election Commission* (2003).

The new reform outlawed soft-money donations to political parties, the loophole that allowed $1.5 billion in unregulated contributions to flow to the two major parties (state and federal) by the 1999–2000 election cycle.[3] When the Bipartisan Campaign Reform Act was passed, Senator McCain warned that in another decade or two, another reform bill would have to be passed to shut down the loopholes that hired-gun lawyers would surely find for wealthy individuals and interest groups. But it didn't take nearly that long for big donors to identify the 527 loophole. In McCain's words, the Bipartisan Campaign Reform Act had been "like putting your thumb in the dike."[4] In the 2004 election, 527s raised $463 million. (Democratic-affiliated 527 groups raised more than Republican-affiliated 527 groups by a margin of almost 2 to 1, partly because Democratic groups mobilized earlier to make up for the huge amounts of money Bush had raised during his presidency. By the end of the campaign, Republican-affiliated groups had learned to exploit this new loophole and were outspending Democratic-affiliated 527s.)[5] 527 groups cannot coordinate their activities with the candidates' campaigns, but there is some evidence from 2004 that key political operatives acted as intermediaries between candidates and 527 campaign organizations.[6]

As of this writing, a proposed bill to close the 527 loophole has been introduced in Congress, with Senator McCain as one of its sponsors. The objective of The 527 Reform Act of 2005 is to subject 527s to the same limits on contributions that currently apply to other federal political committees (PACs). During the 2004 presidential campaign, George W. Bush promised to support legislation closing the newest loophole in campaign finance.

ASSIGNMENT

Table 5.3.1 shows limits on group and individual contributions to candidates, party organizations, and political action committees (PACs), under the Bipartisan Campaign Reform Act of 2002. Study the table and then answer questions 1 and 2.

---

[3] Federal Election Committee website: http://www.fec.gov.

[4] Quoted in Glen Justice, "Even with Campaign Finance Law, Money Talks Louder than Ever," *New York Times*, November 8, 2004, p. A.1.

[5] Gail Russell Chaddock, "Money Lessons from a Year on the Campaign," *Christian Science Monitor*, November 9, 2004, p. 2.

[6] For example, Benjamin Ginsberg, a lawyer for the Bush–Cheney campaign, had also served as an adviser to the Swift Boat Veterans for Truth. He eventually resigned from the Bush–Cheney campaign. See CNN, "Bush–Cheney Lawyer Resigns over Veterans Flap," August 25, 2004, http://www.cnn.com/2004/ALLPOLITICS/08/25/ginsberg.swiftboat/.

TABLE 5.3.1 Contribution Limits

	To each candidate or candidate committee per election	To national party committee per calendar year	To state, district, and local party committee per calendar year	To any other political committee per calendar year[1]	Special Limits on Overall Spending
Individual may give	$2,100*	$26,700*	$10,000 (combined limit)	$5,000	$101,400* overall biennial limit: • $40,000* to all candidates • $61,400* to all PACs and parties[2]
National Party Committee may give	$5,000	No limit	No limit	$5,000	$37,300* to Senate candidate per campaign[3]
State, District, and Local Party Committee may give	$5,000 (combined limit)	No limit	No limit	$5,000 (combined limit)	No limit
PAC (multicandidate)[4] may give	$5,000	$15,000	$5,000 (combined limit)	$5,000	No limit
PAC (not multicandidate) may give	$2,100[5]*	$26,700*	$10,000 (combined limit)	$5,000	No limit

*These contribution limits are increased for inflation in odd-numbered years.

[1] A contribution earmarked for a candidate through a political committee counts against the original contributor's limit for that candidate. In certain circumstances, the contribution may also count against the contributor's limit to the PAC.

[2] No more than $40,000 of this amount may be contributed to state and local party committees and PACs.

[3] This limit is shared by the national committee and the Senate campaign committee.

[4] A multicandidate committee is a political committee with more than 50 contributors which has been registered for at least 6 months and, with the exception of state party committees, has made contributions to 5 or more candidates for federal office.

[5] A federal candidate's authorized committee(s) may contribute no more than $2,000 per election to another federal candidate's authorized committee(s)

SOURCE: Federal Elections Commission.

1. The Bipartisan Campaign Reform Act, like all public policies, encourages some behaviors and discourages others. Consider the contribution limits for each type of donor (first column) and each type of recipient (top row).

   a. Which donors (first column) are the least restricted in overall spending?

   b. Which recipients (top row) are the most restricted in contributions?

2. Individual donors have carved out a loophole all their own. It's called *bundling*, whereby individuals with common interests and goals pool their individual contributions and deliver them to favored candidates, political parties, and PACs. Consider the potential size of this loophole. The National Rife Association has 4 million members.[7] If just one-tenth of 1 percent of the NRA's membership bundled their maximum individual contribution per candidate/election, how much money could they contribute to a candidate who embraced the NRA's positions on gun control?

Table 5.3.2 lists the top ten 527 groups in the 2004 election. Study it and then answer questions 3 and 4.

TABLE 5.3.2 Top Ten 527 Groups

Committee	Total Receipts	Total Expenditures
America Coming Together	$79,795,487	$78,040,480
Joint Victory Campaign 2004	$71,811,666	$72,588,053
Media Fund	$59,404,183	$54,494,698
Progress for America	$44,929,178	$35,631,378
Service Employees International Union	$40,237,236	$39,579,709
American Fedn of St/Cnty/Munic Employees	$22,227,050	$22,332,587
Swift Vets & POWs for Truth	$17,008,090	$22,565,360
College Republican National Cmte	$12,780,126	$17,260,655
New Democrat Network	$12,726,158	$12,524,063
MoveOn.org	$12,558,215	$21,346,380

NOTE: These data are based on records released by the Internal Revenue Service on Monday, May 23, 2005.
SOURCE: opensecrets.org

3. What percentage of the total expenditures of the top ten groups was spent on behalf of Democrats/Kerry, and what percentage was spent on behalf of Republicans/Bush? You can determine the leaning of each group by going to the opensecrets.org website, where you'll find Table 5.3.2: http://www.opensecrets.org/527s/527cmtes.asp?level=C&cycle=2004&format.[8] Pull down the "election cycle" menu to 2004. Pull down the "view by" menu to Top 50. (*Remember you'll be working with only the top ten.*) Click on the title of each group and, where applicable,

---

[7] NRA website: http://www.nraila.org/About/NRAILA.aspx.

[8] Website URLs sometimes change. Try an external search (e.g., Google) to find the website. Configurations of a website often change. Try an internal search of the site to locate the information. Sometimes websites and pages within websites are removed. In that case, move on to the next question.

EXERCISE 5.3 CAMPAIGN FINANCE REFORM AND THE NEWEST LOOPHOLE—527 GROUPS

the X under "major player profile." From that information you will be able to determine which party/presidential candidate each group supported.

Democratic/Kerry: _____

_____

Republican/Bush: _____

_____

4. Would you support a bill to close the 527 loophole in federal campaigns? Why or why not? (You should consider the possibility of political bias in your response: Many Democrats say that President Bush and other Republicans are eager to prohibit 527 money because it worked to the advantage of the Democrats in 2004 and because the Republicans control the White House and Congress, which give them enormous fundraising advantages—even without the 527 loophole.)

_____

_____

_____

_____

Table 5.3.3 shows the total receipts and contributions for the Bush and Kerry campaigns in the 2004 election. Study it and answer questions 5–9. Notice that the rows in the table list each candidate's primary and general election figures separately. The receipts for the general election campaigns of Bush and Kerry also include federal funds for the candidate's convention expenses. The rows labeled GLAC are the candidates' General Legal and Accounting Committees. These are separate funds used to raise money to pay for accounting/legal fees related to running for president. Funds raised don't count toward donors' contribution limits. Remember also that this table does not include unregulated 527 receipts and expenditures.

5. What were the total receipts (not contributions) for Bush? For Kerry?

Bush: _____

Kerry: _____

6. Why does Table 5.3.3 list total contributions as zero for both candidates during the general election?

_____

7. The vast majority of contributions were made during the primary campaigns. Why? (You'll find the answer in the Introduction to this exercise.)

_____

TABLE 5.3.3 Presidential Campaign Finances, 2004

Name	Dates	Total Receipts $	Total Distribution $	From Individuals $	From Party committees $	From PACs $	Total Contributions $	Operating Expenses $
Bush-Cheney (Primary)	4/1/2003–3/31/2005	274,474,421	274,422,767	260,713,618	28,017	2,866,325	263,607,959	230,542,659
Bush-Cheney (General Election)	8/1/2004–3/31/2005	82,322,486	82,242,759	0	0	0	0	75,742,744
Bush-Cheney GLAC	7/1/2003–3/31/2005	19,172,942	5,442,988	11,211,990	0	52,045	11,264,035	5,169,211
Kerry (Primary)	11/27/2002–3/31/2005	249,736,423	241,840,268	216,961,245	967	147,418	217,109,631	182,838,274
Kerry-Edwards (General Election)	7/1/2004–3/31/2005	92,162,141	91,794,336	0	0	0	0	89,635,096
Kerry GLAC	1/1/2003–3/31/2005	13,584,780	7,422,990	8,329,978	0	0	8,329,973	

SOURCE: opensecrets.org. Reprinted with permission.

EXERCISE 5.3 CAMPAIGN FINANCE REFORM AND THE NEWEST LOOPHOLE—527 GROUPS

8. In the 2004 election, 527s spent a total of approximately $107 million to support Bush and approximately $217 million to support Kerry. How do these figures compare with the total distributions by each candidate's campaign?

_____

_____

9. Assuming that all loopholes could be closed, including 527s and independent spending (the latter would require a Supreme Court reversal or a constitutional amendment), and that candidates would have no choice but to accept public funding, would you support public funding of all federal campaigns, presidential and congressional races? Explain and support your position.

_____

_____

_____

_____

_____

CHAPTER 6

Congress

EXERCISE 6.1 What is the Proper Role of the Representative?

INTRODUCTION

Lawmakers must grapple with how to exercise the legislative power vested in them by citizens in their district or state. Should representatives vote the will of their constituents? Or should representatives vote what they believe to be right, regardless of public opinion?

The *delegate model* of legislative representation is most consistent with the definition of democracy—rule by the people. According to this model, representatives look to their constituents for instruction on what issues to promote and, ultimately, on how to vote. Under the delegate model, representatives stand in place of their constituents and do their bidding.

The delegate model of representation raises several difficult issues. Should representatives be bound by the will of the citizens who voted for them, or do they owe consideration to constituents who voted for other candidates? To what extent should campaign contributions—which come from a narrow segment of the constituency—be factored into a representative's decisions? Should representatives actively seek out constituent opinion, or rely only on input that reaches them through letters and phone calls, for example? Should representatives be bound by the opinions and interests of their constituency on all issues or only on those that most directly affect the state or district? Should representatives be more responsive to constituents who have strong convictions on a particular issue? These dilemmas of democratic politics complicate the delegate model of representation.

The *trustee model* of representation is less consistent with the definition of democracy. According to this model, representatives must transcend the short-term particular interests of their constituency and advocate for the long-term comprehensive interests of the nation. To make the trustee model more compatible with democracy, its advocates concede two points. First, representatives remain accountable to their constituents on election day: Representatives who depart from constituent opinion must be prepared to be voted out of office. Second, representatives are obligated to educate their constituents, to convince them that the position of the representative is the correct one.

The trustee model also raises difficult issues. Does the representative really know what's best for her constituents better than they do? What motivates representatives under the trustee model? Is it the genuine conviction that the representative is championing what's best for her constituents? Or might the representative be responding to interest group pressure from outside the representative's state or district?

In practice, the dilemmas posed by the delegate and trustee models of representation are tempered by two realities. First, most voters cast their ballot for someone who represents their political, cultural, and economic interests. Second, many constituents don't know much about the particular bills their representatives vote on, or even how their representative voted. Even so, elected officials know all too well that an attentive group of constituents, by publicizing a vote it objects to, can make that vote a major issue in the next election.

ASSIGNMENT

1. Assume that a coalition of environmental interest groups—worried about global warming—has succeeded in bringing to the floor of the House a bill that would significantly tighten emission standards on automobiles. Many major automobile companies and their suppliers have factories in Michigan. Would a member of the House from a district in Michigan be more likely to follow the delegate or trustee model of representation in deciding how to vote on this bill? Explain and support your answer.

_____

_____

_____

_____

2. In her campaign for election to the House, a candidate we'll call Betty Jones signed a pledge stating that if elected, she'd serve only three terms. Her support for term limits attracted many votes, garnered a generous campaign contribution from the interest group Term Limits Inc., and was instrumental in her victory. Jones had never held political office before. She taught high school government and civics for twenty-five years before seeking election to the House. The centerpiece of her high school courses was the need to restore honesty and credibility to government. Eventually, her students convinced Jones to take her convictions out of the classroom and put them to the test in the House. Jones's tireless focus on restoring honesty and credibility to government proved very popular with her constituents, who reelected her twice. Now at the end of her third term, Jones must decide whether to honor her pledge to serve only three terms. Polls show that 65 percent of the voters in her district are demanding that she disregard the pledge and run for a fourth term.

a. Make an argument that Jones should follow the delegate model in making her decision.

_____

_____

_____

_____

b. Make an argument that Jones should follow the trustee model in making her decision.

3. Nebraska shares many of the characteristics of midwestern farm states: Agriculture provides a significant portion of the state's income, even though fewer than 10 percent of its workers are employed in agriculture; the population is overwhelmingly white (Nebraska has a far lower percentage of minorities than the nation as a whole); and about a third of the state's population can be classified as rural.

a. On a vote to renew U.S. economic and military aid to Israel, would a U.S. senator from Nebraska be more likely to follow the delegate or trustee model? Explain and support your answer.

b. A senator from Nebraska will vote on a bill to expand agricultural trade with Iran—a nation that may be developing nuclear weapons and may be supporting terrorism. The senator has long been a staunch opponent of nuclear proliferation and a strong supporter of the war on terrorism.

Make an argument that the senator should follow the delegate model in casting his vote.

Make an argument that the senator should follow the trustee model in casting his vote.

4. Oregon is a state with vast acreage of old-growth forests. The economy of the state is heavily dependent on the lumber industry. But tourism is important to the state's economy as well, and Oregon has a strong environmental movement. Would a U.S. senator representing Oregon be more likely follow the delegate or trustee model in voting on a bill to ban cutting old-growth forests? Explain and support your answer.

_____

_____

_____

_____

_____

5. In deciding whether to follow the delegate or trustee model of representation, a senator considers many factors, such as public opinion, party politics, the demographic and economic characteristics of the state, and the senator's own political ideology and personal values, among others. For each issue listed here, identify factors that would be likely to cause a senator to adopt the delegate and trustee models of representation. The answer to the first question has been completed for you.

a. Foreign policy

Delegate model: A senator would adopt the delegate model if the public in his or her state was particularly attentive to some controversial foreign policy issue—for example, the war in Iraq. Trustee model: A senator would turn to the trustee model if the public was not engaged or informed on a particular foreign policy issue—for example, the terms of a trade agreement between the United States and the nations of Central and South America.

b. Gay marriage

Delegate model: _____

_____

_____

_____

_____

Trustee model: _____

_____

_____

_____

_____

c. Federal highway construction funds

Delegate model: _____

_____

Trustee model: _____

_____

_____

_____

_____

d. Social Security

Delegate model: _____

_____

_____

_____

_____

Trustee model: _____

_____

_____

_____

_____

6. a. What is the number of your congressional district and the name of your representative in the House? (You can locate your representative by zip code at www.vote-smart.org.)

_____

b. Identify an issue on which your representative would likely vote according to the delegate model of representation and an issue on which he or she would likely follow the trustee model. To do this, you'll need to know something about your representative and the characteristics of your congressional district. You can learn about your representative from his or her congressional homepage at http://clerk.house.gov/members/index.html.[1] Biographical details and information

---

[1] Website URLs sometimes change. Try an external search (e.g., Google) to find the website. Configurations of a website often change. Try an internal search of the site to locate the information. Sometimes websites and pages within websites are removed. In that case, move on to the next question.

on how interest groups rate members of Congress are available at www.vote-smart.org. Explain and support your answer.

Delegate model: _____

Trustee model: _____

EXERCISE 6.2 Why We Hate Congress but Love Our Member of Congress

INTRODUCTION

Incumbents seeking reelection to the House of Representatives almost always win. The astonishing reelection rate of these incumbents highlights the paradoxical voting behavior of many Americans: Voters may hate Congress, but they love their individual member of Congress.

Polls consistently find that the public holds Congress in lower esteem than any other government institution, but no matter: Voters continue to reelect their representatives in Congress. Since 1945, on average, 90 percent of House members seeking reelection won, and about 80 percent of U.S. senators were reelected.[1] Even in 1994, in the midterm election that gave Republicans control of both houses of Congress for the first time since 1954—and that was interpreted by many as an anti-incumbent election—slightly more than 90 percent of House members who ran for reelection won. And an extraordinary number won with 60 percent or more of the vote—for our purposes, the definition of a noncompetitive election.

Primary among the advantages incumbents hold over challengers is a legislative district drawn to include friendly voters. Gerrymandering (see Exercise 4.2) does not apply to U.S. Senate elections, where the district boundaries are the same as the state boundaries. But in House and state legislative races, gerrymandering is an incumbent's best friend. Other advantages of incumbency include commanding more media attention than challengers, greater name recognition, superior fundraising, and the ability to deliver projects to the district and service to individual constituents.

In the early 1990s, several states attempted to restore competition to their elections by imposing term limits on their members in the U.S. House of Representatives and Senate, but the Supreme Court declared those limits unconstitutional.[2] Term limits for state government officeholders, however, have had a better survival rate. Since 1990, twenty-one states have imposed term limits on state legislators. Those limits were overturned by the courts or repealed by the legislature in six states, leaving term limits on the books in fifteen states in 2005. The result is dramatic: In 2004, a total of 261 state legislators were turned out of office because they had served the maximum number of terms allowed.[3]

ASSIGNMENT

Questions 1–4 are based on Table 6.2.1.

TABLE 6.2.1 The 2004 House and Senate Elections

	House	Senate
Number of races	435	34
Number of open races (where incumbent did not seek reelection)	33	8
Number of incumbents seeking reelection who lost to challengers	6	1
Number of incumbents who won with more than 60 percent of the vote	290	17
Number of open races where the winner's margin was more than 60 percent of the vote	14	1

---

[1] See Susan Welch et al., *Understanding American Government*, 6th ed. (Belmont, CA: Wadsworth, 2001), p. 285 and Figure 3.

[2] *U.S. Term Limits, Inc., v. Thornton* (1995).

[3] Information on term limits is available from the National Conference of State Legislatures at http://www.ncsl.org/programs/legman/ABOUT/Termlimit.htm.

134   CHAPTER 6   CONGRESS

1. What were the reelection rates for House and Senate incumbents in 2004? In other words, what percentage of incumbents in the House and Senate were reelected in 2004? To make the calculation, be sure to consider the number of open seats and the number of incumbents defeated. Explain how you made the calculation.

a. House reelection rate: _____

b. Senate reelection rate: _____

c. How you made the calculation: _____

_____

_____

2. In the 2004 House election, four Democratic incumbents seeking reelection in Texas were defeated because Republicans in the Texas state legislature redistricted the state in 2003. That was the second redistricting of the state. The first redistricting occurred shortly after the 2000 census. In the second redistricting, these four Democratic incumbents were placed in districts that had large numbers of Republican voters, thus ensuring their defeat. If the second redistricting in Texas had not occurred and these four Democratic incumbents had not been defeated in the 2004 election, what would have been the reelection rate for House incumbents in 2004? Explain how you made the calculation.

_____

_____

_____

_____

_____

3. In what percentage of the 2004 House and Senate races where incumbents won was the margin of victory over 60 percent? Explain how you made the calculation.

a. House races: _____

b. Senate races: _____

c. How you made the calculation: _____

_____

_____

4. In what percentage of the 2004 open races in the House and Senate was the margin of victory over 60 percent? Explain how you made the calculation.

a. House races: _____

b. Senate races: _____

c. How you made the calculation: _____

_____

_____

d. What conclusion can you draw by comparing the percentage of open races in the House where the winner's margin was over 60 percent with the percentage of open races in the Senate where the winner's margin was over 60 percent?

_____

_____

_____

_____

_____

5. Free-market advocates tell us that competition helps make business accountable to consumers. In your view, does the 2004 reelection rate of House and Senate incumbents pose a problem for representative democracy in the United States? Explain and support your position.

_____

_____

_____

_____

_____

_____

_____

_____

_____

Use Table 6.2.2, "Public Confidence in American Institutions," to answer question 6.

TABLE 6.2.2 Public Confidence in American Institutions

"I am going to read you a list of institutions in American society. Please tell me how much confidence you, yourself, have in each one: a great deal, quite a lot, some, or very little?"

	A Great Deal	Quite A Lot	Some	Very Little	None
The military	36%	39%	19%	5%	—
The police	24	40	26	10	—
The church or organized religion	26	27	28	15	2%
Banks	17	36	36	10	—
The presidency	23	29	25	20	2
The U.S. Supreme Court	16	30	37	14	2
The medical system	15	29	37	17	1
The public schools	16	25	39	18	1
The criminal justice system	10	24	42	22	1

TABLE 6.2.2 (Cont.)

	A Great Deal	Quite A Lot	Some	Very Little	None
Organized labor	12	19	43	22	2
Congress	11	19	48	20	1
Television news	11	19	40	26	3
Newspapers	9	21	44	23	2
Big business	7	17	42	30	3
Health maintenance organizations, HMOs	6	12	39	36	4

SOURCE: The Gallup Poll, May 21–23, 2004. Used by permission of The Gallup Organization.

6. a. Use your answer to question 1 and the data in Table 6.2.2 to calculate the percentage point gap between the 2004 reelection rate for members of the House and Senate and the percentage of Americans who have a great deal of confidence in Congress as an institution.

b. Does that percentage point gap support or refute the notion that Americans hate Congress but love their own representatives in Congress?

7. To explore the fundraising advantage of incumbents, go to www.opensecrets.org.[4] Click on "Congressional Races" and select your state. That takes you to a list of congressional candidates and their spending in the last election.

a. Look at the spending gap between the incumbent and the challenger in each House race for the state you selected. In what percentage of the races did the incumbent raise more money than the challenger?

---

[4] Website URLs sometimes change. Try an external search (e.g., Google) to find the website. Configurations of a website often change. Try an internal search of the site to locate the information. Sometimes websites and pages within websites are removed. In that case, move on to the next question.

b. In what percentage of the races did the incumbent raise at least twice as much money as the challenger?

c. Look next at the race for the congressional district where you reside. (If you don't know your district, go to www.opensecrets.org and enter your zip code.) Assuming that an incumbent was running in your district, did the incumbent raise more money than the challenger? If so, how much more?

In 1992, California voters passed Proposition 164, which limited the number of terms California's delegation in Congress could serve. Three years later, in *U.S. Term Limits, Inc., v. Thornton*, the Supreme Court declared that any attempt to impose term limits by state legislative action (with or without the initiative) was unconstitutional. Arguments for and against Proposition 164 are reproduced in Reading 6.2.1 Study the arguments and then answer question 8.

READING 6.2.1 ARGUMENTS FOR AND AGAINST CALIFORNIA PROPOSITION 164

Argument in Favor of California Proposition 164[5]

Everybody is running for their own survival. The first priority of a member is to stay in office.

—Sixteen-year California Congressman Leon Panetta quoted in USA Today, *April 28, 1992*

Our founding fathers would be shocked at the abuses and attitudes of Congress today. While their policies were sending a record number of Californians to the unemployment line, members of the House voted themselves $40,000 in pay raises and Senate members $27,600. Each one of them now earns more than $129,000 a year. And most of them will be eligible for million dollar tax-subsidized pensions.

Our professional politicians in California's delegation have already given us a $4 trillion dollar national debt, a 9.5% California unemployment rate, 500,000 lost California jobs, banking and postal scandals, and the largest tax increase in U.S. history.

Incumbent politicians have rigged the system to assure their re-election. The longer they are in Washington, the less our career representatives care about us. And the record shows that it's the long-term incumbents who are most likely to be caught in scandals.

California voters launched a national drive for term limits when we passed Prop. 140 in 1990. Term limits are an even better idea for Congress in 1992.

Prop. 164 will put term limits on California's Congress members. The terms of the President, the Governor and the California legislature are already limited; it's time to limit Congressional terms, too.

Prop. 164 will:

- *Increase California's clout in Congress.* Prop. 164 begins to break up the "good ol' boy" seniority system in Congress, which rewards tenure not accomplishment and allows small states enormous power in Congress. With the largest delegation in the country, California's 54

---
[5] Source: Voters' pamphlet, California general election, November 1992.

representatives can work hard for California, instead of taking a backseat to politicians from Mississippi and West Virginia.
- *Give power back to the people of California.* Our representatives will be reminded they are public servants—not masters—who can serve for a definite time and then return home to *live under the laws they made.*
- *Reinvigorate Congress with new blood and new ideas* to tackle the tough problems facing our nation today.
- *Reintroduce courage and honesty* among our representatives by *weakening the hold of special interests, lobbyists and bureaucracy* on Congress. Prop. 164 will force our representatives to face facts, come clean on problems and propose bold new solutions.
- *Protect your right to vote and give you a real choice of candidates.* Incumbents dominate elections with free mail, huge staffs, free travel and PAC funding. Term limits will open up elections to competition and Prop. 164's special write-in provision will allow voters to re-elect exceptional representatives even if their terms have expired.

The dream of our founding fathers has not failed; the careerist politicians we've elected *have* failed. They put their own careers and multi-million dollar retirements ahead of the needs of California and the nation.

Prop. 164 will end political cronyism and reward merit, giving us a Congressional delegation that will solve problems, not add to them.

Argument Against California Proposition 164

No matter how you feel about term limits, vote *no* on Proposition 164. It's not about term limits or Congressional reform; it's about destroying California's clout in Congress.

Proposition 164 will cost California thousands of jobs, weaken our environmental protections, and shift greater burdens onto the backs of California taxpayers.

Proposition 164 only affects *California's own* Members of Congress. It does not apply term limits to *all* Members of Congress.

What's so bad about that? The answer is that California *competes* with other states for Federal dollars—and we are sending more money to Washington than we get back in Federal dollars for California. Proposition 164 means we will pay hundreds of billions of dollars in Federal taxes and get less and less in return.

Powerful members of Congress decide how those Federal dollars are spent. How do they get to be powerful? They stay a long time in Congress. It's called the seniority system. If California limits our terms while Texas, Florida, and New York don't limit theirs, Californians will lose. Our clout in Congress will go to other states, and they will grab more of the hard earned dollars California taxpayers send to Washington.

We need strong California representation to get help for our struggling economy. What happens if we are devastated by another earthquake, or similar disaster? We need Congressional members on the major committees to see that we get help. With California-only term limits, we will end up with a delegation of low ranking members who can't fight for our state against the powerful interests from other states.

Hundreds of thousands of jobs are at stake as cutbacks continue. Who will fight to protect those jobs for California? The Texans, New Yorkers and Floridians will be there for their states. Where will California be?

The Governor's office and the Legislature agree that we need to fight for more Federal help to pay for the immigrant load on California. If we don't get Federal help, California taxpayers must bear a greater burden. Proposition 164 means those Federal dollars will go to other states.

This year we will be electing both U.S. Senators and all California Members of Congress. If we don't like the job incumbents are doing we can vote them out of office. Proposition 164 removes members of Congress without a vote of the people, whether or not they are doing a good job.

To quote the *Sacramento Bee:* "Seniority still counts for a lot in Washington, and if California members of the House are limited to only three two-year terms, and its U.S. Senators to only two six-year terms, the state will have doomed itself to be permanently represented by a bunch of back benchers."

With 54 Members in Congress—the most in the country—we should have the strongest delegation fighting for California in Washington. Proposition 164 assures that we have one of the weakest. Keep California strong. Vote *no* on Proposition 164.

---

8. a. Identify what you think are the three most persuasive arguments on each side of the debate over Proposition 164.

For the proposition: _____

_____

_____

_____

_____

_____

_____

Against the proposition: _____

_____

_____

_____

_____

_____

_____

b. How would you have voted? Explain and support your position.

_____

_____

_____

_____

_____

EXERCISE 6.3 Blacks in Congress

INTRODUCTION

Like every other minority group in America, blacks always have been underrepresented in Congress. The political strength of blacks in the national legislature has never been proportional to the number of African Americans in the general population.

For several reasons, minority groups have long sought to increase their political power in Congress to roughly match their presence in the general population. Proportional representation would boost the ability of minorities to shape the national agenda and address issues of concern, as well as allow minorities in Congress to function as role models, validating and encouraging the aspirations of others.

For African Americans, several obstacles stand in the way of proportional representation in Congress. Efforts to suppress black voting by intimidation and other means remain widespread.[1] Minority candidates face more than their share of difficulty raising campaign funds. And blacks running for office have to grapple with the segment of white voters who shun African-American candidates because of their race.

Representation for African Americans in Congress—let alone proportional representation—never crossed the minds of the framers of the Constitution. Rather, their concern was to strike bargains with the slave states in the South to enable the creation of the new government. Toward that end, key provisions of the Constitution sanctioned and protected the South's system of human bondage. No African American would sit in the U.S. Congress until after slavery was destroyed in the Civil War.

Black Representation in the House Our examination of the struggle of African Americans to capture and hold political power in the House begins with the position of blacks in the South.[2] Before the Civil War, the vast majority of African Americans in the South were slaves; they were defined as property, not citizens. There was a substantial number of free blacks in the South before the Civil War, but most southern states prohibited them from voting. And, in any event, their number was never large enough in any given congressional district to elect a black to the House.

In 1867, Republicans in Congress passed the Reconstruction Acts, laws mandating the use of federal power to establish and protect the voting rights of the freed slaves. That application of federal power in the South on behalf of blacks, combined with the determination of newly enfranchised blacks to vote, sent Joseph Rainey to the House in 1870, the first African American to take a seat there.[3] Rainey was born a slave in South Carolina, but his father later purchased the family's freedom. To avoid being drafted to work for the Confederate Army during the Civil War, Rainey escaped to the West Indies. He returned to South Carolina at the end of the war and held several political positions before being elected to the House. He was reelected four times.

Between 1870 and 1877, thirteen other blacks from southern states served in the House. Together, those fourteen men served a total of twenty-one terms. But those striking gains, the product of the application of federal military force in the South, were short lived. The commitment of whites in the North to the political equality of blacks in the South had always been weak and uncertain, and the national government abandoned the effort in

---

[1] See, for example, "The Long Shadow of Jim Crow: Voter Intimidation and Suppression in America Today" at www.naacp.org.

[2] In this exercise, the South consists of the eleven states of the Confederacy: Alabama, Arkansas, Florida, Georgia, Louisiana, Mississippi, North Carolina, South Carolina, Tennessee, Texas, and Virginia.

[3] Rainey won a special election in 1870 to fill a vacant seat in the House. He took his seat on December 12, 1870. He joined the members of the Forty-First Congress, who had been elected in 1868 and were already in session. The Forty-First Congress had convened in December 1869. Jefferson Long, the second black to take a seat in the House, was also elected in 1870 in a special election. He took his seat on December 22, 1870.

1877. Whites in the South, free to reestablish the traditional racial hierarchy, stripped blacks of their voting rights by wielding the literacy test, the poll tax, and the white primary. The disfranchisement of African Americans, combined with violence, economic intimidation, and Jim Crow segregation,[4] kept blacks in the South from voting and running for Congress until well into the twentieth century.

Paradoxically, African Americans in the North had to wait much longer than southern blacks to capture their first seat in the House. From the time the Constitution was adopted until the ratification of the Fifteenth Amendment in 1870, determining who would vote was strictly a state prerogative. Northern states had a mixed record on black voting: Some allowed blacks to vote; others didn't. Even in northern states where blacks were allowed to vote, African Americans were not elected to the House. That's because blacks were a tiny fraction of the northern population—about 2 percent in 1840, for example—and there were never enough black voters in any given House district to elect an African American.

That changed beginning in about 1900, when many blacks fled the South to escape disfranchisement, economic deprivation, and racial violence—particularly a surge in lynchings. These North-bound blacks laid the groundwork for the return of African Americans to the House. Gathering in congressional districts in Chicago, New York, and Detroit, northern blacks captured their first seat in the House in 1928 with the election of Oscar De Priest, a Republican representing a district on the South Side of Chicago. De Priest served three terms in the House. He was defeated in 1934 by Arthur Mitchell, the first black Democrat elected to the House.

The nation waited almost one hundred years before again using federal power to protect the voting rights of blacks in the South. The Voting Rights Act of 1965 authorized the president to send federal officials to the South to ensure that blacks could vote without interference. President Lyndon Johnson aggressively enforced the new legislation. In 1965, for example, only 6 percent of the blacks eligible to vote in Mississippi were registered; by 1968, that rate had increased to 44 percent. The first blacks from the South to return to the House as a result of the renewed federal commitment to protect African American political equality were Barbara Jordan from Texas and Andrew Young from Georgia, both Democrats and both elected in 1972.

Black Representation in the Senate The underrepresentation of blacks in the U.S. Senate has been staggering. With the adjournment of the 108th Congress late in 2004, the Senate was 216 years old. Blacks have been represented in the Senate during just twenty-five of those years, and at no time have African Americans occupied more than one seat in the Senate.

Prior to the ratification of the Seventeenth Amendment in 1913, Senators were chosen by the members of each state's legislature. As noted below, state legislatures appointed African Americans to the Senate only twice. Both appointments were in the early 1870s when the application of federal power in the South enabled the election of blacks to southern state legislatures in large numbers.

After the ratification of the Seventeenth Amendment, African Americans seeking a seat in the Senate had to stand for election statewide. This remains an obstacle to greater black representation because a statewide electorate is usually more numerous and more diverse than the voters who elect members of the House. In most states, blacks voters simply do not have the numbers to elect black candidates in statewide elections.

Hiram Revels was the first African American to serve in the Senate. He was born in North Carolina in 1827 to parents who were free blacks, which made him free also. After a career in the ministry, Revels settled in Mississippi and was elected to the state legislature in 1869. The

---

[4] The history of Jim Crow segregation is described at www.jimcrowhistory.org.

EXERCISE 6.3 BLACKS IN CONGRESS 143

FIGURE 6.3.1 Black Representation in the House by Region

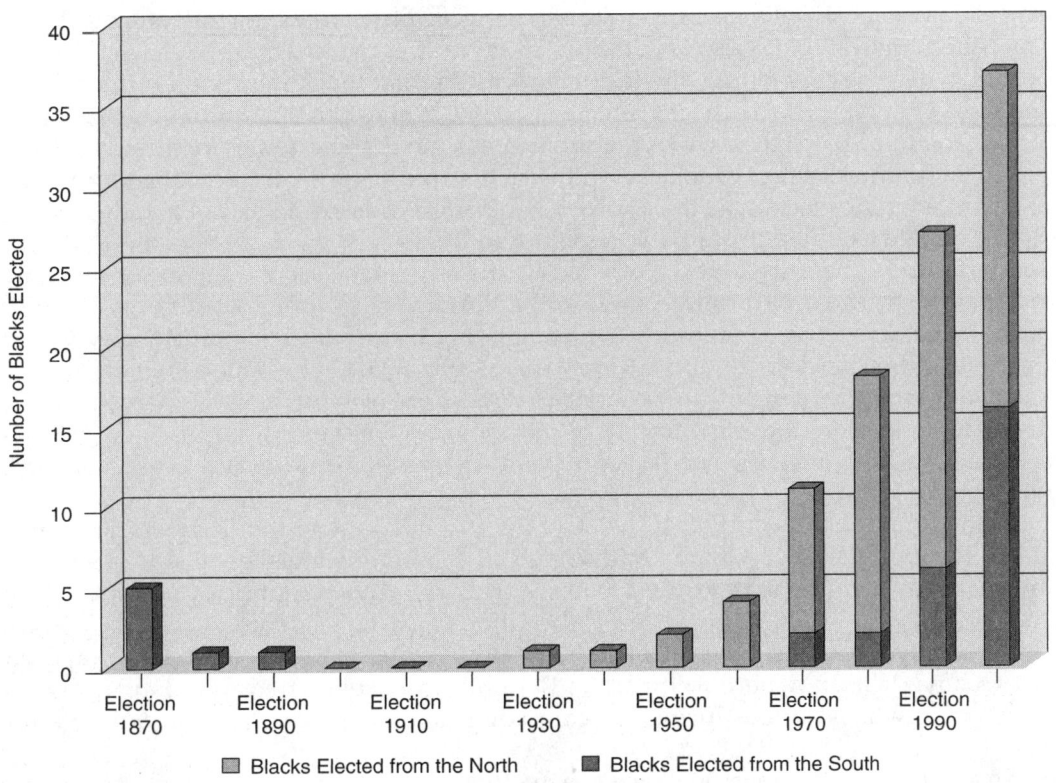

FIGURE 6.3.2 Black Representation in the House by Political Party Affiliation

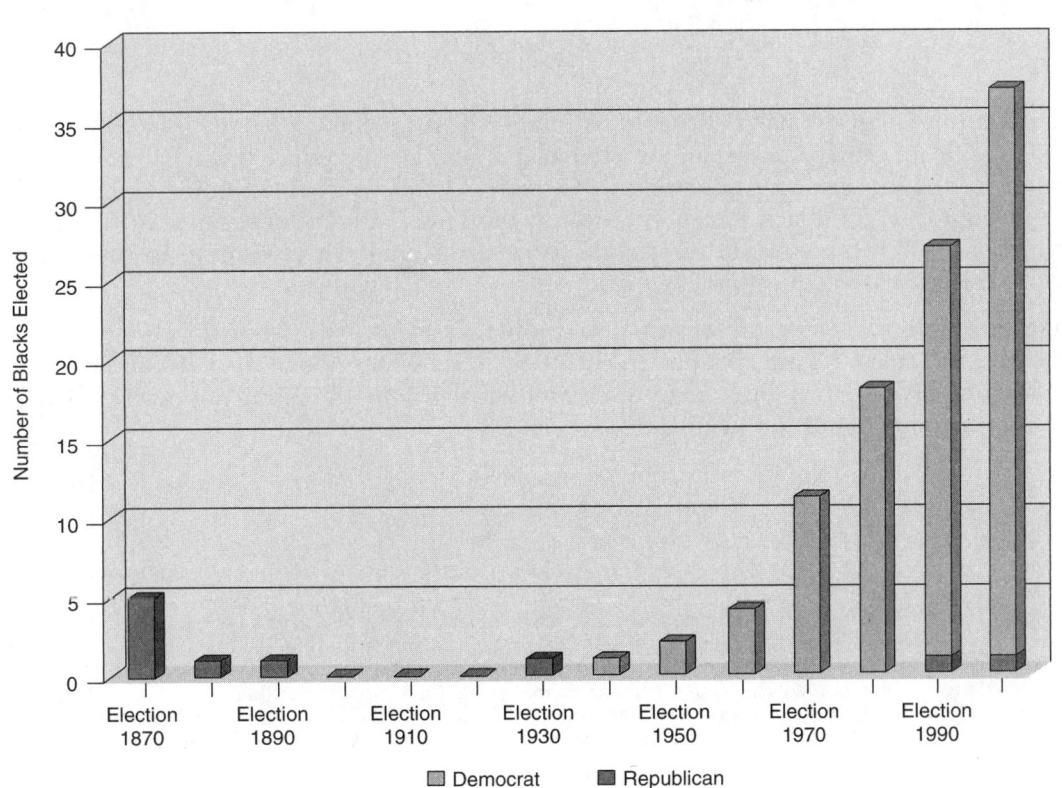

Mississippi legislature chose Revels in 1870 to fill one of the state's two vacant seats in the Senate. Revels served in the Senate from February 1870 until March 1871.[5]

Blanche Bruce, a Republican like Revels, was the second African American to serve in the Senate. Bruce held many local political offices in Mississippi, including registrar of voters and sheriff, and established himself as a wealthy cotton farmer. In 1874, the Mississippi legislature sent Bruce to the Senate, where he served just one term. He was the first black to serve a full term and the only former slave to serve.

Edward Brooke, the third black to serve in the Senate, was the first elected by popular vote and the first to represent a northern state.[6] Brooke served with distinction in World War II and pursued a career in law before winning election as the attorney general of Massachusetts in 1962. In 1966, he won election to the Senate as a Republican and served two terms.

Carol Moseley-Braun is the only black woman and the first black Democrat to serve in the Senate. Before her election, Moseley-Braun served in the Illinois legislature for ten years. In 1992, she won election to the Senate by defeating a white opponent. In that election, Moseley-Braun received 95 percent of the black vote and 48 percent of the white. She failed in her bid for reelection in 1998, attracting 93 percent of the African-American vote but only 36 percent of the white vote. Her challenger in the election, Republican Peter Fitzgerald, capitalized on the fundraising scandals and other controversies that plagued Moseley-Braun and outspent her 2 to 1 in the campaign.

Fitzgerald declined to seek a second term in 2004. Barack Obama won the Democratic Party's nomination to run for the open seat. Obama had served in the Illinois legislature since 1997 and was viewed by many as a rising star in the Democratic Party. The Republican nominee, Jack Ryan, withdrew prior to the election because of allegations that he had pressured his wife to accompany him to kinky sex clubs. Several prominent Illinois Republicans declined to take up the race against Obama. With nowhere to turn, the Republican Party settled for Alan Keyes, an outspoken conservative who asserted during the campaign that Jesus Christ would not vote for Obama.

For the first time, two African Americans faced each other in a race for a seat in the U.S. Senate. Obama routed Keyes, receiving over 70 percent of the votes cast. According to one exit poll, nine out of ten black voters and seven out of ten white voters backed Obama, who became the fifth African American to take a seat in the Senate.

ASSIGNMENT

Black representation in Congress has fluctuated dramatically since the Civil War. Blacks have at times achieved significant representation in the House and Senate only to see those gains erode or vanish. Before answering the questions below, study Figure 6.3.1, "Black Representation in the House by Region," and Figure 6.3.2, "Black Representation in the House by Political Party Affiliation." These depictions of the African-American struggle for proportional representation in the House will assist you in answering the questions below.

1. Use the data in Table 6.3.1 to complete the chart, "Blacks in the House of Representatives." Notice that the data in Table 6.3.1 are grouped to correlate with the periods in the left-hand column of the chart. Your objective: to develop a quantitative measure of how the political power of blacks in the House has fluctuated since the Civil War.

---

[5] Both of Mississippi's U.S. Senate seats had been empty since 1861, when Jefferson Davis and Albert Brown walked out of the Senate to signal Mississippi's secession from the Union. Those seats, and other southern seats, remained vacant for the duration of the Civil War and well into the period of Reconstruction. Congress required that the southern states ratify the Fourteenth and, in some cases, the Fifteenth Amendments as a condition of readmission to the Union and to their vacant seats in the Senate. While the Senate seats of the southern states were vacant, the six-year term carried by all seats in the Senate continued to run. The term for the seat Revels won was 1864–1870, which explains why Revels served just one year in the Senate.

[6] The unamended Constitution provided that senators were chosen by the members of each state's legislature. The Seventeenth Amendment, ratified in 1913, allowed citizens to directly elect senators.

TABLE 6.3.1 Blacks in the House of Representatives

Election	Congress	Size of House	Number of Blacks Elected	Party	Region
1870*	41st	241	2	R	S
1870**	42d	241	5	R	S
1872	43d	292	7	R	S
1874	44th	292	7	R	S
1876	45th	292	3	R	S
1878	46th	292	0		
1880	47th	292	1	R	S
1882	48th	325	2	R	S
1884	49th	325	2	R	S
1886	50th	325	0		
1888	51st	325	3	R	S
1890	52d	325	1	R	S
1892	53d	356	1	R	S
1894	54th	356	1	R	S
1896	55th	356	1	R	S
1898	56th	356	1	R	S
1900	57th	356	0		
1902	58th	386	0		
1904	59th	386	0		
1906	60th	386	0		
1908	61st	386	0		
1910	62d	386	0		
1912	63d	435	0		
1914	64th	435	0		
1916	65th	435	0		
1918	66th	435	0		
1920	67th	435	0		
1922	68th	435	0		
1924	69th	435	0		
1926	70th	435	0		
1928	71st	435	1	R	N
1930	72d	435	1	R	N
1932	73d	435	1	R	N
1934	74th	435	1	D	N
1936	75th	435	1	D	N
1938	76th	435	1	D	N
1940	77th	435	1	D	N
1942	78th	435	1	D	N
1944	79th	435	2	D	N
1946	80th	435	2	D	N
1948	81st	435	2	D	N
1950	82d	435	2	D	N
1952	83d	435	2	D	N
1954	84th	435	3	D	N
1956	85th	435	4	D	N
1958	86th	435	4	D	N
1960	87th	437[†]	4	D	N
1962	88th	435	5	D	N
1964	89th	435	6	D	N
1966	90th	435	6	D	N

TABLE 6.3.1 (Cont.)

Election	Congress	Size of House	Number of Blacks Elected	Party	Region
1968	91st	435	10	D	N
1970	92d	435	11	D	N
1972	93d	435	16	D	2S 14N
1974	94th	435	16	D	3S 13N
1976	95th	435	16	D	3S 13N
1978	96th	435	17	D	2S 15N
1980	97th	435	18	D	2S 16N
1982	98th	435	21	D	2S 19N
1984	99th	435	20	D	2S 18N
1986	100th	435	22	D	4S 18N
1988	101st	435	24	D	5S 19N
1990	102d	453	27	1R 26D	6S 21N
1992	103d	435	39	1R 38D	18S 21N
1994	104th	435	41	2R 39D	17S 24N
1996	105th	435	39	1R 38D	16S 23N
1998	106th	435	37	1R 36D	16S 21N
2000	107th	435	37	1R 36D	16S 21N
2002	108th	435	37	0R 37D	17S 20N
2004	109th	435	40	0R 40D	18S 22N

NOTE: Key: R = Republican; D = Democrat; S = southern state; N = nonsouthern state.

° Special election.

°° Regular election

† To accommodate the admission of Alaska and Hawaii in 1959, the size of the House was increased temporarily to provide each of the new states with one seat. The size of the House returned to 435 after the apportionment based on the 1960 census.

SOURCE: Data come primarily from U.S. Senate, *Biographical Directory of the United States Congress, 1774–1989*, doc. 100–34 (Washington, D.C.: Joint Committee on Printing, 1989).

a. To fill in the chart column headed "Terms of Service in the House," use the data on the size of the House provided in the third column of Table 6.3.1. (The size of the House is the number of seats in the House, which is the same as the number of terms of service in the House.) For each period specified in the left-hand column of the chart, calculate the total number of terms of service in the House and enter your results.

Sessions of Congress run for two years and are numbered sequentially. The 109th Congress, for example, was elected in November 2004 and was seated in January 2005. All 435 House terms in the 109th Congress expire when that Congress adjourns sometime late in 2006. Since the 63rd Congress (1913–1915), the number of seats in the House has been 435. So, for example, in the 91st–108th Congresses (1969–2004), the total number of House terms was 7,830 (18 Congresses multiplied by 435 seats in each Congress).

The calculations for the 91st–108th Congresses, as well as those for the 109th Congress, have been completed for you. In making the calculations for the other periods, remember to factor in changes in the size of the House. The dates in Table 6.3.1 are important. But when making the required calculations, you must rely on *the sessions of Congress* specified by number in the second column of Table 6.3.1.

b. For each period in the left-hand column of the chart, determine the number of House terms blacks served. You can find this information in the fourth column of Table 6.3.1. For each period, total the number of black representatives elected and fill in the chart column headed "Number of House Terms Blacks Served."

c. For each period in the left-hand column of the chart, calculate the percentage of House terms blacks served and enter your results in the chart column headed "Percent of House Terms Blacks Served." To make the calculation, divide the number of terms of service in the House in any period into the number of terms blacks served. The resulting figure is the percentage of total House terms blacks served during that period. Again, the calculations for the 91st–108th Congresses, as well as those for the 109th Congress, have been completed for you.

That figure is useful for two reasons. First, it indicates how the political power of blacks in the House has changed since the Civil War. Second, we can compare that figure with the percentage of blacks in the total population to determine the extent to which black political strength in the House approximates the presence of blacks in the general population.

Looking at the percentage of total terms blacks served in the House is a more accurate measure of black political power than just counting the number of black representatives during a given period, a process that does not capture multiple terms. For example, between 1928 and 1944, a period that includes the 71st–78th Congresses, two blacks were elected to the House: De Priest and Mitchell. But to say that two blacks served during this period is hardly an accurate measure of black representation because De Priest served three terms and Mitchell served four. Looking only at the number of black members who served in the House over a period of multiple Congresses, then, will understate the extent of black representation.

Blacks in the House of Representatives

Congress and Period*	Terms of Service in the House	Number of House Terms Blacks Served	Percent of House Terms Blacks Served	Blacks as a Percent of Total National Population[†]
41st–44th 1869–1877	——	——	——	13
45th–56th 1877–1901	——	——	——	11–13
57th–70th 1901–1929	——	——	——	10–11
71st–90th 1929–1968	——	——	——	10–11
91st–108th 1969–2004	7,830	448	5.7	11–13
109th Congress	435	40	9.2	13

*Prior to the ratification of the Twentieth Amendment in 1933, Congress typically convened in December of the year *following* its election. The 44th Congress, for example, elected in 1874 did not convene until December 1875. Prior to the ratification of the Twentieth Amendment, Congress also typically did not adjourn until early in the year *following* the election of a new Congress. So, for example, the 44th and 45th Congresses were both in session at different times in 1877: the outgoing 44th Congress early in the year and the incoming 45th Congress in December. Since the ratification of the Twentieth Amendment, the incoming Congress convenes on January 3 following the November election, and the outgoing Congress usually adjourns before the election of the new Congress.

[†]According to Census Bureau figures, the black percentage of the nation's population has ranged from about 10 to 13 percent since the Civil War. The geographic distribution of African Americans has changed much more dramatically.

148   CHAPTER 6   CONGRESS

2. From 1869 to 1877, the national government used force to protect black voting rights in the South. How did black representation in the House during that period compare with the succeeding period, 1877–1901, when the power of the national government had been withdrawn? To make the comparison, cite the quantitative measure of black political strength you developed filling in the chart on page 147. It's the column headed "Percent of House Terms Blacks Served."

3. How did black representation in the House from 1929 to 1968 compare with the percentage of blacks in the total population? To make the comparison, cite the quantitative measure of black political strength you developed filling in the chart on page 147. It's the column headed "Percent of House Terms Blacks Served."

4. Table 6.3.1 indicates that no blacks were returned to the House by the elections of 1878 or 1886. Consequently, no blacks served in the House during the 46th and 50th Congresses. There have been two other periods since the Constitution was drafted when there was no African-American representation—from the North or South—in the House. Identify the beginning and ending dates of those periods.

Period 1: _____

Period 2: _____

5. Many believe that minority representation in Congress should approximate a minority's presence in the general population. In the 109th Congress, how far are blacks from achieving that goal? That is, how many more blacks would have had to be elected to the House in 2004 to make black representation there commensurate with the proportion of blacks in the general population? To make the calculation, multiply the number of seats in the House by the percentage of African Americans in the general population. Next, subtract from that figure the number of blacks serving in the House in the 109th Congress.

6. a. For the elections of 1968–2004, what number of blacks would have had to be elected to the U.S. Senate to achieve black representation commensurate with the proportion of blacks in the general population? To find that figure, multiply the number of elections held during the period by the number of senators elected every two years. The product is the total number of Senate seats up for grabs over the period. Next, multiply that figure by the approximate percentage of blacks in the total population over the period. Then subtract from that figure the number of African Americans who served in the Senate during that period.

b. How does the figure from question 6.a. compare with the number of Senate terms blacks were elected to during the period? In other words, how close were African Americans to achieving proportional representation during the period?

7. Examine the data in Table 6.3.2. Notice that the population of congressional districts in Illinois is about 650,000. The total population of Illinois is about nineteen times that of any of its congressional districts. Candidates running to represent Illinois in the Senate face an electorate very different from that faced by candidates running for a seat in the House.

a. Calculate the percentage of blacks in the population for the First and Second Congressional Districts in Illinois, and for the state.

First Congressional District: _____

Second Congressional District: _____

State: _____

b. How does the distribution of the black population within a state help explain why far more blacks have been elected to the House than to the Senate? Explain and support your answer.

TABLE 6.3.2 Illinois Congressional Districts, 106th Congress, by Race

District	Total Population	White	Black	American Indian and Alaska Native	Asian	Native Hawaiian and Other Pacific Islander	Some Other Race	Two or More Races	Hispanic or Latino (of any race)
First	560,239	128,823	393,738	1,017	7,632	150	20,261	8,618	41,866
Second	556,482	100,944	421,557	1,138	2,557	158	22,110	8,018	43,429
Third	629,597	494,324	28,447	1,900	10,439	199	76,261	18,027	153,021
Fourth	625,941	279,763	50,925	4,382	16,256	500	247,567	26,548	438,481
Fifth	635,824	488,185	12,604	2,082	38,819	355	70,734	23,045	159,220
Sixth	615,419	515,468	15,052	1,210	47,630	190	24,349	11,520	66,836
Seventh	569,470	159,378	360,548	890	27,334	305	12,389	8,626	29,724
Eighth	699,513	583,648	18,594	1,478	51,442	256	31,080	13,015	78,895
Ninth	593,205	396,198	72,486	1,838	71,738	480	29,218	21,247	72,793
Tenth	627,793	496,333	41,952	1,420	35,956	299	39,830	12,003	87,548
Eleventh	635,653	504,469	83,999	1,503	4,549	173	30,658	10,302	66,771
Twelfth	560,912	439,366	103,683	1,521	4,959	207	4,356	6,820	11,089
Thirteenth	759,124	651,412	34,298	1,096	46,969	194	13,344	11,811	41,223
Fourteenth	720,663	601,118	32,189	1,869	17,706	253	53,770	13,758	126,383
Fifteenth	595,833	509,612	52,563	1,186	15,652	163	8,303	8,354	17,743
Sixteenth	691,356	614,822	35,236	1,566	9,323	199	20,224	9,986	47,987
Seventeenth	567,712	523,622	21,026	1,145	3,718	134	11,015	7,052	26,098
Eighteenth	597,447	543,086	37,991	1,245	5,569	104	3,394	6,058	9,079
Nineteenth	575,769	539,061	26,604	1,201	2,226	132	1,737	4,808	5,537
Twentieth	601,341	555,839	33,383	1,319	3,129	159	2,112	5,400	6,539
Total	12,419,293	9,125,471	1,876,875	31,006	423,603	4,610	722,712	235,016	1,530,262

SOURCE: U.S. Census Bureau, *Census 2000 Redistricting Data*, summary file, matrices PL1 and PL2.

EXERCISE 6.4 Legislative Apportionment

INTRODUCTION

The process of allocating seats in a legislature—called *legislative apportionment*—is one of the most contentious, politically charged issues in American politics today. But it's not a new issue: Bitter territorial disputes over who would get the seats, the votes, and hence the power in Congress and state legislatures have often marked the Republic's history.

Two of these disputes nearly derailed the Constitutional Convention. States with smaller populations demanded, as their price for joining the union, that they receive the same number of seats in the national legislature as states with much larger populations. That impasse was resolved by the Great Compromise. Whites in the South demanded, as their terms for joining the union, that slaves be counted in apportioning the House. That dispute was finessed by the Three-Fifths Compromise. The Civil War's destruction of slavery ended the advantage in representation the South had carved out in the House. But the terms of the Great Compromise still define the two strikingly different systems of representation in Congress.

In the House, apportionment is population based: Seats are allocated to states in proportion to each state's share of the nation's population. Based on the 2000 census, each of the nation's 435 House districts was drawn to contain about 650,000 people. Because the population of House districts is equal, and because each district has one representative and one vote, the political power of citizens in the House is roughly equal.[1] In contrast to the population-based system in the House, the Senate is state based. The Constitution awards representation in the Senate equally to each state—two seats per state—irrespective of a state's population. In effect, the Constitution treats states as privileged political and geographic units entitled to a fixed amount of political power simply because they exist as states. The approximately 500,000 citizens of Wyoming today have as much clout in the Senate as the approximately 36 million citizens of California.[2]

In deference to the principle of federalism, the framers of the Constitution did not prescribe a system of representation for the state legislatures. The result: States have employed a number of different structures. California's experience highlights many difficult political questions surrounding legislative apportionment at the state level.

In 1849, California's first state constitution established a bicameral (two-house) legislature consisting of a state assembly and a state senate. It specified that "representation shall be apportioned according to population." In 1879, California's second constitution required that state legislative districts be "as nearly equal in population" as possible. The framers of California's constitutions clearly intended that legislative power in the state would be apportioned equally among citizens of the state—a population-based system.

Until the 1880s, northern California had the overwhelming majority of the state's citizens, and hence the most political power in the state. By the 1920s, however, California's population had become predominately southern and urban. As California's population shifted, so did power in the state legislature. Rural interests perceived correctly that population-based apportionment worked against them, and they feared being overwhelmed by the growing political power of urban centers, particularly in southern California. To preserve the power of rural interests, groups such as the California Farm Bureau Federation sponsored Proposition 28, a ballot initiative to amend the state constitution. Approved by voters in November 1926, Proposition 28 fundamentally restructured apportionment by eliminating population-based representation in the state senate. (The assembly remained population based.) The new basis for representation in the California state senate

---

[1] Because the total population of a state is unlikely to be evenly divisible by the population the census establishes for House districts, the number of persons per representative can never be precisely equal. As noted above, the 2000 census established a population of about 650,000 for House districts. States that had fewer than 650,000 people received more than their fair share of political power because the Constitution requires that every state have at least one seat in the House. States with populations greater than 650,000 (or any multiple of 650,000) but less than the number required for an additional seat in the House received less than their fair share of power. More details on apportionment are at http://www.census.gov/population/www/censusdata/apportionment/history.html.

[2] The population numbers here are taken from the 2000 census.

mirrored that in the U.S. Senate: The state's counties would hold the same privileged position that states occupy in the U.S. Senate. California's counties, because they were discrete geographic and political units, were assigned an equal and fixed amount of legislative power in the state senate—whatever their population.

There was one problem: The size of the state senate in California was set at forty seats, and there were fifty-eight counties in the state. The difficulty was dodged by awarding one seat in the state senate to each of the more populous counties and grouping together the less populous counties—but only up to a maximum of three counties per senate district. As Table 6.4.1 makes apparent, twenty-seven senate districts were nothing more or less than the boundaries of a single county. Thirteen senate districts were made up of either two or three counties grouped together. In 1964, in *Reynolds v. Sims*, in response to a legislative apportionment in Alabama, the Supreme Court declared that population parity, not geography, must be used to allocate seats in state legislatures. By 1966, to comply with the Court's ruling, California again returned to a population-based system of representation in its state senate.

ASSIGNMENT

The questions below explore the link between legislative apportionment and political advantage, and the Supreme Court's verdict in 1964 on apportionment in state legislatures.

1. The sixteen smallest (by population) states in the nation are Alaska, Delaware, Hawaii, Idaho, Maine, Montana, Nebraska, Nevada, New Hampshire, New Mexico, North Dakota, Rhode Island, South Dakota, Vermont, West Virginia, and Wyoming. Each of these sixteen states has from one to three members in the House. Together, they have a total of twenty-nine members in the House. Because there are 435 members in the House, these sixteen states have 6.7 percent of the seats in the House (29/435).

a. The nation's population according to the 2000 census is 281,424,177.[3] The population of the sixteen smallest states is 18,259,164. What percentage of the nation's total population do these sixteen states have?

b. Is the voting strength of these sixteen states in the House proportional to their share of the nation's population?

2. a. How many votes do the sixteen smallest (by population) states have in the U.S. Senate?

b. Looking at the census data in question 1, it's clear that the voting strength of these sixteen states in the Senate is *not* proportional to their share of the nation's population. To make the voting strength of the sixteen states proportional to their share of the nation's population, how many Senate seats in total would you assign to these states?

3. The four states with the largest populations in the nation are California, Florida, New York, and Texas. Together these four states have a total of 139 members in the House, or 32 percent of the seats in the House (139/435).

---

[3] This is the total apportionment population. The populations of the District of Columbia, Puerto Rico, and the U.S. Island Areas are excluded from the apportionment population because they do not have voting seats in the U.S. House of Representatives.

a. Again, the nation's total population according to the 2000 census is 281,424,177. The total population of the four largest states is 89,868,655. What percentage of the nation's total population do these four states have?

b. Is the voting strength of these four states in the House proportional to their share of the nation's population?

4. a How many votes do the four most populous states have in the U.S. Senate?

b. Looking at the census data in question 3, it's clear that the voting strength of these four states in the U.S. Senate is *not* proportional to their share of the nation's population. To make the voting strength of these four states proportional to their share of the nation's population, how many Senate seats in total would you assign to them?

Table 6.4.1 lists the populations and geographic sizes of the California state senate districts established in 1961. Use the information in the table to answer questions 5–7, which explore disparities in representation in the California state legislature in the 1960s.

TABLE 6.4.1 Population and Area of California State Senate Districts Established in 1961

District	Counties	Population, 1960	Area, Square Miles
1st	Modoc, Lassen, Plumas	33,525	11,209
2nd	Del Norte, Siskiyou	50,656	7,315
3rd	Humboldt	104,892	3,573
4th	Mendocino, Lake	64,845	4,763
5th	Trinity, Shasta	69,174	6,989
6th	Butte	82,030	1,663
7th	Sierra, Nevada, Placer	80,156	3,360
8th	Colusa, Glenn, Tehama	54,625	5,446
9th	El Dorado, Amador	39,380	2,307
10th	Yuba, Sutter	67,239	1,244
11th	Napa, Yolo	131,617	1,792
12th	Sonoma	147,375	1,579
13th	Marin	146,820	520
14th	San Francisco	740,316	45
15th	Solano	134,597	827
16th	Alameda	908,209	733
17th	Contra Costa	409,030	734
18th	Santa Clara	642,315	1,302
19th	Sacramento	502,778	983
20th	San Joaquin	249,989	1,409
21st	San Mateo	444,387	454
22nd	Stanislaus	157,294	1,500
23rd	Santa Cruz, San Benito	99,615	1,835
24th	Madera, Merced	130,914	2,144
25th	Monterey	198,351	3,324

TABLE 6.4.1 (Cont.)

District	Counties	Population, 1960	Area, Square Miles
26th	Calaveras, Mariposa, Tuolumne	29,757	4,756
27th	Kings	49,954	1,395
28th	Alpine, Inyo, Mono	14,294	13,842
29th	San Luis Obispo	81,044	3,316
30th	Fresno	365,945	5,964
31st	Santa Barbara	168,962	2,738
32nd	Tulare	168,403	4,838
33rd	Ventura	199,138	1,851
34th	Kern	291,984	8,152
35th	Orange	703,925	782
36th	San Bernardino	503,591	20,131
37th	Riverside	306,191	7,177
38th	Los Angeles	6,038,771	4,060
39th	Imperial	72,105	4,284
40th	San Diego	1,033,011	4,255
Total	California State Population	15,717,204	

SOURCE: Adapted from Don A. Allen, Sr., *Legislative Sourcebook* (Assembly of the State of California, 1965).

5. a. Which California state senate district had the lowest population?

b. Which district had the highest population?

c. What is the ratio of population variance between the two districts? To answer this question, divide the smaller population figure into the larger one and express the result as a ratio, such as 30 to 1.

6. The population variance you identified in question 5 is a measure of the disparity in voting power between individual citizens in the two state senate districts. How many times greater is the weight of a vote cast by a citizen in the smallest district than the weight of one cast by a voter in the largest district?

7. According to the 1960 census, California's total population was 15,717,204. The twenty-one state senate districts with the smallest populations had a combined population of 1,684,614.

a. What percentage of California's total population lived in the twenty-one smallest state senate districts?

b. What percentage of the total votes in the California state senate did the twenty-one smallest districts have?

c. What is your assessment of the distribution of political power in California's state senate in the early 1960s?

_____

_____

_____

_____

_____

Excerpts from the Supreme Court's decision, *Reynolds v. Sims*, are included as Reading 6.4.1. In the *Reynolds* case, the plaintiffs argued that the apportionment of the Alabama state legislature deprived citizens of their rights under the equal protection clause of the Fourteenth Amendment. Disparities among districts in population and political power were widespread in state legislatures across the nation in 1964, when the Supreme Court issued its decision. In the Alabama state senate, population variance ratios were as high as 40 to 1. Study Reading 6.4.1, and then answer the questions that follow.

READING 6.4.1 EXCERPTS FROM *REYNOLDS V. SIMS*, 377 U.S. 533 (1964)

Chief Justice Warren delivered the opinion of the Court.

Legislators represent people, not trees or acres. Legislators are elected by voters, not farms or cities or economic interests. As long as ours is a representative form of government, and our legislatures are those instruments of government elected directly by and directly representative of the people, the right to elect legislators in a free and unimpaired fashion is a bedrock of our political system. It could hardly be gainsaid that a constitutional claim had been asserted by an allegation that certain otherwise qualified voters had been entirely prohibited from voting for members of their state legislature. And, if a State should provide that the votes of citizens in one part of the State should be given two times, or five times, or 10 times the weight of votes of citizens in another part of the State, it could hardly be contended that the right to vote of those residing in the disfavored areas had not been effectively diluted. It would appear extraordinary to suggest that a State could be constitutionally permitted to enact a law providing that certain of the State's voters could vote two, five, or 10 times for their legislative representatives, while voters living elsewhere could vote only once. And it is inconceivable that a state law to the effect that, in counting votes for legislators, the votes of citizens in one part of the State would be multiplied by two, five, or 10, while the votes of persons in another area would be counted only at face value, could be constitutionally sustainable. Of course, the effect of ... state legislative districting schemes which give the same number of representatives to unequal numbers of constituents is identical. ... Overweighting and overvaluation of the votes of those living here has the certain effect of dilution and undervaluation of the votes of those living there. The resulting discrimination against those individual voters living in disfavored areas is easily demonstrable mathematically. Their right to vote is simply not the same right to vote as that of those living in a favored part of the State. Two, five, or 10 of them must vote before the effect of their voting is equivalent to that of their favored neighbor. Weighting the votes of citizens differently, by any method or means, merely because of where they happen to reside, hardly seems justifiable. ...

State legislatures are, historically, the fountainhead of representative government in this country. A number of them have their roots in colonial times, and substantially antedate the creation of our Nation and our Federal Government. In fact, the first formal stirrings of American political independence are to be found, in large part, in the views and actions of several of the colonial legislative bodies. With the birth of our National Government, and the adoption and ratification of the Federal Constitution, state legislatures retained a most important place in our Nation's governmental structure. But representative government is in essence self-government through the medium of elected representatives of the people, and each and every citizen has an inalienable right to full and effective participation in the political processes of his State's legislative bodies. Most citizens can achieve this participation only as qualified voters through the election of legislators to represent them. Full and effective participation by all citizens in state government requires, therefore, that each citizen have an equally effective voice in the election of members of his state legislature. Modern and viable state government needs, and the Constitution demands, no less.

Logically, in a society ostensibly grounded on representative government, it would seem reasonable that a majority of the people of a State could elect a majority of that State's legislators. To conclude differently, and to sanction minority control of state legislative bodies, would appear to deny majority rights in a way that far surpasses any possible denial of minority rights that might otherwise be thought to result. Since legislatures are responsible for enacting laws by which all citizens are to be governed, they should be bodies which are collectively responsive to the popular will. And the concept of equal protection has been traditionally viewed as requiring the uniform treatment of persons standing in the same relation to the governmental action questioned or challenged. With respect to the allocation of legislative representation, all voters, as citizens of a State, stand in the same relation regardless of where they live. Any suggested criteria for the differentiation of citizens are insufficient to justify any discrimination, as to the weight of their votes, unless relevant to the permissible purposes of legislative apportionment. Since the achieving of fair and effective representation for all citizens ... is concededly the basic aim of legislative apportionment, we conclude that the Equal Protection Clause guarantees the opportunity for equal participation by all voters in the election of state legislators. Diluting the weight of votes because of place of residence impairs basic constitutional rights under the Fourteenth Amendment just as much as invidious discriminations based upon factors such as race ... or economic status. ... Our constitutional system amply provides for the protection of minorities by means other than giving them majority control of state legislatures. And the democratic ideals of equality and majority rule, which have served this Nation so well in the past, are hardly of any less significance for the present and the future....

To the extent that a citizen's right to vote is debased, he is that much less a citizen. The fact that an individual lives here or there is not a legitimate reason for overweighting or diluting the efficacy of his vote. The complexions of societies and civilizations change, often with amazing rapidity. A nation once primarily rural in character becomes predominantly urban. Representation schemes once fair and equitable become archaic and outdated. But the basic principle of representative government remains, and must remain, unchanged—the weight of a citizen's vote cannot be made to depend on where he lives. Population is, of necessity, the starting point for consideration and the controlling criterion for judgment in legislative apportionment controversies.... A citizen, a qualified voter, is no more nor no less so because he lives in the city or on the farm. This is the clear and strong command of our Constitution's Equal Protection Clause. This is an essential part of the concept of a government of laws and not men. This is at the heart of Lincoln's vision of "government of the people, by the people, [and] for the people." The Equal Protection Clause demands no less than substantially equal state legislative representation for all citizens, of all places as well as of all races.

We hold that, as a basic constitutional standard, the Equal Protection Clause requires that the seats in both houses of a bicameral state legislature must be apportioned on a population basis. Simply stated, an individual's right to vote for state legislators is unconstitutionally impaired when its weight is in a substantial fashion diluted when compared with votes of citizens living in other parts of the State.

8. Identify and explain the reasons for the Court's ruling against geographic-based apportionment.

9. Assume that it is 1964, and that you've been charged with bringing the California state senate into compliance with the Supreme Court's ruling, *Reynolds v. Sims*. Begin your restructuring of the system of representation by capping the number of seats in the state senate at forty. Explain the process you would use to allocate the forty seats in the state senate to California's 15,717,204 citizens to comply with the Court's ruling.

10. The system of representation in the U.S. Senate—two votes per state—clearly violates the one-person, one-vote standard established by the Court in *Reynolds v. Sims*. Why would a citizen of California, disgruntled with the fact that one person's vote has more weight than another's in the U.S. Senate, be unlikely to convince the Supreme Court to extend the one-person, one-vote standard to the U.S. Senate?

11. What would be required to make representation in the U.S. Senate conform to the Supreme Court's one-person, one-vote standard?

CHAPTER 7

The Presidency

EXERCISE 7.1 The Electoral College

INTRODUCTION

The 2000 and 2004 presidential elections demonstrated that the electoral college is no mere historical curiosity. Close observers of presidential elections have long noted the electoral college's power to shape the strategy of presidential campaigns. But who foresaw that the electoral college vote in the 2000 election would produce a constitutional crisis and install in the Oval Office the candidate who received fewer popular votes?

The 2004 election again focused the nation's attention on the system the Constitution prescribes for electing the president. George W. Bush won a second term by capturing the majority of the electoral college vote—and the majority of the popular vote as well. But if just 1 percent of Ohio voters had reversed themselves, John Kerry would have won the electoral vote (with one vote to spare) and been seated in the Oval Office with about 3 million fewer votes than his opponent.

The process for electing the president is set forth in Article II, Section 1 of the Constitution, but key elements of the system developed in the years following the Constitutional Convention of 1787. In fact, the term *electoral college* does not appear in the Constitution and did not become the official designation for the body until 1845.[1] The electoral college has been transformed over the past 200 years but without an overarching plan or philosophy to guide its evolution. To many observers it is a peculiar, even bizarre, system for electing the person who will occupy the most powerful office on the planet. One scholar described the electoral college as "perhaps the world's most important governmental body that has neither meetings nor choices."[2]

---

[1] See *Presidential Elections, 1789–1992* (Washington, DC: Congressional Quarterly Press, 1995) for comprehensive information on the history and functions of the electoral college.

[2] Frank J. Sorauf, *Party Politics in America* (Boston: Little, Brown, 1984), p. 304.

How did the electoral college come into being? The delegates at the Constitutional Convention of 1787 considered four ways to choose a president: by direct popular election, through Congress, through the state legislatures, or through intermediate electors. Direct popular election was ruled out because the vast majority of delegates wanted to restrain—not expand—democracy. They believed that popular elections would arouse the passions and self-interest of the people, destabilize the new government, undermine the public interest, and put demagogues in power. Democracy was so suspect in the framers' minds that only the House was given to the citizens to elect directly, and even there, state laws restricted the franchise to adult, white, male property holders. Election of the president by Congress was rejected because the delegates feared it might compromise the independence of the executive branch. The delegates also rejected election by the state legislatures because they feared it might make the president beholden to the states and undermine the authority of the newly established central government.

For want of a better option, the delegates settled on vesting the power to choose the president in intermediate electors. Because the electoral college was a compromise negotiated among many, it's difficult to say precisely what the framers expected from the institution. But this much seems clear: They intended that the electors would select the president independent of public opinion. The framers assumed the electors would be educated and propertied men of talent and character, men who would be better able than the people at large to judge the qualifications of presidential candidates.

The electors, however, have never been as insulated from public opinion as the framers wanted. In the first presidential election, in 1789, four states held direct popular elections to choose their electors. In other states, the state legislatures picked the electors. As political parties developed and strengthened in the late 1790s, they began to offer voters slates of electors pledged to cast their ballots for the party's presidential and vice presidential candidates. The development of political parties essentially committed the electors to cast their ballots according to the popular will within their respective states. At the same time, direct popular election of electors spread widely and rapidly. By the election of 1836, South Carolina was the only state holding out against direct popular election of its electors: The South Carolina state legislature continued to pick the state's electors through the election of 1860. Since the Civil War, the direct popular election of electors has been virtually universal and has for the most part bound electors to the public will—precisely what the framers wanted to avoid.

In the Constitution, the framers allocated electoral college votes to the states by formula. Every state receives as many electoral votes as it has members in Congress. California, for example, since the 2000 reapportionment has fifty-three seats in the House and two seats in the Senate, netting it fifty-five electoral votes. The Twenty-Third Amendment, ratified in 1961, awarded three electoral votes to the citizens of Washington, DC, bringing the total number of electoral votes to 538 (435 House seats plus 100 seats in the Senate plus three for the nation's capital).[3]

To win the presidency, a candidate must capture an absolute majority of the 538 electoral college votes. That magic number is 270. If no presidential candidate wins 270 votes, the Constitution requires a contingency election in the House of Representatives. The House chooses from among the three candidates who received the most electoral votes. In the House each state gets one vote. According to House rules, that vote is cast by the majority of the state's delegation in the House. The winner must receive a majority of the fifty votes cast by the state delegations. The election of 1824, the last election to be decided in the House, is the best example of this constitutional provision in play. In that election, no candidate received a majority of the electoral college vote or, for that matter, a majority of the popular vote. Andrew Jackson had the most electoral votes and the most popular votes; John Quincy Adams was the runner-up in the electoral and popular vote; and William Crawford came in third. The House considered the three candidates and chose Adams as president. The Constitution does not require that the House choose the candidate with the most electoral or the most popular votes.

If no candidate for the vice presidency reaches the requisite 270 electoral college votes, the U.S. Senate chooses the vice president from the two candidates who have the most electoral votes. Each

---

[3] The District was awarded the same number of votes as the number of seats in Congress it would be entitled to if it were a state.

senator casts one vote, and a majority of the whole number of senators is required. Again, the Constitution does not require that the Senate select the candidate with the most electoral or the most popular votes.

Three elements of the electoral college are essential to understanding how candidates win the presidency. First, the electoral college is state centered. The general election for president is actually fifty separate state elections and one in Washington, DC, held on the same day. The national popular-vote total is constitutionally irrelevant: All that counts is the popular-vote total in each state. Winning in all states except Maine and Nebraska requires a plurality of the statewide popular vote.[4] That's the second key element of the electoral college. Candidates do not need a majority of the popular vote in a state to win—only more popular votes than any other candidate. The third feature is winner-take-all. A state's electoral votes are not divided among the candidates according to the proportion of the popular vote they win. All of a state's electoral votes go to the candidate who wins a plurality of the popular vote in the state. Winner-take-all is not required by the Constitution, but all states except Maine and Nebraska have implemented it.

Interposed between the voters in a presidential election and the candidates seeking the presidency are the members of the electoral college. Some states make this explicit by printing the names of the electoral college members on the ballot under the name of the candidate to whom they are pledged. That would prove impractical, of course, in a large state like California, where fifty-five electors would be named for each presidential candidate on the ballot.

How are electors chosen? How do they carry out their responsibility? State party organizations choose people to serve as electors based on their demonstrated loyalty and service to the party. Before the general election, each state party organization names a number of electors equal to the state's number of electoral votes. Each party's list of electors is called its *slate of electors*. The electors pledge to support the presidential and vice presidential candidates of the party. At this stage, the people named on each party's slate are only potential voting members of the electoral college. Whether they will cast an electoral college ballot depends on the results of the popular vote in their state.

On the first Monday after the second Wednesday in December, the electors pledged to the candidate who won the popular vote in each state go their state capitals, where each elector casts one vote for president and one vote for vice president. Their voting is public; in the 2000 election, it was carried live by C-SPAN and CNN. On January 6, the sitting vice president presides over the official counting of the electoral college votes before a joint session of Congress.

The electors are not obligated by the Constitution or by federal law to cast their votes for the candidate to whom they pledged their support. Electors who break ranks with their party are called *faithless electors*. The practice is not common, and no presidential election has turned on it. Still, many states have passed laws attempting to bind electors to their pledges. Whether those laws are enforceable has yet to be determined. In 1992, presidential candidate Ross Perot tried to bind the electors pledged to him by requiring them to sign notarized oaths promising allegiance. Perot worried more than the major-party candidates about faithless electors because his campaign had to recruit potential electors from the ranks of campaign volunteers who had only a short history of commitment to him.

ASSIGNMENT

Figure 7.1.1 shows how the electoral college worked in the 2004 election in California. This diagram should help you understand the electoral college and answer the questions below. Another resource is the National Archives and Records Administration's electoral college website at www.archives.gov. Several of the questions that follow require a careful reading of the Twelfth Amendment (consult the Constitution in Appendix 3 at the back of this textbook.)

---

[4] Both Maine and Nebraska award their electoral college votes according to what's called the *district system*, one electoral vote to each congressional district in the state. The candidate with a plurality of the popular vote in the district wins that electoral vote. Two electoral votes in each state—those that represent the states' Senate seats—are awarded to the plurality winner of the statewide popular vote.

FIGURE 7.1.1 How the Electoral College Works: The 2004 Election in California

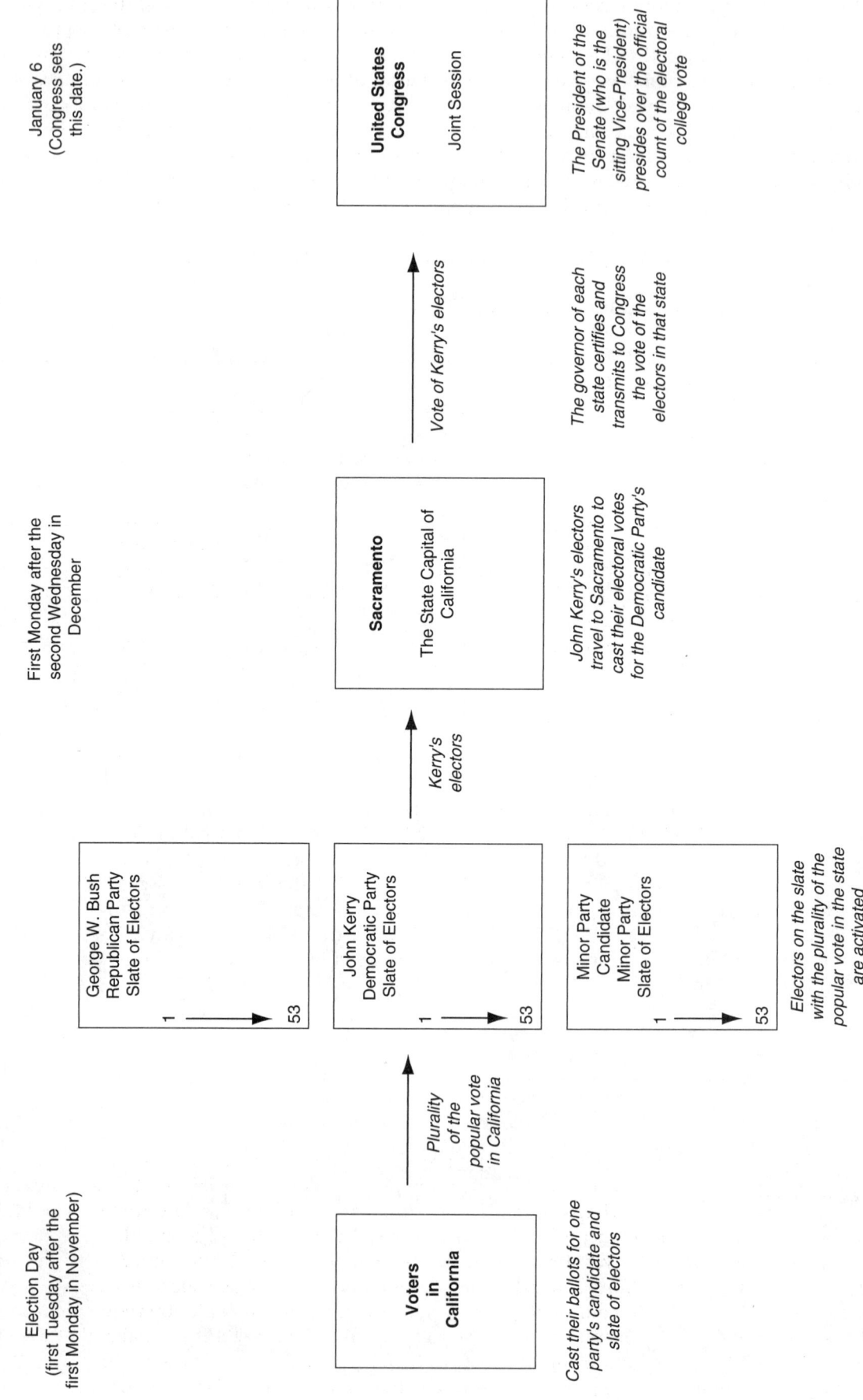

1. State party organizations choose people as electors because of their demonstrated loyalty to the party. Even so, some electors fail to cast their electoral votes as pledged. In 1956, W. F. Turner, an Alabama elector pledged to Democratic presidential candidate Adlai Stevenson, cast his vote for a local judge. (Who knows? Maybe they were fishing buddies.) In the 2000 election, Barbara Lett-Simmons, an elector from Washington, DC, pledged to Al Gore, cast a blank ballot to protest the fact that the District of Columbia has no vote in Congress. What do you think could happen between the general election in November and the electoral vote in December that might lead the electors to install as president the candidate everyone thought had lost the election? Think of an event so significant that it would break the ties of the electors' party loyalty.

2. If no presidential candidate receives a majority of the electoral votes, the election is decided in the House. The development of a strong two-party system has made this contingency less likely: Minor-party candidates are unlikely to win a plurality of the popular vote in enough states to deprive a major-party candidate of an electoral vote majority. In 1968, however, it seemed possible that third-party candidate George Wallace, running on the ticket of the American Independent Party, might do exactly that. And in 1992, at least before Perot dropped out of and then reentered the race, a viable third-party candidacy also seemed possible. (In that election, Perot ran on the United We Stand ticket.) How do today's electoral conditions—that is, weak political parties and little voter loyalty to the major parties—increase the possibility that a presidential election might again be decided in the House of Representatives?

3. In setting up the electoral college, the framers made a mistake. They assigned each elector two votes but did not require that the electors when casting their two votes specify whether they were voting for a candidate to be president or vice president. When the votes were tallied, the candidate with a majority became president and the runner-up became vice president. The framers apparently didn't anticipate—perhaps because they didn't want to contemplate fractious political parties—that a president elected under this system might have as his vice president his opponent in the election. That is exactly what happened in the election of 1796, when John Adams, a Federalist, became president and Thomas Jefferson, a Democratic Republican, became vice president. The Twelfth Amendment (1804) eliminated this politically difficult possibility by requiring that electors cast separate ballots for president and vice president. But the possibility remains that the electoral vote could install a president from one party and a vice president from another. Explain a sequence of events that would be required to produce that result. Begin with a situation in which the

candidates for president and vice president receive fewer than 270 electoral votes and control of Congress is split between the Democrats and the Republicans.

_____
_____
_____
_____
_____
_____
_____

4. In the 1980 presidential election, forty-one electoral votes were at stake in New York. Ronald Reagan, the Republican Party candidate, received 2,893,831 popular votes statewide, or 46.7 percent of the popular vote. Jimmy Carter, the Democratic Party candidate, received 2,728,372 popular votes in the state, or 44.0 percent of the popular vote. John Anderson was the Independent Party candidate; he received 467,801 popular votes, or 7.5 percent of the popular vote.

a. According to the rules for awarding electoral college votes, how were New York's forty-one electoral votes allocated to the candidates?

Reagan: _____

Carter: _____

Anderson: _____

b. Suppose you knew nothing about the rules for awarding electoral votes and had no access to the popular-vote totals in this election. What does the distribution of electoral votes among the three candidates seem to indicate about each candidate's popular support in New York state?

_____
_____
_____

5. Table 7.1.1 shows the popular vote by state in the 1976 presidential election. Jimmy Carter won a slim majority of the popular vote nationwide and 297 electoral votes. Gerald Ford received 240 electoral votes. Notice that one electoral vote is missing. Mike Padden, an elector in Washington state pledged to Ford, cast his electoral vote for Ronald Reagan.

Relatively small changes in the popular vote in 1976 could have given Ford the White House. For example, take 5,559 popular votes in Ohio—about one-tenth of 1 percent of the total votes cast in the state—and move them out of Carter's column and into Ford's. Then give Ford 3,687 of Carter's popular votes in Hawaii, about 1 percent of the total votes cast there.

a. What are the new electoral vote totals?

Carter: _____

Ford: _____

TABLE 7.1.1 Popular and Electoral College Votes, Presidential Election 1976

State	Total Popular Vote	Jimmy Carter (D) Popular Vote	Jimmy Carter (D) Percentage of Total Popular Vote	Jimmy Carter (D) Electoral College Vote	Gerald Ford (R) Popular Vote	Gerald Ford (R) Percentage of Total Popular Vote	Gerald Ford (R) Electoral College Vote
Alabama	1,182,850	659,170	55.7	9	504,070	42.6	
Alaska	123,574	44,058	35.7		71,555	57.9	3
Arizona	742,719	295,602	39.8		418,642	56.4	6
Arkansas	767,535	498,604	65.0	6	267,903	34.9	
California	7,867,117	3,742,284	47.86		3,882,244	49.4	45
Colorado	1,081,554	460,353	42.6		584,367	54.0	7
Connecticut	1,381,526	647,895	46.9		719,261	52.1	8
Delaware	235,834	122,596	52.0	3	109,831	46.6	
DC	168,830	137,818	81.6	3	27,873	16.5	
Florida	3,150,631	1,636,000	51.9	17	1,469,531	46.6	
Georgia	1,467,458	979,409	66.74	12	483,743	33.0	
Hawaii	291,301	147,375	50.6	4	140,003	48.0	
Idaho	344,071	126,549	36.8		204,151	59.3	4
Illinois	4,718,914	2,271,295	48.1		2,364,269	50.1	26
Indiana	2,220,362	1,014,714	45.7		1,183,958	53.3	13
Iowa	1,279,306	619,931	48.5		632,863	49.5	8
Kansas	957,845	430,421	44.9		502,752	52.5	7
Kentucky	1,167,142	615,717	52.8	9	531,852	45.6	
Louisiana	1,278,439	661,365	51.7	10	587,446	46.0	
Maine	483,216	232,279	48.1		236,320	48.9	4
Maryland	1,439,897	759,612	52.8	10	672,661	46.7	
Massachusetts	2,547,558	1,429,475	56.1	14	1,030,276	40.5	
Michigan	3,653,749	1,696,714	46.4		1,893,742	51.8	21
Minnesota	1,949,931	1,070,440	54.9	10	819,395	42.0	
Mississippi	769,361	381,309	49.6	7	366,846	47.7	
Missouri	1,953,600	998,387	51.1	12	927,443	47.5	
Montana	328,734	149,259	45.4		173,703	52.8	4
Nebraska	607,668	233,692	38.5		359,705	59.2	5

TABLE 7.1.1 (Cont.)

		Jimmy Carter (D)			Gerald Ford (R)		
State	Total Popular Vote	Popular Vote	Percentage of Total Popular Vote	Electoral College Vote	Popular Vote	Percentage of Total Popular Vote	Electoral College Vote
Nevada	201,876	92,479	45.8		101,273	50.2	3
New Hampshire	339,618	147,635	43.5		185,935	54.8	4
New Jersey	3,014,472	1,444,653	47.9		1,509,688	50.1	17
New Mexico	418,409	201,148	48.1		211,419	50.5	4
New York	6,534,170	3,389,558	51.9	41	3,100,791	47.5	
North Carolina	1,678,914	927,365	55.2	13	741,960	44.2	
North Dakota	297,188	136,078	45.8		153,470	51.6	3
Ohio	4,111,873	2,011,621	48.9	25	2,000,505	48.7	
Oklahoma	1,092,251	532,442	48.8		545,708	50.0	8
Oregon	1,029,876	490,407	47.6		492,120	47.8	6
Pennsylvania	4,620,787	2,328,677	50.4	27	2,205,604	47.7	
Rhode Island	411,170	227,636	55.4	4	181,249	44.1	
South Carolina	802,583	450,807	56.2	8	346,149	43.1	
South Dakota	300,678	147,068	48.9		151,505	50.4	4
Tennessee	1,476,345	825,879	55.9	10	633,969	42.9	
Texas	4,071,884	2,082,319	51.1	26	1,953,300	48.0	
Utah	541,198	182,110	33.7		337,908	62.4	4
Vermont	187,765	80,954	43.1		102,085	54.4	3
Virginia	1,697,094	813,896	48.0		836,554	49.3	12
Washington	1,555,534	717,323	46.1		777,732	50.0	8
West Virginia	750,964	435,914	58.1	6	314,760	41.9	
Wisconsin	2,104,175	1,040,232	49.4	11	1,004,987	47.8	
Wyoming	156,343	62,239	39.8		92,717	59.3	3
Totals	81,555,889	40,830,763	50.1	297	39,147,793	48.0	240

NOTE: The votes received by minor-party candidates are not noted.
SOURCE: *Dave Leip's Atlas of U.S. Presidential Elections*, "Past Presidential Election Results," at www.uselectionatlas.org.

b. Who is president based on the new electoral college vote? Explain your answer.

c. Where would this election be decided? Why?

d. What three candidates have a chance to win the presidency? Explain your answer.

6. Table 7.1.2 shows the popular vote by state in the 2000 presidential election. Al Gore won a plurality of the popular vote nationwide. George W. Bush lost the popular vote to Gore but managed to win 271 electoral votes—one more than he needed to be president. If just 269 of Bush's popular votes in Florida had gone to Gore, Gore would have been president.

a. In what other state besides Florida did Bush have the smallest margin of victory in the popular vote total?

b. What is the minimum number of popular votes that, if shifted from Bush's column to Gore's, would have made Gore the winner of the state's electoral votes?

c. Would winning this state's electoral votes have made Gore president?

7. Political science professors have long cautioned that in some future presidential election, the winner of the popular vote would not be president. The 2000 election has given those instructors new credibility in the eyes of their students. Even so, it remains difficult for many students to understand how a candidate who loses the nationwide popular vote can win a majority of the electoral college vote. The answer, of course, is that the winner-take-all feature of the electoral college distorts the popular vote instead of taking an accurate account of it.

Careful analysis of the sample data below should reveal why, in the elections of 1888 and 2000, the winners of the popular vote did not win the Oval Office. Apply the rules of the electoral college when answering the questions below.

- State X has fifteen electoral votes. The Republican candidate received 255,000 popular votes; the Democratic candidate received 250,000 popular votes.
- State Y has five electoral votes. The Republican candidate received 50,000 popular votes; the Democratic candidate received 150,000 popular votes.

TABLE 7.1.2 Popular and Electoral College Votes, Presidential Election 2000

State	Total Popular Vote	George W. Bush (R) Popular Vote	Percentage of Total Popular Vote	Electoral College Vote	Al Gore (D) Popular Vote	Percentage of Total Popular Vote	Electoral College Vote
Alabama	1,666,272	941,173	56.5	9	692,611	41.6	
Alaska	285,560	167,398	58.6	3	79,004	27.7	
Arizona	1,532,016	781,652	51.0	8	685,341	44.7	
Arkansas	921,781	472,940	51.3	6	422,768	45.9	
California	10,965,856	4,567,429	41.7		5,861,203	53.5	54
Colorado	1,741,368	883,748	50.8	8	738,227	42.4	
Connecticut	1,459,525	561,094	38.4		816,015	56.0	8
Delaware	327,622	137,288	41.9		180,068	55.0	3
DC	201,894	18,073	9.0		171,923	85.2	2*
Florida	5,963,110	2,912,790	48.9	25	2,912,253	48.8	
Georgia	2,596,804	1,419,720	54.7	13	1,116,230	43.0	
Hawaii	367,951	137,845	37.5		205,286	55.8	4
Idaho	501,621	336,937	67.2	4	138,637	27.6	
Illinois	4,742,123	2,019,421	42.6		2,589,026	54.6	22
Indiana	2,199,302	1,245,836	56.7	12	901,980	41.0	
Iowa	1,315,563	634,373	48.2		638,517	48.5	7
Kansas	1,072,216	622,332	58.0	6	399,276	37.2	
Kentucky	1,544,187	872,492	56.5	8	638,898	41.4	
Louisiana	1,765,656	927,871	52.6	9	792,344	44.9	
Maine	651,817	286,616	44.0		319,951	49.1	4
Maryland	2,025,480	813,797	40.2		1,145,782	56.6	10
Massachusetts	2,702,984	878,502	32.5		1,616,487	59.8	12
Michigan	4,232,711	1,953,139	46.1		2,170,418	51.3	18
Minnesota	2,438,685	1,109,659	45.5		1,168,266	47.9	10
Mississippi	994,184	572,844	57.6	7	404,614	40.7	
Missouri	2,359,892	1,189,924	50.4	11	1,111,138	47.1	
Montana	410,997	240,178	58.4	3	137,126	33.4	
Nebraska	697,019	433,862	62.3	5	231,780	33.3	
Nevada	608,970	301,575	49.5	4	279,978	46.0	

TABLE 7.1.2 (Cont.)

State	Total Popular Vote	George W. Bush (R) Popular Vote	Percentage of Total Popular Vote	Electoral College Vote	Al Gore (D) Popular Vote	Percentage of Total Popular Vote	Electoral College Vote
New Hampshire	569,081	273,559	48.1	4	266,348	46.8	
New Jersey	3,187,226	1,284,173	40.3		1,788,850	56.1	15
New Mexico	598,605	286,417	47.9		286,783	47.9	5
New York	6,821,999	2,403,374	35.2		4,107,697	60.2	33
North Carolina	2,911,262	1,631,163	56.0	14	1,257,692	43.2	
North Dakota	288,256	174,852	60.7	3	95,284	33.1	
Ohio	4,701,998	2,350,363	50.0	21	2,183,628	46.4	
Oklahoma	1,234,229	744,337	60.3	8	474,276	38.4	
Oregon	1,533,968	713,577	46.5		720,342	47.0	7
Pennsylvania	4,913,119	2,281,127	46.4		2,485,967	50.6	23
Rhode Island	409,112	130,555	31.9		249,508	61.0	4
South Carolina	1,382,717	785,937	56.8	8	565,561	40.9	
South Dakota	316,269	190,700	60.3	3	118,804	37.6	
Tennessee	2,076,181	1,061,949	51.2	11	981,720	47.3	
Texas	6,407,637	3,799,639	59.3	32	2,433,746	38.0	
Utah	770,754	515,096	66.8	5	203,053	26.3	
Vermont	294,308	119,775	40.7		149,022	50.6	3
Virginia	2,739,447	1,437,490	52.5	13	1,217,290	44.4	
Washington	2,487,433	1,108,864	44.6		1,247,652	50.2	11
West Virginia	648,124	336,475	51.9	5	295,497	45.6	
Wisconsin	2,598,607	1,237,279	47.6		1,242,987	47.8	11
Wyoming	218,351	147,947	67.8	3	60,481	27.7	
Totals	105,401,849	50,455,156	47.9	271	50,997,335	48.4	266

NOTE: The votes received by minor-party candidates are not noted.

*One Gore elector in Washington, D.C., abstained from voting.

SOURCE: *Dave Leip's Atlas of U.S. Presidential Elections*, "Past Presidential Election Results," at www.uselectionatlas.org.

a. Which candidate won the popular vote?

b. Which candidate won a majority of the electoral vote?

c. To understand the reversal of the popular and electoral college votes, look for patterns in the popular-vote totals within each state and also between the two states. The Republican candidate in state X won a big prize in the electoral college vote by winning narrowly in the popular vote. The Democratic candidate in state Y won a small prize in the electoral college vote by capturing a very wide margin of popular votes. Explain in your own words why the winner of the popular vote did not win the electoral college vote.

8. The mechanics of the electoral college are peculiar. Presidential candidates must take careful account of those peculiarities and shape their electoral strategies around them. An *electoral strategy* is the plan a candidate follows to allocate the campaign's limited resources—the candidate's time and money, for example.

a. How do the mechanics of the electoral college influence candidates' decisions to target certain voters? Explain and support your answer.

b. Looking at Table 7.1.3, which reflects the reapportionment of the House based on the 2000 census, what is the minimum number of states a candidate would need to win to capture the White House? Remember that a state's electoral votes equal its representation in the House plus its two Senate seats.

9. Research carried out by George W. Bush's campaign in the months leading up to the 2004 presidential election showed conclusively—barring some unforeseeable event—that whatever resources he might commit to the state, Bush had no chance of winning the popular vote in California on November 2. Bush's research was confirmed by independent public opinion polls,

TABLE 7.1.3 Population and Representation in the House by State, 2000 Census Data

State	Population	Number of Representatives in the House
Alabama	4,461,130	7
Alaska	628,933	1
Arizona	5,140,683	8
Arkansas	2,679,733	4
California	33,930,798	53
Colorado	4,311,882	7
Connecticut	3,409,535	5
Delaware	785,068	1
Florida	16,028,890	25
Georgia	8,206,975	13
Hawaii	1,216,642	2
Idaho	1,297,274	2
Illinois	12,439,042	19
Indiana	6,090,782	9
Iowa	2,931,923	5
Kansas	2,693,824	4
Kentucky	4,049,431	6
Louisiana	4,480,271	7
Maine	1,277,731	2
Maryland	5,307,886	8
Massachusetts	6,355,568	10
Michigan	9,955,829	15
Minnesota	4,925,670	8
Mississippi	2,852,927	4
Missouri	5,606,260	9
Montana	905,316	1
Nebraska	1,715,369	3
Nevada	2,002,032	3
New Hampshire	1,238,415	2
New Jersey	8,424,354	13
New Mexico	1,823,821	3
New York	19,004,973	29
North Carolina	8,067,673	13
North Dakota	643,756	1
Ohio	11,374,540	18
Oklahoma	3,458,819	5
Oregon	3,428,543	5
Pennsylvania	12,300,670	19
Rhode Island	1,049,662	2
South Carolina	4,025,061	6
South Dakota	756,874	1
Tennessee	5,700,037	9
Texas	20,903,994	32
Utah	2,236,714	3
Vermont	609,890	1
Virginia	7,100,702	11
Washington	5,908,684	9
West Virginia	1,813,077	3
Wisconsin	5,371,210	8
Wyoming	495,304	1
Total	281,424,177*	435

*This is the total apportionment population. The populations of the District of Columbia, Puerto Rico, and the U.S. Island Areas are excluded from the apportionment population because they do not have voting seats in the U.S. House of Representatives.

one of which showed Bush trailing Kerry by 18 percentage points in mid-October. There was precedent: George H. W. Bush (the first President Bush, that is) in 1992, Bob Dole in 1996, and George W. Bush himself in 2000—all Republicans—faced similar situations in California. Their positions on the environment and abortion, to name two examples, were out of sync with most voters in the state, and they found it impossible to remake themselves or adjust their views to win the support of a plurality of California's voters. In 1992, George H. W. Bush lost California to Bill Clinton by 13 percentage points; in 1996, Dole lost the state to Clinton by the same margin; and in 2000, George W. Bush lost to Gore by almost 12 percentage points.

Assume the role of chief campaign adviser to George W. Bush during the 2004 presidential election. Recognizing that Bush is likely to meet a similar fate at the hands of California voters in November 2004, would you direct a substantial amount of the campaign's resources to California in the two months before the election? Cite specific features of the electoral college to explain and support your reasoning.

10. Dispense with the electoral college. Assume that the president is directly elected by a plurality of the popular vote nationwide. Under this system, every popular vote counts, whatever a candidate's prospects of winning a plurality of the popular vote in any particular state. Consider again the situation posed in question 9. Under the direct election system, would you direct a substantial amount of the campaign's resources to California in the two months before the election? Explain and support your position.

11. Returning to the electoral college system for electing the president, assume you're managing George W. Bush's 2004 campaign in Texas. On October 11, about three weeks before the election, your polls show Bush with 60 percent of the popular vote in the state and John Kerry with 37 percent. At a meeting on October 12, the campaign's director of political advertising announces he has developed and tested a series of television advertisements designed to boost Bush's standing over the next three weeks. He claims that the ads will increase Bush's lead to 70 percent by the day of the election, reducing Kerry's standing to 28 percent. The ads will cost $5 million. Assume the polling projections are accurate, that the campaign can afford the $5-million expenditure, and that you have it on good authority that Kerry will not be presenting you with any

surprises in Texas before the election. Should you authorize the $5-million expenditure for the ads? Explain how your decision is derived from an understanding of how the electoral college operates.

_____
_____
_____
_____
_____
_____

12. Dispense again with the electoral college, and assume that the president is directly elected by a plurality of the popular vote nationwide. Would you authorize the $5-million expenditure described in question 11? Explain and support your position.

_____
_____
_____
_____
_____

13. Many advocates of electoral college reform argue that the winner-take-all system for awarding electoral votes should be replaced by a proportional system that would allocate electoral votes to candidates according to the percentage of the popular vote received in each state. For example, based on Table 7.1.2, proportional awarding in California in the 2000 election would have netted George W. Bush twenty-three electoral votes and Al Gore twenty-nine. California's other two electoral votes would have gone to minor-party candidates. What effect would proportional awarding have on the aspects of presidential elections identified below? Explain and support your answers.

a. On the prospects of minor-party candidates: _____

_____
_____
_____

b. On the extent to which candidates target and contest states such as California and Texas:

_____
_____

c. On the likelihood that no candidate receives a majority of the electoral college vote and that the election has to be decided by the House:

EXERCISE 7.2 Evaluating Presidential Performance

INTRODUCTION

No one in the world is evaluated as searchingly, as frequently, or by so many as the president of the United States. A sitting president is scrutinized twenty-four hours a day. The product of all that scrutiny is public opinion, a fickle commodity at best. President Lyndon Johnson's approval rating, for example, was as high as 76 percent in his first year in office, but later fell to 39 percent—dragged down by the widespread perception that the war in Vietnam had become a quagmire. And the scrutiny doesn't end when a president leaves office: Historians and political scientists are at the ready to dissect a former president's every action and decision for centuries to come.

All presidents attempt to shape current and future assessments of their performance. Early in his first term, President Bill Clinton met in the Oval Office with Richard Reeves, an author and historian who had published a study of John Kennedy's presidency.[1] Clinton discussed with Reeves the components of presidential greatness, presumably with the purpose of improving Clinton's own performance. To cement Kennedy's place in history, members of his family and his inner circle of advisers worked diligently after the assassination to perpetuate a number of myths about the Kennedy presidency. Richard Nixon, after resigning from office in disgrace, authored several books that he hoped would rehabilitate his reputation and encourage the public and scholars alike to see him as a great statesman.

People's perceptions of presidential performance are shaped by their expectations, which increased dramatically in the twentieth century. Before about 1900, the national government played an insignificant role in the daily lives of most Americans: Local and state governments provided the few services that governments rendered. It simply would not have occurred to most Americans to look to the president as the source of their prosperity and security.

Public expectations began to grow as Presidents Theodore Roosevelt, William Taft, and Woodrow Wilson led the national government to take on new responsibilities to ensure the nation's welfare. Roosevelt's crusades against abuses by the meat-packing and drug industries, for example, captured the imagination of many Americans and began to reshape their view of the presidency. But no president did more to inflate public expectations than Franklin Delano Roosevelt, who promised that under his leadership the national government would restore security and stability to Americans mired in the Great Depression. Through his skillful use of press conferences and fireside chats broadcast on radio, FDR personalized the presidency and taught the nation to expect a great deal more from the office and its occupant.

In time, inflated by the rhetoric of politicians and the constant glare of the media, public expectations of presidents became unrealistically high. It may be comforting to think that presidents can take the reins of power and dispatch the nation's problems with the stroke of an executive order. But presidential power is much more constrained than that—limited by separation of powers, checks and balances, federalism, public opinion, and myriad other factors. An electorate that expects the president to work miracles is always going to be disappointed.

We expect public opinion of presidential performance to change day to day. Scholars' evaluations of presidential leadership also change, albeit more slowly. Early studies of President Herbert Hoover, for example, portrayed him as a rigid ideologue who was overwhelmed by the economic collapse in 1929 and incapable of making a credible response to the subsequent crisis. In the 1970s, historians began to reexamine Hoover's performance in office.[2] Today, many scholars credit Hoover with making a vigorous, if insufficient, response to the crisis. Those scholars acknowledge the constraints Hoover faced and the unprecedented use he made of the tools available to him. What accounts for the change in thinking? The passing of time yielded historical perspective and judgment. Until the 1970s, scholars seemed unable to evaluate Hoover without comparing him with his successor, Franklin D. Roosevelt. Roosevelt's unprecedented use of the national government—not to mention his personality, his charm, his charisma—obscured Hoover's innovative

---

[1] *President Kennedy: Profile of Power* (New York: Simon & Schuster, 1993).
[2] For example, see Joan Hoff Wilson, *Herbert Hoover: Forgotten Progressive* (Boston: Little, Brown, 1975).

response to the economic crisis. Only decades after Hoover left office were historians able to bring him out from Roosevelt's shadow and judge him on his own merits.

For scholars evaluating presidential performance, time yields not only perspective and judgment but also a more complete record—something essential to informed assessment. Executive branch departments and agencies, particularly the State Department and the CIA, are notoriously slow in declassifying documents. But as the documentary record is filled in, new information may lead scholars to reassess presidential performance. In the 1990s, for example, the Kennedy and Johnson presidential libraries released tape recordings these presidents secretly made in the Oval Office. Diligent historians have performed the difficult task of transcribing the tapes.[3] In Kennedy's case, the tapes reveal the president's skill and luck in negotiating the Cuban missile crisis and bringing the world back from the brink of nuclear destruction. In Johnson's case, the tapes point to the president's desperate search for a politically acceptable alternative to the mounting escalation of the war in Vietnam.

Political scientists, historians, and journalists have long debated which criteria to employ in assessing presidential performance, how to weigh those criteria to produce a balanced evaluation, and how to rank a president in relation to other presidents. The modern version of presidential assessment was pioneered in 1948, in a study by Arthur Schlesinger Sr. His son, Arthur Schlesinger Jr., produced a similar study in 1996.[4] More recently, C-SPAN and the Federalist Society ranked presidents based on surveys of presidential scholars.[5] C-SPAN surveyed fifty-eight scholars, asking them to evaluate the presidents on a number of criteria: public persuasion, crisis leadership, economic management, moral authority, international relations, administrative skills, relations with Congress, vision/agenda setting, pursuit of equal justice for all, and performance within the context of his times. The Federalist Society, with help from the *Wall Street Journal*, asked seventy-eight scholars to rank the presidents on criteria of each scholar's choosing.

ASSIGNMENT

Table 7.2.1 shows data from the C-SPAN and *Wall Street Journal* surveys and places the presidents since Lincoln in historical context. Questions 1–3 are based on the table.

1. In the space below, list the presidents who served during periods when the level of crisis or challenge was low and who attained a near-great or great ranking.

2. What is the highest ranking achieved by a president who served when the level of crisis or challenge was low?

3. What connection exists between the crises or challenges a president faces in office and the possibility of his achieving near-great or great status?

---

[3] Ernest R. May and Philip D. Zelikow, *The Kennedy Tapes: Inside the White House During the Cuban Missile Crisis* (Cambridge, MA: Harvard University Press, 1997); and Michael R. Beschloss, *Reaching for Glory: Lyndon Johnson's Secret White House Tapes, 1964–1965* (New York: Simon & Schuster, 2001).

[4] "The Ultimate Approval Rating," *New York Times Magazine*, December 16, 1996, p. 46.

[5] Both surveys can be found on the Internet: the C-SPAN survey at www.americanpresidents.org, and the *Wall Street Journal* survey at www.opinionjournal.com/hail/.

TABLE 7.2.1 Rankings of Presidential Performance, 1860–2000

Period	Important Issues or Events	Level of Crisis or Challenge	President	C-SPAN Ranking	Wall Street Journal Ranking	Wall Street Journal Category
1860–1865	Civil War	Extreme	Lincoln	1	2	Great
1865–1877	Reconstruction	High	Johnson	40	36	Failure
			Grant	33	32	Below average
1877–1900	Industrialization urbanization, westward expansion	Low	Hayes	26	22	Average
		Low	Garfield	29	*	*
		Low	Arthur	32	26	Average
		Low	Cleveland	17	12	Above average
		Low	Harrison	31	27	Below average
1896–1901	Spanish-American War	High	McKinley	15	14	Above average
1901–1912	Reform, foreign policy	High	Roosevelt	4	5	Near great
		Moderate	Taft	24	19	Average
1912–1920	Reform, World War I	Extreme	Wilson	6	11	Near great
1920–1928	Economic expansion	Low	Harding	38	38	Failure
			Coolidge	27	25	Average
1928–1932	Economic depression	High	Hoover	34	29	Below average
1932–1945	Great Depression, World War II	Extreme	Roosevelt	2	3	Great
1945–1952	Cold war, demobilization, Korean War	High	Truman	5	7	Near great
1952–1960	Cold war, economic expansion	Moderate	Eisenhower	9	9	Near great
1960–1963	Cold war, civil rights	High	Kennedy	8	18	Above average
1963–1968	Vietnam War, civil rights, Great Society	Very high	Johnson	10	17	Above average
1968–1974	Vietnam War, Watergate	Very high	Nixon	25	33	Below average
1974–1980	Cold war	High	Ford	23	28	Below average
	Economic recession, energy crisis		Carter	22	30	Below average

TABLE 7.2.1 (Cont.)

Period	Important Issues or Events	Level of Crisis or Challenge	President	C-SPAN Ranking	WALL STREET JOURNAL	
					Ranking	Category
1980–1988	Cold war	Moderate	Reagan	11	8	Near great
1988–1992	Gulf War, economic recession	Moderate	Bush	20	21	Average
1992–2000	Foreign policy, impeachment	Moderate	Clinton	21	21	Average

°James A. Garfield, elected in 1880, was shot several months into his term by a deranged office seeker and died two months later. Garfield served as president for a little over six months. His early death makes it difficult to evaluate and rank his performance.

SOURCE: Both surveys can be found on the Web: the C-SPAN survey at www.americanpresidents.org and the *Wall Street Journal* survey at www.opinionjournal.com/hail/.

4. Read the essay by Michael Kinsley, "The Power of One."[6] The essay is at http://www.time.com/time/archive/preview/0,10987,443202,00.html, or conduct an Internet search. In Kinsley's view, what is the most important component of presidential leadership? Cite language from the essay to support your answer.

5. Read the essay by Benjamin Schwarz, "Bush Fibbed, and That Might Be OK."[7] The essay is at http://portland.indymedia.org/en/2003/10/274064.shtml,[8] or conduct an Internet search. In Schwarz's view, what is the most important component of presidential leadership? Cite language from the essay to support your answer.

6. The emergence of any single document or piece of information bearing on a president's performance is unlikely to decisively alter scholars' assessment of that president. Of course, we can imagine exceptions to that general rule. For example, almost since the day the Japanese attacked Pearl Harbor (December 7, 1941), some have accused President Franklin D. Roosevelt of knowing in advance that the attack was coming and purposely leaving the nation vulnerable so as to galvanize public opinion behind his objective: to join the world war on the side of the Allies and to defeat Hitler. A clear majority of Americans did not want to enter the war, and Roosevelt, so the

---

[6] *Los Angeles Times*, April 14, 2003.

[7] *Los Angeles Times*, October 30, 2003.

[8] Website URLs sometimes change. Try an external search (e.g., Google) to find the website. Configurations of a website often change. Try an internal search of the site to locate the information. Sometimes websites and pages within websites are removed. In that case, move on to the next question.

argument goes, recognized that only an attack by a foreign power against U.S. territory and citizens—2,400 people died at Pearl Harbor—would shake the public from its isolationist stupor.

Most scholars agree that the charges against Roosevelt are contradicted by the documentary record and are unlikely ever to be substantiated. But suppose the scholars are mistaken; suppose the charges are proved true. In your view, how would the revelation that Roosevelt had prior knowledge of the attack on Pearl Harbor affect scholars' assessment of his presidency?

This question is not as simple as it seems at first glance. One author who believes Roosevelt did know about the attack in advance argues that the president was right to sacrifice Pearl Harbor to achieve a greater good: the defeat of Hitler.[9] Address this author's argument in your answer. Explain and support your position.

_____
_____
_____
_____
_____
_____
_____
_____

7. You'll find the Federalist Society survey, "Hail to the Chief: Scholars Rank the Presidents," at www.opinionjournal.com/hail/. Go to the site, click on Ranking Methodology, and read the introduction to professor James Lindgren's essay. What methods did the survey directors employ to avoid bias in the survey?

_____
_____
_____
_____

8. Read the section of Lindgren's essay that examines America's most controversial presidents. Who are they, and what makes them controversial?

_____
_____
_____
_____

---

[9] Robert B. Stinnett, *Day of Deceit: The Truth about FDR and Pearl Harbor* (New York: Free Press, 2000). David Kahn published a devastating critique of Stinnett's book in the *New York Review of Books*, November 2, 2000.

9. Read the section of Lindgren's essay titled "Comparing the Responses of Scholars in History, Law, and Political Science." Identify two systematic differences between the rankings assigned to presidents by law professors and those assigned by historians.

10. You'll find the C-SPAN Survey of Presidential Leadership at www.americanpresidents.org. Go to the site, scroll down, and under the heading "Resources," click on the C-SPAN Survey of Presidential Leadership and then Historian Survey Results. Notice that you can select a criterion and look at the ranking of every president based on that criterion. Or you can select a president and look at his ranking on all ten criteria.

a. Select Lyndon Johnson. On what criterion did he receive the highest "final score"?

b. On what criterion did Johnson receive the lowest "final score"?

11. Select two other presidents. In the space below, identify the presidents and specify for each the category in which he achieved the highest and lowest "final score."

President 1: _____

President 2: _____

EXERCISE 7.3 The Power of the Sword

INTRODUCTION

Presidents today own the power of the sword. Constitutional checks and balances have repeatedly proven too frail to restrain the war-making power of the executive branch. An order from the commander in chief alone will expend the nation's treasure in combat, spill its citizens' blood on foreign battlefields, inflict the pinpoint destruction of a terrorist safe house, or annihilate the world in a nuclear holocaust. Presidents have wielded this awesome power with mixed results. President Harry Truman's war in Korea, for example, is generally thought to have advanced national security; President Lyndon Johnson's war in Vietnam, by consensus opinion, undermined it.

The framers of the Constitution did not anticipate the concentration of virtually unchecked war-making power in the president's hands. Delegates at the Constitutional Convention took for granted that the power of the sword would be divided between the legislative and executive branches. Vesting all war power in the legislature, as the Articles of Confederation did, would dull the new government's ability to respond decisively to foreign threats. Vesting the power exclusively in the executive, as the English did, risked the president unilaterally embarking on misguided military adventures abroad. The delegates, then, awarded Congress the power to "declare war" and the president the power of "Commander in Chief." But each branch's war powers are wider than these narrow phrases suggest. In Article I, Section 8, the Constitution confers on Congress the power to provide for the common defense of the nation, to raise and support an army and navy, and to fund military operations. Article II, Section 1 grants broad "executive power" to the president, suggesting to some that he would lead in determining matters of peace and war. Additionally, the president's oath of office binds him to "defend the Constitution of the United States."

Just how the two branches would share the war power had to be worked out in practice. One issue to be determined: the extent of executive authority absent a declaration of war from Congress. By commanding military force short of war to protect national security, the nation's first presidents offered an expansive definition of executive war power. President George Washington sent troops to fight Native Americans in the Battle of Fallen Timbers and his own citizens in the Whiskey Rebellion. There was no declaration of war from Congress in either case. In response to French raids on American shipping in the West Indies, President John Adams waged an undeclared naval war against France from 1798 to 1800, with some engagements as far afield as the Indian Ocean and the Mediterranean Sea. On his authority alone, President Thomas Jefferson fought the First Barbary War from 1801 to 1805, dispatching American warships to the Mediterranean with orders to destroy the pirates' vessels and blockade Tripoli. During the Republic's history, presidents have employed armed force abroad over 300 times.[1]

The legislative branch has exercised its war power less frequently. Congress declared war for the first time in 1812 against the British; the second declaration came in 1846 against Mexico; and the third in 1898 against Spain. World Wars I and II were the only declarations of war in the twentieth century, and there have been none since. Neither did Congress advance an expansive interpretation of its war power. The legislature might have claimed that the power to *authorize* war entailed the power to *prosecute* it, even to determine a war's aims, scope, pace, and the deployment of troops. But Congress has generally left these matters to the commander in chief. Why?

The legislature is inherently maladapted—institutionally and politically—to make war. Congress' bicameral division, its size, the diversity of its members' views, and its generally reactive posture make it a poor competitor with the energy and vigor of a singular commander in chief. In the post–World War II era, Congress' lack of instantaneous access to classified information gathered by executive branch agencies and the development of intercontinental ballistic missiles have constrained the legislature. Who besides the president could decide—in only minutes—whether or not to launch America's nuclear weapons? Additionally, the imperative of political

---

[1] For a list and brief description of the use of armed force abroad, see Ellen C. Collier, "Instances of Use of United States Forces Abroad, 1798–1993," at www.history.navy.mil/wars/foabroad. For an analysis of the War Powers Resolution, including a list and brief description of presidents' use of armed force since 1973, see Richard F. Grimmett, "The War Powers Resolution: After Thirty Years," at www.fas.org/man/crsRL32267.

self-preservation has tempered Congress' desire to take the nation to war. Military debacles yank down the public approval ratings of government officeholders and institutions. From the legislative perspective, better to let the president take the fall. Finally, consider this: What if the House and Senate voted a declaration of war and the commander in chief refused to lead the charge? A troubling prospect indeed.

More often than declaring war, Congress has enacted so-called conditional resolutions that authorize the president to use armed force, subject to some specified limitation. Conditional resolutions do not delegate the legislature's power to the executive, but rather provide Congress' assent to military actions the commander in chief undertakes on his own constitutional authority.

When Iraq invaded and occupied Kuwait in 1990, President George H. W. Bush requested a congressional resolution supporting the use of force to implement United Nations Security Council demands that Iraq withdraw. Congress complied but imposed this condition: that prior to using military force, the president report that he had exhausted all diplomatic and other peaceful means to achieve compliance with UN resolutions.

After the September 11, 2001, attacks on the World Trade Center and the Pentagon, Congress passed a resolution authorizing the president

> to use all necessary and appropriate force against those nations, organizations, or persons he determines planned, authorized, committed, or aided the terrorist attacks that occurred on September 11, 2001, or harbored such organizations or persons, in order to prevent any future acts of international terrorism against the United States by such nations, organizations or persons.

Note that this resolution does not contain the type of conditional clause found in the 1990 resolution and that its authorization of military action against unspecified "organizations or persons" is sweeping and unprecedented.

In the summer of 2002, President George W. Bush began to move toward a second war with Iraq, arguing that its possession of weapons of mass destruction posed a threat to the United States. In October, Congress authorized the president to use military force against Iraq, but only after he determined that measures short of war would not protect the United States, and that the use of force was consistent with the war on terrorism.[2]

Among conditional resolutions, the Tonkin Gulf Resolution of 1964 is notorious. President Lyndon Johnson informed the nation on August 4, 1964, that North Vietnamese patrol boats in the Gulf of Tonkin had twice attacked American destroyers on routine patrol there. The next day, Johnson asked Congress to go on record supporting in advance whatever military response he deemed necessary. The resolution stated that "Congress approves and supports the determination of the President, as Commander-in-Chief, to take all necessary measures to repel any armed attack against the Forces of the United States and to prevent further aggression." No conditions were imposed. The vote in the House was 416–0 and in the Senate 82–2. By 1967, Johnson had committed over 500,000 troops to the war in Vietnam. Many members of Congress regretted signing this "blank check," which they came to believe had allowed Johnson to escalate the conflict far beyond what anyone anticipated in 1964. But much postgame congressional criticism of the Tonkin Gulf Resolution was mere political posturing; after all, Congress annually funded every step of the escalation and, by the end of the war, approved drafting over 2.7 million Americans to fight in Vietnam.

In 1968, Senator William Fulbright, Chair of the Senate Foreign Relations Committee, held hearings on the Gulf of Tonkin incident, establishing that Johnson had misrepresented the event and deceived Congress.[3] The war in Vietnam was so unpopular by 1968 that Johnson declined to seek his own party's nomination to run in the November election. Winning that election and taking

---

[2] The 1990 resolution was titled "Authorization of Use of Military Force Against Iraq Resolution." The vote in the house was 250–183; in the Senate 52–47. The 2001 resolution was called "Authorization for Use of Military Force." The vote in the House was 420–1; in the Senate 98–0. The 2002 resolution was titled "Authorization for Use of Military Force Against Iraq Resolution of 2002." The vote in the House was 296–133; in the Senate 77–23.

[3] The hearings determined, among other things, that the USS *Maddox* was not on routine patrol, but rather on an intelligence mission to some extent coordinated with covert South Vietnamese patrol boat raids against North Vietnamese coastal installations. Scholars continue to debate whether the second attack by the North Vietnamese against the *Maddox* and the *C. Turner Joy* on August 4 actually occurred. (The first attack on August 2 against the *Maddox* is beyond question.) For a major study of the incidents, which concludes that the second attack did not occur, see Edwin E. Moise, *Tonkin Gulf and the Escalation of the Vietnam War* (Chapel Hill: University of North Carolina Press, 1996).

office in January 1969, President Richard Nixon continued to wage war even after Congress repealed the Tonkin Gulf Resolution in 1971. By January 1973, when the United States signed a cease-fire agreement with North Vietnam, 20,553 Americans had died under Nixon's prosecution of the conflict. The total number of Americans killed in the war was over 58,000.

In November 1973, Congress overrode Nixon's veto and passed into law the War Powers Resolution (WPR). An excerpt of the law is provided as Reading 7.3.3. Supporters claimed that the WPR would rein in the president's runaway war making, in their view the cause of the debacle in Vietnam. Opponents, including every president since the enactment of the WPR, claimed that the law was a brazenly unconstitutional infringement on the power of the commander in chief. Today, some view the WPR as a principled—if unsuccessful—effort by Congress to recapture war power it had ceded to the executive; others see the WPR as a device further to absolve Congress from political responsibility for military failures.

Whatever the intent and motives of the supporters of the WPR, today the United States is vulnerable to attacks that the framers of the Constitution could not have anticipated. Perhaps more than any other factor, the impress of this vulnerability on the nation's psyche helps explain why Americans accept the president's exercise of sweeping war-making power. Yet, for many the matter remains troubling. By escaping the constitutional restraint that it be shared with the legislature, the war power has effectively become the president's alone—the most potent in his arsenal of powers and a foundation of the modern presidency, eroding the system of checks and balances by which the framers intended to thwart tyranny. The war on terrorism has energized debate on how the power of the sword should properly be shared between the legislative and executive branches. Whether the fight against terrorism leads to a rebalancing of the war power or to even greater concentration in the commander in chief remains to be seen.

ASSIGNMENT

1. Examine the chart "Categorizing and Quantifying the Use of Armed Force Abroad." For each period specified in the left-hand column, calculate the average number of times *per year* that the United States deployed armed force abroad. To make the calculation, divide the number of times armed force was deployed abroad during each period by the number of years in the period. The calculation for the first period, 1788–Civil War, is 59 divided by 78 equals 0.8 times per year. Enter your calculations in the chart's third column.

2. For each period specified in the left-hand column of the chart calculate the ratio of unilateral presidential deployment of armed force abroad to deployments authorized by Congress. We'll call this the "presidential dominance ratio." To make the calculation, divide the number of unilateral presidential deployments by the number of deployments authorized by Congress for each period. The calculation for the first period, 1788–Civil War, is 54 divided by 5 equals 11, for a ratio of 11:1, meaning that the president unilaterally deployed armed force abroad eleven times for every one time that Congress authorized it. Enter your calculations in the chart's right-hand column.

The data in the chart indicate a steady increase since 1788 in the number of military deployments per year, almost all stemming from unilateral presidential action. In *quantitative* terms, then, the president's use of the war power has far outstripped that of Congress. But the data in the chart don't tell us anything about the *qualitative* aspect of unilateral presidential deployments. In assessing the gravitation of war powers into the president's hands, one wants to investigate not merely the frequency of the president's use of armed force, but also how the purpose and nature of presidential military deployments have changed over time. For example, if one were to find that early in the Republic's history, presidential deployments of armed force tended to be long, costly, drawn-out affairs, and that today—in contrast—presidential war making tends to be quick and surgical, then one might be less alarmed by the executive's monopoly of the war power. Examine Reading 7.3.1, "Descriptions of Typical Unilateral Presidential Military Deployments of American Troops." This reading describes five unilateral presidential deployments of armed force from the period before the Civil War and five examples from the period after World War II. Questions 3 and 4 ask you to compare and contrast the different examples.

Categorizing and Quantifying the Use of Armed Force Abroad

Period (and length)	Total number of times armed force deployed abroad	Average number of deployments per year	Number of declarations of war by Congress	Number of conditional use of force resolutions passed by Congress	Number of unilateral presidential deployments	Presidential Dominance Ratio
1788–Civil War (78 years)	59	0.8	2	3	54	11:1
1865–Spanish-American War (33 years)	40	—	1	4	35	—
1899–World War II (47 years)	68	—	8*	0	58	—
1946–Second Iraq War (57 years)	143	—	0	5	138	—

*During World War I, Congress voted separate declarations of war against Germany and Austria–Hungary in 1917. During World War II, Congress voted separate declarations of war against Japan, Germany, and Italy in 1941, and against Bulgaria, Hungary, and Romania in 1942.

READING 7.3.1 Descriptions of Typical Unilateral Presidential Military Deployments of American Troops[4]

Five examples of deployments from the pre–Civil War period:

1813–14—**Marguesas Islands**. U.S. forces built a fort on the island of Nukahiva to protect three prize ships that had been captured from the British.

1818—**Oregon**. The USS *Ontario*, dispatched from Washington, landed at the Columbia River and in August took possession of Oregon territory. Britain had conceded sovereignty, but Russia and Spain asserted claims to the area.

1843—**Africa**, November 29 to December 16. Four U.S. vessels demonstrated and landed various parties (one of 200 marines and sailors) to discourage piracy and the slave trade along the Ivory Coast and to punish attacks by the natives on American seamen and shipping.

1854—**Nicaragua**, July 9 to 15. Naval forces bombarded and burned San Juan del Norte (Greytown) to avenge an insult to the American minister to Nicaragua.

1858—**Uruguay**, January 2 to 27. Forces from two U.S. warships landed to protect American property during a revolution in Montevideo.

Five examples of deployments from the post–World War II period:

1948—**Berlin**. After the Soviet Union established a land blockade of the U.S., British, and French sectors of Berlin on June 24, 1948, the United States and its allies airlifted supplies to Berlin until the blockade was lifted in May 1949.

1962—**Cuba**. President Kennedy instituted a "quarantine" on the shipment of offensive missiles to Cuba from the Soviet Union. He also warned the Soviet Union that the launching of any missile from Cuba against nations in the Western Hemisphere would bring about U.S. nuclear retaliation on the Soviet Union. A negotiated settlement was achieved in a few days.

1975—**South Vietnam**. On April 30, 1975, President Ford reported that a force of 70 evacuation helicopters and 865 Marines had evacuated about 1,400 U.S. citizens and 5,500 third-country nationals and South Vietnamese from landing zones near the U.S. Embassy in Saigon and the Tan Son Nhut Airfield.

1988—**Panama**. In mid-March and April 1988, during a period of instability in Panama and as pressure grew for Panamanian military leader General Manuel Noriega to resign, the United States sent 1,000 troops to Panama to "further safeguard the canal, U.S. lives, property and interests in the area." The forces supplemented 10,000 U.S. military personnel already in Panama.

1999—**Bosnia**. On January 19, 1999, by letter, President Clinton notified Congress "consistent with the War Powers Resolution" that pursuant to his authority as commander in chief, he was continuing to authorize the use of combat-equipped U.S. armed force in Bosnia and other states in the region to participate in and support the NATO-led Stabilization Force. He noted that U.S. SFOR military personnel totaled about 6,900, with about 2,300 U.S. military personnel deployed to Hungary, Croatia, Italy, and other regional states. Also, some 350 U.S. military personnel remain deployed in the former Yugoslav Republic of Macedonia as part of the UN Preventative Deployment Force.

---

[4] These examples are taken from Ellen C. Collier, "Instances of Use of United States Forces Abroad, 1798–1993," at www.history.navy.mil/wars/foabroad; and from Richard F. Grimmett, "The War Powers Resolution: After Thirty Years," at www.fas.org/man/crsRL32267.

3. How does the purpose or objective of unilateral presidential military deployments prior to the Civil War differ from that following World War II?

_____

_____

_____

_____

4. How does the amount of military force applied by the president prior to the Civil War differ from that applied after World War II?

_____

_____

_____

Questions 5–10 are based on Reading 7.3.2, excerpts from the War Powers Resolution (WPR).

READING 7.3.2 EXCERPTS FROM THE WAR POWERS RESOLUTION

Public Law 93-148, passed over President's veto November 7, 1973

JOINT RESOLUTION Concerning the war powers of Congress and the President.

Resolved by the Senate and House of Representatives of the United States of America in Congress assembled,

Short Title

Section 1. This joint resolution may be cited as the "War Powers Resolution".

Purpose and Policy

Sec. 2. (a) It is the purpose of this joint resolution to fulfill the intent of the framers of the Constitution of the United States and insure that the collective judgment of both the Congress and the President will apply to the introduction of United States Armed Forces into hostilities, or into situations where imminent involvement in hostilities is clearly indicated by the circumstances, and to the continued use of such forces in hostilities or in such situations.

(b) Under article I, Section 8, of the Constitution, it is specifically provided that the Congress shall have the power to make all laws necessary and proper for carrying into execution, not only its own powers but also all other powers vested by the Constitution in the Government of the United States, or in any department or officer thereof.

(c) The constitutional powers of the President as Commander-in-Chief to introduce United States Armed Forces into hostilities, or into situations where imminent involvement in hostilities is clearly indicated by the circumstances, are exercised only pursuant to (1) a declaration of war, (2) specific statutory authorization [meaning a law passed by Congress], or (3) a national emergency created by attack upon the United States, its territories or possessions, or its armed forces.

Consultation

Sec. 3. The President in every possible instance shall consult with Congress before introducing United States Armed Forces into hostilities or into situations where imminent involvement in hostilities is clearly indicated by the circumstances, and after every such introduction shall consult regularly with the Congress until United States Armed Forces are no longer engaged in hostilities or have been removed from such situations.

Reporting

Sec. 4. (a) In the absence of a declaration of war, in any case in which United States Armed Forces are introduced-

(1) into hostilities or into situations where imminent involvement in hostilities is clearly indicated by the circumstances;

(2) into the territory, airspace or waters of a foreign nation, while equipped for combat, except for deployments which relate solely to supply, replacement, repair, or training of such forces; or

(3) in numbers which substantially enlarge United States Armed Forces equipped for combat already located in a foreign nation;

the President shall submit within 48 hours to the Speaker of the House of Representatives and to the President pro tempore of the Senate a report, in writing, setting forth-

(A) the circumstances necessitating the introduction of United States Armed Forces;

(B) the constitutional and legislative authority under which such introduction took place; and

(C) the estimated scope and duration of the hostilities or involvement.

(b) The President shall provide such other information as the Congress may request in the fulfillment of its constitutional responsibilities with respect to committing the Nation to war and to the use of United States Armed Forces abroad.

(c) Whenever United States Armed Forces are introduced into hostilities or into any situation described in subsection (a) of this section, the President shall, so long as such armed forces continue to be engaged in such hostilities or situation, report to the Congress periodically on the status of such hostilities or situation as well as on the scope and duration of such hostilities or situation, but in no event shall he report to the Congress less often than once every six months.

Congressional Action

Sec. 5. (b) Within sixty calendar days after a report is submitted or is required to be submitted pursuant to section 4(a)(1), whichever is earlier, the President shall terminate any use of United States Armed Forces with respect to which such report was submitted (or required to be submitted), unless the Congress (1) has declared war or has enacted a specific authorization for such use of United States Armed Forces, (2) has extended by law such sixty-day period, or (3) is physically unable to meet as a result of an armed attack upon the United States. Such sixty-day period shall be extended for not more than an additional thirty days if the President determines and certifies to the Congress in writing that unavoidable military necessity respecting the safety of United States Armed Forces requires the continued use of such armed forces in the course of bringing about a prompt removal of such forces.

(c) Notwithstanding subsection (b), at any time that United States Armed Forces are engaged in hostilities outside the territory of the United States, its possessions and territories without a declaration of war or specific statutory authorization, such forces shall be removed by the President if the Congress so directs by concurrent resolution.

Interpretation of Joint Resolution

Sec. 8. (2) (c) For purposes of this joint resolution, the term "introduction of United States Armed Forces" includes the assignment of members of such armed forces to command, coordinate, participate in the movement of, or accompany the regular or irregular military forces of any foreign country or government when such military forces are engaged, or there exists an imminent threat that such forces will become engaged, in hostilities.

---

5. According to the WPR, the president's legal authority as commander in chief to introduce U.S. armed forces into hostilities, or situations where hostilities are imminent, can be exercised under only three conditions. What are they?

_____

_____

_____

_____

_____

6. What does the WPR require the president to do within forty-eight hours of introducing U.S. armed forces into hostilities or situations where hostilities are imminent?

_____

_____

_____

_____

7. What does the WPR require the president to do within sixty calendar days of introducing U.S. armed forces into hostilities or situations where hostilities are imminent?

_____

_____

8. The WPR lists three conditions under which the president would *not* be required to take the action you identified in question 7 above. List the three exceptions here.

_____

_____

_____

_____

9. Suppose that a cruise ship plying the Mediterranean, and carrying 1,500 Americans, is seized by militants who demand the immediate release of all accused terrorists in U.S. custody. The hijackers immediately behead ten Americans and continue the beheadings at the rate of one every 15 minutes, with the butchery televised worldwide. The terrorists claim they will continue the beheadings until their demand is met or until all the American passengers are dead. Suppose also that Congress is not in session and that it would take the members of the House and Senate 24 hours to convene in special session after receiving the president's call to do so.

a. Would it be legal for the president under the WPR to use the armed forces of the United States—for example, the Navy Seals—to rescue the hostages? Explain why or why not.

b. What action should the president take? What would the political ramifications be?

10. Suppose that the president dispatches 10,000 Marines to kill 2,500 terrorists who have gathered from around the world in the jungles of a remote Philippine island. The president reports the action to Congress according to the requirements of the WPR. Congressional and public opinion is evenly divided between those denouncing the president's adventurism abroad and those praising his aggressive pursuit of terrorists. After 60 days of combat and 500 Marines killed, the president certifies to Congress under Section 5 (b) of the WPR that he needs an additional 30 days to win the fight. He notifies Congress that he's sending 5,000 more troops. But at the end of that 30-day extension (the 90th day of combat), an additional 700 Marines are dead. Public opinion remains divided. The president, however, is determined to proceed—based on intelligence he can't share—indicating that victory is attainable. A majority in Congress sees only a quagmire and, under Section 5 (c) of the WPR, orders the president by concurrent resolution (which does not require the president's signature) to terminate hostilities immediately and remove all U.S. military forces from the Philippines. Congress also declares by concurrent resolution that the president is in violation of Sections 2 (c) and 5 (c) of the WPR and threatens to cut off funding for the military operation.

a. Did the president have legal authority under the WPR to order the Marines to attack the terrorists in the first place? Explain why or why not.

_____

_____

_____

_____

b. What other act of Congress referred to in this exercise might give the president the authority to attack the terrorists?

_____

_____

c. Suppose that the president continues to defy Congress' demands to withdraw the troops, and that he escalates the conflict by introducing more Marines and increased firepower into the theater of combat. In that event, do you think Congress would follow through on its threat to cut off funding for troops in the field as a way to restrain the errant commander in chief?

_____

_____

_____

_____

_____

Questions 11 and 12 are based on Reading 7.3.3, an excerpt from the Report of the Senate Foreign Relations Committee on the War Powers Resolution, February 9, 1972.

READING 7.3.3 EXCERPTS FROM THE REPORT OF THE SENATE FOREIGN RELATIONS COMMITTEE ON THE WAR POWERS RESOLUTION, FEBRUARY 9, 1972

The purpose of the war powers bill... is to fulfill—not to alter, amend, or adjust—the intent of the framers of the United States Constitution in order to insure that the collective judgment of both the Congress and the President will be brought to bear in decisions involving the introduction of the Armed Forces of the United States in hostilities or in situations where imminent involvement in hostilities is indicated by circumstances....

The essential purpose of the bill, therefore, is to reconfirm and to define with precision the constitutional authority of Congress to exercise its constitutional war powers with respect to "undeclared" wars and the way in which this authority relates to the constitutional responsibilities of the President as Commander-in-Chief. The bill is in no way intended to encroach upon, alter or detract from the constitutional powers of the President, in his capacity as Commander-in-Chief, to conduct hostilities authorized by Congress, to repel attacks or the imminent threat of attacks upon the United States or its armed forces, and to rescue endangered American citizens and nationals in foreign countries....

The heart and core of the bill—the provision which will give substance and weight to the Congressional war power—is Section 5, which provides that the use of the armed forces under any of the emergency conditions spelled out in Section 3 shall not be sustained for a period beyond thirty days unless Congress adopts legislation specifically authorizing the continued use of the armed forces. The intended effect of Section 5 is to impose a prior and unalterable restriction on the emergency use of the armed forces by the President. Emergency use of the armed forces by the President—under Section 8—would be undertaken with full knowledge on his part that the operation could be continued beyond a thirty-day period only with the specific authorization of Congress. The President would thereby stand forewarned against any emergency use of the armed forces that did not conform with the law and that he did not feel confident would command the support of majorities of both Houses of Congress....

The Committee concurs in the view expressed by Justice Harlan: that when checks and balances are disrupted in one area of our public policy, all others are affected, and so are the basic rights of the citizens. As Professor Alpheus Thomas Mason said in his testimony before the Committee, "Separation of powers in war making, constitutionally shared by Congress and the President, has all but vanished. The President is in complete, unqualified control." In the Committee's view, as in the view of the framers of the Constitution, "complete, unqualified control" in one area poses the danger, if not indeed the inevitability, of "complete, unqualified control" over all other areas of our national life....

The Committee does not contest the need of "flexibility," nor of adaptability, in our political process in order to accommodate to modern conditions.... What the Committee does contest is that expansive view of Executive prerogative which holds that the President may use the armed forces at will, even in conditions falling short of a genuine national emergency, and that he may sustain that use for as long as he, and he alone, sees fit. Such unrestricted Presidential control of the armed forces is neither necessary or wise in our nuclear age, reconcilable with the Constitution, nor tolerable in a free society....

The framers of the Constitution vested the war power in Congress not primarily because they felt confident that the legislature would necessarily exercise it more wisely but because they expected the legislature to exercise it more *sparingly* than it had been exercised by the Crown [meaning the King of England], or would be likely to be exercised by the President as the successor to the Crown. The framers, it would appear, were concerned with the way in which war would be initiated in making certain that it would not be initiated easily, capriciously, or often....

11. According to the committee's report, what is the "heart and core" of the bill? What's the intended effect of this part of the bill? Cite specific language from the report in your answer.

_____

_____

_____

_____

_____

12. According to the committee's report, the Constitution's system of checks and balances as it relates to war powers is out of order. Explain. Cite specific language from the report in your answer.

_____

_____

_____

_____

_____

Questions 13 and 14 are based on Reading 7.3.4, an excerpt from President Richard Nixon's message on his veto of the War Powers Resolution.

READING 7.3.4 PRESIDENT RICHARD NIXON'S VETO OF THE WAR POWERS RESOLUTION

To the House of Representatives:

I hereby return without my approval House Joint Resolution 542 – the War Powers Resolution. While I am in accord with the desire of the Congress to assert its proper role in the conduct of our foreign affairs, the restrictions which this resolution would impose upon the authority of the President are both unconstitutional and dangerous to the best interests of our Nation.

The proper roles of the Congress and the Executive in the conduct of foreign affairs have been debated since the founding of our country. Only recently, however, has there been a serious challenge to the wisdom of the Founding Fathers in choosing not to draw a precise and detailed line of demarcation between the foreign policy powers of the two branches.

The Founding Fathers understood the impossibility of foreseeing every contingency that might arise in this complex area. They acknowledged the need for flexibility in responding to changing circumstances. They recognized that foreign policy decisions must be made through close cooperation between the two branches and not through rigidly codified procedures.

These principles remain as valid today as they were when our Constitution was written. Yet House Joint Resolution 542 would violate those principles by defining the President's powers in ways which would strictly limit his constitutional authority.

Clearly Unconstitutional

House Joint Resolution 542 would attempt to take away, by a mere legislative act, authorities which the President has properly exercised under the Constitution for almost 200 years. One of its provisions would automatically cut off certain authorities after sixty days unless the Congress extended them. Another would allow the Congress to eliminate certain authorities merely by the passage of a concurrent resolution—an action which does not normally have the force of law, since it denies the President his constitutional role in approving legislation.

I believe that both these provisions are unconstitutional. The only way in which the constitutional powers of a branch of the Government can be altered is by amending the Constitution—and any attempt to make such alterations by legislation alone is clearly without force.

Undermining our Foreign Policy

While I firmly believe that a veto of House Joint Resolution 542 is warranted solely on constitutional grounds, I am also deeply disturbed by the practical consequences of this resolution. For it would seriously undermine this Nation's ability to act decisively and convincingly in times of international crisis. As a result, the confidence of our allies in our ability to assist them could be diminished and the respect of our adversaries for our deterrent posture could decline. A permanent and substantial element of unpredictability would be injected into the world's assessment of American behavior, further increasing the likelihood of miscalculation and war.

If this resolution had been in operation, America's effective response to a variety of challenges in recent years would have been vastly complicated or even made impossible. We may well have been unable to respond in the way we did during the Berlin crisis of 1961, the Cuban missile crisis of 1962, the Congo rescue operation in 1964, and the Jordanian crisis of 1970—to mention just a few examples. In addition, our recent actions to bring about a peaceful settlement of the hostilities in the Middle East would have been seriously impaired if this resolution had been in force.

While all the specific consequences of House Joint Resolution 542 cannot yet be predicted, it is clear that it would undercut the ability of the United States to act as an effective influence for peace. For example, the provision automatically cutting off certain authorities after 60 days unless they are extended by the Congress could work to prolong or intensify a crisis. Until the Congress suspended the deadline, there would be at least a chance of United States withdrawal and an adversary would be tempted therefore to postpone serious negotiations until the 60 days were up. Only after the Congress acted would there be a strong incentive for an adversary to negotiate. In addition, the very existence of a deadline could lead to an escalation of hostilities in order to achieve certain objectives before the 60 days expired.

The measure would jeopardize our role as a force for peace in other ways as well.

It would, for example, strike from the President's hand a wide range of important peacekeeping tools by eliminating his ability to exercise quiet diplomacy backed by subtle shifts in our military deployments. It would also cast into doubt authorities which Presidents have used to undertake certain humanitarian relief missions in conflict areas, to protect fishing boats from seizure, to deal with ship or aircraft hijackings, and to respond to threats of attack.... Finally, since the bill is somewhat vague as to when the 60 day rule would apply, it could lead to extreme confusion and dangerous disagreements concerning the prerogatives of the two branches, seriously damaging our ability to respond to international crises.

Failure to Require Positive Congressional Action

I am particularly disturbed by the fact that certain of the President's constitutional powers as Commander in Chief of the Armed Forces would terminate automatically under this resolution 60 days after they were invoked. No overt Congressional action would be required to cut off these powers—they would disappear automatically unless the Congress extended them. In effect, the Congress is here attempting to increase its policy-making role through a provision which requires it to take absolutely no action at all.

In my view, the proper way for the Congress to make known its will on such foreign policy questions is through a positive action, with full debate on the merits of the issue and with each member taking the responsibility of casting a yes or no vote after considering those merits. The authorization and appropriations process represents one of the ways in which such influence can be exercised. I do not, however, believe that the Congress can responsibly contribute its considered, collective judgment on such grave questions without full debate and without a yes or no vote. Yet this is precisely what the joint resolution would allow. It would give every future Congress the ability to handcuff every future President merely by doing nothing and sitting still. In my view, one cannot become a responsible partner unless one is prepared to take responsible action....

RICHARD NIXON

The White House,
October 24, 1973

---

13. What argument does Nixon make to support his position that the WPR is unconstitutional?

_____
_____
_____
_____
_____

14. What argument does Nixon make to support his position that the WPR undermines the conduct of foreign policy?

_____
_____
_____
_____
_____

EXERCISE 7.4 Distinguishing Fact from Opinion in an American Presidential Campaign

INTRODUCTION

Many Americans take a dim view of their representatives in government, believing that politicians seek nothing more than power and perks and will say anything—even lie—to get elected. But how many citizens undertake the tough task of evaluating the accuracy of candidates' statements? The line between fact and opinion is not always clear, and drawing that line demands more knowledge and understanding of politics and public policy than many citizens have or want to have. Yet democracy hinges on an educated citizenry.

Political campaigns illustrate the difficulty of separating fact from opinion. The first problem is that politicians exaggerate and distort, whether intentionally or not, to cast themselves in a favorable light and their opponents as creatures of the dark. The second hurdle is that, because media coverage of campaigns is often careless, candidates' statements routinely are taken out of context or blown out of proportion. The third obstacle to drawing a clear line between fact and opinion is that many Americans are only marginally attentive to campaign coverage and rarely consult sources of information outside the mainstream media.

The quest for accuracy has been made easier in recent presidential campaigns through the work of newspapers, especially the *New York Times*, the *Washington Post*, and the *Los Angeles Times*, which regularly analyze claims made in political ads and presidential debates. The *Washington Post* was particularly effective in tracking down the Swift Boat Veterans for Truth claim that John Kerry's war record was fabricated. The ad was shown to be inaccurate in every respect. Nevertheless, the "Swifties" purpose had been served: They raised doubts about the candidate's veracity and war-hero status.[1]

ASSIGNMENT

Study Reading 7.4.1, which describes the difference between statements of fact and statements of opinion. The questions that follow ask you to distinguish fact from opinion in candidate statements from the three presidential debates of 2004.

READING 7.4.1 FACT OR OPINION?

A *statement of fact* can be verified as true or refuted as false. In the social sciences, a statement of fact and truth are not necessarily the same. According to one social scientist, "Facts are not to be confused with Truth. A fact is only as good as the means of verification used to establish it, as well as the frame of reference within which it requires meaning. A great deal of science consists of using methodological advances to reverse, modify, or even falsify 'facts' ... formerly verified."[2]

For example, during the first presidential debate of 2004, President Bush, in response to Senator Kerry's accusation that the Bush administration had not vigorously pursued Osama bin Laden and other Al Qaida terrorists, asserted, "Seventy-five percent of known Al Qaida leaders have been brought to justice."[3] Bush's statement can be verified using scientific methods of investigation.

---

[1] Michael Dobbs, "Swift Boat Accounts Incomplete," *Washington Post*, August 22, 2004, p. A01.

[2] Kenneth Hoover and Todd Donovan, *The Elements of Social Scientific Thinking*, 7th ed. (Boston: Bedford, St. Martin's, 2001), p. 132.

[3] Transcript of the First Presidential Debate, website of the Commission on Presidential Debates, http://www.debates.org/. All subsequent debate statements are from the transcript link on this website.

Because Bush qualified the statement to *known* Al Qaida leaders, an investigator could determine whether 75 percent of them had been captured ("brought to justice"). Verification would require investigating how many terrorists the intelligence community had identified as leaders and how many of those had been captured.

A *statement of opinion* is based on personal values, ideology, or wishful prediction. With the passage of time, an opinion may turn out to be true, partially true, or false. But a statement of opinion at the time it's made cannot be verified or refuted scientifically. For example, in the second presidential debate of 2004, President Bush, in response to Senator Kerry's assertion that the Bush administration should have been directly engaged with North Korea to keep that regime from developing nuclear weapons, said, "It is naive and dangerous to take a policy that he suggested the other day, which is to have bilateral relations with North Korea. Remember, he's the person who's accusing me of not acting multilaterally. He now wants to take the six-party talks we have—China, North Korea, South Korea, Russia, Japan, and the United States—and undermine them by having bilateral talks." Whereas parts of the statement are at least partially factual—Kerry did, for example, criticize Bush for not acting multilaterally *in Iraq*—Bush's main point was to establish the peril of Kerry's proposal for bilateral talks with North Korea. Which approach is better—bilateral or multilateral talks with North Korea—is a matter of opinion. Both approaches have their proponents and both have good arguments to support them. Time will tell whether or not the Bush approach was correct. Even if the multilateral approach works, however, we still would not know how the bilateral approach might have fared.

Most statements candidates make about their positions on issues are statements of opinion, even when a candidate has abundant arguments and apparent evidence to support the position. For example, a candidate who says that the media are destroying family values—but who does not preface the statement with "I believe"—is misrepresenting a statement of opinion as a statement of fact. There is no body of evidence or standard of measurement by which that statement of opinion can be verified or refuted.

In questions 1–10, identify each statement as fact—something that can be confirmed or refuted—or opinion. To answer part b of each question ("Why?"), do this: If it's a statement of fact, explain how it could be verified or refuted. If it's a statement of opinion, explain why it cannot be verified or refuted. Some of the statements mix fact and opinion. (You do not have to determine whether or not the statements are accurate.)

---

1. Kerry (Debate 1): "This president has made [in Iraq], I regret to say, a colossal error of judgment. And judgment is what we look for in the president of the United States of America."

a. Statement of fact or of opinion?

b. Why?

2. Bush (Debate 1): "The world is safer without Saddam Hussein."

a. Statement of fact or of opinion?

EXERCISE 7.4 DISTINGUISHING FACT FROM OPINION IN AN AMERICAN PRESIDENTIAL CAMPAIGN

b. Why?

_____

_____

_____

3. Kerry (Debate 2): "The president has presided over an economy where we've lost 1.6 million jobs. The first president in 72 years to lose jobs."

a. Statement of fact or of opinion?

_____

b. Why?

_____

_____

_____

4. Bush (Debate 2): "Government-sponsored health care would lead to rationing. It would ruin the quality of health care in America."

a. Statement of fact or of opinion?

_____

b. Why?

_____

_____

_____

5. Bush (Debate 2): "As a matter of fact, the tools now given to the terrorist fighters are the same tools that we've been using against drug dealers and white-collar criminals."

a. Statement of fact or of opinion?

_____

b. Why?

_____

_____

_____

6. Kerry (Debate 2): "Ladies and gentlemen, in 1985, I was one of the first Democrats to move to balance the budget. I voted for the balanced budget in '93 and '97. We did it. We did it. And I was there."

a. Statement of fact or of opinion?

_____

b. Why?

7. Kerry (Debate 2): "I'm against the partial-birth abortion, but you've got to have an exception for the life of the mother and the health of the mother under the strictest test of bodily injury to the mother."

   a. Statement of fact or of opinion?

   b. Why?

8. Bush (Debate 3): "People need to remember: Six months prior to my arrival, the stock market started to go down. And it was one of the largest declines in our history. And then we had a recession and we got attacked, which cost us 1 million jobs. But we acted. I led the Congress. We passed tax relief. And now this economy is growing. We added 1.9 million new jobs over the last 13 months."

   a. Statement of fact or of opinion?

   b. Why?

9. Kerry (Debate 3): "Under President Bush, the middle class has seen their tax burden go up and the wealthiests' [sic] tax burden has gone down. Now that's wrong."

   a. Statement of fact or of opinion?

   b. Why?

10. Kerry (Debate 3): "It's long overdue time to raise the minimum wage."

a. Statement of fact or of opinion?

_____

b. Why?

_____

_____

_____

11. Read through the transcripts of one of the three presidential debates held during the 2004 campaign. The transcripts are available from the website of the Commission on Presidential Debates: http://www.debates.org.[4]

Choose one statement of fact made by each candidate in one of the debates, and then check the accuracy of those statements of fact. There are a variety of ways to check the accuracy of politicians' statements, but good daily newspapers are one of the best. After each presidential debate, the *New York Times*, the *Washington Post*, and the *Los Angeles Times* published articles about the accuracy of the claims made in the previous debate. The archives of the newspapers are available through ProQuest (National Newspaper Index Database). Your college library likely subscribes to the database. Do a search for full-text articles between October 1, 2004, and October 15, 2004. Begin with the search term "presidential debates 2004," and try others as needed. Another useful resource for checking facts in presidential races is FactCheck.org at http://www.factcheck.org. A useful website for learning more about the presidential candidates' positions on the issues for the purpose of checking whether they were representing their positions accurately during the debates is the On The Issues website at http://www.issues2000.org/George_W_Bush.htm and http://www.issues2000.org/John_Kerry.htm.

a. Debate number (1, 2, or 3):

Bush statement of fact: _____

Accuracy: _____

_____

_____

b. Debate number (1, 2, or 3):

Kerry statement of fact: _____

Accuracy: _____

_____

_____

12. The polling data in Table 7.4.1 indicate the public's knowledge of Bush's and Kerry's positions on major public policy issues. Study the table. Then determine whether a plurality of the

---

[4] Website URLs sometimes change. Try an external search (e.g., Google) to find the website. Configurations of a website often change. Try an internal search of the site to locate the information. Sometimes websites and pages within websites are removed. In that case, move on to the next question.

TABLE 7.4.1 Voters' Knowledge of Candidates' Positions on the Issues, October 14–20, 2004

Who favors completely eliminating the estate tax, that is the tax on property worth more than one and a half million dollars left by people who die—George W. Bush, John Kerry, both or neither?

Bush	46%
Kerry	20%
Both	6%
Neither	10%
Don't know	18%

Which candidate wants to make additional stem cell lines from human embryos available for federally funded research on diseases like Parkinsons?

Bush	9%
Kerry	74%
Both	5%
Neither	5%

Which candidate proposes moving sixty to seventy thousand troops stationed in Europe and South Korea to other locations, including the United States, in the next decade—George W. Bush, John Kerry, both or neither?

Bush	40%
Kerry	31%
Both	9%
Neither	8%

Which candidate has stated he favors reinstating the military draft—George W. Bush, John Kerry, both or neither?

Bush	22%
Kerry	14%
Both	4%
Neither	53%

Which candidate favors placing limits on how much people can collect when a jury finds that a doctor has committed medical malpractice—George W. Bush, John Kerry, both or neither?

Bush	48%
Kerry	16%
Both	11%
Neither	10%

Which candidate favors allowing the federal government to negotiate with drug companies for lower prescription drug prices for senior citizens—George W. Bush, John Kerry, both or neither?

Bush	17%
Kerry	55%
Both	14%
Neither	6%

Which candidate favors increasing the five dollar and fifteen cent minimum wage employers must pay their workers—George W. Bush, John Kerry, both or neither?

Bush	8%
Kerry	66%
Both	13%
Neither	4%

°Those with no opinion are not shown.

SOURCE: Used with permission by the National Annenberg Election Survey of the University of Pennsylvania's Annenberg Public Policy Centre, "Voters Learned Positions on Issues since Presidential Debates," October 23, 2004, http://www.annenbergpublicpolicycenter.org/naes/index.htm.

respondents to the poll correctly identified each candidate's positions and fill in the chart, "Accuracy of Voters' Perception of Candidates' Position," accordingly. Use the On The Issues website (www.issues2000.org/George_W_Bush.htm and www.issues2000.org/John_Kerry.htm) to check the respondents' accuracy.

Accuracy of Voters' Perception of Candidates' Position	
Issue	Plurality (most respondents) Perceived Candidates' Position Correctly? (Yes or No)
Estate tax	
Stem cells	
Troop location	
Reinstating draft	
Limits on medical malpractice suits	
Regulate Rx for lower costs to seniors	
Increase minimum wage	

13. What do Table 7.4.1 and your answers to question 12 tell you about voters' understanding of candidates' positions on major issues?

_____

_____

_____

CHAPTER 8

Bureaucracy and the Regulatory Process

EXERCISE 8.1 The Fourth Branch

INTRODUCTION

The title *chief executive* suggests that the president, in principle, commands and controls the executive branch of the national government. Many presidents have embraced Franklin Delano Roosevelt's view that "the Presidency was established as a single strong Chief Executive in which was vested the entire executive power of the National Government."[1] The framers of the Constitution, however, refused to confer that much power on the president. Instead, the framers divided jurisdiction over the executive branch between Congress and the president, and assigned to Congress a substantial role in executive branch affairs. For example, to staff the highest positions in the executive branch, the president must secure the consent of the Senate. Congress also has the power to create executive branch agencies and departments, and to direct and fund their operations through legislation.

In Article II, Section I, the Constitution vests the executive power in the president. But nowhere does it bestow the title *chief executive* on the president, and it has very little to say about the president's management of the executive branch. There are only three direct references in the Constitution to the president's power over executive branch departments. The first allows the president to "require the Opinion in writing, of the principal Officer in each of the executive Departments, upon any Subject relating to the Duties of their respective Offices." The second gives the president the power to appoint, subject to Senate approval, executive branch officers. In the third reference the president is admonished to "take Care that the Laws be faithfully executed."

Throughout the nineteenth century, the president's position at the head of the executive branch would not have seemed to most Americans to be a fountainhead of power. The national government

---

[1] Quoted in Richard M. Pious, *The American Presidency* (New York: Basic Books, 1979), p. 211.

was largely irrelevant to the conduct of most citizens' lives, and few had direct contact with it. At the time of the Civil War, for example, the federal bureaucracy consisted of just four Cabinet departments: War, State, Treasury, and Interior. Until well into the nineteenth century, the executive branch did little more than deliver the mail, guard the nation's coasts, fight Native Americans, and collect taxes.

In 1789, the president carried out his responsibility as head of the executive branch by supervising about fifty civilian employees: the State Department had nine, the War Department two, and the Treasury Department thirty-nine. By 1900, the number of civilian employees in the executive branch had gone up to about 240,000. By the end of the twentieth century, the federal bureaucracy had become more powerful than any nineteenth-century American could have imagined. Today the executive branch consists of fifteen Cabinet departments, dozens of agencies, commissions, and government corporations, with more than 2.7 million civilian employees and a budget for fiscal year 2004–2005 of about $2.3 trillion. The size and complexity of the federal bureaucracy raise important questions about the president's ability to oversee it. What does it mean to be the chief executive of the federal government? Is it possible for the president to command and control, or even manage and supervise, the federal bureaucracy?

ASSIGNMENT

1. Get acquainted with the federal bureaucracy by going to www.lib.lsu.edu/gov/fedgov, the Louisiana State University Library Federal Agencies Directory.[2] At the top of the page, click on <u>Complete U.S. Federal Government Agencies Directory (Hierarchical)</u>. Here are listed the Cabinet departments and independent agencies of the federal government and their various subunits. The subunits include bureaus, divisions, branches, offices, and services. Each line in the hierarchical list represents one subunit and is a link to that subunit's website.

a. Estimate the total number of subunits of the federal bureaucracy in this hierarchical list.

___

b. Use the links to explore two subunits of your choice. Identify those subunits and their mission or purpose.

Subunit 1: ___

___

___

Subunit 2: ___

___

___

2. Examine the organization chart of the executive branch in Figure 8.1.1. What do the vertical lines in the chart suggest about the president's position and power in the executive branch?

___

___

___

---

[2] Website URLs sometimes change. Try an external search (e.g., Google) to find the website. Configurations of a website often change. Try an internal search of the site to locate the information. Sometimes websites and pages within websites are removed. In that case, move on to the next question.

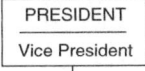

The Executive Branch

```
                         PRESIDENT
                         Vice President

              Executive Office of the President
              White HOuse Office
              Council on Environmental Quality
              Office of Management and Budget
              Office of Science and Technology Policy
              Council of Economic Advisors
              National Security Council
              Office of the United States
              Trade Representative
              Office of Administration
              Office of Policy Development
```

CABINET DEPARTMENTS							
Department of Agriculture	Department of Commerce	Department of Defense	Department of Education	Department of Energy	Department of Health and Human Services	Department of Housing and Urban Development	Department of Homeland Security
Department of The Interior	Department of Justice	Department of Labor	Department of State	Department of Transportation	Department of The Treasury	Department of Veterans Affairs	

INDEPENDENT ESTABLISHMENTS AND GOVERNMENT CORPORATIONS

ACTION	Export-Import Bank of the U.S.	Interstate Commerce Commission	Panama Canal Commisssion
Administrative Conference of the U.S.	Farm Credit Administration	Merit Systems Protection Board	Peace Corps
African Development Foundation	Federal Communications Commission	National Aeronautics and Space Administration	Pennsylvania Avenue Development Corporation
American Battle Monuments Commission	Federal Deposit Insurance Corporation	National Archives and Records Administration	Postal Rate Commission
Appalachian Regional Commisssion	Federal Election Commision	National Capital Planning Commission	Railroad Retirement Board
Board for International Broadcasting	Federal Emergency Management Agency	National Credit Union Administration	Securities and Exchange Commission
Central Intelligence Agency	Federal Home Loan Bank Board	National Foundation on the Arts and the Humanities	Selective Service System
Commission on The Bicentennial of the United States Constitution	Federal Labor Relations Authority	National Labor Relations Board	Small Business Administration
Commission on Civil Rights	Federal Maritime Commission	National Mediation Board	Tennessee Valley Authority
Commission of Fine ARts	Federal Mediation and Conciliation Service	National Science Foundation	U.S. Arms Control and Disarmament Agency
Commodity Futures Trading Commission	Federal Mine Safety and Health Review Commission	National Transportation Safety Board	U.S. Information Agency
Consumer Product Safety Commission	Federal Reserve System, Board of Governors of the	Nuclear Regulatory Commission	U.S. International Development Cooperation Agency
Environmental Protection Agency	Federal Trade Commission	Occupational Safety and Health Review Commission	U.S. International Trade Commission
Equal Employment Opportunity Commission	General Services Administration	Office of Personnel Management	U.S. Postal Service
	Inter-American Foundation	Office of Special Counsel	

3. On Figure 8.1.1 locate the box that contains Executive Office of the President (EOP). The EOP, whose task is to ensure that the departments and agencies in the federal bureaucracy carry out the president's policies, consists of about 1,500 people, compared to the 2.7 million in the federal bureaucracies. Yet, even the relatively small EOP presents problems of management and supervision. For the EOP to function successfully as the president's "watchdog," assisting him to oversee the federal bureaucracy, EOP employees must be responsive to the president's policy preferences. Do you think that the president, with the help of his White House aides and the top officials in the EOP he appoints, would be able effectively to direct these 1,500 employees in the EOP? Explain and support your position.

4. The federal bureaucracy consists of the departments and agencies in the two large lower boxes in Figure 8.1.1. They're labeled "CABINET DEPARTMENTS" and "INDEPENDENT ESTABLISHMENTS AND GOVERNMENT CORPORATIONS." Note that the federal bureaucracy is connected by a vertical line upward through the Executive Office of the President to the "PRESIDENT" himself. How and why would the president's ability to direct the federal bureaucracy differ from his ability to direct the EOP?

5. Locate the Department of Agriculture (USDA) in Figure 8.1.1. In 2005, the USDA had about 100,000 employees and a budget of about $94 billion. How significant a component of the entire executive branch does the USDA appear to be? Explain and support your answer.

6. Figure 8.1.2 is an organization chart of the Department of Agriculture. Note that there are seven major subunits within the USDA, each headed by an undersecretary. One of these subunits is the Under Secretary for Food Safety. Locate the Under Secretary for Natural Resources and Environment. Notice that the Forest Service is one of the agencies charged with overseeing natural resources and the environment. According to the figure, how significant a component of the entire USDA does the Forest Service appear to be? Explain and support your answer.

FIGURE 8.1.2 U.S. Department of Agiculture, 2002

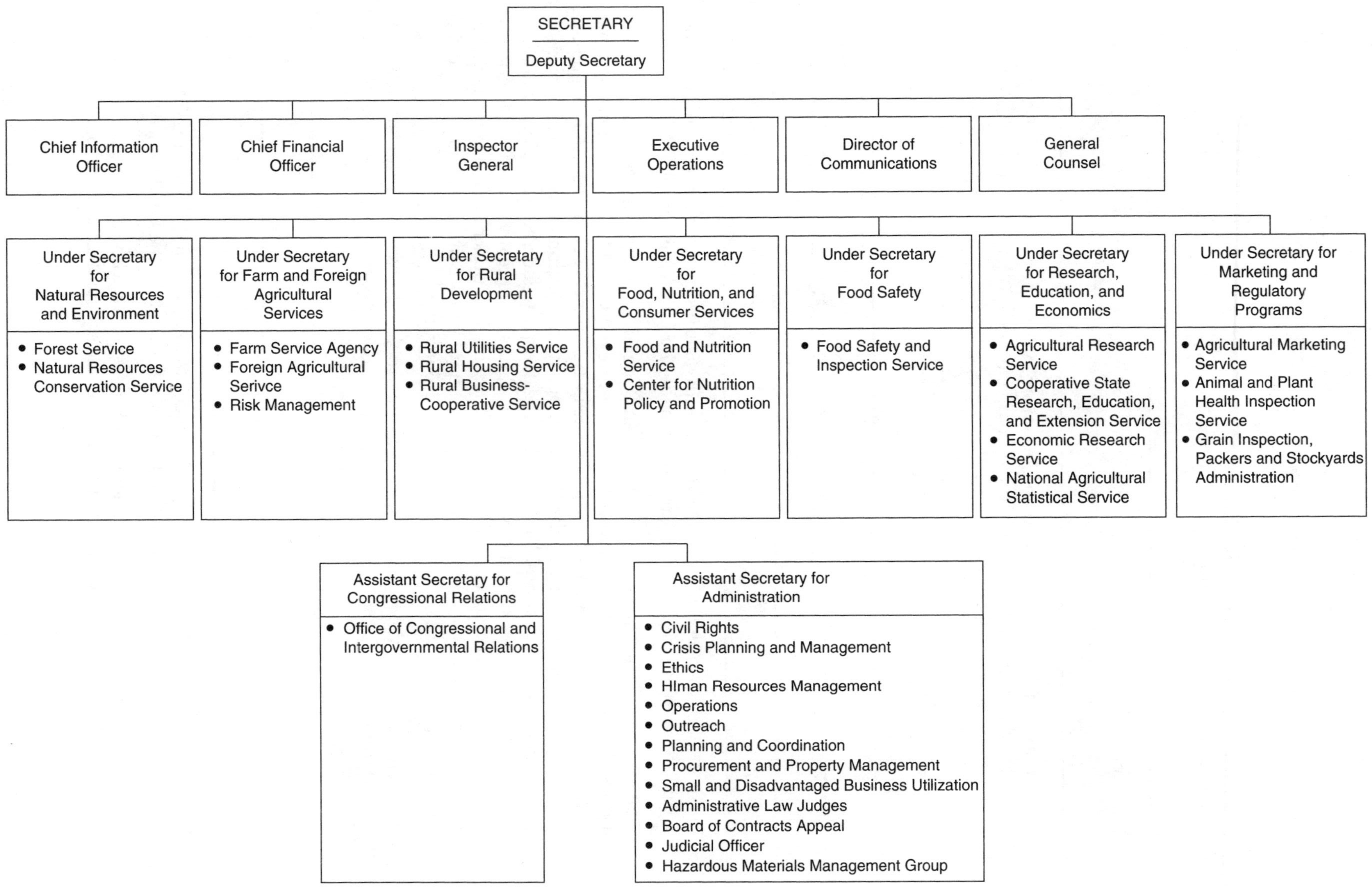

SECRETARY
Deputy Secretary

- Chief Information Officer
- Chief Financial Officer
- Inspector General
- Executive Operations
- Director of Communications
- General Counsel

Under Secretary for Natural Resources and Environment
- Forest Service
- Natural Resources Conservation Service

Under Secretary for Farm and Foreign Agricultural Services
- Farm Service Agency
- Foreign Agricultural Serivce
- Risk Management

Under Secretary for Rural Development
- Rural Utilities Service
- Rural Housing Service
- Rural Business-Cooperative Service

Under Secretary for Food, Nutrition, and Consumer Services
- Food and Nutrition Service
- Center for Nutrition Policy and Promotion

Under Secretary for Food Safety
- Food Safety and Inspection Service

Under Secretary for Research, Education, and Economics
- Agricultural Research Service
- Cooperative State Research, Education, and Extension Service
- Economic Research Service
- National Agricultural Statistical Service

Under Secretary for Marketing and Regulatory Programs
- Agricultural Marketing Service
- Animal and Plant Health Inspection Service
- Grain Inspection, Packers and Stockyards Administration

Assistant Secretary for Congressional Relations
- Office of Congressional and Intergovernmental Relations

Assistant Secretary for Administration
- Civil Rights
- Crisis Planning and Management
- Ethics
- Hlman Resources Management
- Operations
- Outreach
- Planning and Coordination
- Procurement and Property Management
- Small and Disadvantaged Business Utilization
- Administrative Law Judges
- Board of Contracts Appeal
- Judicial Officer
- Hazardous Materials Management Group

7. Now go to the Forest Service's website at www.fs.fed.us. Click on <u>About Us</u>, and then on <u>Meet the Forest Service</u>. Read the material there to better understand the size, scope, and mission of the Forest Service.

a. How many acres of land does the Forest Service administer?

b. What is the title of the head of the Forest Service?

c. How many people work for the Forest Service?

d. The Forest Service is a large and important agency by any standard, yet it doesn't appear in Figure 8.1.1, the organization chart of the executive branch. What does its exclusion from that chart indicate about the executive branch?

8. In the 1930s, when Franklin Delano Roosevelt was president, the federal bureaucracy was less than half its present size. Even so, Roosevelt made the following complaint:

> The Treasury is so large and far-flung and ingrained in its practices that I find it almost impossible to get the action and results I want—even with Henry [Morgenthau] there. But the Treasury is not to be compared with the State Department. You should go through the experience of trying to get any changes in the thinking, policy, and action of the career diplomats and then you'd know what a real problem was. But the Treasury and the State Department put together are nothing compared with the Na-a-vy. The admirals are really something to cope with—and I should know. To change anything in the Na-a-vy is like punching a feather bed. You punch it with your right and you punch it with your left until you are finally exhausted, and then you find the damn bed just as it was before you started punching.[3]

In one sentence, using your own words, state the problem Roosevelt struggled with as head of the executive branch.

9. During Richard Nixon's term in office, this celebrated outburst by the president was recorded for posterity on the taping system he had secretly installed in the Oval Office:

> We have no discipline in this bureaucracy. We never fire anybody. We never reprimand anybody. We never demote anybody. We always promote the sons-of-bitches that kick us in the ass. . . . We

---
[3] Richard E. Neustadt, *Presidential Power: The Politics of Leadership from FDR to Carter* (New York: John Wiley and Sons, 1980), p. 33.

are going to quit being a bunch of goddamn soft-headed managers.... When a bureaucrat deliberately thumbs his nose, we're going to get him.... The little boys over in [the State Department] particularly, that are against us [the Defense Department, the Department of Health, Education, and Welfare]—those three areas particularly.... There are many unpleasant places were civil service people can be sent.... When they don't produce in this administration, somebody's ass is kicked out.... Now, goddamn it, those are the bad guys—the guys down in the woodwork.[4]

a. What did Nixon likely mean by "the guys down in the woodwork"?

_____

_____

_____

b. Identify the problem in contemporary government that triggered Nixon's anger.

_____

_____

_____

10. In recent decades, many political scientists have come to think of the departments and agencies in the executive branch as a fourth branch of government. What evidence can you find in this exercise to support the characterization?

_____

_____

_____

_____

_____

_____

_____

---

[4] J. Anthony Lukas, *Nightmare: The Underside of the Nixon Years* (New York: Viking Press, 1976), p. 18.

EXERCISE 8.2 The National Security State

INTRODUCTION

For most of their history, Americans have had to sacrifice comparatively little to maintain their national security. Much of the work was done for them by nature. Americans fortuitously built their nation in one of the most secure regions of the world. Vast oceans to the east and west have insulated the country for most of its history, protecting it from conflict and turmoil in Europe and Asia and deterring would-be invaders from striking. U.S. national security has been bolstered as well by neighbors to the north and south that pose little threat to America.

That helps explain why many Americans have viewed the military establishment and large standing armed forces with suspicion. For American colonists, the instruments of royal tyranny and the abridgement of their liberties were the British army and navy. Consequently, Americans in the early years of the Republic looked not to a national army to protect them but to their various state militias, whose importance was acknowledged in the Second Amendment to the Constitution. In 1787, the framers were careful to subordinate the military to civilian control and to vest two key powers in the hands of Congress instead of the executive: the power to raise armies and the power to declare war (Article I, Section 8). According to the Constitution, the president's role was limited to commanding the armies raised and authorized by Congress (see Exercise 7.3).

The confidence of Americans in the security of their nation was shattered by the Japanese attack on Pearl Harbor on December 7, 1941. America was no longer a natural fortress. Japanese aircraft carriers had crossed the Pacific undetected, penetrated American defenses, and revealed that U.S. territory was vulnerable to foreign attack.

Technology had played a part in the Japanese attack; it would play a larger part in U.S. security concerns during the cold war. In 1949, the Soviet Union exploded its first atomic bomb and later threatened the United States with its capacity to deliver atomic weapons on intercontinental bombers. That threat paled in comparison with the development of the intercontinental ballistic missile (ICBM) as a vehicle for delivering nuclear weapons. Because it was impossible to defend against incoming ICBMs, America was rendered utterly vulnerable to an attack by the Soviet Union. To limit its vulnerability, the United States adopted the doctrine of mutual assured destruction (MAD): A nuclear attack on the United States by the Soviet Union would trigger a massive nuclear counterattack by the United States. In a classic standoff, the Soviet Union made the same threat.

The Japanese attack on Pearl Harbor and the rise of the Soviet Union as a nuclear superpower led to the conviction that projecting military power abroad was essential to achieving national security at home. Adversaries had to be contained overseas before they could carry their threat to American shores. Consequently, beginning in the late 1940s, the United States developed a series of military alliances with nations in strategic areas of the world. President George Washington, in his farewell address to the nation in 1796, had warned Americans of the dangers of permanent alliances with foreign powers. The nation heeded Washington's advice until 1949, when America joined its first peacetime military alliance—the North Atlantic Treaty Organization (NATO). For a nation so long averse to becoming entangled with foreign powers and so insistent on maintaining its freedom of action in foreign affairs, this was powerful evidence that Americans had embraced a new vision of national security. President George W. Bush has departed from this post–World War II consensus and emphasized a more unilateral approach to national security.

When scholars describe the United States in the post–World War II era, many talk about the *national security state*. A national security state is permanently mobilized for war. That mobilization entails enormous social and economic costs to the nation, costs that Americans would never have accepted before World War II. The foundation of the national security state was laid in 1950, when President Harry Truman approved National Security Council Document 68 (NSC-68) NSC-68 was a blueprint for putting the nation on permanent wartime footing and for obtaining public and congressional approval for the sacrifices that would entail, primary among them a vast increase in military spending and maintenance of large standing military forces. NSC-68's recommendations for massive increases in defense spending were controversial, and Truman at first was reluctant to accept them. But the outbreak of the Korean War in June 1950 cinched the case for constructing the national security state.

The precise costs of the national security state are difficult to determine. Obviously, national security requires the maintenance of large standing military forces as well as the departments and agencies in the executive branch needed to sustain those forces. Other costs are less obvious. In the quest to develop and maintain a nuclear arsenal, the Departments of Energy and Defense contaminated vast swaths of land with nuclear and other wastes. The clean-up costs promise to run into the trillions of dollars. And there are more far-reaching costs as well. The public resources dedicated to the national security state remain unavailable for other uses such as improving the nation's infrastructure, its schools, its health-care system. In the interest of fighting the cold war—and now the war on terrorism—the national security state abridged the civil liberties and civil rights of many citizens. Sustaining the national security state undoubtedly entails other costs that have yet to be revealed.

Despite sustained investment in the national security state, the United States continues to grapple with its vulnerability. President George W. Bush's initiatives to defend the nation against ballistic missile and terrorist attacks are the latest in a long line of efforts to recover the sense of national security that Americans enjoyed before World War II. A terrorist attack on U.S. territory using chemical, biological, or nuclear weapons would pose an unprecedented challenge to national security. Since the end of World War II, the ability of the United States to deliver a punishing military attack has deterred enemy nations from striking U.S. territory. But, because terrorists are an amorphous target beyond the president's reach, they are unlikely to be deterred by military retaliation. Whether the national security state can manage to contain this vulnerability remains to be seen.

ASSIGNMENT

Table 8.2.1 lists data on U.S. military spending from 1791 to 1950 by year or by period. When a period is shown—for example, 1850–1859—the expenditure noted is the yearly average for that period. Notice that the dollar amount of military spending for each year or period is in current dollars, which means that the figures have *not* been adjusted for inflation. A dollar spent on the military in 1820, for example, would have purchased substantially more goods or services than a dollar spent in 1920. But the spending figures in Table 8.2.1 do not compensate for that erosion in value.[1]

TABLE 8.2.1 U.S. Military Spending, 1791–1950, in Current Dollars

Year or Period	Military Spending Per Year	
1791–1799	2,013,000	
1800–1809	2,872,000	
1810	3,948,000	
1811	3,999,000	
1812	15,777,000	War of 1812 begins
1813	26,099,000	
1814	27,662,000	
1815	23,454,000	War of 1812 ends
1816	19,920,000	Demobilization
1817	11,319,000	
1818	8,577,000	
1819	10,350,000	
1820–1829	6,413,000	
1830–1839	12,041,000	
1840–1845	12,240,000	
1846	17,248,000	Mexican War begins
1847	46,207,000	
1848	34,910,000	Mexican War ends

---

[1] Figures adjusted for inflation would allow more accurate comparisons of spending over time, but adjusted figures are not available for the years preceding 1945.

TABLE 8.2.1 (Cont.)

Year or Period	Military Spending Per Year	
1849	24,640,000	Demobilization
1850–1859	24,988,000	
1860	27,925,000	
1861	35,402,000	Civil War begins
1862	437,036,000	
1863	662,521,000	
1864	776,518,000	
1865	1,153,936,000	Civil War ends
1866	327,774,000	Demobilization
1867	126,258,000	
1868	149,023,000	
1869	98,503,000	
1870–1879	53,171,000	
1880–1889	51,756,000	
1890–1895	46,415,000	
1896	77,979,000	
1897	83,512,000	
1898	150,816,000	Spanish-American War
1899	293,783,000	Demobilization
1900	190,728,000	
1901	205,123,000	
1902	180,075,000	
1903–1915	291,294,000	
1916	337,030,000	
1917	617,574,000	U.S. enters World War I
1918	6,148,795,000	World War I ends
1919	11,011,387,000	Demobilization
1920	2,357,974,000	
1921	1,768,450,000	
1922	935,531,000	
1923	730,252,000	
1924–1935	768,382,000	
1936–1940	1,213,587,000	
1941	6,252,001,000	U.S. enters World War II
1942	22,905,097,000	
1943	63,413,912,000	
1944	75,975,964,000	
1945	80,537,254,000	World War II ends
1946	40,184,000,000	Demobilization
1947	13,205,000,000	
1948	10,151,000,000	
1949	11,241,000,000	
1950	11,674,000,000	

NOTE: Current dollars have not been adjusted for inflation.
SOURCE: Adapted from Census Bureau, *Historical Statistics of the United States* (Washington, D.C.: U.S. Government Printing Office, 1975).

1. Use the data in Table 8.2.1 to complete the following chart. Your objective is to compare the average annual military spending in the years immediately preceding and following each war. To determine the *prewar average*, calculate the approximate average annual military spending over the five years preceding the war. The *wartime high* figure is just that, the highest amount spent on

defense in any year during the war. To determine the *postwar average,* calculate the approximate average annual military spending during the four or five years following the war. In your calculation of the postwar average, don't include the figure for the year immediately following the war, the year labeled *demobilization.* Military spending may remain at wartime levels for a brief period after the fighting has stopped, reflecting the costs of demobilizing the forces. Finally, in the right-hand column of the chart, note the ratio of prewar spending to postwar spending. Simply divide the prewar average into the postwar average, rounding the quotient to the nearest tenth. Notice that the ratio tells you how many times greater postwar spending was than prewar spending. We've given you a head start filling in the chart by entering the data for the War of 1812 and the Mexican War.

War	Military Spending			
	Prewar Average	**Wartime High**	**Postwar Average**	**Prewar Average: Postwar Average**
War of 1812	$3,300,000	$27,662,000	$11,000,000	1:3.3
Mexican War	$12,000,000	$46,000,000	$25,000,000	1:2.1
Spanish-American War				
Civil War				
World War I				
World War II				

2. How did the six wars listed in the chart affect the long-term pattern of military spending? Use data from the chart to support your answer.

_____

_____

_____

_____

3. Again looking at the chart in question 1, did defense spending after any of the wars listed ever drop to the prewar spending average?

_____

4. Table 8.2.2 shows annual military spending since 1945. The amounts in the table are in constant 2006 dollars: They've been adjusted for inflation. A dollar adjusted for inflation would purchase the same amount of military supplies or services in 1945 as it would in 2006. Looking at the table, describe briefly and in general terms the trend or pattern in annual military spending since the end of the Korean War.

_____

_____

_____

TABLE 8.2.2	U.S. Military Spending, Fiscal Years 1945–2006, in Constant 2006 Dollars	
1945	1,138,845,000,000	World War II ends
1946	619,120,000,000	Demobilization
1947	191,766,000,000	
1948	140,777,000,000	
1949	149,482,000,000	
1950	146,260,000,000	Korean War begins
1951	221,284,000,000	
1952	382,891,000,000	
1953	411,958,000,000	Korean War ends
1954	388,977,000,000	Demobilization
1955	340,780,000,000	
1956	325,751,000,000	
1957	332,469,000,000	
1958	324,812,000,000	
1959	327,150,000,000	
1960	325,246,000,000	
1961	327,221,000,000	
1962	354,541,000,000	
1963	357,664,000,000	
1964	357,727,000,000	
1965	329,583,000,000	Johnson escalates Vietnam War
1966	361,724,000,000	
1967	423,182,000,000	
1968	461,397,000,000	
1969	448,766,000,000	
1970	417,399,000,000	
1971	381,486,000,000	
1972	355,564,000,000	
1973	326,072,000,000	U.S. troops leave Vietnam
1974	319,830,000,000	
1975–1979	312,469,000,000	
1980–1989	411,916,000,000	
1990–1999	357,993,000,000	
2000	329,425,000,000	
2001	330,739,000,000	9/11 terrorist attacks; Afghanistan War
2002	367,741,000,000	
2003	419,569,000,000	Iraq War
2004	459,402,000,000	
2005	453,848,000,000	
2006	426,287,000,000	

NOTE: These figures are adjusted for inflation.
SOURCE: U.S. Department of Defense, National Defense Budget Estimates for FY 2006, Office of the Undersecretary of Defense (Comptroller), April 2005.

5. a. Estimate the average annual military expenditure since the end of the Korean War for the years the United States was not fighting a major war.

b. What percentage of military spending at the height of the Vietnam War does the average expenditure you calculated in part a represent? To find the figure, divide the average annual military expenditure since the end of the Korean War by the amount of military spending in 1968.

c. What does that comparison indicate about the budget requirements of the national security state—even when the nation is not at war?

_____

_____

_____

6. The cold war between the United States and the Soviet Union ended in 1991 with the collapse of the Soviet Union. Many observers at the time predicted that the end of the cold war would bring a "peace dividend," meaning that spending on the national security state would be cut and the savings redirected to education, the environment, medical care, even reducing taxes.

a. Using Table 8.2.2, compare yearly military expenditures in the 1980s (when the cold war was under way) with those in the 1990s (after the cold war had ended). What is the approximate average annual peace dividend the nation captured in the 1990s?

_____

b. What percentage of yearly military spending in the 1980s does the annual peace dividend represent? To make the calculation, divide the average annual peace dividend by the average yearly military expenditure in the 1980s.

_____

c. What factors might explain the relatively meager peace dividend?

_____

_____

_____

_____

7. President Bush's budget for fiscal year 2003 called for a substantial increase in defense spending. The president's budget message to Congress opened with these lines: "Americans will never forget the murderous events of September 11, 2001. They are for us what Pearl Harbor was to an earlier generation of Americans: a terrible wrong and a call to action." There is some historical basis for the parallel the president cited. The Japanese attack on Pearl Harbor awakened Americans to an unanticipated vulnerability—surprise attack from abroad by a hostile nation-state. The terrorist attacks on September 11 awakened Americans to another vulnerability—surprise attack from within by organized terrorists directed from abroad.

In response to the Japanese attack on Pearl Harbor, U.S. defense spending increased dramatically to prosecute World War II and to build the national security state. Make the following calculations to determine the validity of President Bush's comparison of the 9/11 attacks with Pearl Harbor.

a. Looking at the chart you completed in question 1, how many times greater, on average, was defense spending after World War II than defense spending before the war?

_____

b. Multiply the defense spending listed in Table 8.2.2 for 2002 by the factor you found in part a. Write the product here.

_____

c. The federal expenditures for fiscal year 2003 totaled $2.1 trillion. For 2004, total federal expenditures were $2.3 trillion. Do you think that the so-called war on terrorism will eventually command an increase in defense spending proportionately as great as the increase required to maintain national security after the Japanese attack on Pearl Harbor? Explain and support your answer.

8. The military spending figures in Table 8.2.2 do not include the costs of the wars in Afghanistan and Iraq. The Bush administration requested that spending for those wars be kept off-budget. So far, Congress has agreed. Neither do the figures in Table 8.2.2 include the increased costs of homeland security since the 9/11 attacks.[2] According to one estimate, through the end of fiscal year 2005, the wars in Afghanistan and Iraq—including reconstruction, foreign assistance, and training—have cost $314 billion.[3] To gauge the impact of the wars in Afghanistan and Iraq on military spending and the national security state, make the following calculations.

a. From Table 8.2.2, calculate average annual military spending for the years 2002–2005.

b. Take the $312 billion in special appropriations for the wars in Afghanistan and Iraq, average it over four years (2002–2005), and add that average to the figure you calculated in part a. The average annual amount spent on national security—including the wars in Afghanistan and Iraq—for the years 2002–2005 is:

c. How does average annual military spending for the years 2002–2005—including the costs of the wars in Afghanistan and Iraq—compare with military spending in 1953 at the height of the Korean War, and with military spending in 1968 at the height of the Vietnam War? Remember that because you are working with figures adjusted for inflation, a 1953 dollar, for example, has the same purchasing power as a 2005 dollar.

---

[2] For fiscal year 2006, the Bush administration requested $49.9 billion for homeland security. More information on spending for homeland security is available from the Center for Strategic and Budgetary Assessments at www.csbaonline.org.
[3] James Sterngold, "Casualty of War: The U.S. Economy," *San Francisco Chronicle*, July 17, 2005.

EXERCISE 8.3 How Much Regulation Is Enough? How Much Is Too Much?

INTRODUCTION

The dizzying pace of change in biotechnology has generated conflict between those who see the promise of medical cures and corporate profits, and those who fear the damage emerging technologies might inflict on the public. For federal regulators, the challenge is determining the right amount of regulation—rules that protect the general welfare without imposing undue delay on patients waiting for new treatments or undue costs on industry. For the American people, protection from hazardous therapies and medications is of paramount concern. For the biotechnology and pharmaceutical industries, the bottom line is markets and profits. In recent years, the politics of regulation has become ever more contentious, pitting public interest groups against the deregulatory fervor of the Bush administration.

A case study in the pros and cons of government regulation of new medical technology is gene therapy: "Genes, which are carried on chromosomes, are the basic physical and functional units of heredity.... When genes are altered so that the encoded proteins are unable to carry out their normal functions, genetic disorders can result. Gene therapy is a technique for correcting defective genes responsible for disease development. Researchers may use one of several approaches for correcting faulty genes."[1]

The problem of determining how much regulation is enough in the field of gene therapy was brought to light by the death in 1999 of an 18-year-old patient. Jesse Gelsinger had been undergoing gene therapy for a liver disease in a clinical trial at the University of Pennsylvania's Institute of Gene Therapy. (Many of the human subjects in clinical trials are suffering from life-threatening illnesses; the trials offer them their last hope of a cure.) Federal investigators later determined that the researchers had violated several federal regulations.

Two government offices are responsible for monitoring gene therapy clinical trials. The Food and Drug Administration (FDA) is the primary watchdog; it tracks adverse reactions until the new therapy is approved. The second is the Recombinant DNA Advisory Committee (RAC) of the National Institutes of Health (NIH). The RAC was created to reassure Americans who are wary of genetic engineering; its role is primarily advisory, although it does approve the procedures for clinical trials. After the death of Jesse Gelsinger, the FDA and RAC proposed new rules for gene therapy protocols.

Despite some optimism about gene therapy in the years after the Gelsinger incident, hopes were dashed again when "the FDA placed a temporary halt on all gene therapy trials using retroviral vectors in blood stem cells. The FDA took this action after it learned that a second child treated in a French gene therapy trial had developed a leukemia-like condition."[2] On February 28, 2003, FDA's Biologics Response Modifiers Advisory Committee (now called Cell, Tissue, and Gene Therapies Advisory Committee) issued a report calling for new safeguards in the use of retroviruses in gene therapy.[3] As of this writing, the FDA has not adopted those recommendations.

ASSIGNMENT

Study Readings 8.3.1 and 8.3.2 to answer the questions that follow.

---

[1] Doegenomes.com: http://www.ornl.gov/sci/techresources/Human_Genome/medicine/genetherapy.shtml.
[2] Doegenomes.com: http://www.ornl.gov/sci/techresources/Human_Genome/medicine/genetherapy.shtml.
[3] Report available at: http://www.fdaadvisorycommittee.com/FDC/AdvisoryCommittee/Committees/Cellular%2c+Tissue+and+Gene+Therapies/022803_genetherapy/022803_genetherapyR.htm.

READING 8.3.1 Human Gene Therapy: Harsh Lessons, High Hopes[4]

In the 10 years since that first genetic treatment on Sept. 14, 1990, the hyperbole has exceeded the results. Worldwide, researchers launched more than 400 clinical trials to test gene therapy against a wide array of illnesses. Surprisingly, cancer has dominated the research. Even more surprising, little has worked.

"There was initially a great burst of enthusiasm that lasted three, four years where a couple of hundred trials got started all over the world," says Anderson, now at the University of Southern California in Los Angeles. "Then we came to realize that nothing was really working at the clinical level."

Abbey S. Meyers, president of the National Organization for Rare Disorders Inc., an umbrella organization of patients' groups, is much more blunt. "We haven't even taken one baby step beyond that first clinical experiment," Meyers says. "It has hardly gotten anywhere. Over the last 10 years, I have been very disappointed."

And then things got worse.

In September 1999, a patient died from a reaction to a gene therapy treatment at the University of Pennsylvania's Institute of Human Gene Therapy in Philadelphia. Jesse Gelsinger, an exuberant 18-year-old from Tucson, Arizona, suffered from a broken gene that causes one of those puzzling metabolic diseases of genetic medicine. An optimistic, altruistic Gelsinger went to Philadelphia to help advance the science that might eventually cure his type of illness. Instead, the experiment killed him.

In the aftermath of his death, there has been a flurry of activity to minimize the chance of future accidental deaths. The Food and Drug Administration, along with the National Institutes of Health, launched several investigations of the University of Pennsylvania studies and others. The inquiries provided disappointing news: Gene therapy researchers were not following all of the federal rules requiring them to report unexpected adverse events associated with the gene therapy trials; worse, some scientists were asking that problems not be made public. And then came the allegations that there were other unreported deaths attributed to genetic treatments, at least six in all.

"Probably the clearest evidence of the system not working is that only 35 to 37 of 970 serious adverse events from [a common type of gene therapy trial] were reported to the NIH" as required, says LeRoy Walters, the recently retired head of the Kennedy Institute of Ethics at Georgetown University and former chairman of NIH's Recombinant DNA Advisory Committee. "That is fewer than 5 percent of the serious adverse events."

The news hit the clinical trial community like a thunderclap. The consequences have been immediate and wide-ranging, and may threaten future research.

"Participation in gene therapy trials is way down because the public is not sure what to make of this," says Philip Noguchi, M.D., director of the Cellular and Genetic Therapy Division in FDA's Center for Biologic Evaluation and Research (CBER). "They want to know what the government is doing to help restore the confidence in this field."

Responding to the Crisis

The federal government moved quickly to do just that. FDA immediately shut down the trial in which Gelsinger had volunteered, and all clinical gene transfer trials at the University of Pennsylvania in January. The university went on to severely restrict the research of its once-high-flying gene therapy

---

[4] Source: From Larry Thompson, "Human Gene Therapy: Harsh Lessons, High Hopes," *FDA Consumer Magazine*, September–October 2000: www.fda.gov/fdac/features/2000/500_gene.html.

institute director James Wilson, M.D., announcing in May that all his work would be confined to animal and laboratory experiments and that he would be barred from conducting studies in people.

FDA also suspended gene therapy trials at St. Elizabeth's Medical Center in Boston, a major teaching affiliate of Tufts University School of Medicine, which sought to use gene therapy to reverse heart disease, because scientists there failed to follow protocols and may have contributed to at least one patient death. FDA also temporarily suspended two liver cancer studies sponsored by the Schering-Plough Corporation because of technical similarities to the University of Pennsylvania study.

Moreover, as nervousness spread through the field in the months after revelations about Gelsinger's death, some research groups voluntarily suspended gene therapy studies, including two experiments sponsored by the Cystic Fibrosis Foundation and studies at Beth Israel Deaconess Medical Center in Boston aimed at hemophilia. The scientists paused to review their studies and make sure they learned from the mistakes made at the University of Pennsylvania.

In March, the Department of Health and Human Services announced two initiatives by FDA and NIH. The Gene Therapy Clinical Trial Monitoring Plan is designed to ratchet up the level of scrutiny with additional reporting requirements for study sponsors. A series of Gene Transfer Safety Symposia was designed to get researchers to talk to each other, to share their results about unexpected problems and to make sure that everyone knows the rules.

In addition, FDA launched random inspections of 70 clinical trials in more than two dozen gene therapy programs nationwide and instituted new reporting requirements. "We see the need to get the concept across that this is for keeps," says FDA's Noguchi. "You can be sloppy when you are dealing with a scientific paper, but you can't be sloppy when you are dealing with a human. Everything matters."

So far, the inspections only suggest that one other program appears to be in trouble, he says, but by the fall, "We should be able to say accurately the state of the art of gene therapy and where it needs to improve."

Meanwhile, President Clinton announced more "new actions designed to ensure that individuals are adequately informed about the potential risks and benefits of participating in research... and steps designed to address the potential financial conflicts of interest faced by researchers." In addition, the President said in May, "We are also sending the Congress a new legislative proposal to authorize civil monetary penalties for researchers and institutions found to be in violation of regulations governing human clinical trials." If the legislation passes, FDA will, for the first time for drugs and biologics, have the power to essentially fine researchers and their institutions, up to $250,000 and $1 million, respectively.

"This is a clear message," HHS Secretary Donna E. Shalala, Ph.D., said in May, "that we intend to get serious."...

The Gelsinger Case

When Orkin and Motulsky [Orkin and Motulsky were two doctors who had been appointed to an FDA committee to review the efficacy of the NIH's investment in gene therapy trials] reported on the technical limitations of gene transfer techniques five years ago, they virtually predicted problems in the clinic. During that same December meeting at which Orkin and Motulsky made their disheartening report, the RAC approved the University of Pennsylvania gene therapy trial for ornithine transcarboxylase deficiency (OTCD). FDA, too, allowed the study to proceed.

The treatment idea was fairly straightforward. OTCD occurs when a baby inherits a broken gene that prevents the liver from making an enzyme needed to break down ammonia. With the OTCD gene isolated, the University of Pennsylvania researchers packaged it in a replication-defective adenovirus. To reach the target cells in the liver, the Philadelphia scientists wanted to inject the adenovirus directly into the hepatic artery that leads to that organ. Some members of the NIH RAC objected, fearing that direct delivery to the liver was dangerous. Nonetheless, after a vigorous public discussion with the University of Pennsylvania researchers, the RAC voted for approval of the study.

At age 18, Jesse Gelsinger was in good health, but was not truly a healthy teenager. He had a rare form of OTCD that appeared not to be linked to his parents, but the genetic defect arose spontaneously in his body after birth. During his youth, he had many episodes of hospitalization, including an incident just a year before the OTCD trial in which he nearly died from a coma induced by liver failure. But a strict diet that allowed only a few grams of protein per day and a pile of pills controlled his disease to the point where he appeared to be a normally active teenager. With the encouragement of his father, Paul Gelsinger, Jesse volunteered for the study, and when he was initially evaluated, his medical condition qualified him to participate. Gelsinger received the experimental treatment in September 1999. Four days later, he was dead. No one is really sure exactly why the gene therapy treatment caused his death, but it appears that his immune system launched a raging attack on the adenovirus carrier. Then an overwhelming cascade of organ failures occurred, starting with jaundice, and progressing to a blood-clotting disorder, kidney failure, lung failure, and ultimately brain death.

In its investigation, FDA found a series of serious deficiencies in the way that the University of Pennsylvania conducted the OTCD gene therapy trial, some more serious than others. For example, researchers entered Gelsinger into the trial as a substitute for another volunteer who dropped out, but Gelsinger's high ammonia levels at the time of the treatment should have excluded him from the study. Moreover, the university failed to immediately report that two patients had experienced serious side effects from the gene therapy, as required in the study design, and the deaths of monkeys given a similar treatment were never included in the informed consent discussion.

FDA's discussions with the university remain ongoing.

READING 8.3.2 ENHANCING THE PROTECTION OF HUMAN SUBJECTS IN GENE TRANSFER RESEARCH AT THE NIH[5]

Protocol Review

- Safety will be best protected if subjects are not enrolled in novel gene transfer trials until RAC [Recombinant DNA Advisory Committee] discussion has occurred and the investigator has responded to the RAC recommendations.
- The timing of review of gene transfer protocols by RAC, the local IRB [Institutional Review Board] and IBC [Institutional Biosafety Committee], and FDA should be altered to ensure that RAC can function as an effective advisory committee to investigators, institutional IRBs and IBCs, and FDA. Specifically,
- The requirement that the investigator obtain IRB approval prior to submission to OBA [Office of Biotechnology Activities]/RAC should be eliminated. This change would allow investigators to receive RAC input at an earlier stage of protocol development.
- IBC approval should be withheld until RAC review is complete. In the case of non-novel protocols, IBC approval can be granted as soon as the IBC is notified that the protocol has been deemed non-novel.
- In the case of novel protocols, IBC approval must be withheld until after RAC discussion and the investigator has responded to the review, thereby, preventing the initiation of a trial prior to RAC review.

---

[5] Source: Advisory Committee to the Director, Working Group on NIH Oversight of Clinical Gene Transfer Research, "Executive Summary," in *Enhancing the Protection of Human Subjects in Gene Transfer Research at the National Institutes of Health*, July 12, 2000: www.nih.gov/about/director/07122000.htm.

- RAC should complete its review and revision of the definition of "novel" gene transfer protocols and the process/mechanism for determining whether or not a protocol is "novel." Public comment and input should be solicited.
- To clarify the types of research that are subject to the NIH Guidelines, RAC should complete its review and revision of the definition of gene transfer research to ensure that all applicable and appropriate areas of research are subject to oversight and review.

Serious Adverse Event Reporting

- Public discussion of serious adverse events is an important component of the oversight process.
- NIH/OBA should continue to receive from investigators reports of serious adverse events. The Working Group acknowledged that FDA is working on a proposed rule to make public some information regarding serious adverse events in gene transfer, and encourages the agency to move expeditiously in meeting this goal.
- Serious adverse events should not be considered trade secrets or proprietary, and must be reported to RAC.
- Data in aggregate made available to the public should be analyzed and interpreted.
- All reasonable measures must be taken to protect the privacy of the individual(s) who suffered the adverse event, without compromising the health of others in similar trials.
- A majority of the Working Group recommended that NIH and FDA must work together to simplify, streamline, and harmonize reporting of serious adverse events. This includes clarification of the timing requirements for reporting specific types of serious adverse events.
- NIH should work with FDA to expand and enhance education and outreach programs to investigators and sponsors conducting gene transfer research to inform them of their reporting obligations.
- NIH should explore ways for promoting the communication of serious adverse events to the relevant IBCs and IRBs.
- A standing body should be established to conduct ongoing analyses of adverse event data. This body should include basic scientists, clinicians, patient advocates, and ethicists. Additional ad hoc members can be appointed for their expertise on an as needed basis. This group would:
  —review all reports of adverse events,
  —analyze the data for trends,
  —develop a cumulative report that would be presented annually at a public RAC meeting and made available to the public, and
  —identify trends or even single events that may warrant further public discussion or federal action.

Professional and Public Education

- NIH/OBA should target education efforts at specialty clinical centers where gene transfer studies are likely to be conducted or subjects recruited, such as CF centers or hemophilia clinics. In addition, OBA/RAC should produce a pamphlet or brochure on gene transfer research targeted to families and consumers and post such information on its website.
- In collaboration with [Office for Human Research Protections (OHRP)] and other relevant groups, OBA should continue its initiatives for a series of workshops for IRBs and IBCs on gene transfer research.
- OBA should work with OHRP to encourage IRB cooperation in ensuring that human subjects are not enrolled in gene transfer trials until RAC deems a protocol non-novel, or if novel, the protocol has completed the RAC review process.
- NIH should work with OHRP to encourage the inclusion of additional resource sites for information regarding participation in clinical trials in the informed consent form. For gene transfer clinical trials, this information should include a reference to the RAC review process and directions regarding how to obtain relevant information from OBA/RAC.

1. Which federal rules did the gene therapy researchers who treated Jesse Gelsinger violate?

2. How did the FDA respond to the discovery of rule violations in gene therapy clinical trials?

3. Jesse Gelsinger volunteered for gene therapy in hopes of curing his liver disease. Families like the Gelsingers, along with researchers and biotechnology companies, often argue that increased federal regulations—such as those proposed in Reading 8.3.2—impede scientific progress and unduly limit the number of clinical trials available to people who are critically ill. They also argue that the federal government overreacted to Jesse Gelsinger's death when the FDA and NIH closed down the University of Pennsylvania's clinical trials and then issued new regulations and guidelines. Others argue, however, that the public at large requires vigorous protection by governmental agencies that have the scientific expertise to assess the merits of new medical protocols and the independence to regulate researchers who have too much at stake in the success of their own protocols. Do you think the FDA and NIH regulatory response to the Gelsinger death was justified? Explain and support your answer.

CHAPTER 9

The Judiciary

EXERCISE 9.1 Establishing Judicial Review

INTRODUCTION

Wielding the power of judicial review, courts today routinely strike down as unconstitutional legislative and executive branch actions at the national, state, and local levels of government. For critics of the nation's courts, judicial review is antidemocratic: When politically unaccountable federal courts, for example, invalidate legislation passed by duly elected members of Congress and signed into law by the president of the United States, the will of the people is denied. For proponents, judicial review is an essential restraint on the will of the majority, and a safeguard of individual liberties and minority rights.

Dramatic controversies over the Supreme Court's exercise of judicial review punctuate the Republic's history. Two examples: In 1857, in *Dred Scott v. Sanford*, the Court declared unconstitutional a federal law—the Missouri Compromise—banning slavery in the northern territories. The ruling inflamed northern opinion, discredited the Court in the eyes of many, and hurled the nation toward civil war. Senator John P. Hale of New Hampshire responded by introducing a resolution to abolish the Supreme Court! Disputes over judicial review flared again in the 1930s, when the Supreme Court declared unconstitutional many New Deal measures aimed at rescuing the nation from the depths of the Great Depression. President Franklin D. Roosevelt counterattacked by demanding that Congress enact legislation that would have created six new seats on the Court so that Roosevelt could fill them with justices who would affirm the constitutionality of his legislative program.

When the framers took up judicial review at the Constitutional Convention in Philadelphia in 1787, it proved less divisive; the vast majority of delegates supported the principle that the federal judiciary would be the final authority interpreting law and the Constitution.[1] Several clauses in the

---

[1] Henry J. Abraham, *The Judicial Process*, 7th ed. (New York: Oxford University Press, 1998), pp. 335–336

Constitution allude to judicial review, but the framers declined to spell out the power because it raised an unsettling question: Would judicial supremacy over *the text* of the Constitution entail a "judicial veto" over *the actions* of the legislative and executive branches? James Madison rejected such a broad notion of judicial supremacy, but other Constitution-makers claimed in their state ratifying conventions that the judicial check would indeed limit the national government. Alexander Hamilton, in "Federalist No. 78," asserted that the Supreme Court must be vested with the power of judicial review, but that even so armed, it would remain the weakest of the branches.

The Supreme Court established its power to declare an act of Congress unconstitutional in *Marbury v. Madison* (1803) by ruling that Section 13 of the Judiciary Act of 1789—a federal law—was contradicted, and trumped, by the Constitution. At stake in the case: whether a Federalist Party appointee, William Marbury, would serve—or be denied—a five-year term as a justice of the peace on a Washington, DC, court. Few disputes to reach the Supreme Court have been substantively so insignificant; yet because of the participants' stature, the high political drama of the case, and the force of Chief Justice John Marshall's opinion, few cases have commanded as much attention from scholars and students.

In the election of 1800, for the first time, the Federalist Party lost control of Congress and the presidency. Federalists feared that the victorious Republican Party—led by Thomas Jefferson, the new president—would savage the young government and bring the nation to ruin. To preserve Federalist influence as a bastion against the Republican tide, the outgoing Federalist president, John Adams, joined with the lame-duck[2] Federalist Congress to create fifty-nine new positions in the judiciary. Adams filled these posts with loyal Federalist Party judges, often referred to as "midnight appointments" to indicate the desperate and last-minute nature of Adams's gambit.

John Marshall, a Federalist and Adams's secretary of state, was responsible for certifying and delivering to the new appointees their judicial commissions, documents authorizing them to take their seats on the bench. Unfortunately for seventeen of the new appointees, Marshall was in a hurry. Adams had nominated and the Federalist Congress had confirmed Marshall as the new chief justice of the Supreme Court. In his rush to step down as secretary of state and take up his new post, Marshall left seventeen judicial commissions on his desk, undelivered. The new Republican president, Jefferson, found the commissions and ordered his secretary of state, James Madison, not to deliver them—thereby retaliating against the Federalist effort to pack the judiciary and setting the stage for a confrontation between the executive and judicial branches.

William Marbury and three other Adams appointees waiting to receive their commissions sued to force Madison to deliver the documents. They took their case directly to the Supreme Court and demanded that the Court issue an order, called a *writ of mandamus*, compelling Madison to carry out his duty as secretary of state. Because Marshall agreed to hear Marbury's case before any lower court had examined it, the Supreme Court exercised original jurisdiction.[3]

Presiding over the case spawned by his own negligence, Marshall appeared trapped. If he issued the writ, Madison would defy it. Having no way to physically compel Madison, Marshall and the Court would appear impotent. Declining to issue the writ, on the other hand, would appear a cowardly endorsement by default of Madison's dereliction of his duty as secretary of state.

Marshall extricated the Court from this dilemma by ruling that Section 13 of the Judiciary Act of 1789 had unconstitutionally bestowed on the Supreme Court a new power: to issue writs of mandamus—*under its original jurisdiction*—to public officials who failed to perform their official duties. Marshall argued that Section 13 expanded the original jurisdiction of the Supreme Court beyond that specified in the Constitution, and that when an act of Congress conflicts with the

---

[2] Before the Twentieth Amendment was ratified in 1933, Congress would typically not adjourn until March of the year following the election. Since the new president was not sworn in until March, Adams had several months after his defeat to push legislation through the still-Federalist Congress.

[3] Many aspects of Marshall's decision and the events surrounding it remain disputed by scholars. A close examination of Section 13 of the Judiciary Act of 1789 indicates that it did not broaden the Court's original jurisdiction. Marshall may have recognized this because he did not even cite in his decision the language in Section 13 that he was declaring unconstitutional. Furthermore, Article III, Section 2 of the Constitution does not stipulate that the Court has original jurisdiction *only* in cases "affecting Ambassadors, other public Ministers and Consuls, and those in which a State shall be a Party." Scholars have pointed out that because many members of the Congress that drafted and enacted the Judiciary Act of 1789 had been delegates to the Constitutional Convention, they probably would not have passed a law that conflicted with the Constitution. See, for example, "The 200th Anniversary of *Marbury v. Madison*: The Reasons We Should Still Care About the Decision, and the Lingering Questions It Left Behind," by Joel B. Grossman, at http://writ.news.findlaw.com/commentary/20030224_grossman.html.

Constitution, that legislation must not be allowed to stand. Marshall's interpretation of the Constitution circumscribed Congress' power and expanded that of his own Court.

Today, no act of Congress or the president, or of state and local governments, is immune to judicial scrutiny. The bracing, panoramic scope of judicial review and the centralization of power in the nation's highest court would shock even those who struggled early in the Republic's history with defining the Court's power. However, the full potential of judicial review took time to develop. After *Marbury*, the Court waited over half a century before striking down another act of Congress. In the late nineteenth century, the Court exercised judicial review more frequently, but limited its reach mainly to the problem of state government regulation of private economic matters. In the twentieth century, and especially in the 1950s–1970s, the Court discarded restraint and vastly expanded its jurisdiction into the realms of civil rights and civil liberties, fundamentally reshaping American society. Today's justices, and many observers of the Court, are divided over the wisdom of this course. Do the justices too often *make* law instead of *interpret* law? Dissenting from the majority opinion in *Webster v. Reproductive Health Services* (1989), an abortion rights case, Justice Antonin Scalia wrote that the majority were needlessly prolonging "this Court's self-awarded sovereignty over a field where it has little proper business since the answers to most of the cruel questions posed are political and not judicial."

In the *Marbury* case, recognizing the comparative weakness of the Court, Marshall deftly avoided confrontations with the legislative and executive branches. By the late twentieth century, however, with its power handsomely enlarged, the Court stood as an equal and coordinate—not inferior—branch of the federal government. So confident were the justices in the power and position of the Court that they waged battle directly with President Richard Nixon. In *The United States v. Nixon* (1974), the Court ordered Nixon to turn over secretly recorded tapes containing material politically fatal to him. The president yielded to the Court's order, affirming that the justices of the High Court were indeed the final arbiters of the Constitution—even in a direct confrontation with the chief executive.

ASSIGNMENT

Study Reading 9.1.1, an excerpt from *Marbury v. Madison*, and Reading 9.1.2, an excerpt from "Federalist No. 78," and answer the questions that follow.

READING 9.1.1 *MARBURY V. MADISON*, 5 U.S. 137 (1803)

That the people have an original right to establish, for their future government, such principles as, in their opinion, shall most conduce to their own happiness, is the basis on which the whole American fabric has been erected. The exercise of this original right is a very great exertion; nor can it nor ought it to be frequently repeated. The principles, therefore, so established are deemed fundamental. And as the authority, from which they proceed, is supreme, and can seldom act, they are designed to be permanent.

This original and supreme will organizes the government, and assigns to different departments their respective powers. It may either stop here; or establish certain limits not to be transcended by those departments.

The government of the United States is of the latter description. The powers of the legislature are defined and limited; and that those limits may not be mistaken or forgotten, the constitution is written. To what purpose are powers limited, and to what purpose is that limitation committed to writing; if these limits may, at any time, be passed by those intended to be restrained? The distinction between a government with limited and unlimited powers is abolished, if those limits do not confine the persons on whom they are imposed, and if acts prohibited and acts allowed are of equal obligation. It is a proposition too plain to be contested, that the constitution controls any legislative act repugnant to it; or, that the legislature may alter the constitution by an ordinary act.

Between these alternatives there is no middle ground. The constitution is either a superior, paramount law, unchangeable by ordinary means, or it is on a level with ordinary legislative acts, and like other acts, is alterable when the legislature shall please to alter it.

If the former part of the alternative be true, then a legislative act contrary to the constitution is not law: if the latter part be true, then written constitutions are absurd attempts, on the part of the people, to limit a power in its own nature illimitable.

Certainly all those who have framed written constitutions contemplate them as forming the fundamental and paramount law of the nation, and consequently the theory of every such government must be, that an act of the legislature repugnant to the constitution is void.

This theory is essentially attached to a written constitution, and is consequently to be considered by this court as one of the fundamental principles of our society....

It is emphatically the province and duty of the judicial department to say what the law is. Those who apply the rule to particular cases, must of necessity expound and interpret that rule. If two laws conflict with each other, the courts must decide on the operation of each. So if a law be in opposition to the constitution: if both the law and the constitution apply to a particular case, so that the court must either decide that case conformably to the law, disregarding the constitution; or conformably to the constitution, disregarding the law: the court must determine which of these conflicting rules governs the case. This is of the very essence of judicial duty.

If then the courts are to regard the constitution; and the constitution is superior to any ordinary act of the legislature; the constitution, and not such ordinary act, must govern the case to which they both apply.

Those then who controvert the principle that the constitution is to be considered, in court, as a paramount law, are reduced to the necessity of maintaining that courts must close their eyes on the constitution, and see only the law.

This doctrine would subvert the very foundation of all written constitutions. It would declare that an act, which, according to the principles and theory of our government, is entirely void, is yet, in practice, completely obligatory. It would declare, that if the legislature shall do what is expressly forbidden, such act, notwithstanding the express prohibition, is in reality effectual. It would be giving to the legislature a practical and real omnipotence with the same breath which professes to restrict their powers within narrow limits. It is prescribing limits, and declaring that those limits may be passed at pleasure....

It is also not entirely unworthy of observation, that in declaring what shall be the supreme law of the land, the constitution itself is first mentioned; and not the laws of the United States generally, but those only which shall be made in pursuance of the constitution, have that rank.

Thus, the particular phraseology of the constitution of the United States confirms and strengthens the principle, supposed to be essential to all written constitutions, that a law repugnant to the constitution is void, and that courts, as well as other departments, are bound by that instrument.

The rule [meaning the law] must be discharged.

READING 9.1.2 ALEXANDER HAMILTON, "FEDERALIST NO. 78"

... Whoever attentively considers the different departments of power must perceive, that, in a government in which they are separated from each other, the judiciary, from the nature of its functions, will always be the least dangerous to the political rights of the Constitution; because it will be least in a capacity to annoy or injure them. The Executive not only dispenses the honors, but holds the sword of the community. The legislature not only commands the purse, but prescribes the rules by which the duties and rights of every citizen are to be regulated. The judiciary, on the contrary, has no influence over either the sword or the purse; no direction either of the strength or of the wealth of the society; and can take no active resolution whatever. It may truly be said to have neither FORCE nor WILL, but merely judgment; and must ultimately depend upon the aid of the executive arm even for the efficacy of its judgments.

This simple view of the matter suggests several important consequences. It proves incontestably, that the judiciary is beyond comparison the weakest of the three departments of power; that it can never attack with success either of the other two; and that all possible care is requisite to enable it to defend itself against their attacks. It equally proves, that though individual oppression may now and then proceed from the courts of justice, the general liberty of the people can never be endangered from that quarter; I mean so long as the judiciary remains truly distinct from both the legislature and the Executive. For I agree, that "there is no liberty, if the power of judging be not separated from the legislative and executive powers."

And it proves, in the last place, that as liberty can have nothing to fear from the judiciary alone, but would have every thing to fear from its union with either of the other departments; that as all the effects of such a union must ensue from a dependence of the former on the latter, notwithstanding a nominal and apparent separation; that as, from the natural feebleness of the judiciary, it is in continual jeopardy of being overpowered, awed, or influenced by its co-ordinate branches; and that as nothing can contribute so much to its firmness and independence as permanency in office, this quality may therefore be justly regarded as an indispensable ingredient in its constitution, and, in a great measure, as the citadel of the public justice and the public security.

The complete independence of the courts of justice is peculiarly essential in a limited Constitution. By a limited Constitution, I understand one which contains certain specified exceptions to the legislative authority; such, for instance, as that it shall pass no bills of attainder, no ex post facto laws, and the like. Limitations of this kind can be preserved in practice no other way than through the medium of courts of justice, whose duty it must be to declare all acts contrary to the manifest tenor of the Constitution void. Without this, all the reservations of particular rights or privileges would amount to nothing.

Some perplexity respecting the rights of the courts to pronounce legislative acts void, because contrary to the Constitution, has arisen from an imagination that the doctrine would imply a superiority of the judiciary to the legislative power. It is urged that the authority which can declare the acts of another void, must necessarily be superior to the one whose acts may be declared void. As this doctrine is of great importance in all the American constitutions, a brief discussion of the ground on which it rests cannot be unacceptable.

There is no position which depends on clearer principles, than that every act of a delegated authority, contrary to the tenor of the commission under which it is exercised, is void. No legislative act, therefore, contrary to the Constitution, can be valid. To deny this, would be to affirm, that the deputy is greater than his principal; that the servant is above his master; that the representatives of the people are superior to the people themselves; that men acting by virtue of powers, may do not only what their powers do not authorize, but what they forbid.

If it be said that the legislative body are themselves the constitutional judges of their own powers, and that the construction they put upon them is conclusive upon the other departments, it may be answered, that this cannot be the natural presumption, where it is not to be collected from any particular provisions in the Constitution. It is not otherwise to be supposed, that the Constitution could intend to enable the representatives of the people to substitute their will to that of their constituents. It is far more rational to suppose, that the courts were designed to be an intermediate body between the people and the legislature, in order, among other things, to keep the latter within the limits assigned to their authority. The interpretation of the laws is the proper and peculiar province of the courts. A constitution is, in fact, and must be regarded by the judges, as a fundamental law. It therefore belongs to them to ascertain its meaning, as well as the meaning of any particular act proceeding from the legislative body. If there should happen to be an irreconcilable variance between the two, that which has the superior obligation and validity ought, of course, to be preferred; or, in other words, the Constitution ought to be preferred to the statute [meaning the law], the intention of the people to the intention of their agents....

---

1. According to the excerpts from Marshall's ruling in Reading 9.1.1 and from "Federalist No. 78" in Reading 9.1.2, if the Constitution says one thing and a law passed by Congress says another, which must give way and why? Cite passages from each reading to support your answer.

2. According to Marshall's ruling, the clause in Article III, Section 2 that specifies the original jurisdiction of the Court is restrictive—meaning that the types of original jurisdiction authorized are the only ones granted by the Constitution to the Court. But some scholars assert that Marshall and his colleagues misinterpreted the Constitution, and that this clause in Article III, Section 2 does not necessarily preclude Congress from adding to the original jurisdiction of the Supreme Court. Examine carefully this excerpt of Article III, Section 2:

"In all cases affecting Ambassadors, other public Ministers and Consuls, and those in which a State shall be a Party, the supreme Court shall have original jurisdiction. In all the other Cases before mentioned, the supreme Court shall have appellate Jurisdiction, both as to Law and Fact, with such Exceptions, and under such Regulations as the Congress shall make."

Do you think that Marshall or his critics have the stronger argument? Cite specific language—or the lack thereof—in the excerpt above to support your position.

3. If you sided with Marshall in question 2, rewrite the passage in Article III, Section 2 to *expressly preclude* the Supreme Court from exercising original jurisdiction in cases other than those specified. If you sided with Marshall's critics in question 2, rewrite the passage in Article III, Section 2 to *expressly authorize* the Supreme Court to exercise original jurisdiction in cases other than those specified.

_____

_____

_____

_____

_____

_____

4. In Readings 9.1.1 and 9.1.2, do Marshall and Hamilton suggest that judicial review is a narrow power that must be exercised cautiously, or a broad, unlimited power? Cite specific language—or the lack thereof—in each reading to support your answer.

_____

_____

_____

_____

_____

_____

_____

5. In Reading 9.1.2, Hamilton argues that the courts are the weakest of the three departments of power (branches of government). How does Hamilton support his argument? Cite specific language in Reading 9.1.2 to support your answer.

_____

_____

_____

_____

_____

_____

6. The threat that judicial review poses to the legislative and executive branches depends on the significance of the legislation the Court strikes down and on how frequently the Court exercises the power of judicial review. Consider the quantitative aspect of judicial review. Between 1803 and 1899, for example, the Court declared unconstitutional in whole or in part twenty-six acts of Congress.[4] Between 1986 and its decision in *McConnell v. FEC* in 2003, the Court presided over by Chief Justice William Rehnquist declared unconstitutional in whole or in part forty acts of Congress.

a. Describe how the frequency with which the Court strikes down acts of Congress has changed.

b. Does the change you described in part a support or undermine Hamilton's prediction that the judiciary would be the weakest of the three departments of power? Explain and support your answer.

7. We take for granted today that the Supreme Court exclusively has the power to determine what's constitutional and what's not. But a judicial monopoly on constitutional interpretation was not inevitable. In Reading 9.1.3, President Thomas Jefferson suggested two alternative approaches to constitutional interpretation. Identify each approach and explain its strengths and weaknesses.

a. Jefferson's first approach and its strengths and weaknesses:

---

[4] A list of the acts of Congress held unconstitutional in whole or in part by the Supreme Court is at http://www.gpoaccess.gov/constitution/html/acts.html. Number 1 is listed as an "Act of September 24, 1789 (1 Stat. 81, Sec. 13, in part)." This is the Judiciary Act of 1789. Under a brief description of the act, you'll find the citation of the Supreme Court decision that struck down the act. In this case, of course, the decision is "*Marbury v. Madison*, 5 U.S. (1 Cir.) 137 (1803)."

b. Jefferson's second approach and its strengths and weaknesses:

READING 9.1.3 THOMAS JEFFERSON TO W. H. TORRANCE, MONTICELLO, JUNE 11, 1815

... whether the judges are invested with exclusive authority to decide on the constitutionality of a law, has been heretofore a subject of consideration with me in the exercise of official duties. Certainly there is not a word in the constitution which has given that power to them more than to the executive or legislative branches. Questions of property, of character and of crime being ascribed to the judges, through a definite course of legal proceeding, laws involving such questions belong, of course, to them; and as they decide on them ultimately and without appeal, they of course decide *for themselves*. The constitutional validity of the law or laws again prescribing executive action, and to be administered by that branch ultimately and without appeal, the executive must decide for *themselves* also, whether, under the constitution, they are valid or not. So also as to laws governing the proceedings of the legislature, that body must judge *for itself* the constitutionality of the law, and equally without appeal or control from its co-ordinate branches. And, in general, that branch which is to act ultimately, and without appeal, on any law, is the rightful expositor of the validity of the law, uncontrolled by the opinions of the other co-ordinate authorities. It may be said that contradictory decisions may arise in such case, and produce inconvenience. This is possible, and is a necessary failing in all human proceedings. Yet the prudence of the public functionaries, and authority of public opinion, will generally produce accommodation.... This is what I believe myself to be sound. But there is another opinion entertained by some men of such judgment and information as to lessen my confidence in my own. That is, that the legislature alone is the exclusive expounder of the sense of the constitution, in every part of it whatever. And they allege in its support, that this branch has authority to impeach and punish a member of either of the others acting contrary to its declaration of the sense of the constitution. It may indeed be answered, that an act may still be valid although the party is punished for it, right or wrong. However, this opinion which ascribes exclusive exposition to the legislature, merits respect for its safety, there being in the body of the nation a control over them, which, if expressed by rejection on the subsequent exercise of their elective franchise, enlists public opinion against their exposition, and encourages a judge or executive on a future occasion to adhere to their former opinion. Between these two doctrines, every one has a right to choose, and I know of no third meriting any respect.

EXERCISE 9.2 Judicial Activism Versus Judicial Restraint: The Supreme Court and the Juvenile Death Penalty

INTRODUCTION

The debate between proponents of judicial activism and advocates of judicial restraint is as old as the Republic. The debate centers on this question: What is the proper role of the federal courts, particularly the Supreme Court, in the American constitutional system? The answer to this question cannot be found in the Constitution because the framers did not spell out the judicial powers. In fact, even judicial review—the extraordinary power of the federal courts to decide the constitutionality of legislative and executive branch actions—is missing from the Constitution. It was Chief Justice John Marshall, ruling in *Marbury v. Madison* (1803), who bestowed judicial review on the courts (see Exercise 9.1).

That decision sparked an early debate about the role of the Supreme Court, with detractors claiming that the Court had overreached in declaring an act of Congress unconstitutional and in claiming for itself a power that is nowhere specified in the Constitution. Controversy over the role of the Supreme Court in the constitutional system flared again in 1857, when the Court waded into the great controversy of the day—the question of slavery in the western territories. In *Scott v. Sanford* the Court ruled that slaves are not citizens of the United States under the provisions of the Constitution and went on to declare the Missouri Compromise unconstitutional. For the first time since *Marbury*, the Court exercised the power of judicial review, igniting a firestorm of controversy that propelled the nation toward civil war. It would take the Civil War and the Thirteenth and Fourteenth Amendments (ratified in 1865 and 1868, respectively) to fix what judicial activists had broken.

The debate between judicial activism and judicial restraint continues. The modern controversy can be traced to 1953, when President Dwight D. Eisenhower appointed Earl Warren chief justice of the Court. Under Warren's leadership, from 1953 to 1969, a solid majority of the Court initiated extraordinary changes in our understanding of constitutional liberties and rights, especially the rights of the accused. And for the first time, the Court ruled that a number of provisions of the Bill of Rights must be applied to protect citizens from the actions of state governments. Inevitably the Court's activism generated a political reaction. Conservatives, who felt the Court was undermining law and order, called for Warren's impeachment. In 1968 presidential candidate Richard Nixon ran on a promise to appoint "strict constructionists" to the federal courts, by which he meant judges who would not read their own political agenda into the language of the Constitution and who generally would defer to the will of the people—or at least to the will of elected officials. Presidents Ronald Reagan, George Bush Sr., and George W. Bush repeated Nixon's pledge to appoint strict constructionists to the bench.

Behind the debate between judicial activism and judicial restraint is lots of hypocrisy. Conservatives bitterly criticize activist judges for establishing abortion and homosexual rights, but they are ready and willing to enlist federal judicial intervention in right-to-life cases—for example, the much-publicized battle in 2005 between Terri Schiavo's parents and her husband over the removal of her life support. Liberals sharply criticize judges who yoke themselves to the framers' intent, but they are not beyond invoking the framers' intent themselves when activist judges overrule certain state prerogatives—for example, the Supreme Court's decision to overrule the Florida courts and to put George W. Bush in the White House in *Bush v. Gore* (2000). Judges and law professors may care deeply about the tenets of constitutional interpretation, but politicians usually care more about promoting their own agenda, whether it's advanced by judicial activism or restraint. Not surprisingly, Americans' views of the courts are more likely informed by their policy preferences than by their preference for a particular method of constitutional interpretation.

BOX 9.2.1 Tenets of Judicial Activism and Judicial Restraint

JUDICIAL ACTIVISM

- *The Constitution is a living document.* Its meaning is not fixed and therefore cannot always conform to the intentions of its authors. Indeed, on many constitutional matters the intention of the framers cannot be discerned. The principles set forth in the Constitution are timeless, but the language of the document must be adapted to new times and conditions. The framers used general and often ambiguous language to allow future generations of Americans to create their own politics. They did not intend for the Constitution to become a straitjacket. An activist judiciary plays an essential role in the process of adapting the Constitution to new political problems and dilemmas.
- *A constitutional system ultimately depends on the federal courts to protect minority and individual rights.* Elected officials need to be in sync with the majority to get reelected. It's not surprising, then, that they may neglect minority and individual rights. Because federal judges are appointed, not elected, and because they have life tenure as long as they behave well, they are less likely to succumb to the tyranny of the majority. In the long run, an activist judiciary, insulated from majority public opinion, is the only branch of government that can be counted on to protect minority and individual rights.

JUDICIAL RESTRAINT

- *The job of judges is to apply the Constitution, not rewrite it.* Judges are obligated to interpret the Constitution with scrupulous regard for the meaning of its language and by adhering strictly to the intent of the framers. When judges go beyond these parameters, they inevitably and improperly substitute their own personal views and preferences for those specified in the Constitution. To correctly interpret the Constitution, judges must restrain themselves from acting as though they know better than the Constitution itself or the people who wrote it.
- *Judges must defer to the elected representatives of the people and to the people themselves.* Unless a law clearly violates specific language in the Constitution, democracy requires that judges defer to the elected representatives of the people. Judges cannot and should not protect the people from poorly conceived laws; in the spirit of democracy, the people themselves must act to correct laws that they find to be unwise. There is a manifest difference between bad public policy and unconstitutional public policy. Republican government will not long survive if the people look to the courts for redress rather than to themselves and to their elected representatives. In James Madison's words in "Federalist No. 10," "The ultimate repository of liberty is in the people."

ASSIGNMENT

Reading 9.2.1, from the Court's decision in *Roper v. Simmons* (2005), illustrates the conflict between judicial activism and judicial restraint. In 1993, at the age of 17, Christopher Simmons and a friend broke into the home of St. Louis County homemaker, Shirley Cook, intending to rob her while she slept. Cook awoke and recognized Simmons. The two teenagers then bound Cook with duct tape and electrical wire and threw her from a bridge into the river below. Simmons had previously told friends he wanted to commit a murder and that as a juvenile he could get away with it.

At 18, Simmons was tried, convicted, and sentenced to death under Missouri state law, which allowed the execution of those who committed certain crimes as juveniles. The Supreme Court had ruled in *Stanford v. Kentucky* (1989) that state death penalty laws for juveniles were not in violation of the Eighth Amendment's prohibition against cruel and unusual punishment. Based on that U.S. Supreme Court ruling, the Missouri Supreme Court turned down Simmons's appeal. In 2002, the U.S. Supreme Court, in *Atkins v. Virginia*, ruled that capital punishment for the mentally retarded did violate the Eighth Amendment. Based on the Court's reasoning in that case, Simmons filed a writ of *habeas corpus* to the Missouri Supreme Court arguing that his conviction also violated the Eighth Amendment. The Missouri Supreme Court agreed. The state of Missouri then appealed to the U.S. Supreme Court, which by a vote of 5–4 ruled that the death penalty as applied to juveniles was unconstitutional. At the time of the Court's ruling, nineteen states permitted the execution of juvenile murderers, and seventy-two inmates were on death rows in twelve states for murders they committed as juveniles. Study Reading 9.2.1 and answer the questions that follow.

READING 9.2.1 From *Roper v. Simmons*, 000 U.S. 03-633 (2005)

From Justice Kennedy's Opinion of the Court

The prohibition against "cruel and unusual punishments," like other expansive language in the Constitution, must be interpreted according to its text, by considering history, tradition, and precedent, and with due regard for its purpose and function in the constitutional design. To implement this framework we have established the propriety and affirmed the necessity of referring to "the evolving standards of decency that mark the progress of a maturing society" to determine which punishments are so disproportionate as to be cruel and unusual.... The inquiry into our society's evolving standards of decency did not end there.... Instead we returned to the rule, established in decisions predating Stanford, that "the Constitution contemplates that in the end our own judgment will be brought to bear on the question of the acceptability of the death penalty under the Eighth Amendment."...

A majority of States have rejected the imposition of the death penalty on juvenile offenders under 18, and we now hold this is required by the Eighth Amendment....

Our determination that the death penalty is disproportionate punishment for offenders under 18 finds confirmation in the stark reality that the United States is the only country in the world that continues to give official sanction to the juvenile death penalty. This reality does not become controlling, for the task of interpreting the Eighth Amendment remains our responsibility. Yet ... the Court has referred to the laws of other countries and to international authorities as instructive for its interpretation of the Eighth Amendment's prohibition of "cruel and unusual punishments."...

Over time, from one generation to the next, the Constitution has come to earn the high respect and even, as Madison dared to hope, the veneration of the American people. See *The Federalist* No. 49. The document sets forth, and rests upon, innovative principles original to the American experience, such as federalism; a proven balance in political mechanisms through separation of powers; specific guarantees for the accused in criminal cases; and broad provisions to secure individual freedom and preserve human dignity. These doctrines and guarantees are central to the American experience and remain essential to our present-day self-definition and national identity. Not the least of the reasons we honor the Constitution, then, is because we know it to be our own. It does not lessen our fidelity to the Constitution or our pride in its origins to acknowledge that the express affirmation of certain fundamental rights by other nations and peoples simply underscores the centrality of those same rights within our own heritage of freedom.

From Justice Scalia's Dissenting Opinion

In urging approval of a constitution that gave life-tenured judges the power to nullify laws enacted by the people's representatives, Alexander Hamilton assured the citizens of New York that there was little risk in this, since "[t]he judiciary ... ha[s] neither FORCE nor WILL but merely judgment." [*The Federalist*, No. 78] But Hamilton had in mind a traditional judiciary, "bound down by strict rules and precedents which serve to define and point out their duty in every particular case that comes before them." Bound down, indeed. What a mockery today's opinion makes of Hamilton's expectation, announcing the Court's conclusion that the meaning of our Constitution has changed over the past 15 years—not, mind you, that this Court's decision 15 years ago was *wrong*, but that the Constitution *has changed*. The Court reaches this implausible result by purporting to advert, not to the original meaning of the Eighth Amendment, but to "the evolving standards of decency,"...of our national society. It then finds, on the flimsiest of grounds, that a national consensus which could not be perceived in our people's laws barely 15 years ago now solidly exists. Worse still, the Court says in so many words that what our people's laws say about the issue does not, in the last analysis, matter: "[I]n the end our own judgment will be brought to bear on the question of the acceptability of the death penalty under the Eighth Amendment." The Court thus proclaims itself sole arbiter of our Nation's moral standards—and in the course of discharging that awesome responsibility purports to take guidance from the views of foreign courts and legislatures. Because I do not believe that the meaning of our Eighth Amendment, any more than the meaning of other provisions of our Constitution, should be determined by the subjective views of five Members of this Court and like-minded foreigners, I dissent.

1. Based on your examination of Justice Kennedy's opinion of the court, would you identify him as a practitioner of judicial activism or judicial restraint? Cite specific language in his opinion to support your position.

2. Justice Scalia did not vote with the majority; he justified his decision in a *dissenting opinion*. Based on your examination of Justice Scalia's opinion, would you identify him as a practitioner of judicial activism or judicial restraint? Cite specific language in his dissenting opinion to support your position.

3. In your view, should the Supreme Court justices factor into their decision on the juvenile death penalty today's standards of decency and even how other nations handle the issue? Explain and support your position.

4. In your view, what role should the Supreme Court play in the American political system? Should the justices practice judicial activism or judicial restraint? Explain and support your position.

5. Reflect carefully and honestly on this question: Was the preference you expressed for judicial activism or judicial restraint in question 4 influenced by your personal view of whether the juvenile death penalty is right or wrong? Explain and support your answer.

EXERCISE 9.3 What Role Should the Senate Play in Judicial Appointments?

INTRODUCTION

The power to determine who sits on the nation's highest courts has always been contested. Today, it's a bitter battleground between the political parties. That's because federal judges reach into every aspect of social and economic life and are the final arbiters of what the law means. Serving for life, they will leave their impress on the nation long after the president who nominated them and the senators who confirmed them are no longer in office.

Article II, Section 2 of the Constitution specifies that the president "shall nominate, and by and with the Advice and Consent of the Senate, shall appoint ... Judges of the Supreme Court, and all other Officers of the United States; whose Appointments are not herein otherwise provided for; and which shall be established by Law." (The appointment power was extended to all federal judgeships in the Federal Judiciary Act of 1789.) The president alone controls who is nominated to the federal courts; the Senate alone controls who is confirmed. To place a president's nominee on a federal court requires a simple majority vote (50 percent plus one vote) in the Senate. Although we often speak of the president's power to appoint federal judges, the Constitution divides that power between the president and the Senate.

The politics surrounding appointments to the federal judiciary—already contentious—have been further polarized during George W. Bush's presidency. President Bush, a conservative determined to appoint conservative judges, confronted a Senate in which the minority Democratic Party was equally determined to deny Bush his more controversial conservative nominees. President Bill Clinton was often forced to compromise by nominating federal judges who were more moderate than he would have preferred had his Democratic Party controlled the Senate.

Because the Democrats were the minority party in the Senate in the 108th and 109th Congresses (2003 and 2005), they were unable to use the Senate Judiciary Committee to block Bush nominees. Instead, Democrats resorted to a less commonly used procedure—the *filibuster*. The Republican majority in the Senate lacked the required number of votes to shut down these Democratic filibusters—a procedure known as *cloture*.[1]

BOX 9.3.1 Filibuster and Cloture

FILIBUSTER

- The filibuster is a procedural feature that highlights the Senate's tradition of unlimited debate.
- Filibustering is the use of dilatory or obstructive tactics to block a measure by preventing it from coming to a vote.
- The possibility of filibusters exists because Senate rules place few limits on senators' rights. A senator who seeks recognition usually has a right to the floor if no other senator is speaking, and then may speak for as long as he or she wishes.

CLOTURE

- Senate Rule XXII, known as the "cloture rule," enables senators to terminate a filibuster.
- Sixteen senators initiate cloture by presenting a motion to end debate.
- The senate does not vote on the cloture motion until the second day after the motion is made. Three-fifths of the votes of all senators—that's sixty votes—is required to invoke cloture.

---

[1] Congressional Research Service, Library of Congress, "Filibusters and Clotures in the Senate," March 28, 2003: http://www.senate.gov/reference/resources/pdf/RL30360.pdf.

Because the Constitution gives Congress the authority to "determine the Rules of its Proceedings" (Article I, Section 5), the majority leader of the Senate, Dr. Bill Frist (Republican, Tennessee), threatened in 2005 to change Senate rules to prohibit the filibuster of judicial nominations. Frist's threat became known as the "nuclear option" because it would compromise the Senate's tradition of unlimited debate and lead to war between Republicans and Democrats in the Senate at the expense of Bush's legislative agenda. Frist and most Senate Republicans argued that the president's judicial nominees are entitled to an up or down vote; Democrats argued that the filibuster was an important tradition in the Senate, especially as it protected minority rights. On May 23, 2005, moderate Democrats and moderate Republicans agreed to a compromise by which three of the president's filibustered nominees would be given up or down votes. Democrats, according to the agreement, would still be allowed to filibuster judicial nominees in "extraordinary circumstances." As of this writing, the Senate has confirmed the three appointments, but the "extraordinary circumstances" exception has not been tested.

The controversy over the Democrats' use of the filibuster against some of Bush's judicial nominees has opened a wider constitutional debate about the Senate's role in the judicial appointment process and the meaning of the phrase "by and with the advice and consent of the Senate."

ASSIGNMENT

Reading 9.3.1 is an excerpt from the debates about advice and consent at the Constitutional Convention of 1787. Reading 9.3.2 is selections from *The Federalist*, specifically Alexander Hamilton's analysis of the Senate's power of advice and consent. Judges and scholars still refer to the proceedings of the Constitutional Convention and *The Federalist* authors' arguments for ratification of the Constitution to interpret ambiguous language in the Constitution. Readings 9.3.3 and 9.3.4 bring the debate into the present. They are excerpts from testimony at a Senate hearing (108th Congress, May 6, 2003) on the role of the Senate in judicial appointments. Reading 9.3.3 is an argument for a relatively weak Senate role of advice and consent, whereas Reading 9.3.4 is an argument for a strong Senate role. The questions that follow the readings ask you to assess contrasting views on the meaning of "advice and consent."

READING 9.3.1 JAMES MADISON, "DEBATES AT FEDERAL CONVENTION, 1787"

June 13, 1787

Mr. Madison [James Madison, delegate from Virginia]: [He] objected to an appt. by the whole Legislature. Many of them were incompetent Judges of the requisite qualifications. They were too much influenced by their partialities. The candidate who was present, who had displayed a talent for business in the legislative field, who had perhaps assisted ignorant members in business of their own, or of their Constituents, or used other winning means, would without any of the essential qualifications for an expositor of the laws prevail over a competitor not having these recommendations, but possessed of every necessary accomplishment. He proposed that the appointment should be made by the Senate, which as a less numerous & more select body, would be more competent judges, and which was sufficiently numerous to justify such a confidence in them.

July 21, 1787

Col. Mason [George Mason, delegate from Virginia]: Notwithstanding the form of the proposition by which the appointment seemed to be divided between the Executive & Senate, the appointment was substantially vested in the former alone.... He considered the appointment by the Executive as a dangerous prerogative. It might even give him an influence over the Judiciary department itself.

September 7, 1787

Col. Mason: He took occasion to express his dislike of any reference whatever of the power to make appointments to either branch of the Legislature. On the other hand he was averse to vest so dangerous a power in the President alone.

Mr. Hamilton [Alexander Hamilton, delegate from New York]: The nomination to offices will give great weight to the President. Here then is a mutual connection & influence, that will perpetuate the President, and aggrandize both him & the Senate.

READING 9.3.2 EXCERPTS FROM *THE FEDERALIST* ON ADVICE AND CONSENT

Alexander Hamilton, "Federalist No. 66"

It will be the office of the President to NOMINATE, and, with the advice and consent of the Senate, to APPOINT. There will, of course, be no exertion of CHOICE on the part of the Senate. They may defeat one choice of the Executive, and oblige him to make another; but they cannot themselves CHOOSE, they can only ratify or reject the choice of the President. They might even entertain a preference to some other person, at the very moment they were assenting to the one proposed, because there might be no positive ground of opposition to him; and they could not be sure, if they withheld their assent, that the subsequent nomination would fall upon their own favorite, or upon any other person in their estimation more meritorious than the one rejected. Thus it could hardly happen, that the majority of the Senate would feel any other complacency towards the object of an appointment than such as the appearances of merit might inspire, and the proofs of the want of it destroy.

Alexander Hamilton, "Federalist No. 76"

The sole and undivided responsibility of one man [the president] will naturally beget a livelier sense of duty and a more exact regard to reputation. He will, on this account, feel himself under stronger obligations, and more interested to investigate with care the qualities requisite to the stations to be filled, and to prefer with impartiality the persons who may have the fairest pretensions to them. He will have FEWER personal attachments to gratify, than a body of men who may each be supposed to have an equal number; and will be so much the less liable to be misled by the sentiments of friendship and of affection. A single well-directed man, by a single understanding, cannot be distracted and warped by that diversity of views, feelings, and interests, which frequently distract and warp the resolutions of a collective body. There is nothing so apt to agitate the passions of mankind as personal considerations whether they relate to ourselves or to others, who are to be the objects of our choice or preference. Hence, in every exercise of the power of appointing to offices, by an assembly of men, we must expect to see a full display of all the private and party likings and dislikes, partialities and antipathies, attachments and animosities, which are felt by those who compose the assembly. The choice which may at any time happen to be made under such circumstances, will of course be the result either of a victory gained by one party over the other, or of a compromise between the parties. In either case, the intrinsic merit of the candidate will be too often out of sight. In the first, the qualifications best adapted to uniting the suffrages of the party, will be more considered than those which fit the person for the station. In the last, the coalition will commonly turn upon some interested equivalent: "Give us the man we wish for this office, and you shall have the one you wish for that." This will be the usual condition of the bargain. And it will rarely happen that the advancement of the public service will be the primary object either of party victories or of party negotiations....

But might not his nomination be overruled? I grant it might, yet this could only be to make place for another nomination by himself. The person ultimately appointed must be the object of his preference, though perhaps not in the first degree. It is also not very probable that his nomination would often be overruled. The Senate could not be tempted, by the preference they might feel to another, to reject the one proposed; because they could not assure themselves, that the person they might wish would be brought forward by a second or by any subsequent nomination. They could not even be certain, that a future nomination would present a candidate in any degree more acceptable to them; and as their dissent might cast a kind of stigma upon the individual rejected, and might have the appearance of a reflection upon the judgment of the chief magistrate, it is not likely that their sanction would often be refused, where there were not special and strong reasons for the refusal.

To what purpose then require the co-operation of the Senate? I answer, that the necessity of their concurrence would have a powerful, though, in general, a silent operation. It would be an excellent check upon a spirit of favoritism in the President, and would tend greatly to prevent the appointment of unfit characters from State prejudice, from family connection, from personal attachment, or from a view to popularity. In addition to this, it would be an efficacious source of stability in the administration.

Alexander Hamilton, "Federalist No. 77"

To this union of the Senate with the President, in the article of appointments, it has in some cases been suggested that it would serve to give the President an undue influence over the Senate, and in others that it would have an opposite tendency—a strong proof that neither suggestion is true. To state the first in its proper form is to refute it. It amounts to this: the President would have an improper influence over the Senate, because the Senate would have the power of restraining him. This is an absurdity in terms. It cannot admit of a doubt that the entire power of appointment would enable him much more effectually to establish a dangerous empire over that body than a mere power of nomination subject to their control.

Let us take a view of the converse of the proposition: "the Senate would influence the Executive." As I have had occasion to remark in several other instances, the indistinctness of the objection forbids a precise answer. In what manner is this influence to be exerted? In relation to what objects? The power of influencing a person, in the sense in which it is here used, must imply a power of conferring a benefit upon him. How could the Senate confer a benefit upon the President by the manner of employing their right of negative upon his nominations? If it be said they might sometimes gratify him by an acquiescence in a favorite choice, when public motives might dictate a different conduct, I answer that the instances in which the President could be personally interested in the result would be too few to admit of his being materially affected by the compliances of the Senate. Besides this, it is evident that the POWER which can originate the disposition of honors and emoluments is more likely to attract than to be attracted by the POWER which can merely obstruct their course. If by influencing the President be meant restraining him, this is precisely what must have been intended. And it has been shown that the restraint would be salutary, at the same time that it would not be such as to destroy a single advantage to be looked for from the uncontrolled agency of that magistrate. The right of nomination would produce all the good, without the ill. Upon a comparison of the plan for the appointment of the officers of the proposed government with that which is established by the constitution of this State, a decided preference must be given to the former. In that plan the power of nomination is unequivocally vested in the executive. And as there would be a necessity for submitting each nomination to the judgment of an entire branch of the legislature, the circumstances attending an appointment, from the mode of conducting it, would naturally become matters of notoriety, and the public would be at no loss to determine what part had been performed by the different actors. The blame of a bad nomination would fall upon the President singly and absolutely. The censure of rejecting a good one would lie entirely at the door of the Senate, aggravated by the consideration of their having counteracted the good intentions of the executive. If an ill appointment should be made, the executive, for nominating, and the Senate, for approving, would participate, though in different degrees, in the opprobrium and disgrace.

READING 9.3.3 Excerpts from the Testimony of Dr. John Eastman, Professor, Chapman University School of Law, Senate Hearings on Judicial Nominations and the Filibuster[2]

I. The Constitutional Structure of the Appointment Process Envisions a More Limited Role for the Senate than is Currently Claimed, and None for a Minority Faction of the Senate. As is well known to this body, Article II of the Constitution provides that the President "shall nominate, and by and with the Advice and Consent of the Senate, shall appoint, . . . Judges of the Supreme Court" and of such inferior courts as Congress has ordained and established. This is one of the fundamental components of the separation of powers mechanism devised by our nation's founders to protect against governmental tyranny. By it, the Senate provides an important check on the power of the President, but it is only a check; recent claims that the advice and consent clause gives to the Senate a co-equal role in the appointment of federal judges simply are not grounded either in the Constitution's text or in the history and theory of the appointments process. Necessarily, the claim that such power exists in less than a majority of the Senate is even more problematic.

    A. The Framers of the Constitution Assigned to the President the Pre Eminent Role in Appointing Judges.

    1. The President Alone Has the Power to Nominate

Article II of the Constitution provides that the President "shall nominate, and by and with the Advice and Consent of the Senate, shall appoint . . . Judges of the supreme [sic] Court [and such inferior courts as the Congress may from time to time ordain and establish]." As the text of the provision makes explicitly clear, the power to choose nominees—to "nominate"—is vested solely in the President, and the President also has the primary role to "appoint," albeit with the advice and consent of the entire Senate. The text of the clause itself thus demonstrates that the role envisioned for the Senate was a much more limited one than is currently being claimed by some, and it was, in any event, a role assigned to the entire Senate, not to a minority faction. . . . In Federalist 76, for example, Alexander Hamilton explained at length that "one man of discernment is better fitted to analyze and estimate the peculiar qualities adapted to particular offices, than a body of men of equal or perhaps even of superior discernment." . . .

Note the very limited role that the Senate serves in Hamilton's view—which, of course, echoes the views expressed at the Constitutional Convention by both those who defended and those who opposed giving the appointment power to the President. In the founders' view, the Senate acts as a brake on the President's ability to fill offices with his own friends and family members rather than qualified nominees, but beyond that, the element of choice—the essence of the power to fill the office—belongs to the President alone. The Senate has the power to refuse nominees, but in the Constitutional scheme it has no proper authority in picking the nominees—either through direct choice or through logrolling and deal-making of the kind that the modern filibuster encourages. . . .

    2. The Framers Envisioned A Narrow Role for The Senate in The Confirmation Process.

Of course, there is more to the appointment power than the power to nominate, and the Senate unquestionably has a role to play in the confirmation phase of the appointment process. But the role envisioned by the framers was as a check on improper appointments by the President, one that would not undermine the President's ultimate responsibility for the appointments he made. The Senate's confirmation power therefore acts only as a relatively minor check on the President's authority—it exists only to prevent the President from selecting a nominee who "does not possess

---

[2] Senate Hearing 108-227, "Judicial Nominations, Filibusters, and the Constitution, When a Majority Is Denied the Right to Consent," Subcommittee on the Constitution, Civil Rights, and Property Rights of the Senate Judiciary Committee, May 6, 2003: http://frwebgate.access.gpo.gov/cgi-bin/getdoc.cgi?dbname=108_senate_hearings&docid=f:90460.wais.

due qualifications for office." Essentially, it exists to prevent the President from being swayed by nepotism or mere political opportunism. Assessing a candidate's "qualifications for office" arguably did not give the entire Senate grounds for imposing an ideological litmus [test] on the President's nominees, at least where the questioned ideology did not prevent a judge from fulfilling his oath of office. It necessarily did not give such a power to a small faction of the Senate, as has become the practice through the use of ideologically-grounded holds or filibusters.

READING 9.3.4 EXCERPTS FROM THE STATEMENT OF SENATOR TED KENNEDY (DEMOCRAT, MASSACHUSETTS), SENATE HEARINGS ON JUDICIAL NOMINATIONS AND THE FILIBUSTER[3]

It is always interesting in a hearing such as this, as we are trying to find out where authority and responsibilities lie, to look back at the Constitutional Convention itself. In the Constitutional Convention, when it met in Philadelphia from late May until mid September in 1787, on May 29th the Convention began its work on the Constitution with the Virginia Plan introduced by Governor Randolph, which provided that a national judiciary be established or be chosen by the national legislature, and under this plan the President had no role at all, in the selection of judges.

When this provision came before the Convention on June 5th, several members were concerned that having the whole legislature select judges was to [sic] unwieldy and James Wilson suggested an alternative proposal that the President be given the sole power to appoint judges. That idea had no support. Rutledge of South Carolina said that he was by no means disposed to grant so great a power to any single person. James Madison agreed that the legislature was too large a body, and stated that he was rather inclined to give the appointment power to the Senatorial Branch of the legislative group, "sufficiently stable and independent to provide deliberate judgments," were the words he used. A week later Madison offered a formal motion to give the Senate the sole power to appoint judges, and this motion was adopted without any objection whatsoever at the Constitutional Convention.

On June 19th the Convention formally adopted the working draft of the Constitution, and it gave the Senate the exclusive power to appoint the judges. July 18th the Convention reaffirmed its decision to grant the Senate its exclusive power. James Wilson again proposed judges be appointed by the Executive, and again his motion was defeated overwhelmingly. The issue was considered again on July 21st, and the Convention again agreed to the exclusive Senate appointment of judges. In a debate concerning the provision, George Mason called the idea of Executive appointment of Federal judges a dangerous precedent. Not until the final days of the Convention was the President given power to nominate the judges. So on September 4th, two weeks before the Convention's work was completed, the last important decision made by the founding fathers, the Committee proposed that the President should have a role in selecting judges. It stated the President shall "nominate, and by and with the advice and consent of the Senate, shall appoint the judges of the Supreme Court." The debates make clear that while the President had the power to nominate, the Senate still had a central role. Governor [sic] Morris of Pennsylvania described the provision as giving the Senate the power to appoint the judges nominated to them by the President. And the Convention, having repeatedly rejected the proposals that would lodge exclusive power to select judges to the Executive Branch, could not possibly have intended to reduce the Senate to a rubber stamp role.

---

[3] Senate Hearing 108-227, "Judicial Nominations, Filibusters, and the Constitution, When a Majority Is Denied the Right to Consent," Subcommittee on the Constitution, Civil Rights, and Property Rights of the Senate Judiciary Committee, May 6, 2003: http://frwebgate.access.gpo.gov/cgi-bin/getdoc.cgi?dbname=108_senate_hearings&docid=f:90460.wais.

It is important that Americans understand what our founding fathers deliberated, what they believed, what they thought they were achieving with the power of the United States Senate not to be a rubber stamp for the presidency, and they also expected advice and consent.... We have had an amazing life experience for this country and when you review what the founding fathers had intended and expected and what the rules had shown, it is clear that it was the function of advice and consent. It was the involvement of the United States Senate in the consideration and voting of various nominees on it in this process, that has contributed to this experience. We should all take the time to review that, because it has been the experience in the United States when this process has worked. That is not the way it is working at the present time. We would be failing our responsibilities if we were just to be a rubber stamp. We certainly have no obligation to ignore or suspend our long-standing rules and become a rubber stamp.

---

1. Based on Readings 9.3.1–9.3.4, identify three arguments that support an extensive role for the Senate in its exercise of the power of advice and consent over judicial nominations, including arguments for the use of the filibuster. Cite the reading(s) each argument is derived from.

2. Based on Readings 9.3.1–9.3.4, identify three arguments that support a minimal role for the Senate in its exercise of the power of advice and consent over judicial nominations, including arguments for prohibiting the filibuster. Cite the reading(s) each argument is derived from.

3. In your view, should senators be allowed to use the filibuster to block a president's judicial nominations to federal courts? Explain and support your position by citing specific passages in the readings.

4. Many observers claim that the controversy over the filibuster of judicial nominees is not about the constitutional role of the Senate or about minority rights. Rather, the conflict is a partisan effort to gain political advantage. Because the Republicans have a majority in the Senate and because they hold the presidency, they want presidential power and majority rule to prevail; because the Democrats are the minority in the Senate and are facing a conservative Republican president, they want Senate power and minority rights to carry the day. If the parties' status were reversed, it is argued, their positions on the role of the Senate and the use of the filibuster would be reversed as well. To what extent do you think your answer to question 3 was affected by your political views and, more specifically, by whether you support Bush's appointment of conservative judges to the federal courts?

EXERCISE 9.4 Beating the Odds on Judicial Appointments

INTRODUCTION

When it comes to the exercise of judicial power, nothing counts more than who sits on the nation's highest court. Justices arrive on the Supreme Court with political views and positions on constitutional interpretation. Their personal experience and political bias affect how they decide cases involving volatile social issues like abortion—about which the Constitution has nothing direct to say. Liberal justices, for example, find in the Constitution a right to abortion; conservative justices do not.

Presidents and their advisers calculate carefully in selecting a nominee to the Supreme Court, especially since a nominee will have life tenure and carry a president's legacy for years to come. Political considerations include whether the president is in his first term, thinking of reelection, or in his second term—freer from interest group pressure and public opinion. Today presidents often consider diversity—race, ethnicity, gender, religion. When Thurgood Marshall, the first African American appointed to the Court, retired in 1991, President George H. W. Bush continued black representation by naming Clarence Thomas as Marshall's replacement. Institutionally, the president's support in the Senate must be calibrated, since a majority vote is required to elevate the nominee to a life term. Given the rancor over judicial nominations that has persisted since the defeat of Robert Bork's nomination in 1987, the president must ask himself whether he has the stomach and political capital for a possibly bruising fight.

Presidents' policy considerations include finding a nominee who fits a particular ideological profile, although some presidents have been more insistent on an ideological litmus test than others. President George W. Bush stated that his ideal nominee would be another Antonin Scalia or Clarence Thomas—judges known for their conservative decisions. In addition to seeking a nominee to match the president's ideology and policy positions, the president must consider the aims of the varied constituencies in the president's coalition. In the case of the Republican Party, for example, conservative Christians expect a president's nominee to be soundly anti-abortion; the Chamber of Commerce and the National Association of Manufacturers are concerned about the nominee's record on government regulation.

Finally, the professional qualifications of nominees are assessed. Beginning in the Eisenhower administration, presidents sought the advice of the American Bar Association's Standing Committee of Federal Judiciary before making judicial nominations. The committee rates judicial candidates as "well qualified," "qualified," or "not qualified." A unanimous rating of "well qualified" for President Bill Clinton nominees Ruth Bader Ginsburg and Stephen Breyer, for example, eased their Senate confirmation. But a unanimous ABA rating of "qualified"[1] (the highest rating available at the time) was of little help to Harrold G. Carswell, one of President Richard Nixon's nominees. Carswell had served only six months on the U.S. Court of Appeals prior to his nomination to the Supreme Court. Critics charged that his credentials were too thin to warrant a seat on the Court and that his record on civil rights was suspect. Carswell's confirmation prospects weren't advanced when the floor manager of the nomination, Senator Roman Hruska (Republican, Nebraska), endorsed Carswell's mediocrity: "Even if he is mediocre there are a lot of mediocre judges and people and lawyers. They are entitled to a little representation, aren't they, and a little chance?"[2] The Senate rejected Carswell's nomination by a vote of 51 to 45. President George W. Bush, in 2001, ended the traditional practice of consulting the ABA on all federal judicial nominations. Bush's action stemmed from Republican criticism that the ABA was biased against conservative nominees and from the desire to bring conservative groups such as the Federalist Society into the evaluation of prospective nominees.

---

[1] Prior to voting on Carswell's rating, the ABA committee instituted a new system that rated the nominee as either "qualified" or "not qualified."

[2] Richard Harris, *Decision* (New York: E. P. Dutton, 1971), p. 110.

The Constitution's framers chose life tenure as the foundation of an independent judiciary to insulate justices from majority public opinion and the political considerations of elective office.[3] For presidents, life tenure holds out the promise that an appointee will protect and extend the president's legacy long after he's departed from the White House. William O. Douglas, one of President Franklin D. Roosevelt's appointments, served thirty-six years on the Supreme Court—clear into Gerald Ford's presidency. William H. Rehnquist carried President Richard M. Nixon's legacy across the presidencies of Ford, Carter, Reagan, Bush I, Clinton, and into the presidency of Bush II.

Life tenure, however, has proved a curse for some presidents. Several Supreme Court justices have surprised the presidents who appointed them—and the senators who confirmed them—by recasting themselves under the cloak of life tenure. Nominees who were thought to be reliably liberal discovered themselves to be conservatives—and vice versa. Although presidents might view these transformations as betrayal, the view from the Court is different. Even a loyal ally of the president may be moved by institutional influences such as the traditional and fiercely guarded independence of the Court, the legal arguments of the justices and law clerks, and the respect often accorded to prior court rulings. At the end of his sixteen-year term as chief justice, Earl Warren stated that he did not "see how a man could be on the Court and not change his views substantially over a period of years... for change you must if you are to do your duty on the Supreme Court."[4]

After leaving office, former president Harry Truman observed that "packing the Supreme Court simply can't be done.... I've tried and it won't work.... Whenever you put a man on the Supreme Court he ceases to be your friend. I'm sure of that."[5] President Dwight D. Eisenhower agreed: His appointment of Chief Justice Earl Warren went notoriously awry. As governor of California, Warren helped Eisenhower secure the Republican Party's nomination at the 1952 convention. In return, Eisenhower promised Warren the first vacancy on the Court. After Chief Justice Fred Vinson died of a heart attack in 1953, Warren held Eisenhower to the promise. Warren's record as attorney general and governor of California indicated political compatibility with Eisenhower's brand of moderate Republicanism. As chief justice, however, Warren angered the president and conservatives across the nation by embracing judicial activism to advance individual rights and social justice in the areas of racial discrimination, criminal procedures, and personal privacy, to name a few. Indeed, less than a year after taking his seat on the bench, Warren brilliantly orchestrated a unanimous decision declaring unconstitutional state laws mandating racially segregated schools. *Brown v. Board of Education of Topeka* inflamed the South, alarmed conservatives in both parties, and helped launch a revolution in race relations.

After Eisenhower had left office and the extent of the Warren Court's revolution had become clear, Eisenhower often remarked that his biggest mistake was "the appointment of that dumb son of a bitch Earl Warren."[6]

To ensure that its Supreme Court appointments didn't backfire, the Reagan administration screened its nominees for ideological compatibility more carefully and aggressively than any previous presidency. The process included thorough scrutiny of candidates' speeches, articles, and court opinions, day-long interviews with Department of Justice officials, and deliberations by the White House Judicial Selection Committee to determine which candidates to recommend for the president's consideration. The interviews were particularly controversial. Some potential nominees cried foul at being asked directly about their view on issues such as abortion. After all, most judges consider it a violation of their impartiality and neutrality to commit to a position before they have considered the particulars of a case.

---

[3] The Constitution does not use the term *life tenure* but states that judges "shall hold their Offices during good Behaviour." Federal court judges may be removed from office for violating the "good behavior" standard. The removal process is as follows: The House of Representatives must vote by simple majority to impeach the judge, who would then be tried in the Senate where a two-thirds vote is required to convict and remove the judge. The vice president presides over the trial in the Senate. In the Republic's history, only one Supreme Court justice—Samuel Chase, in 1805—has been impeached. He was acquitted in the Senate.

[4] Anthony Lewis, "A Talk with Warren on Crime, the Court, the Country," *The New York Times Magazine*, October 19, 1969, pp. 128–29.

[5] Lecture at Columbia University, New York City, April 28, 1959. Quoted in Henry J. Abraham, *The Judicial Process*, 7th ed. (New York: Oxford University Press, 1998), p. 79.

[6] Stephen E. Ambrose, *Eisenhower: The President* (New York: Simon & Schuster, 1984), p. 190.

Political scientists continue to investigate and debate how recent presidents have fared in their efforts to use the judicial appointment power to protect and extend their legacies. The questions that follow examine a slice of that debate.

ASSIGNMENT

Table 9.4.1 ranks three presidents on their liberalism in social and economic policy (0 = extremely conservative; 100 = extremely liberal). Table 9.4.2 ranks selected Supreme Court justices on their liberalism in civil liberties and economic cases (0 = extremely conservative; 100 = extremely liberal). In the area of civil liberties—for example, First Amendment rights and privacy—liberal presidents and Supreme Court justices would favor individual rights over government intrusion. In economics cases, liberals would favor government regulations and union rights over private and corporate interests.[7] Use the tables to answer the questions that follow.

TABLE 9.4.1 Presidential Social and Economic Liberalism

President	Social and Economic Liberalism Ranking
Ronald Reagan	17.8
George H. W. Bush	33.0
Bill Clinton	67.6

TABLE 9.4.2 Supreme Court Justices' Liberalism in Civil Liberties and Economics Cases*

Supreme Court Justice	Civil Liberties Cases	Economic Cases
O'Connor	34.6	42.7
Rehnquist†	23.1	46.5
Scalia	29.7	44.1
Kennedy	36.5	45.4
Souter	54.0	53.8
Thomas	27.0	36.5
Ginsburg	61.4	59.0
Breyer	63.4	42.9

* The data give equal weight to Supreme Court cases. Clearly, from the president's and his constituents' perspectives, some cases are much more important than others. Pro-life groups, for example, have been bitterly disappointed that Justices Kennedy and O'Connor have not voted to overturn *Roe v. Wade.*

† These data are for Rehnquist's votes as a Reagan appointee to chief justice. The rankings for his votes as a Nixon appointee are 19.3 in civil liberties cases and 42.2 in economics cases.

1. In his two terms as president, Ronald Reagan appointed three justices to the Court: Sandra Day O'Connor, Antonin Scalia, and Anthony M. Kennedy. Reagan also elevated William H. Rehnquist from associate justice to chief justice.

a. Examine the liberalism rankings for Reagan's appointees in Table 9.4.2 on civil liberties and economic cases and compare them with Reagan's ranking on social and economic liberalism in

---

[7] The data in Tables 9.4.1 and 9.4.2 are adapted from Jeffrey A. Segal, Richard J. Timpone, and Robert M. Howard, "Buyer Beware? Presidential Success through Supreme Court Appointments," *Political Quarterly Research*, Vol. 53 (Sept. 2000), pp. 557–573, and from http://www.sunysb.edu/polsci/jsegal/data/pressc_main.htm. The authors thank Professor Jeffrey A. Segal for permission to adapt and reprint the data.

Table 9.4.1. Does your comparison indicate that Reagan's appointees are more liberal or more conservative than Reagan?

b. In civil liberties cases, which of Reagan's four appointees comes closest to practicing Reagan's brand of conservatism?

c. In civil liberties cases, which of Reagan's four appointees is farthest from practicing Reagan's brand of conservatism?

d. What is the average liberalism ranking of all four Reagan appointees on civil liberties and economic cases?

e. The *presidential compatibility gap* is the point spread between the rankings of a justice and those of the president who appointed that justice. The higher the number, the more disappointed a president would likely be with the rulings of his nominee. What is the presidential compatibility gap between the average ranking of Reagan's appointees (which you calculated in part d) and Reagan's ranking on social and economic liberalism?

2. President George H. W. Bush served one term as president and made two appointments to the Court: David H. Souter and Clarence Thomas.

a. What's the presidential compatibility gap for Souter? To find the presidential compatibility gap, calculate the average of Souter's rankings in civil liberties and economic cases. Then calculate the difference between Souter's average ranking and the ranking of George H. W. Bush.

b. What's the presidential compatibility gap for Thomas?

c. Which of Bush's appointees comes closest to practicing Bush's brand of conservatism?

3. President Bill Clinton served two terms as president and made two appointments to the Court: Ruth Bader Ginsburg and Stephen G. Breyer.

a. Are the rulings of these appointees more liberal or more conservative than Clinton's ranking?

b. What's the presidential compatibility gap for Ginsburg?

c. What's the presidential compatibility gap for Breyer?

4. a. Find the average presidential compatibility gap for each president's appointees. (You already calculated the average for Reagan's appointees in question 1.e.)

Ronald Reagan: _____

George H. W. Bush: _____

Bill Clinton: _____

b. Which president would likely be most disappointed in the rulings of his appointees to the Supreme Court?

_____

5. Consider the following example of the complex factors that contribute to the presidential compatibility gap. Supreme Court Justice Lewis F. Powell Jr. retired in June 1987. President Ronald Reagan nominated Federal Appeals Court Judge Robert Bork to fill the vacancy. On October 23, 1987, the Senate defeated Bork's nomination by a vote of 58 to 42. At the time of Bork's defeat, the Democrats held fifty-five seats in the Senate; the Republicans held forty-five. Factors in Bork's defeat included the unprecedented mobilization of civil rights, labor, and women's organizations opposed to Bork's conservative political and legal views, as well as disarray in the Reagan administration resulting from the Iran-Contra scandal and the consequent failure of the White House to fully mobilize conservative resources on Bork's behalf.

On October 29, 1987, less than a week after Bork's defeat, Reagan announced that he would nominate Federal Appeals Court Judge Douglas Howard Ginsburg to fill the still-vacant seat. Ginsburg, however, was forced to withdraw his nomination before Reagan formally submitted it to the Senate because of the disclosure that Ginsburg had smoked marijuana while a student and faculty member at Harvard Law School. The disclosure embarrassed Reagan, whose "just say no to drugs campaign" was in full swing at the time.

Consider Reagan's political position as he attempted for the third time to fill the seat vacated by Powell. Reagan was undoubtedly aware that only one other president in the twentieth century—Richard M. Nixon—had failed twice in a row to elevate his nominees to a vacant seat on the Court. If Reagan failed a third time, he would have the distinction of being the first president since the Civil War to do so.

How would you advise Reagan to proceed? Would you recommend that Reagan nominate again a conservative whose record indicates that he or she would practice the president's brand of conservatism? Or would you recommend that Reagan compromise his political principles and nominate a more moderate candidate who could attract enough Democratic votes to be confirmed? Explain and support your recommendation.

_____

_____

_____

_____

_____

_____

Study Reading 9.4.1, excerpts from Reagan's news conference announcing his third nominee, and answer the questions that follow.

READING 9.4.1 REMARKS ANNOUNCING THE NOMINATION OF ANTHONY M. KENNEDY TO BE AN ASSOCIATE JUSTICE OF THE SUPREME COURT OF THE UNITED STATES, NOVEMBER 11, 1987[8]

The President: It's not just in fulfillment of my constitutional duty but with great pride and respect for his many years of public service, that I am today announcing my intention to nominate United States Circuit Judge Anthony Kennedy to be an Associate Justice of the Supreme Court. Judge Kennedy represents the best tradition of America's judiciary....

During his 12 years on the Nation's second highest court, Judge Kennedy has participated in over 1400 decisions and authored over 400 opinions. He's a hard worker and, like Justice Powell, whom he will replace, he is known as a gentleman. He's popular with colleagues of all political persuasions. And I know that he seems to be popular with many Senators of varying political persuasions as well....

Judge Kennedy is what many in recent weeks have referred to as a true conservative—one who believes that our constitutional system is one of enumerated powers—that it is we, the people who have granted certain rights to the Government, not the other way around. And that unless the Constitution grants a power to the Federal Government, or restricts a State's exercise of that power, it remains with the States or the people....

Judge Kennedy has participated in hundreds of criminal law decisions during his tenure on the Ninth Circuit Court of Appeals. In that time he's earned a reputation as a courageous, tough, but fair jurist. He's known to his colleagues and to the lawyers who practiced before him as diligent, perceptive, and polite. The hallmark of Judge Kennedy's career has been devotion—devotion to his family, devotion to his community and his civic responsibility, and devotion to the law. He's played a major role in keeping our cities and neighborhoods safe from crime. He's that special kind of American who's always been there when we needed leadership. I'm certain he will be a leader on the Supreme Court.

The experience of the last several months has made all of us a bit wiser. I believe the mood and the time is now right for all Americans in this bicentennial year of the Constitution to join together in a bipartisan effort to fulfill our constitutional obligation of restoring the United States Supreme Court to full strength. By selecting Anthony M. Kennedy, a superbly qualified judge whose fitness for the high court has been remarked upon by leaders of the Senate in both parties, I have sought to ensure the success of that effort.

I look forward, and I know Judge Kennedy is looking forward, to prompt hearings conducted in the spirit of cooperation and bipartisanship. I'll do everything in my power as President to assist in that process....

Q [question from reporter]: Mr. President, throughout this whole process, Senator Hatch says there have been a lot of gutless wonders in the White House. Do you know who they are, who he is referring to, why he would say such a thing since he is such a devoted conservative?

The President: ...when these ceremonies here this morning are over, I'm going to try to find out where he gets his information because, you know something, I haven't been able to find a gutless wonder in the whole place.

Q: Do you know why he was so upset?

The President: I don't know. I don't know, unless he's been reading the paper too much.

---

[8] Go to http://www.reagan.utexas.edu/archives/speeches/1987/111187a.htm.

Q: Mr. President, you said that Judge Kennedy is popular with people of all political persuasions. What happened to your plan to give the Senate the nominee that they would object to just as much as Judge Bork?

The President: Maybe it's time that I did answer on that, where that was said and why—and it was humorously said. I was at a straight party organization affair, a dinner. And when I finished my remarks, which were partisan, a woman, down in front, member there, just called out above all the noise of the room, "What about Judge Bork?" And she got great applause for saying that. And then the questions came. Was I going to give in and try to please certain elements in the Senate? And I made that—intended to be facetious answer to her. And so, as I say, it was—sometimes you make a facetious remark and somebody takes it seriously and you wish you'd never said it, and that's one for me. ...

Q: Did you cave into the liberals, Mr. President? Some conservatives are saying you caved into the liberals, appointing someone who can be confirmed, but not appointing someone who is going to turn the Court around.

The President: When the day comes that I cave in to the liberals, I will be long gone from here. [*Laughter*]

Q: Judge Kennedy, did they ask you if you'd ever smoked marijuana?

Q: Did you ever smoke marijuana?

Q: Did they ask you?

Judge Kennedy: They asked me that question, and the answer was no, firmly, no.

Q: Mr. President, do you think conservatives, sir, will back this nominee? You know, Senator Helms, at one point, is alleged to have said, "No way, Jose," to Judge Kennedy.

The President: We'll find out about that in the coming days ahead. ...

Note: The President spoke at 11:30 a.m. in the Briefing Room at the White House. Marlin Fitzwater was Assistant to the President for Press Relations.

---

6. a. Did Reagan follow the recommendation you made in question 5?

_____

b. How did Reagan describe Kennedy's political ideology?

_____

_____

_____

c. What evidence do you find in Reagan's remarks that Kennedy was a compromise nominee—in other words, not the "true conservative" Reagan would have preferred?

_____

_____

d. What questions did reporters raise indicating that Kennedy was not a "true conservative"?

CHAPTER 10

Civil Rights

EXERCISE 10.1 Mandating Racial Segregation by State Law

INTRODUCTION

Blacks liberated from slavery by the Civil War defined *freedom* in expansive terms, arguing that freedom necessarily includes the right to vote and hold political office, equality before the law, and the ownership of land. Many whites, North and South, defined freedom for blacks in the most narrow, restrictive terms, arguing that freedom is nothing more than the absence of slavery. The battle over the meaning of freedom for African Americans raged during the late nineteenth century, throughout the twentieth, and into the twenty-first century as the United States continues its painful and drawn-out adjustment to the end of slavery.

In 1867 Congress, under the leadership of the Radical Republicans, passed the Reconstruction Acts, legislation that secured for blacks in the South the right to vote and a measure of legal equality. African Americans were elected to political office throughout the South and in 1870, for the first time, took seats in the U.S. House of Representatives and Senate (see Exercise 6.3). Those gains were made possible by the use of military power on behalf of African Americans in the South. In 1877, however, the North pulled its troops out of the South. Unencumbered, white southerners reasserted supremacy by passing state laws to disfranchise and segregate blacks. Among the devices employed to strip African Americans of their voting rights were the literacy test, the poll tax, the grandfather clause, and the white primary. Jim Crow laws buttressed white supremacy by mandating the separation of whites and blacks in almost every public and private area of life. Blacks were relegated to separate and inferior schools, restrooms, parks, restaurants, hotels, trains, streetcars, swimming pools, and even cemeteries.

In 1890 the Louisiana state legislature required railroads to provide "equal but separate accommodations for the white and colored races" and prohibited travelers from riding in railcars designated for the other race. A group of blacks from New Orleans challenged the law in court. They received some support from railroad companies, which objected to the additional expense of providing separate cars for black and white passengers. The dispute eventually made its way to the Supreme Court in the case *Plessy v. Ferguson* (1896).

In 1909 blacks and whites, alarmed at the deteriorating position of African Americans, formed an interest group called the National Association for the Advancement of Colored People (NAACP). Its mission: to secure full rights of citizenship for black Americans. The legal arm of the NAACP filed a series of lawsuits challenging the system of racial separation mandated by state law in the South. Those suits made inroads against segregation in the South, particularly in the areas of graduate education and interstate transportation, but progress was slow. Segregation was pervasive and firmly entrenched.

Beginning in the late 1940s, the NAACP challenged segregation in public schools. One case, *Briggs v. Elliott* (1952), was initiated by black parents in Clarendon County, South Carolina, where the school board in the 1949–1950 term spent $43 per black child and $179 per white child. The Supreme Court consolidated *Briggs* with three other challenges to school segregation under the name of a case from Kansas, *Brown v. Board of Education of Topeka* (1954). The case was argued before the Court by Thurgood Marshall, the lead attorney for the NAACP's Legal and Educational Defense Fund, who was later appointed by President Lyndon Johnson to a seat on the Supreme Court. Earl Warren, the chief justice who engineered the Court's unanimous decision in *Brown*, had been appointed to the Court by President Dwight Eisenhower in 1953.

ASSIGNMENT

Study Reading 10.1.1, an excerpt from *Plessy v. Ferguson*, and Reading 10.1.2, an excerpt from *Brown v. Board of Education of Topeka*, and answer the questions that follow.

READING 10.1.1 *Plessy v. Ferguson*, 163 U.S. 537 (1896)

Mr. Justice Brown delivered the opinion of the court.

The constitutionality of this act is attacked upon the ground that it conflicts both with the thirteenth amendment of the constitution, abolishing slavery, and the fourteenth amendment, which prohibits certain restrictive legislation on the part of the states.

1. That it does not conflict with the thirteenth amendment, which abolished slavery and involuntary servitude, except a punishment for crime, is too clear for argument....

2. ... The object of the [fourteenth] amendment was undoubtedly to enforce the absolute equality of the two races before the law, but, in the nature of things, it could not have been intended to abolish distinctions based upon color, or to enforce social, as distinguished from political, equality, or a commingling of the two races upon terms unsatisfactory to either. Laws permitting, and even requiring, their separation, in places where they are liable to be brought into contact, do not necessarily imply the inferiority of either race to the other, and have been generally, if not universally, recognized as within the competency of the state legislatures in the exercise of their police power. The most common instance of this is connected with the establishment of separate schools for white and colored children, which have been held to be a valid exercise of the legislative power even by courts of states where the political rights of the colored race have been longest and most earnestly enforced....

We think the enforced separation of the races, as applied to the internal commerce of the state, neither abridges the privileges or immunities of the colored man, deprives him of his property without due process of law, nor denies him the equal protection of the laws, within the meaning of the fourteenth amendment....

In this connection, it is also suggested by the learned counsel for the plaintiff in error that the same argument that will justify the state legislature in requiring railways to provide separate accommodations for the two races will also authorize them to require separate cars to be provided for people whose hair is of a certain color, or who are aliens, or who belong to certain nationalities, or to enact laws requiring colored people to walk upon one side of the street, and white people upon the other, or requiring white men's houses to be painted white, and colored men's black, or their vehicles or business signs to be of different colors, upon the theory that one side of the street is as good as the other, or that a house or vehicle of one color is as good as one of another color. The reply to all this is that every exercise of the police power must be reasonable, and extend only to such laws as are enacted in good faith for the promotion of the public good, and not for the annoyance or oppression of a particular class....

We consider the underlying fallacy of the plaintiff's argument to consist in the assumption that the enforced separation of the two races stamps the colored race with a badge of inferiority. If this be so, it is not by reason of anything found in the act, but solely because the colored race chooses to put that construction upon it. The argument necessarily assumes that if, as has been more than once the case, and is not unlikely to be so again, the colored race should become the dominant power in the state legislature, and should enact a law in precisely similar terms, it would thereby relegate the white race to an inferior position. We imagine that the white race, at least, would not acquiesce in this assumption. The argument also assumes that social prejudices may be overcome by legislation, and that equal rights cannot be secured to the negro except by an enforced commingling of the two races. We cannot accept this proposition. If the two races are to meet upon terms of social equality, it must be the result of natural affinities, a mutual appreciation of each other's merits, and a voluntary consent of individuals.... Legislation is powerless to eradicate racial instincts, or to abolish distinctions based upon physical differences, and the attempt to do so can only result in accentuating the difficulties of the present situation. If the civil and political rights of both races be equal, one cannot be inferior to the other civilly or politically. If one race be inferior to the other socially, the constitution of the United States cannot put them upon the same plane....

Mr. Justice Harlan dissenting.

In respect of civil rights, common to all citizens, the constitution of the United States does not, I think, permit any public authority to know the race of those entitled to be protected in the enjoyment of such rights.... Indeed, such legislation as that here in question is inconsistent not only with that equality of rights which pertains to citizenship, national and state, but with the personal liberty enjoyed by every one within the United States.

It was said in argument that the statute of Louisiana does not discriminate against either race, but prescribes a rule applicable alike to white and colored citizens. But this argument does not meet the difficulty. Every one knows that the statute in question had its origin in the purpose, not so much to exclude white persons from railroad cars occupied by blacks, as to exclude colored people from coaches occupied by or assigned to white persons. Railroad corporations of Louisiana did not make discrimination among whites in the matter of accommodation for travelers. The thing to accomplish was, under the guise of giving equal accommodation for whites and blacks, to compel the latter to keep to themselves while traveling in railroad passenger coaches. No one would be so wanting in candor as to assert the contrary. The fundamental objection, therefore, to the statute, is that it interferes with the personal freedom of citizens.... If a white man and a black man choose to occupy the same public conveyance on a public highway, it is their right to do so; and no government, proceeding alone on grounds of race, can prevent it without infringing the personal liberty of each.

It is one thing for railroad carriers to furnish, or to be required by law to furnish, equal accommodations for all whom they are under a legal duty to carry. It is quite another thing for government to forbid citizens of the white and black races from traveling in the same public conveyance, and to punish officers of railroad companies for permitting persons of the two races to occupy the same passenger coach....

Our constitution is color-blind, and neither knows nor tolerates classes among citizens. In respect of civil rights, all citizens are equal before the law. The humblest is the peer of the most powerful. The law regards man as man, and takes no account of his surroundings or of his color when his civil rights as guaranteed by the supreme law of the land are involved. It is therefore to be regretted that this high tribunal, the final expositor of the fundamental law of the land, has reached the conclusion that it is competent for a state to regulate the enjoyment by citizens of their civil rights solely upon the basis of race....

The destinies of the two races, in this country, are indissolubly linked together, and the interests of both require that the common government of all shall not permit the seeds of race hate to be planted under the sanction of law. What can more certainly arouse race hate, what more certainly create and perpetuate a feeling of distrust between these races, than state enactments which, in fact, proceed on the ground that colored citizens are so inferior and degraded that they cannot be allowed to sit in public coaches occupied by white citizens? That, as all will admit, is the real meaning of such legislation as was enacted in Louisiana....

The arbitrary separation of citizens, on the basis of race, while they are on a public highway, is a badge of servitude wholly inconsistent with the civil freedom and the equality before the law established by the constitution. It cannot be justified upon any legal grounds.

READING 10.1.2 *Brown v. Board of Education of Topeka*, 347 U.S. 483 (1954)

Mr. Chief Justice Warren delivered the opinion of the Court.

These cases come to us from the States of Kansas, South Carolina, Virginia, and Delaware. They are premised on different facts and different local conditions, but a common legal question justifies their consideration together in this consolidated opinion.

In each of the cases, minors of the Negro race, through their legal representatives, seek the aid of the courts in obtaining admission to the public schools of their community on a nonsegregated basis. In each instance, they had been denied admission to schools attended by white children under laws requiring or permitting segregation according to race. This segregation was alleged to deprive the plaintiffs of the equal protection of the laws under the Fourteenth Amendment. In each of the cases other than the Delaware case, a three-judge federal district court denied relief to the plaintiffs on the so-called "separate but equal" doctrine announced by this Court in *Plessy v. Ferguson*. Under that doctrine, equality of treatment is accorded when the races are provided substantially equal facilities, even though these facilities be separate....

The plaintiffs contend that segregated public schools are not "equal" and cannot be made "equal," and that hence they are deprived of the equal protection of the laws. Because of the obvious importance of the question presented, the Court took jurisdiction. Argument was heard in the 1952 Term, and reargument was heard this Term on certain questions propounded by the Court.

Reargument was largely devoted to the circumstances surrounding the adoption of the Fourteenth Amendment in 1868. It covered exhaustively consideration of the Amendment in Congress, ratification by the states, then existing practices in racial segregation, and the views of proponents and opponents of the Amendment. This discussion and our own investigation convince us that, although these sources cast some light, it is not enough to resolve the problem with which we are faced. At best, they are inconclusive. The most avid proponents of the post-War Amendments undoubtedly intended them to remove all legal distinctions among "all persons born or naturalized in the United States." Their opponents, just as certainly, were antagonistic to both the letter and the spirit of the Amendments and wished them to have the most limited effect. What others in Congress and the state legislatures had in mind cannot be determined with any degree of certainty.

An additional reason for the inconclusive nature of the Amendment's history, with respect to segregated schools, is the status of public education at that time. In the South, the movement toward free common schools, supported by general taxation, had not yet taken hold. Education of white children was largely in the hands of private groups. Education of Negroes was almost nonexistent, and practically all of the race were illiterate. In fact, any education of Negroes was forbidden by law in some states. Today, in contrast, many Negroes have achieved outstanding success in the arts and sciences as well as in the business and professional world. It is true that public school education at the time of the Amendment had advanced further in the North, but the effect of the Amendment on Northern States was generally ignored in the congressional debates. Even in the North, the conditions of public education did not approximate those existing today. The curriculum was usually rudimentary; ungraded schools were common in rural areas; the school term was but three months a year in many states; and compulsory school attendance was virtually unknown. As a consequence, it is not surprising that there should be so little in the history of the Fourteenth Amendment relating to its intended effect on public education....

In the instant cases, that question [of whether *Plessy v. Ferguson* should be held inapplicable to public education] is directly presented. Here...there are findings below that the Negro and white schools involved have been equalized, or are being equalized, with respect to buildings, curricula, qualifications and salaries of teachers, and other "tangible" factors. Our decision, therefore, cannot turn on merely a comparison of these tangible factors in the Negro and white schools involved in each of the cases. We must look instead to the effect of segregation itself on public education.

In approaching this problem, we cannot turn the clock back to 1868 when the Amendment was adopted, or even to 1896 when *Plessy v. Ferguson* was written. We must consider public education in the light of its full development and its present place in American life throughout the Nation. Only in this way can it be determined if segregation in public schools deprives these plaintiffs of the equal protection of the laws.

Today, education is perhaps the most important function of state and local governments. Compulsory school attendance laws and the great expenditures for education both demonstrate our recognition of the importance of education to our democratic society. It is required in the performance of our most basic public responsibilities, even service in the armed forces. It is the very foundation of good citizenship. Today it is a principal instrument in awakening the child to cultural values, in preparing him for later professional training, and in helping him to adjust normally to his environment. In these days, it is doubtful that any child may reasonably be expected to succeed in life if he is denied the opportunity of an education. Such an opportunity, where the state has undertaken to provide it, is a right which must be made available to all on equal terms.

We come then to the question presented: Does segregation of children in public schools solely on the basis of race, even though the physical facilities and other "tangible" factors may be equal, deprive the children of the minority group of equal educational opportunities? We believe that it does....

To separate [children in grade and high schools] from others of similar age and qualifications solely because of their race generates a feeling of inferiority as to their status in the community that may affect their hearts and minds in a way unlikely ever to be undone. The effect of this separation on their educational opportunities was well stated by a finding in the Kansas case by a court which nevertheless felt compelled to rule against the Negro plaintiffs:

"Segregation of white and colored children in public schools has a detrimental effect upon the colored children. The impact is greater when it has the sanction of the law; for the policy of separating the races is usually interpreted as denoting the inferiority of the negro group. A sense of inferiority affects the motivation of a child to learn. Segregation with the sanction of law, therefore, has a tendency to [retard] the educational and mental development of negro children and to deprive them of some of the benefits they would receive in a racial[ly] integrated school system."

Whatever may have been the extent of psychological knowledge at the time of *Plessy v. Ferguson*, this finding is amply supported by modern authority. Any language in *Plessy v. Ferguson* contrary to this finding is rejected.

We conclude that in the field of public education the doctrine of "separate but equal" has no place. Separate educational facilities are inherently unequal. Therefore, we hold that the plaintiffs and others similarly situated for whom the actions have been brought are, by reason of the segregation complained of, deprived of the equal protection of the laws guaranteed by the Fourteenth Amendment....

It is so ordered.

---

1. In one sentence, state the Supreme Court's decision in *Plessy v. Ferguson*.

2. Briefly describe what you think are the most important arguments made by the majority to justify its decision in *Plessy*.

3. Briefly describe what you think are the most important arguments made by Justice John Marshall Harlan in his dissent in *Plessy*.

4. How does the majority opinion in *Plessy* differ from Justice Harlan's dissent on the important question of the Louisiana state legislature's intent in enacting the law that segregated railcars? Explain and support your answer.

5. In one sentence, state the Supreme Court's decision in *Brown v. Board of Education of Topeka*.

6. Briefly describe what you think are the most important arguments made by the Supreme Court to justify its decision in *Brown*.

7. Before *Brown* reached the Supreme Court, many school districts in the South dramatically increased their spending on black schools, hoping to stop the Court from ruling that segregated schools are unconstitutional. The strategy didn't work: Despite an influx of funds, most black schools remained patently inferior to white schools. In 1954, for example, public funding per pupil for black schools in the South was only 60 percent of funding for white schools. But what if the strategy had worked? Suppose that southern whites had spent enough to make black schools the equivalent of white schools. Suppose that the defendants in *Brown* were able to demonstrate conclusively to the justices on the Supreme Court that schools for African Americans across the South were in every tangible and measurable way equal to schools for whites. In the *Brown* opinion, what do the justices say that indicates

whether real equality between black and white schools would have altered their decision? Cite language from *Brown* to support your answer.

8. In the early 1950s, the judiciary was the only branch of the national government to act against segregation in the South. Both the executive and the legislative branches studiously avoided the issue. And when the Supreme Court ruled in *Brown*, its decision was vehemently opposed in the South. What characteristics of the Court give it the freedom to make unpopular decisions?

9. Go to http://www.civilrightsproject.harvard.edu/research/reseg04/brown50.pdf.[1] There you'll find a report on school segregation titled, "*Brown* at 50: King's Dream or *Plessy's* Nightmare," by Gary Orfield and Chungmei Lee. Read these sections of the report: Introduction: Dreams and Realities, pp. 4–5; *Brown* and King's Dream of Justice, pp. 5–9; and The Fate of the *Brown* Districts, pp. 11–13.

a. According to authors of the report, is segregation today in the nation's public school's increasing or decreasing?

b. Briefly describe Dr. Martin Luther King's "nightmare."

---

[1] Website URLs sometimes change. Try an external search (e.g., Google) to find the website. Configurations of a website often change. Try an internal search of the site to locate the information. Sometimes websites and pages within websites are removed. In that case, move on to the next question.

c. Describe, using percentages, the state of integration today in Clarendon County schools, one of the *Brown* districts.

EXERCISE 10.2 Same-Sex Marriage: The New Civil Right?

INTRODUCTION

The gay rights movement began with a riot in New York City in 1969, when city police raided the Stonewall Inn, a gay bar. At that time, it was illegal for people of the same gender to dance together. Since then many have suggested parallels between the struggle for gay rights and the battles still being waged for the civil rights of ethnic and racial minorities and women.

The legal battle in the fight for gay rights contests the application of the Fourteenth Amendment. Even though many states and localities have protected gays and lesbians from employment and housing discrimination, and even though many cities and businesses have adopted policies that extend medical insurance and other benefits to those in same-sex domestic partnerships, gay and lesbian rights have not been protected by federal statute, nor has the U.S. Supreme Court included gays and lesbians as a protected group under the *equal protection clause* of the Fourteenth Amendment. The closest the Court has come to linking the equal protection clause and sexual orientation is *Romer v. Evans* (1996). In that case, the Court struck down Colorado's Amendment 2 (a voter initiative) because it singled out gays and lesbians as a class and denied them protection under Colorado's constitution. (Ordinances protecting gays and lesbians from discrimination in cities like Denver, Boulder, and Aspen had been nullified under the Colorado initiative.) The Court did not decide whether the Fourteenth Amendment protected gays and lesbians, but ruled that no state could *a priori* exclude a class of people from such protection.

In *Lawrence v. Texas* (2003), the Supreme Court struck down antisodomy laws as an unconstitutional violation of the liberties included in the *due process clause* of the Fourteenth Amendment. The issue that commanded a majority vote of the Court was not discrimination against gays and lesbians, but rather the right to private sexual relations among consenting adults, whether heterosexual or homosexual (see Exercise 11.3). Justice Antonin Scalia, however, in a dissenting opinion, predicted with trepidation that the decision in *Lawrence* would eventually be used as a precedent to establish a right to same-sex marriage.

Some advocates of a civil right to same-sex marriage believe that the Civil Rights Act of 1964 and other federal statutes that prohibit discrimination based on sex should apply to discrimination against gays, lesbians, and transgendered people as well. Cass Sunstein, a professor of law at the University of Chicago, argues that discrimination against homosexuals is rooted in the fear that gay rights will undermine traditional male and female gender roles. Because homosexuals do not conform to those role expectations, they become the object of discrimination.[1]

The political controversy over same-sex marriage intensified in 1993, when the Hawaii Supreme Court ruled that denying gays and lesbians the right to marry violated the Hawaii constitution. (In 1998, Hawaii voters reversed that decision by ratifying an amendment to the state's constitution that defined marriage as a union between a man and a woman.) The 1993 decision by the Hawaii court engendered an outcry in state capitals and in Washington, DC. Some feared that states would be forced to recognize same-sex marriages under the full faith and credit clause of Article IV, Section 1 of the Constitution: "Full faith and credit shall be given in each state to the public acts, records, and judicial proceedings of every other state. And the Congress may by general laws prescribe the manner in which such acts, records, and proceedings shall be proved, and the effect thereof."

To calm those fears, Congress passed the Defense of Marriage Act (DOMA) in 1996, which (1) granted states the authority to exempt themselves from same-sex marriages recognized by other states and (2) defined marriage as a union between a man and a woman under federal law. Forty-six states now ban recognition of same-sex marriage.[2] In 2000, Vermont became the first state to recognize same-sex unions, granting homosexual partners legal benefits under state law similar to those of marriage.

---

[1] Cass R. Sunstein, *Designing Democracy: What Constitutions Do* (New York: Oxford University Press, 2001).

[2] A few states had bans in place before DOMA. Most of the bans have been enacted by state legislatures under DOMA or by voter initiative. Some laws and initiatives are being challenged in federal and state courts. See: http://www.answers.com/topic/same-sex-marriage-in-the-united-states.

In November 2003, the controversy over same-sex marriage erupted again when the Massachusetts Supreme Court, in *Goodridge v. Dept. of Health*, ruled that the Massachusetts state constitution prohibited discrimination on the basis of sexual orientation in the issuing of marriage licenses.[3] As the campaign for the presidency heated up late in 2004, President George W. Bush announced that he favored an amendment to the U.S. Constitution to define marriage as a union between a man and a woman. Presidential candidate John Kerry stated that he too opposed same-sex marriage but thought that the issue should be left up to each state—consistent with the constitutional principle of federalism. Exit polls from the 2004 presidential election suggested that the same-sex marriage issue helped Bush mobilize and win the support of the vast majority of conservative Christian voters, especially in the eleven states that had ballot measures prohibiting same-sex marriage (see Exercise 4.1).[4]

Nevertheless, in 2005 Congress remained short of the two-thirds majority in the House and Senate required to propose a constitutional amendment restricting the right to gay marriage. Even if Congress proposed such an amendment, three-fourths of the state legislatures would have to ratify it. The framers of the Constitution made it exceedingly difficult to amend the Constitution; they did not want the "passions and prejudices" of the moment frozen into the nation's fundamental law. There's only one constitutional amendment that restricted rather than enlarged the realm of freedom for citizens: the Eighteenth, which ushered in prohibition. Not surprisingly, that's the only amendment that has been repealed (the Twenty-First Amendment; see Exercise 2.4).

The contemporary controversy over same-sex marriage is so heated because the prospect of same-sex marriage challenges deeply embedded moral and cultural norms. But all civil rights movements challenge traditional values. At one time, military leaders maintained that the integration of African Americans into the armed forces would undermine morale, just as many military leaders argue today against the enlistment of openly homosexual men and women.

ASSIGNMENT

On March 7, 2000, California voted to define marriage as a union between a man and a woman. The ballot measure, Proposition 22, passed by a margin of 61 percent to 39 percent.[5] Reading 10.2.1 includes the language of the ballot measure, followed by pro and con ballot arguments. Study the reading and answer the questions that follow.

READING 10.2.1 CALIFORNIA PROPOSITION 22: LIMIT ON MARRIAGE INITIATIVE STATUTE

Proposed Law

SECTION 1. This act may be cited as the "California Defense of Marriage Act."

SECTION 2. Section 308.5 is added to the Family Code, to read:

308.5. Only marriage between a man and a woman is valid or recognized in California.

---

[3] At this writing, the Massachusetts state legislature has placed on hold attempts to amend the state constitution to prohibit gay marriage.

[4] All eleven measures to prohibit same-sex marriage passed. Kerry won only one of those states—Oregon.

[5] On March 14, 2004, a judge of a California superior court struck down Proposition 22 as a violation of the California constitution. As of this writing, that decision is on appeal. In the meantime, Proposition 22 is still being enforced.

Ballot Argument for Proposition 22

Dear Fellow Voter:

I'm a 20-year-old woman voting for only the second time on March 7th. I'm proud, excited, and a bit nervous, because I take my civic responsibilities seriously. Not only that, but among millions of people supporting Proposition 22, the *Protection of Marriage Initiative*, I have the honor of writing you to explain why Californians should vote "Yes" on 22.

Proposition 22 is exactly 14 words long: *"Only marriage between a man and a woman is valid or recognized in California."*

That's it! No legal doubletalk, no hidden agenda. Just common sense: Marriage should be between a man and a woman.

It does not take away anyone's right to inheritance or hospital visitation.

When people ask, "Why is this necessary?" I say that even though California law already says only a man and a woman may marry, it also recognizes marriages from other states. However, judges in some of those states want to define marriage differently than we do. If they succeed, California may have to recognize new kinds of marriages, even though most people believe marriage should be between a man and a woman.

California is not alone in trying to keep marriage between a man and a woman. In 1996, *Democrats and Republicans in Congress overwhelmingly passed a bill* saying that the U.S. government defines marriage as between a man and a woman only, and said each state could do the same.

President Clinton signed the bill the day after he received it. So far, 30 states have passed laws defining marriage as between a man and a woman.

Now it's our turn, and I'm voting "Yes" on 22 to ensure that decisions affecting California are voted on by Californians ... like us.

It's Our State, it should be Our Choice.

But some people today think marriage doesn't matter anymore. They say I have to accept that marriage can mean whatever anyone says it means, and if I don't agree then I'm out of touch, even an extremist.

My family taught me to respect other people's freedoms. Everyone should. But that's a two way street. If people want me to respect their opinions and lifestyles, then they should grant me the same courtesy by respecting MY beliefs. And I believe that marriage should stay the way it is.

It's tough enough for families to stay together these days. Why make it harder by telling children that marriage is just a word anyone can re-define again and again until it no longer has any meaning?

Marriage is an important part of our lives, our families and our future. Someday I hope to meet a wonderful man, marry and have children of my own. By voting "Yes" on 22, I'm doing *my part today* to keep that dream alive. *Please, for all future generations, vote "Yes" on 22.*

Miriam G. Santacruz

We couldn't have said it better! As representatives of *seniors, teachers and parents*, we're proud to join Californians from all walks of life voting "Yes" on 22.

Jeanne Murray

Field Director, 60 Plus Association

Gary Beckner

Executive Director, Association of American Educators

Thomas Fong

President, Chinese Family Alliance

Ballot Argument Against Proposition 22

The California Interfaith Alliance

The League of Women Voters of California

The California Teachers Association

Senator Dianne Feinstein

Senator Barbara Boxer

Congressman Tom Campbell

Vice President Al Gore

Senator Bill Bradley

The California Republican League

And thousands of husbands, wives, mothers and fathers from across California oppose Proposition 22.

THE PURPOSE OF PROPOSITION 22 IS NOT TO BAN MARRIAGE FOR SAME-SEX COUPLES IN CALIFORNIA. IT IS ALREADY BANNED.

You don't need to support marriage for gay and lesbian couples to oppose Proposition 22, the "Knight Initiative". You just have to believe in a few basic values— keeping government out of our personal lives, respecting each other's privacy, and not singling out one group for discrimination or for special rights.

VOTING NO ON 22 WILL *NOT* LEGALIZE SAME-SEX MARRIAGE, NO MATTER WHAT THE SUPPORTERS OF PROPOSITION 22 SAY.

The real purpose is to use Proposition 22 as a tool in court to deny basic civil rights to lesbians and gays and their families. Proposition 22 will be used, as similar laws have been in other states, to deny the right of partners to visit their sick or injured companion in hospitals, to deny the right to inheritance, and even to deny the right of a remaining companion to live in their home.

PROPOSITION 22 WILL RESULT IN UNNECESSARY GOVERNMENT INTERFERENCE.

Whether we think homosexuality is right or wrong, we should stay out of other people's private lives and let people make their own decisions about moral values and commitments. Californians treasure our right to be left alone and to lead our lives the way we wish. Adding more laws about private behavior and personal relationships isn't a solution to anything.

PROPOSITION 22 DIVIDES US. Californians have seen too many efforts in recent years to pick on specific groups of people and single them out for discrimination. Supporters of Proposition 22 are spending millions of dollars to convince you that basic rights should be denied to a group of Californians. They want us to believe that attacking same-gender couples will solve problems instead of causing them. But we've seen what spreading fear and hatred has already done. According to the Attorney General, more than 2,000 Californians were victimized by hate crimes last year alone. California has had enough of the politics of fear and hate. Voting "No" on 22 will send that message.

PROPOSITION 22 IS UNFAIR. Even when gay or lesbian couples have been together for many years, one companion often has no right to visit a sick or injured companion in the hospital. They often can't get basic health insurance for dependents. They have no inheritance rights. That's wrong. And Proposition 22 will make it more difficult to right this wrong— by singling out lesbians and gays for discrimination.

Proposition 22 doesn't solve any problems ...

It adds more government interference to our lives ...

It singles out one group for attack ...

It tears us apart instead of bringing us together.

VOTE NO ON 22.

Antonio R. Villaraigosa

Assembly Speaker, California State Legislature

The Right Reverend William E. Swing

Bishop of the Episcopal Diocese of California

Krys Wulff

---

1. Would you have voted for or against Proposition 22? Explain and support your answer by referring to the ballot arguments that you find most convincing.

2. On November 2, 2004, eleven states voted to prohibit same-sex marriages. One of those states was Ohio. Its ballot measure contained language that might also prohibit civil unions—legally sanctioned partnerships between homosexuals that are not recognized as marriages. The ballot measure read: "Only a union between one man and one woman may be a marriage valid in or recognized by this state and its political subdivisions. This state and its political subdivisions shall not create or recognize a legal status for relationships of unmarried individuals that intends to approximate the design, qualities, significance or effect of marriage." What is the specific language that could be interpreted to restrict or prohibit civil unions?

3. If you would have voted *against* California Proposition 22, banning same-sex marriages, skip this question. If you would have voted *for* California Proposition 22, would you have also voted to ban civil unions? Explain and support your answer.

4. On July 14, 2004, Senator Allard (Republican, Colorado) introduced a constitutional amendment to prohibit same-sex marriage. A motion that would have brought the proposed amendment to the floor of the Senate for a vote was defeated 48–50 (60 senators would have been necessary to permit an up or down vote). The proposed amendment read: "Marriage in the United States shall consist only of the union of a man and a woman. Neither this Constitution, nor the constitution of any State, shall be construed to require that marriage or the legal incidents thereof be conferred upon any union other than the union of a man and a woman." Some senators who opposed the proposed amendment believed that it went too far: They argued that it would prohibit the states from allowing civil unions or any legal rights for homosexual partners. What language in the proposed amendment were they concerned about?

5. Some critics of the proposed constitutional amendment maintain that their opposition stems from their commitment to protect the traditional powers and prerogatives of state governments—not from support for same-sex marriage. They argue that the regulation of marriage is a reserved power of the states and that the federal government has no business telling the states who should or should not be granted marriage licenses. Do you think that the same-sex marriage/civil union issue should be left up to the states? Explain and support your position.

_____

_____

_____

_____

_____

In 1967, the Supreme Court, in *Loving v. Virginia*, decided that laws prohibiting interracial marriage (antimiscegenation laws) violated the Fourteenth Amendment to the Constitution. Reading 10.2.2 includes the language of the two Virginia statutes under which the Lovings, an interracial couple, were prosecuted and which the Supreme Court later nullified in the *Loving* decision. Study the reading and then answer question 6.

READING 10.2.2 VIRGINIA ANTIMISCEGENATION STATUTES

The Lovings were convicted of violating 20-58 of the Virginia Code:

> "Leaving State to evade law.... If any white person and colored person shall go out of this State, for the purpose of being married, and with the intention of returning, and be married out of it, and afterwards return to and reside in it, cohabiting as man and wife, they shall be punished as provided in 20-59, and the marriage shall be governed by the same law as if it had been solemnized in this State. The fact of their cohabitation here as man and wife shall be evidence of their marriage."

Section 20–59, which defines the penalty for miscegenation, provides:

> "Punishment for marriage.... If any white person intermarry with a colored person, or any colored person intermarry with a white person, he shall be guilty of a felony and shall be punished by confinement in the penitentiary for not less than one nor more than five years."

6. Randall Kennedy, a professor of law at Harvard University, makes the following analogy between laws that once banned interracial marriages and laws that now prohibit same-sex marriage: "The ... significance of *Loving* today is that it helps to buttress the case for tolerating same-sex marriages. Just as many people once found trans-racial marriage to be a loathsome potentiality well-worth prohibiting, so, too, do many people find same-sex marriage to be an abomination. This frightened, reflexive reaction will likely dissipate in many of the same ways that antipathy to the idea of trans-racial marriage has dissipated."[6] Do you agree or disagree with Professor Kennedy that discrimination against same-sex marriage is analogous to antimiscegenation laws? Explain and support your position.

_____

_____

_____

_____

_____

---

[6] Randall Kennedy, "*Loving v. Virginia* at 30," February 6, 1997. See SpeakOut.com: http://speakout.com/activism/opinions/3208-1.html.

EXERCISE 10.3 The Gender Wage Gap

INTRODUCTION

All paychecks are not created equal: Since 2000, women have earned about 75 cents for every dollar men earned.[1]

Imbedded in the gender wage gap are difficult and contentious issues such as the roles of men and women in society, undervaluing women's work, and even globalization. With the exception of agreement that the gender wage gap exists, there is today little consensus about it: Is the gap narrowing? What causes the wage gap? What's to be done about it?

Most parties to the debate agree that the gender wage gap has a number of sources. Among them:

- Differences in the age, education, skill, experience, job tenure, and marital status of men and women workers
- Social norms and expectations—for example, the notion that some occupations are "men's work" and others "women's work" or that traditional "women's work" (nursing, teaching, etc.) and the skills and training necessary to perform it are simply undervalued
- The different choices men and women make regarding family—for example, whether to marry, whether to have children, and how to share childrearing responsibilities
- The proportions of men and women working part-time versus full-time
- The proportions of men and women workers who are union versus nonunion

Researchers who study the gender wage gap have attempted to control for the variables identified above using statistical analysis. Even so, a portion of the gap remains unaccounted for.[2] Many suspect that this unexplained portion of the gap stems from discrimination against women workers—discrimination that's illegal under federal law and court rulings.[3] There is no doubt that discrimination against women and minorities in pay and advancement exists in the workplace. Companies frequently settle lawsuits by admitting discriminatory practices and by paying cash settlements.[4]

ASSIGNMENT

Questions 1–6 are based on data from the Department of Labor in Table 10.3.1 "Median Weekly Earnings of Full-Time and Salary Workers by Occupation and Sex, 2004."

---

[1] This figure comes from the Current Population Survey and is based on the female-to-male earnings ratio at the median for year-round, full-time workers. See Census Bureau, Census 2000 Special Reports, "Evidence from Census 2000 About the Earnings by Detailed Occupation for Men and Women," issued May 2004, p. 11. The report is at http://www.census.gov/prod/2004pubs/censr-15.pdf.

[2] See for example, "Women's Earnings: Work Patterns Partially Explain Difference between Men's and Women's Earnings," General Accounting Office Report, October 2003. The report is available at http://www.gao.gov/. Type in the search engine: GAO-04-35.

[3] Title VII of the Civil Rights Act of 1964 was the first federal legislation to address systematically race and gender discrimination in the workplace. In *Reed v. Reed* (1971), the Supreme Court ruled for the first time that statutory gender discrimination violated the equal protection clause of the Fourteenth Amendment.

[4] In July 2004, Boeing agreed to pay up to $70 million and change some of its employment practices to settle a gender discrimination case. Home Depot, Lucky Stores, Smith Barney, and other prominent employers have recently settled gender discrimination cases.

TABLE 10.3.1 Median Weekly Earnings of Full-Time and Salary Workers by Occupation and Sex, 2004

Occupation	Men		Women	
	Number of Workers (in thousands)	Median Weekly Earnings	Number of Workers (in thousands)	Median Weekly Earnings
Management Occupations				
Chief executives	802	$1,875	248	$1,310
Human resource managers	90	1,259	171	958
Food service managers	336	713	232	598
Accountants and auditors	543	1,016	842	757
Professional Occupations				
Computer programmers	371	1,151	145	1,006
Social workers	148	720	472	689
Lawyers	412	1,710	208	1,255
Elementary school teachers	435	917	1,772	776
Pharmacists	90	1,684	72	1,432
Physical therapists	50	955	70	900
Service Occupations				
Police and sheriff officers	571	845	83	841
Waiters and waitresses	261	399	538	327
Maids and housekeeping	95	402	723	324
Sales and Office Occupations				
Real estate sales	197	834	233	663
Postal Service mail carriers	203	834	112	743
Secretaries and administrative assistants	87	598	2,570	550
Production Occupations				
Butchers	209	488	51	369
Laundry and dry cleaning	62	460	74	323
Sewing machine operators	56	381	186	319
Bus drivers	215	588	152	440
Driver/sales and truck drivers	2,494	613	93	476
Packers and packagers	143	373	206	333
Construction Occupations				
Carpenters	1,149	576	21	n.d.*
Electricians	655	718	14	n.d.
Roofers	184	482	3	n.d.

TABLE 10.3.1 (Cont.)

	MEN		WOMEN	
Occupation	Number of Workers (in thousands)	Median Weekly Earnings	Number of Workers (in thousands)	Median Weekly Earnings
Installation, Repair, and Maintenance Occupations				
Aircraft mechanics	113	856	3	n.d.
Automotive mechanics	723	639	12	n.d.
Telecommunication line installers and repairers	127	771	7	n.d.

° No data are shown where the number of workers in the occupation is less than 50,000.
SOURCE: Bureau of Labor Statistics, http://www.bls.gov/cps/cpsaat39.pdf.

1. Identify two occupations in which women are significantly overrepresented, meaning that the number of women in the occupation is much larger than the number of men.

2. Identify two occupations in which women are significantly underrepresented.

3. In how many of the occupations listed in Table 10.3.1 do the median weekly earnings of women exceed those of men?

4. Identify an occupation in which the median weekly earnings of men and women are nearly equal.

5. Identify an occupation in which the median weekly earnings of men and women are far from equal.

6. The gender wage gap is the difference between the earnings of men and women in a given occupation or group of occupations.

a. What's the weekly earnings gap between men and women lawyers?

b. What would be the approximate yearly earnings gap between men and women lawyers?

In April 2005, Senator Tom Harkin (Democrat, Iowa) and several Democratic cosponsors introduced the Fair Pay Act in the House and Senate. The introduction of the bill coincided with Equal Pay Day, an event coordinated by the National Committee on Pay Equity (NCPE), a coalition of dozens of labor unions, women's and civil rights organizations, and other associations and commissions. The NCPE was founded in 1979 with the purpose of eliminating sex- and race-based wage discrimination and achieving pay equity. In introducing the Fair Pay Act of 2005, Senator Harkin said: "We simply must do something about the longtime pattern of wage discrimination. We can start closing the pay gap right now by simply paying women what they're worth." Legislation similar to the Fair Pay Act of 2005 was introduced in Congress during the 1990s and in 2001 and 2003, but failed to pass. The last major legislation passed by Congress on the issue of pay equity was the 1963 Pay Equity Act, signed into law by President John F. Kennedy. Questions 7 and 8 are based on Reading 10.3.1, an excerpt from the Fair Pay Act of 2005.

READING 10.3.1 H.R. 1697, Fair Pay Act of 2005

Section 1. Short Title and Reference.

(a) Short Title—This Act may be cited as the 'Fair Pay Act of 2005'....

Section 2. Findings.

Congress finds the following:

1. Wage rate differentials exist between equivalent jobs segregated by sex, race, and national origin in Government employment and in industries engaged in commerce or in the production of goods for commerce.
2. The existence of such wage rate differentials—
   A. depresses wages and living standards for employees necessary for their health and efficiency;
   B. prevents the maximum utilization of the available labor resources;
   C. tends to cause labor disputes, thereby burdening, affecting, and obstructing commerce;
   D. burdens commerce and the free flow of goods in commerce; and
   E. constitutes an unfair method of competition.
3. Discrimination in hiring and promotion has played a role in maintaining a segregated work force.
4. Many women and people of color work in occupations dominated by individuals of their same sex, race, and national origin.
5. A 2000 study conducted by the Census Bureau of 400 fields that employed 10,000 full-time, year-round workers found that women were able to earn at least as much as men in just 5 fields: hazardous material removal, telecommunications line installation and repair, meeting and convention planning, food preparation, and construction trade assistant work.
6. In 2004, an Institute for Women's Policy Research analysis of data collected in the Current Population Survey by the Bureau of Labor Statistics found that women were paid only 76 cents for every dollar that a man is paid.
7. Section 6(d) of the Fair Labor Standards Act of 1938 (29 U.S.C. 206(d)) prohibits discrimination in compensation for 'equal work' on the basis of sex.
8. Title VII of the Civil Rights Act of 1964 (42 U.S.C. 2000e et seq.) prohibits discrimination in compensation because of race, color, religion, national origin, and sex. The Supreme Court, in its decision in *County of Washington v. Gunther*, 452 U.S. 161 (1981), held that title VII's prohibition against discrimination in compensation also applies to jobs that do not constitute 'equal work' as defined in section 6(d) of the Fair Labor Standards Act of 1938 (29 U.S.C. 206(d)). Decisions of lower courts, however, have demonstrated that further clarification of existing legislation is necessary in order effectively to carry out the intent of Congress to implement the Supreme Court's holding in its Gunther decision.
9. Artificial barriers to the elimination of discrimination in compensation based upon sex, race, and national origin continue to exist more than 3 decades after the passage of section 6(d) of the Fair Labor Standards Act of 1938 (29 U.S.C. 206(d)) and the Civil Rights Act of 1964. Elimination of such barriers would have positive effects, including—

A. providing a solution to problems in the economy created by discrimination through wage rate differentials;
B. substantially reducing the number of working women and people of color earning low wages, thereby reducing the dependence on public assistance; and
C. promoting stable families by enabling working family members to earn a fair rate of pay.

Section 3. Equal Pay for Equivalent Jobs.

(a) Amendment—Section 6 (29 U.S.C. 206) is amended by adding at the end the following:

'(h)(1)(A) Except as provided in subparagraph (B), no employer having employees subject to any provision of this section shall discriminate, within any establishment in which such employees are employed, between employees on the basis of sex, race, or national origin by paying wages to employees in such establishment in a job that is dominated by employees of a particular sex, race, or national origin at a rate less than the rate at which the employer pays wages to employees in such establishment in another job that is dominated by employees of the opposite sex or of a different race or national origin, respectively, for work on equivalent jobs.

'(B) Nothing in subparagraph (A) shall prohibit the payment of different wage rates to employees where such payment is made pursuant to—

  '(i) a seniority system;
  '(ii) a merit system;
  '(iii) a system that measures earnings by quantity or quality of production; or
  '(iv) a differential based on a bona fide factor other than sex, race, or national origin, such as education, training, or experience, except that this clause shall apply only if—
    '(I) the employer demonstrates that?
      '(aa) such factor—
      '(AA) is job-related with respect to the position in question; or
      '(BB) furthers a legitimate business purpose, except that this item shall not apply if the employee demonstrates that an alternative employment practice exists that would serve the same business purpose without producing such differential and that the employer has refused to adopt such alternative practice; and
      '(bb) such factor was actually applied and used reasonably in light of the asserted justification; and
    '(II) upon the employer succeeding under subclause (I), the employee fails to demonstrate that the differential produced by the reliance of the employer on such factor is itself the result of discrimination on the basis of sex, race, or national origin by the employer.

'(C) The Equal Employment Opportunity Commission shall issue guidelines specifying criteria for determining whether a job is dominated by employees of a particular sex, race, or national origin. Such guidelines shall not include a list of such jobs.

'(D) An employer who is paying a wage rate differential in violation of subparagraph (A) shall not, in order to comply with the provisions of such subparagraph, reduce the wage rate of any employee....'

---

7. Study Section 2 of the Fair Pay Act, "Findings."

a. In your view, which finding is most persuasive? Explain your position.

_____

_____

_____

_____

b. In your view, which finding is least persuasive? Explain your position.

8. One aspect of the gender wage gap is that women often are not paid the same as men for the same work. The problem of comparable worth is another aspect of the gender wage gap. Occupations dominated by women pay less—and often a lot less—than occupations with comparable education and skill requirements dominated by men. For example, a study by the National Women's Law Center found that women make up 86 percent of the students enrolled in child care courses. Men, on the other hand, make up 94 percent of the students training to become plumbers. Students entering the field of child care can expect to earn a median salary of $7.43 an hour; the top 10 percent of child care workers earn $10.71 an hour. The median pay for plumbers is $18.19 an hour; the top 10 percent of plumbers make $30.06 an hour.[5]

Study Section 3 of the Fair Pay Act, "Equal Pay for Equivalent Jobs." Carefully examine the following sentence from Section 3, and particularly the use of the word *equivalent*: "no employer ... shall discriminate ... between employees on the basis of sex, race, or national origin by paying wages ... in a job that is dominated by employees of a particular sex, race, or national origin at a rate less than the rate at which the employer pays wages to employees ... in another job that is dominated by employees of the opposite sex or of a different race or national origin ... for work on equivalent jobs."

a. Identify and explain a significant objection that employers would likely raise to this provision of the proposed legislation.

---

[5] "Title IX and Equal Opportunity in Vocational and Technical Education: A Promise Still Owed to the Nation's Young Women," A Report by the National Women's Law Center, June 2002. The report is at www.nwlc.org/pdf/TitleIXCareerEducationReport.pdf.

b. Referring to Section 3, in your own words, explain when the payment of different wage rates for men and women is permitted under the bill.

9. Go to http://www.epf.org/pubs/newsletters/2000/compworth.asp.[6] Study the article "Background on Comparable Worth" by Anita U. Hattiangadi, an economist at the Employment Policy Foundation. Identify two important objections Hattiangadi raises against pay equity and comparable-worth legislation.

10. According to Hattiangadi, what factors beside gender discrimination in the workplace account for the pay gap between men and women?

11. Go to http://www.aflcio.org/issuespolitics/women/equalpay/CaseForEqualPay.cfm. Study "The Case for Equal Pay," in which the AFL-CIO identifies several arguments made by the opponents of equal pay and counters each of those arguments.

---

[6] Website URLs sometimes change. Try an external search (e.g., Google) to find the website. Configurations of a website often change. Try an internal search of the site to locate the information. Sometimes websites and pages within websites are removed. In that case, move on to the next question.

a. In your view, for which argument against equal pay is the AFL-CIO's counterargument most persuasive? Explain and support your answer.

b. In your view, for which argument against equal pay is the AFL-CIO's counterargument least persuasive? Explain and support your answer.

EXERCISE 10.4 The End of Affirmative Action?

INTRODUCTION

Affirmative action refers to government or private-sector programs in employment, higher education admissions, and government contracting that give preference to *underrepresented groups*—those that have suffered a pattern of historical disadvantage and discrimination. Underrepresented groups are those whose numbers in a college, university, or place of employment are disproportionately low compared to their numbers in the general population that the institution or employer serves. Affirmative action initially focused on African Americans, but in time it was applied to members of other minority groups and women.

In 1965, President Lyndon B. Johnson issued Executive Order 11246, making affirmative action official government policy. Johnson believed that the Civil Rights Act of 1964 (CRA), which prohibiting discrimination in employment, would be slow to achieve racial equality. That's because the CRA placed the burden on individuals to prove discrimination and because discrimination in individual cases is difficult to prove. Therefore, Johnson decided that the federal government must make an affirmative effort to hire African Americans. The federal government later required affirmative-action programs to be in place for businesses contracting with the government and for colleges and universities receiving federal aid. From there, affirmative-action programs were adopted by the private sector, often voluntarily. (Many corporations became convinced that affirmative action was good business; the addition of women and minorities to the workplace enabled businesses to penetrate new markets.) Proponents of affirmative action assumed that as minority representation in colleges, universities, and the workplace increased, the need for affirmative-action policies would disappear. This has happened in some cases; for example, women no longer receive preference in admission to law schools because they now make up about half of first-year law school students, but they continue to receive preference in engineering programs.

Affirmative-action programs never enjoyed widespread support for several reasons. First, there had never been a legislative debate about them. Affirmative action was instituted by executive action—and later the courts—so the public was not adequately educated about the rationale for the programs. Second, many whites charged that they had become the victims of so-called reverse discrimination—that affirmative action penalized whites in its attempt to remediate the effects of centuries of discrimination. Third, early affirmative-action programs that set quotas for minority representation were vigorously contested. For example, a medical school might reserve a certain number of first-year slots exclusively for members of minority groups, in the process denying admission to what might have been, by traditional criteria, better-qualified white applicants. Even after the Supreme Court declared the use of quotas unconstitutional in most cases, opponents of affirmative action insisted that quotas were still in effect—under the guise of goals.

The U.S. Supreme Court first addressed affirmative action in 1978, in *Regents of the University of California v. Bakke*. Alan Bakke was twice rejected for admission to the UC-Davis medical school. The university had reserved sixteen of the one hundred openings for applicants who were economically or educationally "disadvantaged." Because some minority applicants who were statistically less qualified were accepted under the special admissions program, Bakke charged that his equal protection rights under the Fourteenth Amendment had been violated. The Court agreed with Bakke. A plurality of the justices held that quotas were unacceptable, although they also agreed that race and other nonacademic factors could be considered as one of many criteria in the admissions process.

In 1996, California voters approved a ballot measure, the California Civil Rights Initiative (CCRI, Proposition 209), that abolished preferences for any individual or group on the basis of race, sex, color, ethnicity, or national origin in public employment, public education, or public contracting. Proponents of the measure argued that the initial goals of affirmative action had been subverted over the years, that thirty years of preferential programs had leveled the playing field, and that the programs were demeaning to minorities. Opponents countered that the programs had helped women and minorities overcome the effects of past and present discrimination and that the CCRI promoted racial divisiveness.[1]

---

[1] A. G. Bloc, "Proposition 209: Affirmative Action," *California Journal*, September 1996, pp. 8–10.

Shortly thereafter, the University of California initiated a policy of guaranteeing admission to one of its nine campuses to the top 4 percent of the graduating class of each high school in the state, so long as a student had successfully completed the prerequisite courses. When this policy failed to maintain diversity at the most competitive campuses in the system, the university decided in 2001 to replace the Scholastic Aptitude Test, on which minorities commonly have low scores, with achievement tests that measure subject matter and skill preparation. Additionally, the university is engaging in a more comprehensive review of applicants, a review that includes other indicators of potential—for example, hardships overcome—not just grades and test scores.

ASSIGNMENT

The most recent affirmative-action cases decided by the Supreme Court are *Gratz v. Bollinger* (2003) and *Grutter v. Bollinger* (2003). Both cases came from the University of Michigan—the first involving its undergraduate admissions program and the second its law school admissions program. Readings 10.4.1 and 10.4.2 describe the affirmative-action admissions programs at University of Michigan Law School and University of Michigan undergraduate admissions. Reading 10.4.3 outlines the criteria the Court uses in determining the constitutionality of affirmative-actions programs. Study the readings and answer the questions that follow.

READING 10.4.1 DESCRIPTION OF AFFIRMATIVE-ACTION PROGRAM AT UNIVERSITY OF MICHIGAN LAW SCHOOL (*GRUTTER* CASE)[2]

The University of Michigan Law School (Law School), one of the nation's top law schools, follows an official admissions policy that seeks to achieve student body diversity through compliance with *Regents of Univ. of Cal. v. Bakke*, 438 U.S. 265. Focusing on students' academic ability coupled with a flexible assessment of their talents, experiences, and potential, the policy requires admissions officials to evaluate each applicant based on all the information available in the file, including a personal statement, letters of recommendation, an essay describing how the applicant will contribute to Law School life and diversity, and the applicant's undergraduate grade point average (GPA) and Law School Admissions Test (LSAT) score. Additionally, officials must look beyond grades and scores to so-called "soft variables," such as recommenders' enthusiasm, the quality of the undergraduate institution and the applicant's essay, and the areas and difficulty of undergraduate course selection. The policy does not define diversity solely in terms of racial and ethnic status and does not restrict the types of diversity contributions eligible for "substantial weight," but it does reaffirm the Law School's commitment to diversity with special reference to the inclusion of African-American, Hispanic, and Native-American students, who otherwise might not be represented in the student body in meaningful numbers. By enrolling a "critical mass" of underrepresented minority students, the policy seeks to ensure their ability to contribute to the Law School's character and to the legal profession. When the Law School denied admission to petitioner Grutter, a white Michigan resident with a 3.8 GPA and 161 LSAT score, she filed this suit, alleging that respondents had discriminated against her on the basis of race in violation of the Fourteenth Amendment, Title VI of the Civil Rights Act of 1964, and 42 U.S.C. §1981; that she was rejected because the Law School uses race as a "predominant" factor, giving applicants belonging to certain minority groups a significantly greater chance of admission than students with similar credentials from disfavored racial groups; and that respondents had no compelling interest to justify that use of race.

---

[2] *Grutter v. Bollinger*, 000 U.S. 02-241 (2003).

READING 10.4.2 Description of Affirmative-Action Program in University of Michigan's Undergraduate Admissions (GRATZ CASE)[3]

Caucasian, applied for admission to the University of Michigan's (University) College of Literature, Science, and the Arts (LSA) in 1995 and 1997, respectively. Although the LSA considered Gratz to be well qualified and Hamacher to be within the qualified range, both were denied early admission and were ultimately denied admission. In order to promote consistency in the review of the many applications received, the University's Office of Undergraduate Admissions (OUA) uses written guidelines for each academic year. The guidelines have changed a number of times during the period relevant to this litigation. The OUA considers a number of factors in making admissions decisions, including high school grades, standardized test scores, high school quality, curriculum strength, geography, alumni relationships, leadership, and race. During all relevant periods, the University has considered African-Americans, Hispanics, and Native Americans to be "under-represented minorities," and it is undisputed that the University admits virtually every qualified applicant from these groups. The current guidelines use a selection method under which every applicant from an underrepresented racial or ethnic minority group is automatically awarded 20 points of the 100 needed to guarantee admission.

Petitioners filed this class action alleging that the University's use of racial preferences in undergraduate admissions violated the Equal Protection Clause of the Fourteenth Amendment, Title VI of the Civil Rights Act of 1964, and 42 U.S.C. §1981. They sought compensatory and punitive damages for past violations, declaratory relief finding that respondents violated their rights to nondiscriminatory treatment, an injunction prohibiting respondents from continuing to discriminate on the basis of race, and an order requiring the LSA to offer Hamacher admission as a transfer student.

READING 10.4.3 Criteria the Supreme Court Uses to Determine Constitutionality of Affirmative-Action Programs

- The program must be *benign*. A benign program is one that is designed not to hinder or degrade a group but, rather, to advance it—to create conditions of equal opportunity for it. The primary effect must not be to harm or discriminate against others, though that may be an unavoidable secondary effect.
- If the program uses *suspect classifications*—race, national origin, or sex—those suspect classifications are constitutional only if they can withstand *strict scrutiny*.
- Suspect classifications can only withstand strict scrutiny if they meet the following criteria:
  1. There must be a *compelling government interest*; for example, improving education or providing educational opportunity.
  2. The program must be *narrowly tailored* to achieve the government's interest. The program can go no further than is absolutely necessary to accomplish that compelling interest.
     - Admission policies that seek the proportional representation of minorities are not narrowly tailored; those that seek to prevent minorities from being isolated and becoming "spokespersons for their race" are narrowly tailored.
     - Admission policies that consider race or ethnicity alone are not narrowly tailored; those that consider a variety of elements of diversity in individual cases (for example, geography and economic hardship) are narrowly tailored.

---

[3] *Gratz v. Bollinger*, 000 U.S. 02-516 (2003).

1. Apply the criteria in Reading 10.4.3 to the affirmative-action program described in Reading 10.4.1 (*Grutter* case) to determine whether that affirmative-action program might have been found constitutional or unconstitutional.

   a. Is the program benign? Explain and support your answer.

   _____

   _____

   _____

   b. Can the suspect classification withstand strict scrutiny? Is there a compelling government interest? Is the program narrowly tailored? Explain and support your answer.

   _____

   _____

   _____

   c. How do you think the Supreme Court ruled in *Grutter v. Bollinger*—for Grutter or for Bollinger (University of Michigan Law School)? Explain your answer by showing what criteria you applied.

   _____

   _____

   _____

   _____

   _____

   _____

   _____

2. You can find the *Grutter* case on findlaw.com: http://caselaw.lp.findlaw.com/scripts/getcase.pl?court=us&vol=000&invol=02-241.[4] (Read the "Held" section of the decision to find the answer.) Did you correctly predict the ruling in the case?

   _____

3. Apply the criteria in Reading 10.4.3 to the affirmative-action program described in Reading 10.4.2 (*Gratz* case) to determine whether that affirmative-action program might have been found constitutional or unconstitutional.

---

[4] Website URLs sometimes change. Try an external search (e.g., Google) to find the website. Configurations of a website often change. Try an internal search of the site to locate the information. Sometimes websites and pages within websites are removed. In that case, move on to the next question.

a. Is the program benign? Explain and support your answer.

b. Can the suspect classification withstand strict scrutiny? Is there a compelling government interest? Is the program narrowly tailored? Explain and support your answer.

c. How do you think the Supreme Court ruled in *Gratz v. Bollinger*—for Gratz or for Bollinger (University of Michigan's undergraduate admissions)? Explain your answer by showing what criteria you applied.

4. You can find the *Gratz* case on findlaw.com: http://caselaw.lp.findlaw.com/scripts/getcase.pl?court=us&vol=000&invol=02-516. (Read the "Held" section of the decision to find the answer.) Did you correctly predict the ruling in the case?

5. Some critics of race-based affirmative-action programs argue that they're racially divisive and they do little for the underclass. Those critics have called for affirmative action based on economic need, particularly in college and professional school admissions, as the most effective and fair way to promote equal opportunity.[5] Do you think it's appropriate for a state university system to use economic disadvantage as a criterion for admissions to diversify its professional programs—for example, its engineering and law programs? Explain and support your answer.

---

[5] See, for example, Shelby Steele, *The Content of Our Character* (New York: St. Martin's Press, 1990).

CHAPTER 11

Civil Liberties

EXERCISE 11.1 The Tension between Civil Liberties Advocates and Civil Rights Advocates: Campus Hate Speech Codes

INTRODUCTION

For most of twentieth-century American history, advocates of civil liberties, like the American Civil Liberties Union (ACLU), and advocates of civil rights, like the National Association for the Advancement of Colored People (NAACP), have been allies in numerous causes. Those and other groups fought together to defend racial, ethnic, and ideological minorities against overbearing majorities and against government repression of dissent. Beginning in the 1970s, however, some hot-button issues, such as school busing, affirmative action, and hate speech codes, created tension between these old allies. Hate speech codes promulgated by many colleges, universities, and cities brought into stark contrast—and sometimes conflict—the often contradictory values of freedom and equality espoused by civil liberties and civil rights advocates.

Civil liberties are anchored in the freedoms granted in the Bill of Rights. The first ten amendments to the Constitution involve the right to be left alone, to be free from government interference and arbitrary government action. Typically, civil liberties cases involve an individual asserting the right to live and express herself freely. According to civil libertarians, only a compelling government interest may restrict—or trump—those liberties.

Civil rights are constitutionally based in the equal protection clause of the Fourteenth Amendment. Rather than asserting the right to be left alone by the state, advocates of civil rights have pressured the national government—particularly the Supreme Court—to dismantle political and social systems of discrimination and oppression. According to civil rights advocates, government enforcement of the equal protection clause is essential for minorities' attainment of the full rights of citizenship.

BOX 11.1.1

Hate Speech Codes as a Civil Liberties Issue

- Based on the First Amendment (freedom of speech)
- The emphasis is on the right to *individual* expression—to think and to believe as one wants.
- There is value in a free and open debate—even if the speech is offensive.

Hate Speech Codes as a Civil Rights Issue

- Based on the equal protection clause of the Fourteenth Amendment
- Groups that have suffered a historical pattern of discrimination seek protection under the Fourteenth Amendment.
- The group objective is to achieve full participation in the educational community and to achieve educational objectives, not to be marginalized and made to feel uncomfortable in the classroom, on campus, and in college housing.

Most civil libertarians oppose hate speech codes. They believe that the right to freedom of speech overrides the objections of those offended by hate speech. Democratic public life, they argue, requires an open, vigorous debate, unimpeded by university authorities. Hate speech should be combated not by suppressing it, but rather by subjecting it to unyielding criticism and scrutiny in the marketplace of ideas. Civil libertarians do not, of course, defend the right of anyone to attack specific individuals with racist, sexist, homophobic, or religious epithets—so-called *fighting words*.

Civil rights advocates believe that hate speech by its very nature dehumanizes and undermines the equality of citizens. In the university setting, hateful attacks on minority students deny them the right to an equal education. At the very least, hate speech marginalizes those it targets, making them uncomfortable in the classroom and impairing their success. According to civil rights advocates, college and university campuses should provide a refuge for minorities from odious speech.

The constitutionality of hate speech codes has remained an issue, particularly at public institutions. (Private colleges and universities have much greater leeway in defining prohibited behavior.) Federal district courts found unconstitutional hate speech codes at the University of Michigan and the University of Wisconsin.[1] The courts found the codes to be overly broad—meaning that the codes were so sweeping that they banned protected speech, such as speech that is merely offensive. In the courts' view, codes must be drawn narrowly to address "only the specific evil at hand." The courts also found the codes vague and imprecise, so that men or women with "common intelligence must necessarily guess at [their] meaning." Courts declare codes "void for vagueness" when reasonable people cannot determine from the language of the code whether or not their actions are likely subject to the code's provisions. After these court cases, public universities narrowed the focus of their hate speech codes or dropped them altogether.

ASSIGNMENT

Study Reading 11.1.1. Then answer question 1.

READING 11.1.1 Case Studies of Campus Hate Speech

Case 1

The members of a prominent fraternity held an "ugly woman" contest in a university building. One of the contestants donned a black wig with curlers, painted his face black, and used pillows to simulate an exaggerated bust and buttocks. Several weeks later, the university dean, at the urging of

---

[1] 721 F. Supp. 852 (E.D. Mich, 1989); 774 F. Supp. 1163 (E.D. Wis, 1991).

several student leaders, disciplined the fraternity for engaging in behavior that perpetuated racial and sexual stereotypes. The fraternity appealed the discipline, contending that the expression—though perhaps offensive to some—was harmless and therefore protected by the First Amendment. University rules specifically prohibit speech and conduct that demean others on the basis of race, ethnicity, sexual orientation, or gender. A hearing has been scheduled for the appeal.

Case 2

A female student at a community college in Texas charged that her English professor's continual references to sexual topics and use of profanity in class constituted sexual harassment. The college's recently enacted sexual harassment policy reads in part: "Conduct is prohibited that has the purpose or effect of unreasonably interfering with an individual's academic performance or creating an intimidating, hostile, or offensive learning environment." The professor acknowledged that his teaching style is sometimes provocative and confrontational, but argued that he has taught this way effectively for years. The college administration put the professor on unpaid leave for one semester and required that he attend sensitivity-training workshops. After a lower court upheld the administration's actions, the professor appealed on the grounds that the college's sexual harassment policy violated his First Amendment rights.

Case 3

A public university adopted a speech code that punished students "for racist or discriminatory comments, epithets or other expressive behavior directed at an individual or on separate occasions at different individuals, or for physical conduct, if such comments, epithets or other expressive behavior or physical conduct intentionally:

1. demean the race, sex, religion, color, creed, disability, sexual orientation, national origin, ancestry or age of the individual or individuals; or
2. create an intimidating, hostile or demeaning environment for education, university-related work, or other university-authorized action."

A student in a sociology class, during a discussion of homosexual marriage, stated, "If we allow gays and lesbians to marry, what's next? People will have the right to marry dogs and adults will have the right to marry children—even their own children." The professor and several students filed a complaint against the student for violating the university's speech code. He was subsequently expelled. The student challenged the expulsion in federal court on the grounds that the speech code was overly broad and vague, and therefore unconstitutionally restricted his First Amendment right to free speech. He argued in court that his comments should not have come under the purview of the university's speech code because they were part of a classroom discussion of an academic issue. The university defended the code and its application of it on the grounds that it had a compelling interest in maintaining a campus climate free from discrimination and intimidation.

---

1. For each of the three cases, identify the civil liberties arguments and the civil rights arguments that apply (see the Introduction and Box 11.1.1).

Case 1

Civil liberties arguments:

_____

_____

_____

_____

Civil rights arguments:

_____
_____
_____
_____
_____

Case 2

Civil liberties arguments:

_____
_____
_____
_____
_____

Civil rights arguments:

_____
_____
_____
_____
_____

Case 3

Civil liberties arguments:

_____
_____
_____
_____

Civil rights arguments:

_____
_____
_____

Reading 11.1.2 presents some arguments for and against a proposed hate speech code at the University of Michigan. Study the arguments and consider them as you answer question 2.

READING 11.1.2 THE PROS AND CONS OF A POLICY COVERING HATE SPEECH AT THE UNIVERSITY OF MICHIGAN[2]

Pros

1. Universities have a right and duty to provide an educational environment, a climate of civility, where all students can learn and live free from bigotry.
2. A university's objective is to educate and to instill within students fundamental values of human decency.
3. Numerous responses from students to the rights and responsibilities document last summer indicated that a significant proportion of the harassment experienced by U-M students comes from faculty. They described in-class harassment, racial harassment at a public event, harassment based on ethnic origin, and clear cultural bias in classroom settings.
4. Speech codes publicly announce a university's support of civil rights and equal dignity of all persons; the failure to adopt a speech code implies that the University condones hate speech.
5. The University may be held liable for damages by persons who were subjected to harassment, if the University knowingly tolerates such conduct.
6. Faculty and staff, as well as students, should be prohibited from violating the rights of other members of the University community.
7. While harassment by faculty may be quite rare, it is important to have a mechanism for dealing with reported incidents and resolving misunderstandings that may be interpreted as harassment.

Cons

1. Any regulation of speech thwarts the truth-seeking process, inhibits the sharing of knowledge and encroaches on academic freedom.
2. The toleration of hate speech is the price to be paid for individual liberty.
3. Restrictions on hate speech represent a step down the slippery slope toward censorship and, ultimately, totalitarianism.
4. Universities are the last place where speech should be restricted, since the essence of a university is the free and unfettered exchange of ideas.
5. Those who are disciplined by codes become martyrs for the cause of free speech despite their hate-filled message.
6. Those victimized by hate speech are overly sensitive and self-conscious, the university's role not being to protect students.
7. Codes are not an effective means to stop hate, and only strong counter-speech prevents hate.

---

[2] *The [Michigan] University Record*, February 8, 1993. Reprinted with permission.

2. How would you decide each of the three cases in Reading 11.1.1? Consider Reading 11.1.2 as you explain and support your answer.

Case 1

Case 2

Case 3

EXERCISE 11.1   THE TENSION BETWEEN CIVIL LIBERTIES ADVOCATES AND CIVIL RIGHTS ADVOCATES

Questions 3 and 4 are based on the American Civil Liberties Union's position on hate speech codes. You will find that position at http://www.aclu.org/StudentsRights/StudentsRights.cfm?ID=9004&c=159.[3]

3. a. Why does the ACLU oppose hate speech codes?

___

b. Do you agree with the ACLU's position? Why or why not?

___

4. The ACLU affirms that racism, sexism, and homophobia are problems on college campuses.

a. How does the ACLU propose to address these problems while preserving free-speech rights?

___

b. Do you agree with the ACLU's recommendations? Why or why not?

___

[3] Website URLs sometimes change. Try an external search (e.g., Google) to find the website. Configurations of a website often change. Try an internal search of the site to locate the information. Sometimes websites and pages within websites are removed. In that case, move on to the next question.

EXERCISE 11.2 Random Drug Testing in Public Schools

INTRODUCTION

According to civil libertarians, efforts to curb drug use often threaten individual privacy, especially when authorities search for and seize drugs in a person's home or automobile or on one's own body. One privacy issue involves drug testing and the language in the Fourth Amendment that protects people "against unreasonable searches and seizures" except when there is "probable cause." According to the Supreme Court, drug testing is reasonable for employees in "safety-sensitive" jobs—railroad engineers and airline pilots, for example—as well as for those who carry firearms. The Court also recognizes that some forms of drug testing are more intrusive than others. For example, breath and urine tests are less intrusive than blood tests, which require penetration of the skin. Many companies routinely test prospective employees for drugs as a condition for working. Private businesses have more latitude in drug testing because the Bill of Rights protects citizens against the invasion of their civil liberties by government to a greater extent than by private entities.

But the Court has not given a green light to drug testing under all circumstances. In 1997, in *Chandler v. Miller*, the Court struck down a Georgia law that required candidates for public office to pass a drug test to qualify for a spot on the ballot. According to the Court, the drug-testing requirement was not reasonable because the state of Georgia failed to demonstrate that drug use plagued a significant number of candidates for state office. In 2001, in *Ferguson v. City of Charleston*, the Court invalidated drug testing for indigent pregnant women who sought the medical services of city hospitals. A public hospital in Charleston, South Carolina, tested pregnant women for drugs—without their knowledge—to identify crack babies. The results of all positive tests were passed on to the police. In a 6–3 decision, the justices held that the hospital's failure to inform the women of the test, not to mention tipping off the police, violated the women's rights under the Fourth Amendment.

Mandatory random drug testing in public school grades K–12 raises controversial questions about the privacy rights of students. In the precedent-setting case, *Vernonia School District v. Acton* (1995), the Supreme Court ruled that schools did not exceed their constitutional authority by requiring random drug tests in a noncompulsory, after-school, competitive athletic program. Since that decision, courts have expanded random drug testing in extracurricular activities. Courts have been willing to permit public schools much constitutional leeway in random drug testing, locker searches, censorship of school newspapers, and weapons searches because the judiciary is reluctant "to become a national school board" micromanaging the nation's schools. Critics of the courts' position contend that the judiciary has suspended the Constitution at the schoolhouse door.

ASSIGNMENT

Study Reading 11.2.1, which is an excerpt from the Supreme Court's opinion in *Vernonia School District v. Acton* (1995). Then answer questions 1–4. The selection focuses on the Court's response to the claim that the student's privacy rights had been infringed on, that the privacy of the student's own body had been violated by the "search for and seizure of" his bodily fluids.

READING 11.2.1 *Vernonia School District v. Acton*, 515 U.S. 646 (1995)

The first factor to be considered is the nature of the privacy interest upon which the search here at issue intrudes. The Fourth Amendment does not protect all subjective expectations of privacy, but only those that society recognizes as "legitimate." What expectations are legitimate varies, of course, with context, depending, for example, upon whether the individual asserting the privacy interest is at home, at work, in a car, or in a public park. Central, in our view, to the present case is the fact that the subjects of the Policy are (1) children, who (2) have been committed to the temporary custody of the State as schoolmaster.

Traditionally at common law, and still today, unemancipated minors lack some of the most fundamental rights of self-determination—including even the right of liberty in its narrow sense, i.e., the right to come and go at will. They are subject, even as to their physical freedom, to the control of their parents or guardians. [A] parent "may ... delegate part of his parental authority, during his life, to the tutor or schoolmaster of his child; who is then in loco parentis, and has such a portion of the power of the parent committed to his charge, viz. that of restraint and correction, as may be necessary to answer the purposes for which he is employed." Thus, while children assuredly do not "shed their constitutional rights ... at the schoolhouse gate," the nature of those rights is what is appropriate for children in school.

Fourth Amendment rights, no less than First and Fourteenth Amendment rights, are different in public schools than elsewhere; the "reasonableness" inquiry cannot disregard the schools' custodial and tutelary responsibility for children. For their own good and that of their classmates, public school children are routinely required to submit to various physical examinations, and to be vaccinated against various diseases. Particularly with regard to medical examinations and procedures, therefore, "students within the school environment have a lesser expectation of privacy than members of the population generally."

Legitimate privacy expectations are even less with regard to student athletes. School sports are not for the bashful. They require "suiting up" before each practice or event, and showering and changing afterwards. Public school locker rooms, the usual sites for these activities, are not notable for the privacy they afford. The locker rooms in Vernonia are typical: no individual dressing rooms are provided; shower heads are lined up along a wall, unseparated by any sort of partition or curtain; not even all the toilet stalls have doors. There is an additional respect in which school athletes have a reduced expectation of privacy. By choosing to "go out for the team," they voluntarily subject themselves to a degree of regulation even higher than that imposed on students generally. In Vernonia's public schools, they must submit to a preseason physical exam (James testified that his included the giving of a urine sample), they must acquire adequate insurance coverage or sign an insurance waiver, maintain a minimum grade point average, and comply with any "rules of conduct, dress, training hours and related matters as may be established for each sport by the head coach and athletic director with the principal's approval."

Having considered the scope of the legitimate expectation of privacy at issue here, we turn next to the character of the intrusion that is complained of. We recognized in *Skinner* that collecting the samples for urinalysis intrudes upon "an excretory function traditionally shielded by great privacy." We noted, however, that the degree of intrusion depends upon the manner in which production of the urine sample is monitored. Under the District's Policy, male students produce samples at a urinal along a wall. They remain fully clothed and are only observed from behind, if at all. Female students produce samples in an enclosed stall, with a female monitor standing outside listening only for sounds of tampering. These conditions are nearly identical to those typically encountered in public restrooms, which men, women, and especially school children use daily. Under such conditions, the privacy interests compromised by the process of obtaining the urine sample are in our view negligible. The other privacy-invasive aspect of urinalysis is, of course, the information it discloses concerning the state of the subject's body, and the materials he has ingested. In this regard it is significant that the tests at issue here look only for drugs, and not for whether the student is, for example, epileptic, pregnant, or diabetic. And finally, the results of the tests are disclosed only to a limited class of school personnel who have a need to know; and they are not turned over to law enforcement authorities or used for any internal disciplinary function.

Taking into account all the factors we have considered above—the decreased expectation of privacy, the relative unobtrusiveness of the search, and the severity of the need met by the search—we conclude Vernonia's Policy is reasonable and hence constitutional. We caution against the assumption that suspicionless drug testing will readily pass constitutional muster in other contexts. The most significant element in this case is the first we discussed: that the Policy was undertaken in furtherance of the government's responsibilities, under a public school system, as guardian and tutor of children entrusted to its care. We find insufficient basis to contradict the judgment of Vernonia's parents, its school board, and the District Court, as to what was reasonably in the interest of these children under the circumstances.

1. On what basis does the Court claim that there is less right to privacy behind the schoolhouse door than beyond it?

_____

_____

_____

2. What are the special circumstances in Veronica School District's program that make the program constitutionally permissible?

_____

_____

_____

3. How does the school district seek to protect the students' privacy?

_____

_____

_____

4. Do you agree with the Court's decision in *Veronica*, or would you have voted to decide the case differently? Explain and support your position.

_____

_____

_____

_____

_____

_____

Study Reading 11.2.2, which is an excerpt from *Board of Education of Independent School District No. 92 of Pottawatomie County v. Earls* (2002). Then answer questions 5 and 6. In this case, the Supreme Court faced the question of whether random drug testing was permissible in *all* extracurricular activities, not just for athletics, as in *Vernonia*. (In practice, the drug testing in the Oklahoma school district had been limited to *competitive* extracurricular activities—for example, cheerleading.)

READING 11.2.2 *Board of Education of Pottawatomie County v. Earls*, 000 U.S. 01-332 (2002)

We first consider the nature of the privacy interest allegedly compromised by the drug testing. As in *Vernonia*, the context of the public school environment serves as the backdrop for the analysis of the privacy interest at stake and the reasonableness of the drug testing policy in general.

A student's privacy interest is limited in a public school environment where the State is responsible for maintaining discipline, health, and safety. Schoolchildren are routinely required to submit to physical examinations and vaccinations against disease. Securing order in the school environment sometimes requires that students be subjected to greater controls than those appropriate for adults. ("Without first establishing discipline and maintaining order, teachers cannot begin to educate their students. And apart from education, the school has the obligation to protect pupils from mistreatment by other children, and also to protect teachers themselves from violence by the few students whose conduct in recent years has prompted national concern").

Respondents argue that because children participating in nonathletic extracurricular activities are not subject to regular physicals and communal undress, they have a stronger expectation of privacy than the athletes tested in *Vernonica*. This distinction, however, was not essential to our decision in *Vernonia*, which depended primarily upon the school's custodial responsibility and authority.

In any event, students who participate in competitive extracurricular activities voluntarily subject themselves to many of the same intrusions on their privacy as do athletes. Some of these clubs and activities require occasional off-campus travel and communal undress. All of them have their own rules and requirements for participating students that do not apply to the student body as a whole. For example, each of the competitive extracurricular activities governed by the Policy must abide by the rules of the Oklahoma Secondary Schools Activities Association, and a faculty sponsor monitors the students for compliance with the various rules dictated by the clubs and activities. This regulation of extracurricular activities further diminishes the expectation of privacy among schoolchildren. We therefore conclude that the students affected by this Policy have a limited expectation of privacy.

Respondents also argue that the testing of nonathletes does not implicate any safety concerns, and that safety is a "crucial factor" in applying the special needs framework. They contend that there must be "surpassing safety interests," or "extraordinary safety and national security hazards," in order to override the usual protections of the Fourth Amendment. Respondents are correct that safety factors into the special needs analysis, but the safety interest furthered by drug testing is undoubtedly substantial for all children, athletes and nonathletes alike. We know all too well that drug use carries a variety of health risks for children, including death from overdose.

---

5. Explain the reasoning the Court used to determine that random drug testing in all extracurricular activities is not significantly different from drug testing in competitive athletics (*Vernonia*) and is therefore constitutional.

Question 6 is based on both the *Vernonia* and *Earls* decisions.

6. Do you think the Court's decisions in *Vernonia* and *Earls* have opened the door for random drug testing for *all* K–12 public school students? Explain and support you answer by citing specific language from the Court's decisions.

Question 7 asks you to consider the pros and cons of random drug testing for public school students (K–12). The position in favor of random testing is stated in Reading 11.2.3. The position against random testing is at the American Civil Liberties Union's website: http://www.aclu.org/DrugPolicy/DrugPolicy.cfm?ID=11002&c=79.[1]

READING 11.2.3 WHAT ARE THE BENEFITS OF RANDOM DRUG TESTING?[2]

Drug use can quickly turn to dependence and addiction, trapping users in a vicious cycle that destroys families and ruins lives. Students who use drugs or alcohol are statistically more likely to drop out of school than their peers who don't. Dropouts, in turn, are more likely to be unemployed, to depend on the welfare system, and to commit crimes. If drug testing deters drug use, everyone benefits—students, their families, their schools, and their communities. Drug and alcohol abuse not only interferes with a student's ability to learn, it also disrupts the orderly environment necessary for all students to succeed. Studies have shown that students who use drugs are more likely to bring guns and knives to school, and that the more marijuana a student smokes, the greater the chances he or she will be involved in physical attacks, property destruction, stealing, and cutting

---

[1] Website URLs sometimes change. Try an external search (e.g., Google) to find the website. Configurations of a website often change. Try an internal search of the site to locate the information. Sometimes websites and pages within websites are removed. In that case, move on to the next question.

[2] Source: Office of National Drug Control Policy: http://news.findlaw.com/hdocs/docs/drugs/schldrgtst802whrpt.pdf.

classes. Just as parents and students can expect schools to offer protection from violence, racism, and other forms of abuse, so do they have the right to expect a learning environment free from the influence of illegal drugs.

---

7. Do you favor the extension of mandatory random drug testing to all students in grades K–12? Explain and support your position.

EXERCISE 11.3 Homosexuals and the Right to Privacy

INTRODUCTION

Americans take for granted that a constitutional right to privacy shields them from a wide array of intrusions by the state. Many citizens bemoan the erosion of the right to privacy, a perennial topic of national political discourse. A close reading of the Constitution, however, reveals no explicit grant of a right to privacy.[1] The Supreme Court has inferred the right to privacy from certain language in the Bill of Rights (see Box 11.3). In *Griswold v. Connecticut* (1965), the High Court held that a Connecticut statute that prohibited a married couple from obtaining information about the use of contraceptives violated the couple's right to privacy. In *Stanley v. Georgia* (1969), the Court found that people have a privacy right to watch sexually explicit movies in their own homes. The Court also employed the concept of privacy to support a woman's right to an abortion (*Roe v. Wade*, 1973). However, the right to privacy does not protect the contents of trash bags left at the curb for pickup (*California v. Greenwood*, 1988). The Court used the right to privacy to allow the withdrawal of artificial life-sustaining measures, so long as there is "informed consent," such as a living will, in *Cruzan v. Director, Missouri Department of Health* (1990). But the Court has not extended privacy rights to protect physician-assisted suicide, *Washington v. Glucksberg* (1997).

The Court has applied privacy rights to consensual heterosexual sex between adults. The Court, however, ruled in *Bowers v. Hardwick* (1986), by a slim 5–4 majority, that homosexual sex was not protected by the Constitution, thereby upholding the constitutionality of Georgia's antisodomy law, a law that applied to both hetero- and homosexual sodomy but that was enforced—albeit rarely—against gays only.

In a landmark reversal of *Bowers*, the Court, in *Lawrence v. Texas* (2003), struck down a Texas antisodomy statute that had been aimed exclusively at gays. Responding to a reported weapons disturbance in a private residence, Houston police entered Lawrence's apartment and saw him and another adult man engaging in a private, consensual sexual act. Under the Texas penal code, Lawrence and his partner were charged with "deviate sexual intercourse, namely anal sex, with a member of the same sex (man)."

BOX 11.3.1 The Right to Privacy

- The right to privacy was announced by the Supreme Court in a 1965 case involving access to birth control devices: privacy of "marital bedroom."
- The Supreme Court based the right to privacy on inferences from the following amendments: 1 (e.g., "freedom of association"); 3 (prohibition against forced quartering of soldiers); 5 (e.g., prohibition against self-incrimination—"freedom of conscience"); and especially 4 (e.g., the right of the people to be secure in their persons, houses, papers, and effects). The Court also based the right on Amendment 9 ("the enumeration of certain rights [in the first eight amendments] does not disparage or deny others retained by the people").
- The right to privacy was later applied in abortion rights (*Roe v. Wade*, 1973)—that is, the privacy of a woman's body and the private relationship between a woman and her physician.
- The right to privacy, some argue, is also applicable to the "right to die (physician-assisted suicide)", random drug testing (see Exerise 11.2), and sexual relations among consenting adults (this exercise).

---

[1] Some state constitutions explicitly grant a right to privacy. Article 1, Section 1 of the California state constitution, for example, reads: "All people are by nature free and independent and have inalienable rights. Among these are enjoying and defending life and liberty, acquiring, possessing, and protecting property, and pursuing and obtaining safety, happiness, and privacy."

ASSIGNMENT

Reading 11.3.1 includes excerpts from the Supreme Court's opinion in *Lawerence v. Texas*. Justice Anthony Kennedy, usually a conservative voice on the Court, wrote the opinion of the Court. Reading 11.3.2 includes excerpts from Justice Antonin Scalia's stinging dissent from the Court's decision. Study both opinions, and then answer the questions that follow.

READING 11.3.1 JUSTICE KENNEDY'S OPINION OF THE COURT IN *LAWRENCE V. TEXAS*, 000 U.S. 02-102 (2003)

We deem it necessary to reconsider the Court's holding in *Bowers*. To say that the issue in *Bowers* was simply the right to engage in certain sexual conduct demeans the claim the individual put forward, just as it would demean a married couple were it to be said marriage is simply about the right to have sexual intercourse. The laws involved in *Bowers* and here are, to be sure, statutes that purport to do no more than prohibit a particular sexual act. Their penalties and purposes, though, have more far-reaching consequences, touching upon the most private human conduct, sexual behavior, and in the most private of places, the home. The statutes do seek to control a personal relationship that, whether or not entitled to formal recognition in the law, is within the liberty of persons to choose without being punished as criminals.

This, as a general rule, should counsel against attempts by the State, or a court, to define the meaning of the relationship or to set its boundaries absent injury to a person or abuse of an institution the law protects. It suffices for us to acknowledge that adults may choose to enter upon this relationship in the confines of their homes and their own private lives and still retain their dignity as free persons. When sexuality finds overt expression in intimate conduct with another person, the conduct can be but one element in a personal bond that is more enduring. The liberty protected by the Constitution allows homosexual persons the right to make this choice.

It must be acknowledged, of course, that the Court in *Bowers* was making the broader point that for centuries there have been powerful voices to condemn homosexual conduct as immoral. The condemnation has been shaped by religious beliefs, conceptions of right and acceptable behavior, and respect for the traditional family. For many persons these are not trivial concerns but profound and deep convictions accepted as ethical and moral principles to which they aspire and which thus determine the course of their lives. These considerations do not answer the question before us, however. The issue is whether the majority may use the power of the State to enforce these views on the whole society through operation of the criminal law. "Our obligation is to define the liberty of all, not to mandate our own moral code."

The present case does not involve minors. It does not involve persons who might be injured or coerced or who are situated in relationships where consent might not easily be refused. It does not involve public conduct or prostitution. It does not involve whether the government must give formal recognition to any relationship that homosexual persons seek to enter. The case does involve two adults who, with full and mutual consent from each other, engaged in sexual practices common to a homosexual lifestyle. The petitioners are entitled to respect for their private lives. The State cannot demean their existence or control their destiny by making their private sexual conduct a crime. Their right to liberty under the Due Process Clause gives them the full right to engage in their conduct without intervention of the government. "It is a promise of the Constitution that there is a realm of personal liberty which the government may not enter." The Texas statute furthers no legitimate state interest which can justify its intrusion into the personal and private life of the individual.

The judgment of the Court of Appeals for the Texas Fourteenth District is reversed, and the case is remanded for further proceedings not inconsistent with this opinion. It is so ordered.

READING 11.3.2 JUSTICE SCALIA'S DISSENTING OPINION IN *LAWRENCE V. TEXAS*, 000 U.S. 02-102 (2003).

I turn now to the ground on which the Court squarely rests its holding: the contention that there is no rational basis for the law here under attack. This proposition is so out of accord with our jurisprudence, indeed, with the jurisprudence of *any* society we know—that it requires little discussion.

The Texas statute undeniably seeks to further the belief of its citizens that certain forms of sexual behavior are "immoral and unacceptable," the same interest furthered by criminal laws against fornication, bigamy, adultery, adult incest, bestiality, and obscenity. *Bowers* held that this *was* a legitimate state interest. The Court today reaches the opposite conclusion. The Texas statute, it says, "furthers *no legitimate state interest* which can justify its intrusion into the personal and private life of the individual." The Court embraces instead *Justice Stevens*' declaration in his *Bowers* dissent, that "the fact that the governing majority in a State has traditionally viewed a particular practice as immoral is not a sufficient reason for upholding a law prohibiting the practice." This effectively decrees the end of all morals legislation.

Today's opinion is the product of a Court, which is the product of a law-profession culture, that has largely signed on to the so-called homosexual agenda, by which I mean the agenda promoted by some homosexual activists directed at eliminating the moral opprobrium that has traditionally attached to homosexual conduct. I noted in an earlier opinion the fact that the American Association of Law Schools (to which any reputable law school *must* seek to belong) excludes from membership any school that refuses to ban from its job-interview facilities a law firm (no matter how small) that does not wish to hire as a prospective partner a person who openly engages in homosexual conduct.

One of the most revealing statements in today's opinion is the Court's grim warning that the criminalization of homosexual conduct is "an invitation to subject homosexual persons to discrimination both in the public and in the private spheres." It is clear from this that the Court has taken sides in the culture war, departing from its role of assuring, as neutral observer, that the democratic rules of engagement are observed. Many Americans do not want persons who openly engage in homosexual conduct as partners in their business, as scoutmasters for their children, as teachers in their children's schools, or as boarders in their home. They view this as protecting themselves and their families from a lifestyle that they believe to be immoral and destructive. The Court views it as "discrimination" which it is the function of our judgments to deter. So imbued is the Court with the law profession's anti-anti-homosexual culture, that it is seemingly unaware that the attitudes of that culture are not obviously "mainstream"; that in most States what the Court calls "discrimination" against those who engage in homosexual acts is perfectly legal.

Let me be clear that I have nothing against homosexuals, or any other group, promoting their agenda through normal democratic means. Social perceptions of sexual and other morality change over time, and every group has the right to persuade its fellow citizens that its view of such matters is the best. That homosexuals have achieved some success in that enterprise is attested to by the fact that Texas is one of the few remaining States that criminalize private, consensual homosexual acts. But persuading one's fellow citizens is one thing, and imposing one's views in absence of democratic majority will is something else. I would no more *require* a State to criminalize homosexual acts—or, for that matter, display *any* moral disapproval of them—than I would *forbid* it to do so. What Texas has chosen to do is well within the range of traditional democratic action, and its hand should not be stayed through the invention of a brand-new "constitutional right" by a Court that is impatient of democratic change. It is indeed true that "later generations can see that laws once thought necessary and proper in fact serve only to oppress," *ante*, at 18; and when that happens, later generations can repeal those laws. But it is the premise of our system that those judgments are to be made by the people, and not imposed by a governing caste that knows best.

One of the benefits of leaving regulation of this matter to the people rather than to the courts is that the people, unlike judges, need not carry things to their logical conclusion. The people may feel that their disapprobation of homosexual conduct is strong enough to disallow homosexual marriage, but not strong enough to criminalize private homosexual acts—and may legislate accordingly. The Court today pretends that it possesses a similar freedom of action, so that we need not fear judicial imposition of homosexual marriage, as has recently occurred in Canada (in a decision that the Canadian Government has chosen not to appeal). At the end of its opinion—after having laid waste the foundations of our rational-basis jurisprudence—the Court says that the present case "does not involve whether the government must give formal recognition to any relationship that homosexual persons seek to enter." Do not believe it. More illuminating than this bald, unreasoned disclaimer is the progression of thought displayed by an earlier passage in the Court's opinion, which notes the constitutional protections afforded to "personal decisions relating to *marriage*, procreation, contraception, family relationships, child rearing, and education," and then declares that "[p]ersons in a homosexual relationship may seek autonomy for these purposes, just as heterosexual persons do." Today's opinion dismantles the structure of constitutional law that has permitted a distinction to be made between heterosexual and homosexual unions, insofar as formal recognition in marriage is concerned. If moral disapprobation of homosexual conduct is "no legitimate state interest" for purposes of proscribing that conduct; and if, as the Court coos (casting aside all pretense of neutrality), "[w]hen sexuality finds overt expression in intimate conduct with another person, the conduct can be but one element in a personal bond that is more enduring"; what justification could there possibly be for denying the benefits of marriage to homosexual couples exercising "[t]he liberty protected by the Constitution." Surely not the encouragement of procreation, since the sterile and the elderly are allowed to marry. This case "does not involve" the issue of homosexual marriage only if one entertains the belief that principle and logic have nothing to do with the decisions of this Court. Many will hope that, as the Court comfortingly assures us, this is so. The matters appropriate for this Court's resolution are only three: Texas's prohibition of sodomy neither infringes a "fundamental right" (which the Court does not dispute), nor is unsupported by a rational relation to what the Constitution considers a legitimate state interest, nor denies the equal protection of the laws. I dissent.

---

1. In *Bowers*, the Court ruled that the Constitution gives no protection to the practice of homosexual sodomy. In the *Lawrence* case, Justice Kennedy asserts that the real constitutional issue posed by Texas's antisodomy law has nothing to do with specific sexual practices. What does he think the real constitutional issue is? Cite specific language from the decision to support your answer.

2. a. Justice Kennedy concedes that many people (maybe even a majority) have a deeply ingrained moral aversion to homosexuality. According to Kennedy, why is it improper to base the Court's decision on such moral objections? Cite specific language from the decision to support your answer.

b. According to Kennedy, what *should* be the basis for the Court's decision? Cite specific language from the decision to support your answer.

3. a. On what grounds does Scalia criticize the Court's majority for maintaining that the state of Texas has no legitimate interest in prohibiting homosexual sodomy?

b. What, according to Scalia, is the legitimate state interest that justifies prohibiting homosexual sodomy?

4. Scalia accuses the Court's majority of pursuing a political agenda. What is the basis for that claim?

5. Scalia believes that the majority opinion opens the door to the constitutional expansion of gay rights. What specific "right" does he fear that the Court may in the future confer on homosexuals?

6. Do you agree with the Court's decision in *Lawrence* that private sexual relations among consenting adults—whether heterosexual or homosexual—should not be a concern of the government? Or do you agree with Justice Scalia that the government has a legitimate interest in the regulation of morals, so long as there is no specific constitutional prohibition against such regulation? Explain and support your answer.

EXERCISE 11.4 Jerry Falwell and *Hustler* Magazine: Libel and the Slippery Slope of Censorship

INTRODUCTION

Where does the right of the press to criticize—and even to mock—public figures end, and the right of the state to censor the press begin?

Censorship is an odious matter, conjuring ingrained fears of the state waging war against the right of free expression. But the First Amendment's freedom of speech protection demands that the nation's courts grapple with a thorny question: Which is the greater threat to the republic—the damage done by reckless, outlandish journalism, or the chilling effect of state censorship on public discourse?

The Supreme Court consistently has held that libel is not protected expression under the First Amendment. *Libel* is the defamation of character in print or by other visual means; *slander* is oral defamation. The Supreme Court has established the following categories of libel as it applies to individuals:

- *Public officials* are those who are elected or appointed to public office. In a landmark decision, *New York Times v. Sullivan* (1964), the Court held that a public official could not recover damages for libel unless that individual could prove actual malice or that an article was printed or a statement made "with knowledge that it was false or with reckless disregard of whether it was false or not." The Court's decision was based on the principle that public debate about a public official needs to be free, open, and uninhibited, even if that means a public official's reputation is tarnished. The necessity of a free press in a free society means that the public's right to know prevails over a public official's reputation. (*Public figures*, such as movie stars and other celebrities, are considered to have the same burden of proof as public officials.)
- The *Sullivan* standard does not apply to *private individuals*. In *Gertz v. Welch* (1974), a 5–4 majority of the Court held that private individuals do not have to prove malice or reckless disregard for the truth in a libel action. The effect of *Gertz* is to give private citizens more protection from defamatory statements than public officials or public figures have. In a libel or slander suit, private individuals need to prove only that a statement was defamatory and false.

The problem for the Court has been defining *defamation* in a way that does not undermine the First Amendment right to freedom of speech. The Court fears that defining defamation to encompass speech that is merely offensive will lead to a "slippery slope of censorship." If the Court allows the government to punish speech that is merely offensive, or a jury to award damages to those who find speech merely offensive, then all speech may eventually be regulated because someone, somewhere will find someone else's speech offensive. Concern about the slippery slope of censorship affected the Court's decision in the *Falwell* case in Reading 11.4.2.

ASSIGNMENT

Study Readings 11.4.1 and 11.4.2. Then answer the questions that follow.

READING 11.4.1 REVEREND JERRY FALWELL AND *HUSTLER* MAGAZINE[1]

Hustler magazine is best known for its photographs of naked women in explicit sexual poses, not for satire. But in 1983, *Hustler* published a parody of an ad for Campari, an alcoholic beverage. The original series of Campari ads, which appeared in a number of magazines but never in *Hustler*, featured celebrities who, in interview format, talked about their "first time." At first glance, it

---

[1] Source: Based on material in Lee Epstein and Thomas G. Walker, *Constitutional Law for a Changing America: Rights, Liberties, and Justice* (Washington, DC. CQ Press, 1992), pp. 261–265. A reprint of the *Hustler* parody appears on page 262 of the book.

looked as though the "first time" was referring to the interviewee's first sexual experience, but it was clear in reading the ads that the interviewees actually were talking about the first time they had experienced Campari.

In the *Hustler* parody, Reverend Jerry Falwell was the celebrity and his answers to the interviewer's questions were of a decidedly sexual nature. In the parody, Falwell spoke of getting drunk on Campari and having sex with his mother in an outhouse. He also was quoted saying he often got drunk before delivering his Sunday sermons. At the bottom of the ad, in small but legible print, ran this statement: AD PARODY—NOT TO BE TAKEN SERIOUSLY.

Not surprisingly, Falwell, a televangelist and conservative commentator on politics and morality, took issue with the parody. He filed suit against *Hustler* and its publisher, Larry Flynt, seeking damages for invasion of privacy, libel, and intentional infliction of emotional distress. The jury found the parody was not libelous because no reader would have believed the words or the behavior attributed to Falwell in the ad. But the jury awarded Falwell $200,000 in damages for "the intentional infliction of emotional distress." After the award was upheld by a court of appeals, Flynt appealed to the U.S. Supreme Court. In *Hustler Magazine v. Falwell* (1988), the Supreme Court reversed the award for emotional distress in an 8–0 vote.

READING 11.4.2 *Hustler Magazine, Inc. et al. v. Jerry Falwell*, 485 U.S. 46 (1988)

Chief Justice Rehnquist delivered the opinion of the Court.

This case *Hustler Magazine, Inc. et al. v. Jerry Falwell* presents us with a novel question involving First Amendment limitations upon a State's authority to protect its citizens from the intentional infliction of emotional distress. We must decide whether a public figure may recover damages for emotional harm caused by the publication of an ad parody offensive to him, and doubtless gross and repugnant in the eyes of most. Respondent would have us find that a State's interest in protecting public figures from emotional distress is sufficient to deny First Amendment protection to speech that is patently offensive and is intended to inflict emotional injury, even when that speech could not reasonably have been interpreted as stating actual facts about the public figure involved. This we decline to do.

At the heart of the First Amendment is the recognition of the fundamental importance of the free flow of ideas and opinions on matters of public interest and concern.

> [T]he fact that society may find speech offensive is not a sufficient reason for suppressing it. Indeed, if it is the speaker's opinion that gives offense, that consequence is a reason for according it constitutional protection. For it is a central tenet of the First Amendment that the government must remain neutral in the marketplace of ideas.

It is firmly settled that ... the public expression of ideas may not be prohibited merely because the ideas are themselves offensive to some of their hearers.

[Falwell] is thus relegated to his claim for damages awarded by the jury for the intentional infliction of emotional distress by "outrageous" conduct [because he does not meet the constitutional standard for libel]. But for reasons heretofore stated this claim cannot, consistently with the First Amendment, form a basis for the award of damages when the conduct in question is the publication of a caricature such as the ad parody involved here. The judgment of the Court of Appeals is accordingly Reversed.

1. According to Supreme Court precedents explained in the Introduction, what characteristics of the *Hustler* Campari ad made it impossible for the jury to find libel damages against *Hustler*?

2. Jerry Falwell is clearly a public figure. Is it likely that the jury would have found against *Hustler* if Falwell had been a private individual? Explain and support your position.

3. If *Hustler* had *not* included the disclaimer, AD PARODY—NOT TO BE TAKEN SERIOUSLY, would the jury have likely found *Hustler* guilty of libel? Explain and support your position.

4. Because the jury did not find libel against *Hustler*, the Supreme Court had to decide the case solely on the constitutionality of the jury's verdict that the parody inflicted *emotional distress* on Falwell. Why did the Court reject the argument that the infliction of emotional distress entitled Falwell to monetary damages from *Hustler*? Cite specific language from the Court's decision to support your answer.

5. If you were on the federal court jury in Virginia that initially decided the case, would you have voted to award monetary damages to Falwell for suffering the infliction of emotional distress? Explain and support your position.

APPENDIX 1

For Instructors: A Guide to Using This Textbook

Critical Thinking and American Government was designed to provide maximum flexibility for its adopters. In this appendix the authors offer suggestions on effectively using the text.

SELECTING AND ASSIGNING EXERCISES

The exercises differ significantly in length, level of difficulty, type of skill development, and subject. Several exercises are divided into two or three parts to provide flexibility in making assignments.

In our courses we assign about a dozen exercises during a semester-long course in American Government and Politics. We explain to our students at the beginning of the course that only selected exercises from the text will be assigned.

GETTING STUDENTS STARTED

It's not uncommon for students to struggle with the first couple of exercises assigned. Depending on the skill level of your students, it may be advisable to discuss with them in advance the first couple of exercises assigned. It's been our experience that students become more comfortable with, and skilled at, the exercises as the semester progresses. You might elect to post on the MyCourse website (explained below) answers to some exercises as you assign them. This can build student confidence and reassure students that they are capable of completing the work.

INTEGRATING THE CRITICAL THINKING EXERCISES INTO CLASSROOM TEACHING

Many exercises can be easily and productively employed to supplement and enhance subjects taught in class. Student completion of an exercise prior to class will provide the instructor with many openings to elaborate, clarify, and discuss the exercise in relation to the subject being studied in class. For example, Exercise 2.4, "Who's in Charge of the Minimum Drinking Age—The Federal Government or the States?," can be employed to clarify how the federal government uses categorical and block grant aid to secure state or local compliance with federal policy objectives. Another example, Exercise 7.2, "Evaluating Presidential Performance," can add a valuable dimension to the study of presidential power.

EMPLOYING THE EXERCISES AS GROUP WORK

The exercises are ideally suited to group work either in or outside of class. The questions are focused to avoid the pitfalls of overly broad group discussion. At the same time, the questions invite collaboration and discussion. "Reading the Constitution," Exercise 1.1, is a good example. Some students will miss items when reading the Constitution that will be picked up by others. Exercise 4.2, "Gerrymandering," should spur student collaboration as well. Some students will be more adept at grasping the political nature of gerrymandering than others, who may get tripped up by the concept of wielding political power by drawing district lines on a map.

The advantages of "collaborative learning" are well documented. So too is a major disadvantage: the lack of individual responsibility and accountability within the group. Too often the group's workload is not shared equally. This can build resentment and dampen enthusiasm for group work. Too often the brightest and most diligent students do the difficult thinking for the group.

We offer the following suggestions for overcoming the perils and pitfalls of group work.

1. Assign students to groups randomly, and reconstitute groups periodically.
2. Evaluate group work by having individual students answer written questions on quizzes or exams.
3. Evaluate group work by asking individual students to answer oral questions in class. Guard against the often-unwitting tendency to call on attentive and engaged students to the exclusion of those not so well prepared or forthcoming.
4. Ask students to evaluate their group. The questionnaire should identify the group, but individual responses should be anonymous.

EVALUATING THE EXERCISES

Whether assigned for completion by groups or by individual students, the exercises may be evaluated in a number of ways.

1. If instructors collect completed exercises from groups or individual students, the evaluation process will be speeded by scoring only selected questions. We usually tell students in advance if this will be the grading mode, but we don't tell them which questions will be scored. Some questions are more significant than others and more clearly reflect a student's understanding of the material. As well, some questions are more difficult than others and minimizing or not scoring these may reassure students that the instructor's expectations are reasonable and achievable.
2. If instructors do not collect completed exercises for evaluation, students' comprehension can be checked with a brief written quiz in class. Take Exercise 1.1, for example, "Reading the Constitution." One could select a few of the more significant and easily grasped questions, put them on an overhead screen, and ask the students to provide short written answers. For this exercise, an obvious candidate would be: "Identify one enumerated power of the president." Another might be: "Identify one power the Constitution prohibits to the states." Informing students in advance of this mode of evaluation and assuring them that the quiz will focus on the most important questions in the exercise may encourage students to approach the text.
3. Another option for instructors who don't collect the written exercises is to formulate variations on one or more questions in an exercise and distribute this as a written quiz to the class. This has worked well, for example, with Exercise 7.1, "The Electoral College." Questions 9–13 in this exercise ask students to apply their understanding of the mechanics of the electoral college to electoral strategy. Instructors can vary the specifics of these questions to present students with different situations that probe their understanding of the material.
4. Of course, instructors who don't collect the written exercises can formulate written or multiple-choice questions based on assigned exercises to integrate into their standard exams.

USING THE INSTRUCTOR'S MANUAL

The answers to each exercise are in the Instructor's Manual available on Wadsworth's E-bank. Please contact your sales representative for access. These answers can be downloaded and posted for student use. As noted above, we have sometimes made the answers available to students at the time of assigning an exercise to facilitate their working through the questions. In this case, we explain how they will be tested on the exercise and caution them that—even though the answers are there for the taking—they must do the hard work of learning the material and how to apply it. Other times, we have withheld posting answers on the website until the exercise has been turned in or until students have been tested in class on the material. Each approach has it benefits and drawbacks.

APPENDIX 2

Tools in Political Analysis

NORMATIVE AND EMPIRICAL THEORIES

Social scientists formulate theories to explain relationships or linkages between events and behavior. Usually expressed in generalizations and propositions, a theory offers a coherent explanation of "why events occur in the manner that they do."[1] The value of a theory is twofold: It provides a general explanation for certain types of behavior, and the explanation can be tested. In political science the acid test of a theory is its ability to explain and ultimately predict.

There is no shortage of theories to explain voter apathy, or how reform-minded political candidates are presumed to moderate their views once elected to legislative bodies, or why some presidents are more effective than others, or why courts in one region of the country are more receptive to environmental litigation than those in other regions. Just as medical researchers attempt to build theories on how lifestyles, blood pressure, age, and eating habits cause (or inhibit) certain kinds of illnesses in humans, political scientists employ this same strategy in studying the political behavior and actions of people, institutions, and countries.

Two dominant theoretical approaches guide how political scientists conceptualize political behavior. Those who utilize *normative theories* emphasize value judgments. Their focus is on how people *should* behave, what governments *should* do, and how countries *should* interact with each other under different conditions. In contrast, *empirical theories* address what actually occurs without making value judgments about the behavior under study. Because normative theories are value based, they cannot be tested scientifically in the manner of empirical theories.

The dividing line between these two approaches is not always clear. Much social science research blends the two together by ascribing certain expectations to behavior and then testing them to see whether they are valid. Political scientist Darrell West's study (1994–1995) of television ads in election campaigns illustrates the mix of the empirical and normative approaches. West examined the television ads run by candidates in several presidential races,

---

[1] Kenneth Hoover and Todd Donovan, *The Elements of Social Scientific Thinking* (New York: St. Martin's Press, 1995), p. 38.

presidential primaries, and U.S. Senate campaigns. He wanted to determine what impact, if any, these ads had on viewers. West's theoretical foundation for his study was based on what others had written about the effects of the media on ordinary citizens, particularly the assumption that television campaign ads have more influence on viewers than does television news coverage of elections and candidates. The empirical aspect of his research involved analyzing campaign articles in several prominent newspapers, data on the number and substance of television campaign ads, and public opinion surveys. Based on his empirical results, West found that political advertisements did have an impact on viewers by shaping their perceptions of the candidates. West proceeded to discuss the implications of candidates being able, via television ads, to shape citizens' perceptions of them. He added the normative element by concluding that the ads, which usually focus on the personal characteristics of the candidates—not their policy stances—are important to candidates, but that their influence "is not always positive from the standpoint of representative democracy."[2]

HYPOTHESES AND VARIABLES

Scientists use *hypotheses* (singular is *hypothesis*) to guide their research. Hypotheses, derived from common sense and casual observation, suggest relationships between two or more variables in which one is thought to influence the other. For example, medical scientists for years have studied the effects of smoking on health. The preliminary hypothesis in this situation would be something like "Smoking has negative consequences on a person's health." More specifically, one could hypothesize "Smoking has a negative effect on a person's cardiovascular and respiratory systems." To determine whether there is a relationship between smoking and health consequences, one would examine the physical conditions of smokers and nonsmokers. In this instance, smoking and nonsmoking would be one variable, and the health of the cardiovascular and respiratory systems would be another. There are, however, other *variables* that influence a person's physical health, including weight, age, eating and drinking habits, cholesterol levels, exercise, and heredity. Since other variables may affect health, the researcher must attempt to control for—meaning to account for, or factor in—the nonsmoking variables. This can be a formidable task. Even in medical research under laboratory conditions, establishing a causal relationship between variable X (smoking) and variable Y (health) is no easy matter.

In trying to develop a theory of voting behavior, political scientists examine key characteristics of voters, such as their age, race-ethnicity, religion, income, education, gender, and geographic location. These characteristics are *independent variables* that can influence a voter's decision. The choice of the voter at election time, whether he or she votes for a Democrat or Republican presidential candidate, is the *dependent variable*. In other words, we hypothesize that independent variables have an influence on the dependent variable (party preference in voting). If we look at race and voting preferences, we see that African Americans are much more likely to vote for Democratic than Republican presidential candidates. It makes sense to assume that racial experience does influence voting. But, what if we reverse the dependent and independent variables? Does it seem logical to hypothesize that voting influences one's racial experience? The critical feature of any variable is that it can be used to classify something along a dimension. Thus, although sex is a variable in many studies, it makes sense to divide it into male and female subsets to see whether there are differences along the dimension "gender." Similarly, people can be grouped into different age brackets. If we were looking at religion as a variable, we would include categories for Catholics, Eastern Orthodox, Protestants, Jews, Moslems, Buddhists, Hindus, and "none of the above." Some of the variables affecting voting behavior are linked. For example, we can compare voting preferences (Democrat or Republican) by income levels (low, middle, and high) and by education (high school degree, some college, college degree, graduate degree). Yet, we know that education and income are linked: In general, the higher one's level of education, the higher one's income is likely to be.

---

[2] Darrell M. West, "Television Advertising in Election Campaigns," *Political Science Quarterly* 109 (Winter 1994–1995), pp. 789–809.

We need to add two cautionary notes here. First, in most research involving political behavior and attitudes, we are not talking about *causation*. Social science research is unlike natural science research, where one can reasonably expect to identify a cause in a controlled laboratory environment. The variables that affect human behavior cannot be controlled for or reproduced in the laboratory. Scientists studying the material and physical world do not labor under this handicap. Chemists, for example, can strictly control and isolate variables in the laboratory—for example, by adding one compound to another and then measuring what happens when a third compound is added to the mix. In this fashion the chemist has control over *intervening variables*. Because human behavior is subject to influences from numerous sources, it is exceedingly difficult to identify one or two variables as having caused a particular action and thus to establish causal relationships between variables. In most cases, political scientists, like most social scientists, can establish only that particular independent variables are more or less likely to explain the dependent variable. Political scientists must usually be content with establishing *correlations* rather than causes.

Second, a hypothesis must be based on a reasonable and plausible connection between the variables under study. One might be able to show that a candidate whose last name has seven letters has been elected governor of a state every twenty-four years. However, one doubts that any actual causation is at work here because there is no plausible reason for hypothesizing a connection between the number of characters in the last names of gubernatorial candidates and voting behavior. Yet, one could formulate a hypothesis that "odd" names are not politically attractive to voters in general. The names of candidates may provide subtle "cues" to voters about ethnicity, gender, and perhaps religion, and thereby shape voting behavior by attracting voters to, or dissuading them from, particular candidates. However, that a particular number of letters in one's last name would influence voting behavior is outside the area of reasonable inquiry.

CASE STUDIES AND COMPARATIVE STUDIES

Studies that focus on the dynamics of one election contest, the impact of an anticrime program in one city, the record of a particular mayor or governor or president, or the political and social views of students at one college campus are regarded as *case studies* because their focus is on behavior in a limited environment. Case studies abound in social science research for reasons of economy, interest, and the attention and resources that can be focused on the carefully limited subject or question at hand. Case studies can also serve as a theoretical foundation for subsequent studies that are comparative in focus by contrasting behavior with other environments. For example, a case study of the Reagan presidency (1981–1988) might assess the foreign and defense policies of his administration during a period of economic and political change in the United States and rapidly changing conditions in the Soviet Union. But to gain a more comprehensive picture of Reagan's foreign policy, a *comparative study* might include the foreign and defense policies of other contemporary presidents as well. The comparative perspective is thus valuable for increasing our ability to make generalizations about political behavior over time and space.

CREATING AN INDEX (INDICES)

We encounter indices in all realms of study and everyday life. An index is a single value that summarizes a number of related variables. For example, suppose you were the chair of a college committee assigned the task of selecting the "outstanding senior of the year" for special recognition at commencement exercises. You could, of course, simply identify the graduating senior with the highest grade point average. However, you might wish to be more comprehensive by looking for attributes other than just scholastic achievement. In addition to high grades, you could identify seniors who were recognized for accomplishments such as community service or achievement in extracurricular activities. To create an index for the "outstanding senior of the year" based on multiple criteria, you would identify several categories and then assign a number to each level in that category. You would then be able to summarize and compare the candidates' scores across the categories. For example, the category of GPA would be broken down into levels of very high (3.75–4.00), high (3.5–3.74), above average (3.0–3.49), average (2.5–2.99), and below average (2.49 and lower). Then each level would be assigned a number from 5 (very high) to 1 (below average).

The same kind of ranking would then be done for the other categories that were deemed relevant to the award.

The consumer price index (CPI) is a summary score created by governments to measure the changing price of consumer goods over a period of time. In the United States, the CPI is based on prices of 400 items in eighty-five cities measured monthly. This index tells us whether inflation is up, down, or holding steady compared with previous periods. Similarly, the FBI's crime index is based on the eight categories of serious crimes reported to the police monthly. FBI analysts summarize the frequency of these crimes, usually the number of crimes per 100,000 population, and issue reports that show whether crime in general is up, down, or unchanged compared with some previous time period. These reports also allow for a comparison of crime rates between states and cities as well as across various time periods.

MEASURES OF CENTRAL TENDENCY

The mode, median, and mean are commonly employed in elementary analysis of data. These statistics, sometimes referred to as measures of centrality, provide basic information about patterns with data combined in a single number. The mode, median, or mean is used depending on what tendency in the data the social scientist wishes to describe. The mode, median, and mean provide different snapshots of a data-based pattern.

The *mode* is the number that occurs most frequently in a distribution. In Table A.1 below, the mode is 78; more students received a score of 78 than any other grade.

The *median* is the middle value in a frequency distribution: Half of the cases are above the median figure and half are below it. The formula to calculate the median for the data in Table 1 is $(N + 1)/2$, where N is the number of values in the data set. We have 80 scores, so $(80 + 1)/2 = 40.5$. With the scores ranked in ascending order, 40.5 takes us to the point between the scores of 79 and 80. The median is therefore 79.5 (40 students received 79 or fewer points and 40 received 80 or more points). (If the data in Table A.1 were grouped in categories—60–69 points, 70–79 points, and

TABLE A.1 Grade Distribution on Examination 1

Points	Number of Students
66	1
70	3
72	4
75	3
76	6
77	9
78	12
79	2
80	7
81	1
82	2
83	5
84	4
85	2
86	5
87	3
88	2
89	3
90	1
91	1
92	1
93	2
95	1

so on—then the formula is more complex. None of the exercises in this textbook require this calculation.)

The *mean* is calculated by adding all of the scores in the frequency distribution and dividing the sum by the number of cases. The resulting number is the average score on the exam. In Table A.1, the mean is 78.5 (sum of the scores, 6280, divided by the number of students who took the exam, 80).

It is easy to be overwhelmed by statistics, especially those derived from complex models and tests. The exercises in this workbook that require data analysis employ elementary statistics, such as those described above.

APPENDIX 3

Constitution of the United States

We the People of the United States, in Order to form a more perfect Union, establish Justice, insure domestic Tranquility, provide for the common defence, promote the general Welfare, and secure the Blessings of Liberty to ourselves and our Posterity, do ordain and establish this Constitution for the United States of America.

ARTICLE I

Section 1   All legislative Powers herein granted shall be vested in a Congress of the United States, which shall consist of a Senate and House of Representatives.

Section 2   The House of Representatives shall be composed of Members chosen every second Year by the People of the several States, and the Electors in each State shall have the Qualifications requisite for Electors of the most numerous Branch of the State Legislature.

No Person shall be a Representative who shall not have attained to the Age of twenty-five Years, and been seven Years a Citizen of the United States, and who shall not, when elected, be an Inhabitant of that State in which he shall be chosen.

Representatives and direct Taxes shall be apportioned among the several States which may be included within this Union, according to their respective Numbers, which shall be determined by adding to the whole Number of free Persons, including those bound to Service for a Term of Years, and excluding Indians not taxed, three fifths of all other Persons.
The actual Enumeration shall be made within three Years after the first Meeting of the Congress of the United States, and within every subsequent Term of ten Years, in such Manner as they shall by Law direct. The Number of Representatives shall not exceed one for every thirty Thousand, but each State shall have at Least one Representative; and until such enumeration shall be made, the State of New Hampshire shall be entitled to chuse three, Massachusetts eight,

Rhode Island and Providence Plantations one, Connecticut five, New York six, New Jersey four, Pennsylvania eight, Delaware one, Maryland six, Virginia ten, North Carolina five, South Carolina five and Georgia three.

When vacancies happen in the Representation from any State, the Executive Authority thereof shall issue Writs of Election to fill such Vacancies.

The House of Representatives shall chuse their Speaker and other Officers; and shall have the sole Power of Impeachment.

Section 3   The Senate of the United States shall be composed of two Senators from each State, chosen by the Legislature thereof, for six Years; and each Senator shall have one Vote.

Immediately after they shall be assembled in Consequence of the first Election, they shall be divided as equally as may be into three Classes. The Seats of the Senators of the first Class shall be vacated at the Expiration of the second Year, of the second Class at the Expiration of the fourth Year, and of the third Class at the Expiration of the sixth Year, so that one third may be chosen every second Year; and if Vacancies happen by Resignation, or otherwise, during the Recess of the Legislature of any State, the Executive thereof may make temporary Appointments until the next Meeting of the Legislature, which shall then fill such Vacancies.

No person shall be a Senator who shall not have attained to the Age of thirty Years, and been nine Years a Citizen of the United States, and who shall not, when elected, be an Inhabitant of that State for which he shall be chosen.

The Vice President of the United States shall be President of the Senate, but shall have no Vote, unless they be equally divided.

The Senate shall chuse their other Officers, and also a President pro tempore, in the absence of the Vice President, or when he shall exercise the Office of President of the United States.

The Senate shall have the sole Power to try all Impeachments. When sitting for that Purpose, they shall be on Oath or Affirmation. When the President of the United States is tried, the Chief Justice shall preside: And no Person shall be convicted without the Concurrence of two thirds of the Members present.

Judgment in Cases of Impeachment shall not extend further than to removal from Office, and disqualification to hold and enjoy any Office of honor, Trust or Profit under the United States: but the Party convicted shall nevertheless be liable and subject to Indictment, Trial, Judgment and Punishment, according to Law.

Section 4   The Times, Places and Manner of holding Elections for Senators and Representatives, shall be prescribed in each State by the Legislature thereof; but the Congress may at any time by Law make or alter such Regulations, except as to the Places of chusing Senators.

The Congress shall assemble at least once in every Year, and such Meeting shall be on the first Monday in December, unless they shall by Law appoint a different Day.

Section 5   Each House shall be the Judge of the Elections, Returns and Qualifications of its own Members, and a Majority of each shall constitute a Quorum to do Business; but a smaller number may adjourn from day to day, and may be authorized to compel the Attendance of absent Members, in such Manner, and under such Penalties as each House may provide.

Each House may determine the Rules of its Proceedings, punish its Members for disorderly Behavior, and, with the Concurrence of two-thirds, expel a Member.

Each House shall keep a Journal of its Proceedings, and from time to time publish the same, excepting such Parts as may in their Judgment require Secrecy; and the Yeas and Nays of the Members of either House on any question shall, at the Desire of one fifth of those Present, be entered on the Journal.

Neither House, during the Session of Congress, shall, without the Consent of the other, adjourn for more than three days, nor to any other Place than that in which the two Houses shall be sitting.

Section 6   The Senators and Representatives shall receive a Compensation for their Services, to be ascertained by Law, and paid out of the Treasury of the United States. They shall in all Cases, except Treason, Felony and Breach of the Peace, be privileged from Arrest during their Attendance at the Session of their respective Houses, and in going to and returning from the same; and for any Speech or Debate in either House, they shall not be questioned in any other Place.

No Senator or Representative shall, during the Time for which he was elected, be appointed to any civil Office under the Authority of the United States which shall have been created, or the Emoluments whereof shall have been increased during such time; and no Person holding any Office under the United States, shall be a Member of either House during his Continuance in Office.

Section 7   All bills for raising Revenue shall originate in the House of Representatives; but the Senate may propose or concur with Amendments as on other Bills.

Every Bill which shall have passed the House of Representatives and the Senate, shall, before it become a Law, be presented to the President of the United States; If he approves he shall sign it, but if not he shall return it, with his Objections to that House in which it shall have originated, who shall enter the Objections at large on their Journal, and proceed to reconsider it. If after such Reconsideration two thirds of that House shall agree to pass the Bill, it shall be sent, together with the Objections, to the other House, by which it shall likewise be reconsidered, and if approved by two thirds of that House, it shall become a Law. But in all such Cases the Votes of both Houses shall be determined by Yeas and Nays, and the Names of the Persons voting for and against the Bill shall be entered on the Journal of each House respectively. If any Bill shall not be returned by the President within ten Days (Sundays excepted) after it shall have been presented to him, the Same shall be a Law, in like Manner as if he had signed it, unless the Congress by their Adjournment prevent its Return, in which Case it shall not be a Law.

Every Order, Resolution, or Vote to which the Concurrence of the Senate and House of Representatives may be necessary (except on a question of Adjournment) shall be presented to the President of the United States; and before the Same shall take Effect, shall be approved by him, or being disapproved by him, shall be repassed by two thirds of the Senate and House of Representatives, according to the Rules and Limitations prescribed in the Case of a Bill.

Section 8   The Congress shall have Power To lay and collect Taxes, Duties, Imposts and Excises, to pay the Debts and provide for the common Defence and general Welfare of the United States; but all Duties, Imposts and Excises shall be uniform throughout the United States;

To borrow money on the credit of the United States;

To regulate Commerce with foreign Nations, and among the several States, and with the Indian Tribes;

To establish an uniform Rule of Naturalization, and uniform Laws on the subject of Bankruptcies throughout the United States;

To coin Money, regulate the Value thereof, and of foreign Coin, and fix the Standard of Weights and Measures;

To provide for the Punishment of counterfeiting the Securities and current Coin of the United States;

To establish Post Offices and Post Roads;

To promote the Progress of Science and useful Arts, by securing for limited Times to Authors and Inventors the exclusive Right to their respective Writings and Discoveries;

To constitute Tribunals inferior to the supreme Court;

To define and punish Piracies and Felonies committed on the high Seas, and Offenses against the Law of Nations;

To declare War, grant Letters of Marque and Reprisal, and make Rules concerning Captures on Land and Water;

To raise and support Armies, but no Appropriation of Money to that Use shall be for a longer Term than two Years;

To provide and maintain a Navy;

To make Rules for the Government and Regulation of the land and naval Forces;

To provide for calling forth the Militia to execute the Laws of the Union, suppress Insurrections and repel Invasions;

To provide for organizing, arming, and disciplining the Militia, and for governing such Part of them as may be employed in the Service of the United States, reserving to the States respectively, the Appointment of the Officers, and the Authority of training the Militia according to the discipline prescribed by Congress;

To exercise exclusive Legislation in all Cases whatsoever, over such District (not exceeding ten Miles square) as may, by Cession of particular States, and the acceptance of Congress, become the Seat of the Government of the United States, and to exercise like Authority over all Places purchased by the Consent of the Legislature of the State in which the Same shall be, for the Erection of Forts, Magazines, Arsenals, dock-Yards, and other needful Buildings;—And

To make all Laws which shall be necessary and proper for carrying into Execution the foregoing Powers, and all other Powers vested by this Constitution in the Government of the United States, or in any Department or Officer thereof.

Section 9 The Migration or Importation of such Persons as any of the States now existing shall think proper to admit, shall not be prohibited by the Congress prior to the Year one thousand eight hundred and eight, but a tax or duty may be imposed on such Importation, not exceeding ten dollars for each Person.

The privilege of the Writ of Habeas Corpus shall not be suspended, unless when in Cases of Rebellion or Invasion the public Safety may require it.

No Bill of Attainder or ex post facto Law shall be passed. No capitation, or other direct, Tax shall be laid, unless in Proportion to the Census or Enumeration herein before directed to be taken.

No Tax or Duty shall be laid on Articles exported from any State.

No Preference shall be given by any Regulation of Commerce or Revenue to the Ports of one State over those of another: nor shall Vessels bound to, or from, one State, be obliged to enter, clear, or pay Duties in another.

No Money shall be drawn from the Treasury, but in Consequence of Appropriations made by Law; and a regular Statement and Account of the Receipts and Expenditures of all public Money shall be published from time to time.

No Title of Nobility shall be granted by the United States: And no Person holding any Office of Profit or Trust under them, shall, without the Consent of the Congress, accept of any present, Emolument, Office, or Title, of any kind whatever, from any King, Prince or foreign State.

Section 10 No State shall enter into any Treaty, Alliance, or Confederation; grant Letters of Marque and Reprisal; coin Money; emit Bills of Credit; make any Thing but gold and silver Coin a Tender in Payment of Debts; pass any Bill of Attainder, ex post facto Law, or Law impairing the Obligation of Contracts, or grant any Title of Nobility.

No State shall, without the Consent of the Congress, lay any Imposts or Duties on Imports or Exports, except what may be absolutely necessary for executing it's inspection Laws: and the net Produce of all Duties and Imposts, laid by any State on Imports or Exports, shall be for the Use of the Treasury of the United States; and all such Laws shall be subject to the Revision and Controul of the Congress.

No State shall, without the Consent of Congress, lay any duty of Tonnage, keep Troops, or Ships of War in time of Peace, enter into any Agreement or Compact with another State, or with a foreign Power, or engage in War, unless actually invaded, or in such imminent Danger as will not admit of delay.

ARTICLE II

Section 1 The executive Power shall be vested in a President of the United States of America. He shall hold his Office during the Term of four Years, and, together with the Vice President chosen for the same Term, be elected, as follows:

Each State shall appoint, in such Manner as the Legislature thereof may direct, a Number of Electors, equal to the whole Number of Senators and Representatives to which the State may be entitled in the Congress: but no Senator or Representative, or Person holding an Office of Trust or Profit under the United States, shall be appointed an Elector.

The Electors shall meet in their respective States, and vote by Ballot for two persons, of whom one at least shall not be an Inhabitant of the same State with themselves. And they shall make a List of all the Persons voted for, and of the Number of Votes for each; which List they shall sign and certify, and transmit sealed to the Seat of the Government of the United States, directed to the President of the Senate. The President of the Senate shall, in the Presence of the Senate and House of Representatives, open all the Certificates, and the Votes shall then be counted. The Person having the greatest Number of Votes shall be the President, if such Number be a Majority of the whole Number of Electors appointed; and if there be more than one who have such Majority, and have an equal Number of Votes, then the House of Representatives shall immediately chuse by Ballot one of them for President; and if no Person have a Majority, then from the five highest on the List the said House shall in like Manner chuse the President. But in chusing the President, the Votes shall be taken by States, the Representation from each State having one Vote; a quorum for this Purpose shall consist of a Member or Members from two-thirds of the States, and a Majority of all the States shall be necessary to a Choice. In every Case, after the Choice of the President, the Person having the greatest Number of Votes of the Electors shall be the Vice President. But if there should remain two or more who have equal Votes, the Senate shall chuse from them by Ballot the Vice President.

The Congress may determine the Time of chusing the Electors, and the Day on which they shall give their Votes; which Day shall be the same throughout the United States.

No person except a natural born Citizen, or a Citizen of the United States, at the time of the Adoption of this Constitution, shall be eligible to the Office of President; neither shall any Person be eligible to that Office who shall not have attained to the Age of thirty-five Years, and been fourteen Years a Resident within the United States.

In Case of the Removal of the President from Office, or of his Death, Resignation, or Inability to discharge the Powers and Duties of the said Office, the same shall devolve on the Vice President, and the Congress may by Law provide for the Case of Removal, Death, Resignation or Inability, both of the President and Vice President, declaring what Officer shall then act as President, and such Officer shall act accordingly, until the Disability be removed, or a President shall be elected.

The President shall, at stated Times, receive for his Services, a Compensation, which shall neither be increased nor diminished during the Period for which he shall have been elected, and he shall not receive within that Period any other Emolument from the United States, or any of them.

Before he enter on the Execution of his Office, he shall take the following Oath or Affirmation:— "I do solemnly swear (or affirm) that I will faithfully execute the Office of President of the United States, and will to the best of my Ability, preserve, protect and defend the Constitution of the United States."

Section 2 The President shall be Commander in Chief of the Army and Navy of the United States, and of the Militia of the several States, when called into the actual Service of the United States; he may require the Opinion, in writing, of the principal Officer in each of the executive Departments, upon any Subject relating to the Duties of their respective Offices, and he shall have Power to Grant Reprieves and Pardons for Offences against the United States, except in Cases of Impeachment.

He shall have Power, by and with the Advice and Consent of the Senate, to make Treaties, provided two thirds of the Senators present concur; and he shall nominate, and by and with the Advice and Consent of the Senate, shall appoint Ambassadors, other public Ministers and Consuls, Judges of the Supreme Court, and all other Officers of the United States, whose Appointments are not herein otherwise provided for, and which shall be established by Law: but the Congress may by Law vest the Appointment of such inferior Officers, as they think proper, in the President alone, in the Courts of Law, or in the Heads of Departments.

The President shall have Power to fill up all Vacancies that may happen during the Recess of the Senate, by granting Commissions which shall expire at the End of their next Session.

Section 3 He shall from time to time give to the Congress Information of the State of the Union, and recommend to their Consideration such Measures as he shall judge necessary and expedient; he may, on extraordinary Occasions, convene both Houses, or either of them, and in Case of Disagreement between them, with Respect to the Time of Adjournment, he may adjourn them to such Time as he shall think proper; he shall receive Ambassadors and other public Ministers; he shall take Care that the Laws be faithfully executed, and shall Commission all the Officers of the United States.

Section 4 The President, Vice President and all civil Officers of the United States, shall be removed from Office on Impeachment for, and Conviction of, Treason, Bribery, or other high Crimes and Misdemeanors.

ARTICLE III

Section 1 The judicial Power of the United States, shall be vested in one supreme Court, and in such inferior Courts as the Congress may from time to time ordain and establish. The Judges, both of the supreme and inferior Courts, shall hold their Offices during good Behaviour, and shall, at stated Times, receive for their Services, a Compensation, which shall not be diminished during their Continuance in Office.

Section 2 The judicial Power shall extend to all Cases, in Law and Equity, arising under this Constitution, the Laws of the United States, and Treaties made, or which shall be made, under their Authority;—to all Cases affecting Ambassadors, other public Ministers and Consuls;—to all Cases of admiralty and maritime Jurisdiction;—to Controversies to which the United States shall be a Party;—to

Controversies between two or more States;—between a State and Citizens of another State;—between Citizens of different States;—between Citizens of the same State claiming Lands under Grants of different States, and between a State, or the Citizens thereof, and foreign States, Citizens or Subjects.

In all Cases affecting Ambassadors, other public Ministers and Consuls, and those in which a State shall be Party, the supreme Court shall have original Jurisdiction. In all the other Cases before mentioned, the supreme Court shall have appellate Jurisdiction, both as to Law and Fact, with such Exceptions, and under such Regulations as the Congress shall make.

Trial of all Crimes, except in Cases of Impeachment, shall be by Jury; and such Trial shall be held in the State where the said Crimes shall have been committed; but when not committed within any State, the Trial shall be at such Place or Places as the Congress may by Law have directed.

Section 3   Treason against the United States, shall consist only in levying War against them, or in adhering to their Enemies, giving them Aid and Comfort. No Person shall be convicted of Treason unless on the Testimony of two Witnesses to the same overt Act, or on Confession in open Court.

The Congress shall have power to declare the Punishment of Treason, but no Attainder of Treason shall work Corruption of Blood, or Forfeiture except during the Life of the Person attainted.

ARTICLE IV

Section 1   Full Faith and Credit shall be given in each State to the public Acts, Records, and judicial Proceedings of every other State. And the Congress may by general Laws prescribe the Manner in which such Acts, Records and Proceedings shall be proved, and the Effect thereof.

Section 2   The Citizens of each State shall be entitled to all Privileges and Immunities of Citizens in the several States.

A Person charged in any State with Treason, Felony, or other Crime, who shall flee from Justice, and be found in another State, shall on demand of the executive Authority of the State from which he fled, be delivered up, to be removed to the State having Jurisdiction of the Crime.

No Person held to Service or Labour in one State, under the Laws thereof, escaping into another, shall, in Consequence of any Law or Regulation therein, be discharged from such Service or Labour, but shall be delivered up on Claim of the Party to whom such Service or Labour may be due.

Section 3   New States may be admitted by the Congress into this Union; but no new States shall be formed or erected within the Jurisdiction of any other State; nor any State be formed by the Junction of two or more States, or Parts of States, without the Consent of the Legislatures of the States concerned as well as of the Congress.

The Congress shall have Power to dispose of and make all needful Rules and Regulations respecting the Territory or other Property belonging to the United States; and nothing in this Constitution shall be so construed as to Prejudice any Claims of the United States, or of any particular State.

Section 4   The United States shall guarantee to every State in this Union a Republican Form of Government, and shall protect each of them against Invasion; and on Application of the Legislature, or of the Executive (when the Legislature cannot be convened) against domestic Violence.

ARTICLE V

The Congress, whenever two thirds of both Houses shall deem it necessary, shall propose Amendments to this Constitution, or, on the Application of the Legislatures of two thirds of the several States, shall call a Convention for proposing Amendments, which, in either Case, shall be valid to all Intents and Purposes, as Part of this Constitution, when ratified by the Legislatures of three fourths of the several States, or by Conventions in three fourths thereof, as the one or the other Mode of Ratification may be proposed by the Congress; Provided that no Amendment which may be made prior to the Year One thousand eight hundred and eight shall in any Manner affect the first and fourth Clauses in the Ninth Section of the first Article; and that no State, without its Consent, shall be deprived of its equal Suffrage in the Senate.

ARTICLE VI

All Debts contracted and Engagements entered into, before the Adoption of this Constitution, shall be as valid against the United States under this Constitution, as under the Confederation.

This Constitution, and the Laws of the United States which shall be made in Pursuance thereof; and all Treaties made, or which shall be made, under the Authority of the United States, shall be the supreme Law of the Land; and the Judges in every State shall be bound thereby, any Thing in the Constitution or Laws of any State to the Contrary notwithstanding.

The Senators and Representatives before mentioned, and the Members of the several State Legislatures, and all executive and judicial Officers, both of the United States and of the several States, shall be bound by Oath or Affirmation, to support this Constitution; but no religious Test shall ever be required as a Qualification to any Office or public Trust under the United States.

ARTICLE VII

The Ratification of the Conventions of nine States, shall be sufficient for the Establishment of this Constitution between the States so ratifying the Same.

Done in Convention by the Unanimous Consent of the States present the Seventeenth Day of September in the Year of our Lord one thousand seven hundred and Eighty seven and of the Independence of the United States of America the Twelfth. In Witness whereof we have hereunto subscribed our Names.

Go. Washington—Presid. and deputy from Virginia
New Hampshire—John Langdon, Nicholas Gilman
Massachusetts—Nathaniel Gorham, Rufus King
Connecticut—Wm. Saml. Johnson, Roger Sherman
New York—Alexander Hamilton
New Jersey—Wil. Livingston, David Brearley, Wm. Paterson, Jona. Dayton
Pensylvania—B. Franklin, Thomas Mifflin, Robt. Morris, Geo. Clymer, Thos. FitzSimons, Jared Ingersoll, James Wilson, Gouv. Morris
Delaware—Geo. Read, Gunning Bedford jun, John Dickinson, Richard Bassett, Jaco. Broom
Maryland—James McHenry, Dan of St. Tho. Jenifer, Danl. Carroll
Virginia—John Blair, James Madison Jr.
North Carolina—Wm. Blount, Richd. Dobbs Spaight, Hu. Williamson
South Carolina—J. Rutledge, Charles Cotesworth Pinckney, Charles Pinckney, Pierce Butler
Georgia—William Few, Abr. Baldwin
Attest: William Jackson, Secretary

AMENDMENT I

Congress shall make no law respecting an establishment of religion, or prohibiting the free exercise thereof; or abridging the freedom of speech, or of the press; or the right of the people peaceably to assemble, and to petition the Government for a redress of grievances.

AMENDMENT II

A well regulated Militia, being necessary to the security of a free State, the right of the people to keep and bear Arms, shall not be infringed.

AMENDMENT III

No Soldier shall, in time of peace be quartered in any house, without the consent of the Owner, nor in time of war, but in a manner to be prescribed by law.

AMENDMENT IV

The right of the people to be secure in their persons, houses, papers, and effects, against unreasonable searches and seizures, shall not be violated, and no Warrants shall issue, but upon probable cause, supported by Oath or affirmation, and particularly describing the place to be searched, and the persons or things to be seized.

AMENDMENT V

No person shall be held to answer for a capital, or otherwise infamous crime, unless on a presentment or indictment of a Grand Jury, except in cases arising in the land or naval forces, or in the Militia, when in actual service in time of War or public danger; nor shall any person be subject for the same offense to be twice put in jeopardy of life or limb; nor shall be compelled in any criminal case to be a witness against himself; nor be deprived of life, liberty, or property, without due process of law; nor shall private property be taken for public use, without just compensation.

AMENDMENT VI

In all criminal prosecutions, the accused shall enjoy the right to a speedy and public trial, by an impartial jury of the State and district wherein the crime shall have been committed, which district shall have been previously ascertained by law, and to be informed of the nature and cause of the accusation; to be confronted with the witnesses against him; to have compulsory process for obtaining witnesses in his favor, and to have the Assistance of Counsel for his defence.

AMENDMENT VII

In Suits at common law, where the value in controversy shall exceed twenty dollars, the right of trial by jury shall be preserved, and no fact tried by a jury, shall be otherwise re-examined in any Court of the United States, than according to the rules of the common law.

AMENDMENT VIII

Excessive bail shall not be required, nor excessive fines imposed, nor cruel and unusual punishments inflicted.

AMENDMENT IX

The enumeration in the Constitution, of certain rights, shall not be construed to deny or disparage others retained by the people.

AMENDMENT X

The powers not delegated to the United States by the Constitution, nor prohibited by it to the States, are reserved to the States respectively, or to the people. [The first ten amendments were ratified in 1791.]

AMENDMENT XI

The Judicial power of the United States shall not be construed to extend to any suit in law or equity, commenced or prosecuted against one of the United States by Citizens of another State, or by Citizens or Subjects of any Foreign State. [Ratified in 1795]

AMENDMENT XII

The Electors shall meet in their respective states, and vote by ballot for President and Vice-President, one of whom, at least, shall not be an inhabitant of the same state with themselves; they shall name in their ballots the person voted for as President, and in distinct ballots the person voted for as Vice-President, and they shall make distinct lists of all persons voted for as President, and of all persons voted for as Vice-President and of the number of votes for each, which lists they shall sign and certify, and transmit sealed to the seat of the government of the United States, directed to the President of the Senate;—
The President of the Senate shall, in the presence of the Senate and House of Representatives, open all the certificates and the votes shall then be counted;—
The person having the greatest Number of votes for President, shall be the President, if such number be a majority of the whole number of Electors appointed; and if no person have such majority, then from the persons having the highest numbers not exceeding three on the list of those voted for as President, the House of Representatives shall choose immediately, by ballot, the President. But in choosing the President, the votes shall be taken by states, the representation from each state having one vote; a quorum for this purpose shall consist of a member or members from two-thirds of the states, and a majority of all the states shall be necessary to a choice. And if the House of Representatives shall not choose a President whenever the right of choice shall devolve upon them, before the fourth day of March next following, then the Vice-President shall act as President, as in the case of the death or other constitutional disability of the President.—
The person having the greatest number of votes as Vice-President, shall be the Vice-President, if such number be a majority of the whole number of Electors appointed, and if no person have a majority, then from the two highest numbers on the list, the Senate shall choose the Vice-President; a quorum for the purpose shall consist of two-thirds of the whole number of Senators, and a majority of the whole number shall be necessary to a choice. But no person constitutionally ineligible to the office of President shall be eligible to that of Vice-President of the United States. [Ratified in 1804]

AMENDMENT XIII

Section 1 Neither slavery nor involuntary servitude, except as a punishment for crime whereof the party shall have been duly convicted, shall exist within the United States, or any place subject to their jurisdiction.

Section 2 Congress shall have power to enforce this article by appropriate legislation. [Ratified in 1865]

AMENDMENT XIV

Section 1 All persons born or naturalized in the United States, and subject to the jurisdiction thereof, are citizens of the United States and of the State wherein they reside. No State shall make or enforce any law which shall abridge the privileges or immunities of citizens of the United States; nor shall any State deprive any person of life, liberty, or property, without due process of law; nor deny to any person within its jurisdiction the equal protection of the laws.

Section 2 Representatives shall be apportioned among the several States according to their respective numbers, counting the whole number of persons in each State, excluding Indians not taxed. But when the right to vote at any election for the choice of electors for President and Vice President of the United States, Representatives in Congress, the Executive and Judicial officers of a

State, or the members of the Legislature thereof, is denied to any of the male inhabitants of such State, being twenty-one years of age, and citizens of the United States, or in any way abridged, except for participation in rebellion, or other crime, the basis of representation therein shall be reduced in the proportion which the number of such male citizens shall bear to the whole number of male citizens twenty-one years of age in such State.

Section 3   No person shall be a Senator or Representative in Congress, or elector of President and Vice- President, or hold any office, civil or military, under the United States, or under any State, who, having previously taken an oath, as a member of Congress, or as an officer of the United States, or as a member of any State legislature, or as an executive or judicial officer of any State, to support the Constitution of the United States, shall have engaged in insurrection or rebellion against the same, or given aid or comfort to the enemies thereof. But Congress may by a vote of two-thirds of each House, remove such disability.

Section 4   The validity of the public debt of the United States, authorized by law, including debts incurred for payment of pensions and bounties for services in suppressing insurrection or rebellion, shall not be questioned. But neither the United States nor any State shall assume or pay any debt or obligation incurred in aid of insurrection or rebellion against the United States, or any claim for the loss or emancipation of any slave; but all such debts, obligations and claims shall be held illegal and void.

Section 5   The Congress shall have power to enforce, by appropriate legislation, the provisions of this article. [Ratified in 1868]

AMENDMENT XV

Section 1   The right of citizens of the United States to vote shall not be denied or abridged by the United States or by any State on account of race, color, or previous condition of servitude.

Section 2   The Congress shall have power to enforce this article by appropriate legislation. [Ratified in 1870]

AMENDMENT XVI

The Congress shall have power to lay and collect taxes on incomes, from whatever source derived, without apportionment among the several States, and without regard to any census or enumeration. [Ratified in 1913]

AMENDMENT XVII

The Senate of the United States shall be composed of two Senators from each State, elected by the people thereof, for six years; and each Senator shall have one vote. The electors in each State shall have the qualifications requisite for electors of the most numerous branch of the State legislatures.

When vacancies happen in the representation of any State in the Senate, the executive authority of such State shall issue writs of election to fill such vacancies: Provided, That the legislature of any State may empower the executive thereof to make temporary appointments until the people fill the vacancies by election as the legislature may direct.

This amendment shall not be so construed as to affect the election or term of any Senator chosen before it becomes valid as part of the Constitution. [Ratified in 1913]

AMENDMENT XVIII

Section 1   After one year from the ratification of this article the manufacture, sale, or transportation of intoxicating liquors within, the importation thereof into, or the exportation thereof from the United States and all territory subject to the jurisdiction thereof for beverage purposes is hereby prohibited.

Section 2 The Congress and the several States shall have concurrent power to enforce this article by appropriate legislation.

Section 3 This article shall be inoperative unless it shall have been ratified as an amendment to the Constitution by the legislatures of the several States, as provided in the Constitution, within seven years from the date of the submission hereof to the States by the Congress. [Ratified in 1919]

AMENDMENT XIX

The right of citizens of the United States to vote shall not be denied or abridged by the United States or by any State on account of sex.

Congress shall have power to enforce this article by appropriate legislation. [Ratified in 1920]

AMENDMENT XX

Section 1 The terms of the President and Vice President shall end at noon on the 20th day of January, and the terms of Senators and Representatives at noon on the 3d day of January, of the years in which such terms would have ended if this article had not been ratified; and the terms of their successors shall then begin.

Section 2 The Congress shall assemble at least once in every year, and such meeting shall begin at noon on the 3d day of January, unless they shall by law appoint a different day.

Section 3 If, at the time fixed for the beginning of the term of the President, the President elect shall have died, the Vice President elect shall become President. If a President shall not have been chosen before the time fixed for the beginning of his term, or if the President elect shall have failed to qualify, then the Vice President elect shall act as President until a President shall have qualified; and the Congress may by law provide for the case wherein neither a President elect nor a Vice President elect shall have qualified, declaring who shall then act as President, or the manner in which one who is to act shall be selected, and such person shall act accordingly until a President or Vice President shall have qualified.

Section 4 The Congress may by law provide for the case of the death of any of the persons from whom the House of Representatives may choose a President whenever the right of choice shall have devolved upon them, and for the case of the death of any of the persons from whom the Senate may choose a Vice President whenever the right of choice shall have devolved upon them.

Section 5 Sections 1 and 2 shall take effect on the 15th day of October following the ratification of this article.

Section 6 This article shall be inoperative unless it shall have been ratified as an amendment to the Constitution by the legislatures of three-fourths of the several States within seven years from the date of its submission. [Ratified in 1933]

AMENDMENT XXI

Section 1 The eighteenth article of amendment to the Constitution of the United States is hereby repealed.

Section 2 The transportation or importation into any State, Territory, or possession of the United States for delivery or use therein of intoxicating liquors, in violation of the laws thereof, is hereby prohibited.

Section 3 The article shall be inoperative unless it shall have been ratified as an amendment to the Constitution by conventions in the several States, as provided in the Constitution, within seven years from the date of the submission hereof to the States by the Congress. [Ratified in 1933]

AMENDMENT XXII

Section 1   No person shall be elected to the office of the President more than twice, and no person who has held the office of President, or acted as President, for more than two years of a term to which some other person was elected President shall be elected to the office of the President more than once. But this Article shall not apply to any person holding the office of President, when this Article was proposed by the Congress, and shall not prevent any person who may be holding the office of President, or acting as President, during the term within which this Article becomes operative from holding the office of President or acting as President during the remainder of such term.

Section 2   This article shall be inoperative unless it shall have been ratified as an amendment to the Constitution by the legislatures of three-fourths of the several States within seven years from the date of its submission to the States by the Congress. [Ratified in 1951]

AMENDMENT XXIII

Section 1   The District constituting the seat of Government of the United States shall appoint in such manner as the Congress may direct:

A number of electors of President and Vice President equal to the whole number of Senators and Representatives in Congress to which the District would be entitled if it were a State, but in no event more than the least populous State; they shall be in addition to those appointed by the States, but they shall be considered, for the purposes of the election of President and Vice President, to be electors appointed by a State; and they shall meet in the District and perform such duties as provided by the twelfth article of amendment.

Section 2   The Congress shall have power to enforce this article by appropriate legislation. [Ratified in 1961]

AMENDMENT XXIV

Section 1   The right of citizens of the United States to vote in any primary or other election for President or Vice President, for electors for President or Vice President, or for Senator or Representative in Congress, shall not be denied or abridged by the United States or any State by reason of failure to pay any poll tax or other tax.

Section 2   The Congress shall have power to enforce this article by appropriate legislation. [Ratified in 1964]

AMENDMENT XXV

Section 1   In case of the removal of the President from office or of his death or resignation, the Vice President shall become President.

Section 2   Whenever there is a vacancy in the office of the Vice President, the President shall nominate a Vice President who shall take office upon confirmation by a majority vote of both Houses of Congress.

Section 3   Whenever the President transmits to the President pro tempore of the Senate and the Speaker of the House of Representatives his written declaration that he is unable to discharge the powers and duties of his office, and until he transmits to them a written declaration to the contrary, such powers and duties shall be discharged by the Vice President as Acting President.

Section 4   Whenever the Vice President and a majority of either the principal officers of the executive departments or of such other body as Congress may by law provide, transmit to the President pro tempore of the Senate and the Speaker of the House of Representatives their written declaration that the President is unable to discharge the powers and duties of his office, the Vice President shall immediately assume the powers and duties of the office as Acting President.

Thereafter, when the President transmits to the President pro tempore of the Senate and the Speaker of the House of Representatives his written declaration that no inability exists, he shall resume the powers and duties of his office unless the Vice President and a majority of either the principal officers of the executive department or of such other body as Congress may by law provide, transmit within four days to the President pro tempore of the Senate and the Speaker of the House of Representatives their written declaration that the President is unable to discharge the powers and duties of his office. Thereupon Congress shall decide the issue, assembling within forty eight hours for that purpose if not in session. If the Congress, within twenty one days after receipt of the latter written declaration, or, if Congress is not in session, within twenty one days after Congress is required to assemble, determines by two thirds vote of both Houses that the President is unable to discharge the powers and duties of his office, the Vice President shall continue to discharge the same as Acting President; otherwise, the President shall resume the powers and duties of his office. [Ratified in 1967]

AMENDMENT XXVI

Section 1   The right of citizens of the United States, who are eighteen years of age or older, to vote shall not be denied or abridged by the United States or by any State on account of age.

Section 2   The Congress shall have power to enforce this article by appropriate legislation. [Ratified in 1971]

AMENDMENT XXVII

No law, varying the compensation for the services of the Senators and Representatives, shall take effect, until an election of Representatives shall have intervened. [Ratified in 1992]